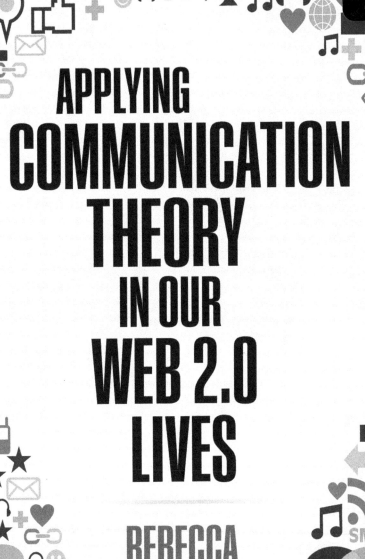

APPLYING
COMMUNICATION
THEORY
IN OUR
WEB 2.0
LIVES

REBECCA
M.L. CURNALIA
Youngstown State University

Kendall Hunt
publishing company

Book Team

Chairman and Chief Executive Officer Mark C. Falb
President and Chief Operating Officer Chad M. Chandlee
Vice President, Higher Education David L. Tart
Director of Publishing Partnerships Paul B. Carty
Senior Developmental Coordinator Angela Willenbring
Vice President, Operations Timothy J. Beitzel
Permissions Editor Carla Kipper
Cover Designer Suzanne Millius

The following interior images are from Shutterstock.com: red lightbulb © Blan-k; blue lightbulb © FMStox; orange lightbulb © Blan-k.

Cover image © Shutterstock.com

www.kendallhunt.com
Send all inquiries to:
4050 Westmark Drive
Dubuque, IA 52004-1840

DEDICATION

To my husband, Jim. He has been a true partner to me since I took
my first communication theory class many, many years ago.

Thanks also to my dear friend and colleague,
Dorian Mermer, who reviewed this book for me.

BRIEF CONTENTS

CONTENTS

ABOUT THE AUTHOR

Dr. Curnalia's background in journalism and politics shaped her scholarly and teaching interests in people's attitudes, beliefs, knowledge, and decision-making. She is intrigued by discrepancies between real and perceived knowledge, the conditions that affect rational decision-making, and how media affect learning and political participation, such as news, satire, infotainment, and engagement via social media. She also explores these constructs in instructional contexts by participating in scholarship and service related to teaching and assessing students' critical thinking, information literacy, and digital literacy. Dr. Curnalia was a member of the National Communication Association's Learning Outcomes Committee; is the author of three textbooks on media, information, and digital literacy; and has published extensively on fear tactics in politics and the uses and effects of political news. She is also an award-winning educator, recognized for her distance education courses, innovation in updating the communication studies curriculum, and for her distinguished service and scholarship during her time at YSU. She currently directs the Master of Arts program in the Department of Communication at Youngstown State University where she is an Associate Professor and teaches classes in communication theory, research methods, and senior capstone.

INTRODUCTION

WELCOME TO *INSIGHT INTO INNOVATION!*

After over a decade of teaching communication theory courses and having received feedback ranging from "Loved it!" to "OMG! So boring," I decided it was time to update the course. As instructors, our first question when we design a new course is typically something along the lines of "what do my students need to learn?" Clearly, students need to learn theories and some basic research methods. But just knowing the concepts, assumptions, and research methods for a theory doesn't really get at my students' *needs*. My students also need skills and applications that will help them in their modern personal and professional lives. More importantly, I reasoned, theory would be more interesting to learn if it fit with what my students and I do every day: using and interacting via mediated channels like social networks, websites, texts, and e-mail.

Insight into Innovation is an introduction to communication theories, concepts, and research that applies to Web 2.0 technologies. Web 2.0 technologies allow for user-generated content and interactivity among creators and users. These technologies include social networking sites and apps; dating websites and apps; social games that we play online; the broad range of user-generated content available online like blogs, Instagram, and YouTube; and websites that allow us to comment on and review content and products, such as Yelp!, comments on articles, and even comments and ratings on retail websites. Before we get into the theories and methods covered in this textbook, let's look first at why I wrote a theory-focused book rather than a user's guide to current Web 2.0 technologies.

WHY I LOVE THEORY: LENSES FOR SEEING LIFE

Throughout this textbook, we use theories as lenses to look closely at different types of Web 2.0 technologies, their uses and their effects. Think for a moment about *lenses*: They help us see more clearly, often helping us see things we wouldn't have been able to see with our naked eye. Lenses can also focus our attention on specific things, sometimes small details, that prove to be very important. If the lens does its job, it can help us see things more clearly, but some lenses aren't a good fit, and they can obscure what we're trying to see. Theories are like this too: they can help us see things we wouldn't have noticed before, sometimes they focus on very specific details, but they can also obscure what we're looking at because not all theories apply equally well to all people and situations.

Thus, theories are like lenses through which we can examine our lives and ourselves and also better understand other people. Theories can help us see the complexities of human communication and new technologies as they affect our own and others' sense of self, relationships, and our society. Each theory offers unique insight into an aspect of human communication by focusing our attention on some aspect or type of human communication.

Micro-level theories, like microscopes, are very narrow and look at a specific type of communication in a specific context, such as theories that focus on a single type of interaction or specific communication strategies. On the other hand, **macro-level theories** help us see the "big picture," such as how each of us affect and are affected by norms and social structures that permeate every aspect of our lives.

In research, when we use a theory or concepts from a theory to analyze a new technology or event, we call it a **case study**. Case studies are sometimes **illustrative** because the technology or event serves as an example—an illustration—of the theory in real life. Case studies may also be **critical**, where we use a theory or concepts from a theory to critique or evaluate a technology or event. Lastly, case studies may be **explanatory**, where we use the predictions from a theory to explain what has happened. In each type of case study, theory is used as a lens to apply, critique, or explain real communication events and technologies.

Using theory to apply, critique, and explain theory should help you learn the concepts and assumptions the theories covered in this book. I also challenge you, as a learner, to use a case study approach as you think about the theories in this book and complete the activities in each chapter. Ultimately, there are two goals of this approach: to help you learn theory and research in communication, and to apply theory and research to become a more competent user and a critical consumer of mediated content. So, now that we are thinking about theories as lenses for understanding our own and others' communication, let's look at some of the specific learning outcomes associated with this approach to theory.

WHAT YOU'LL LEARN: LEARNING OUTCOMES ASSOCIATED WITH *INSIGHT INTO INNOVATION*

In 2014 through 2015, while I was writing the first draft of this book, I also participated in the National Communication Association's Learning Outcomes Project. Communication faculty from across the country came together to discuss what students in communication should know and what they should be able to do upon graduation. The discussions that we had informed my teaching and writing significantly, and so let's look at how the content covered in this book fits with the outcomes that the committee proposed:

1. **Describe the communication discipline, the questions we ask, and our history.** Before we delve into theories, *Insight into Innovation* begins with an overview of the history, methods, and diverse perspectives in the communication discipline. In these chapters, we go over how communication branched off from English departments, incorporated research methods from fields as diverse as English, psychology, and philosophy, and how those historical roots led to the areas of study and diverse research methods in modern communication studies.

2. **Explain, synthesize, and apply communication theory and concepts.** Each unit introduction, and the introduction to each chapter, should help us synthesize theory by seeing how theories and research methods fit together to help us understand ourselves, others, and our society. In the first half of each chapter, I begin by going over the central tenets and concepts from the theory or theories being applied in that chapter. This should help students learn, and be able to explain, the theories and concepts that are central to research in our discipline. Each unit opens with a discussion of how the theories in that unit work together to help us understand an aspect of our lives—our sense of self, how we formulate and interpret messages, how interpersonal relationships form and dissolve, how people interact in groups and organizations, and the uses and effects of mass media. Lastly, the second half of each chapter focuses on applying communication theories and concepts to specific technological innovations by drawing on the most recent research in communication and related disciplines.

3. **Create messages using appropriate modalities to fit your goals, purpose, audience, and context.** As I mentioned in my discussion of case studies, one of the reasons I love theory is because it is useful in everyday life. Communication theories and research in particular can help us adapt to diverse audiences and contexts by teaching us about ourselves and the limitations of our perceptions, by teaching us about others, and by highlighting the affordances and limitations of different technologies that affect communication processes. In several chapters in this book, we will discuss the features of communication competence, such as the process of active listening, how to engage in mindful interaction, and essential digital literacies. These discussions, which are grounded in theory and research, should help us become better communicators across a broad range of modalities, including Web 2.0.

4. **Be an active listener, critical of the layers of meaning in your own and others' messages, and mindfully respond.** In addition to the ability to communicate our ideas, effective communicators are also mindful listeners. We seek to understand not just what someone says or what they post, but also the needs, goals, emotions, and thoughts that are the driving force behind their behavior. The theories we cover related to message formulation and interpretation challenge us to think about how we construct messages, but also to consider how other people see the world. This requires that we listen carefully, that we be present in the moment, and we consider not just what is said or posted, but the implications and latent, underlying meanings in messages.

5. **Recognize, respect, and adapt to individual differences in culture, gender, needs, demographics, and traits.** Effective communicators are aware of cultural types and norms, gendered styles and norms, the relationship between demographics and communication, and common traits that affect how we formulate, send, and interpret messages. This means that we avoid "snap judgments" and reliance on stereotypes based on a person's visible characteristics. Instead, we appreciate that people are complex, and that their view of reality is unique, and seek to understand others in terms of the social norms that may affect and constrain their behavior. Throughout the chapters in this book, we will discuss individual differences such as gender, culture, traits, and socioeconomic circumstances, which affect how people communicate and interpret messages. It was important to me that the discussion of individual differences be integrated throughout the explanation and application of theories, rather than covered solely in units on gender and culture theories, because these differences are essential to understanding ourselves and others across all communication contexts.

6. **Understand the role of communication in shaping, framing, and influencing our sense of self and our society.** Communication is how we express our sense of self: how we talk, our posture, gestures, movements, vocal tone, even our choice of clothing and accessories, reflect who we are and how we see ourselves. How people respond to us, talk about us, and what we observe others doing and the consequences of their choices, all inform our sense of who we are and who we should be. I explain it to my students this way: Our sense of self is formed by how people communicate with us, about us, and around us. These interactions frame our perception of who we should be and what we should do, how we should not be and what we should not do, and who others are. Thus, how we communicate has wide-ranging implications, as we are the outcomes of the communication we receive and we also reinforce norms and social structures by how we communicate with, about, and among other people. In short, communication affects both the self and our society in a dynamic, ongoing process.

7. **Actively participate in public discourse to improve civic life and help resolve the challenges facing our society.** Knowing that communication is central to the formation of the self and the shaping and reshaping of our society, we should all strive to use our communication skills to promote positive change in our society. A common adage, "be the change you want to see in the world," is meaningful in terms of taking the theories and concepts in this book and using them to shape a better, more equitable and just society for ourselves and for others. We can learn about gender norms and roles and how those restrict people's choices in group, organizational, and public contexts, but unless we take it upon ourselves to improve our interactions and correct our misperceptions, those inequities cannot be corrected.

HOW YOU'LL LEARN: LAYOUT AND FEATURES OF *INSIGHT INTO INNOVATION*

Chapter Structure. Each chapter opens with a one-paragraph summary of the theory or theories that will be covered in that chapter, then covers the concepts and assumptions of each theory, offers an applied example that applies theory to a current event or new technology, and reviews typical research methods used to test or apply the theory. Thus, the first half of each chapter provides a thorough, organized discussion of what each theory is all about.

In the second part of each chapter, recent scholarship that tests or applies the theory in the Web 2.0 environment is discussed. These discussions typically focus on one or more communication applications, competencies, or skills that we can apply to our use of Web 2.0 technologies. The applications are rooted in academic scholarship, but are discussed in a way that should promote self-reflection on our own uses of technology and critical thinking about the effects of new technologies.

Chapter Features. You'll notice several features throughout the text to help you engage with the material and think critically about the applications of theory and research in our Web 2.0 lives. There are examples, activities, and links throughout the text to relevant research and resources. The examples are meant to serve as one instance or event where a theory can be used as a lens for more fully understanding what happened or is happening. Activities, articles, videos, and images are provided as an opportunity for you to use a theory as a lens to analyze or think about a problem or event.

Insight into Innovation Activity: Watch *Frontline's "Generation Like."* This episode of Frontline offers insight into the personal, social, and societal implications of ubiquitous social media use: http://www.pbs.org/wgbh/pages/frontline/generation-like/

As you watch the episode, reflect on the learning outcomes for this text:

1. How does the prevalence of social media affect our everyday communication?
2. How might an understanding of theories and research in communication help us become more effective users of this technology?
3. Is social media making us more or less mindful of others?
4. How does the introduction and mass adoption of social media affect our ability to really *know* other people?
5. How has social media shaped and reframed our sense of self, our relationships with other people, and the organization of our society?
6. How has social media affected our knowledge of individual differences in culture, gender, and traits? Has it helped us or hindered us in appreciating individual differences?
7. What features of social media might help us participate more in civic life and promote a more just, equitable society?

Taken together, the discussion of theory, research, and communication competencies, along with the use of real examples and applied activities throughout this textbook, should help you learn theory and meet the learning outcomes outlined in this introduction. Most importantly, I hope that this approach to communication theory and research builds your appreciation for the practical value of theory and scholarship in our everyday lives, particularly as those lives are increasingly lived through mediated channels like smartphones and computers.

CHAPTER 1

WHO WE ARE AND WHAT WE DO: THE COMMUNICATION DISCIPLINE

OUTCOMES

- *Knowledge:* Learn about the fields of study in communication, perspectives on theory, and what a "theory" is.
- *Skill:* Think about communication like a theorist, recognizing the numerous variables that affect people's interaction and the different approaches to understanding interaction.

The Huffington Post reported that communication studies have shown "strong growth" because it is "the right offering at the right time" (Schmitt, 2014, para. 1 and 3). Schmitt attributes our growth as a discipline to "the broad nature and breadth of coursework in the discipline," such as our focus on social networks, groups, and media. The areas of study in the broader discipline provide students in communication studies "vitally relevant knowledge" for use in our new media society (para. 3).

As Schmitt (2014) noted, the communication discipline is broad. We include fields of study such as intrapersonal, interpersonal, group, organizational, persuasive, and mass/mediated communication. Given the nature of Web 2.0 technologies, we are all shaping who we are, building relationships, social networks, professional networks, and can participate in creating and disseminating mass media at the same time. Communication studies, particularly our theories and research methods, can help people be better communicators both face-to-face and online.

Within each field of study, there are theories that explain communication concepts, and each theory comes from a particular perspective or tradition in communication. Even though the discipline is diverse, each field of study and perspective on communication processes gives us unique insight into the personal, professional, and societal changes that are ongoing in our technology-rich lives.

We know that communication is important, and it is something that everyone does. Employers regularly rank communication as one of the top skills they need in employees. Skilled use of communication technologies is essential as well in the modern workplace, and it is equally important

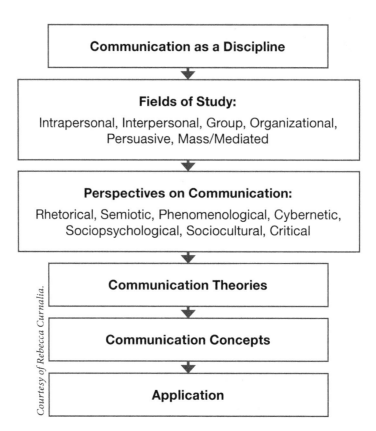

```
┌─────────────────────────────────────────────┐
│          Communication as a Discipline        │
└─────────────────────────────────────────────┘
                      ↓
┌─────────────────────────────────────────────┐
│               Fields of Study:                │
│ Intrapersonal, Interpersonal, Group, Organizational, │
│           Persuasive, Mass/Mediated            │
└─────────────────────────────────────────────┘
                      ↓
┌─────────────────────────────────────────────┐
│         Perspectives on Communication:         │
│ Rhetorical, Semiotic, Phenomenological, Cybernetic, │
│      Sociopsychological, Sociocultural, Critical  │
└─────────────────────────────────────────────┘
                      ↓
┌─────────────────────────────────────────────┐
│            Communication Theories              │
└─────────────────────────────────────────────┘
                      ↓
┌─────────────────────────────────────────────┐
│            Communication Concepts              │
└─────────────────────────────────────────────┘
                      ↓
┌─────────────────────────────────────────────┐
│                 Application                    │
└─────────────────────────────────────────────┘
```

Courtesy of Rebecca Curnalia.

in our personal and social lives. In this book, we focus on three areas of study in communication: the **self** (norms, gender, culture, and traits), **social and professional relationships** (interpersonal, group, and organizational communication), and **society** (persuasion and mass media).

Think of the theories in this book as lenses for interpreting, evaluating, and practicing competent communication, and the foundation in these first few chapters is a lens through which we can interpret, analyze, and critique theories. As you read through the following chapters, which cover theories and related concepts and apply those concepts to new communication technologies, consider how these theories might help you make more effective communication decisions in your personal and professional life and how they relate to being an engaged and informed citizen. Also consider the relative strengths and weaknesses of each theory—how well it fits the discipline, how it is limited by its perspective (Chapter 1), where it fits in our discipline's history and future (Chapter 2), and how the methods used to discover and explore the theory are relevant and applicable to numerous personal and professional contexts (Chapter 3).

🗨️ THE DISCIPLINE: WHAT IS COMMUNICATION?

Defining the discipline is a difficult task, given the breadth of fields of study and diverse research traditions we include. The National Communication Association (2014) defines the communication discipline as the study of "…how people use messages to generate meanings within and across various contexts, cultures, channels, and media" (para. 1). To explore the many things we theorize about and research in communication, it is helpful to think of what happens when we communicate.

The transactional model of communication is a good starting point for thinking about the process of communication. Communication is **transactional** because it occurs among people. It is a **process** because it is an ongoing sequence of events: **encoding**, or creating a message and formulating responses to messages; transmitting the **message** via a **channel**; **decoding**, or interpreting received messages; all within a **context**, or situation, where there is **noise** that may interfere with the interaction.

Communication also is **symbolic**. This means that we are using symbols—spoken words, nonverbal behaviors, and written words—to represent something else. When we encode, we are taking what we want to communicate and translating that meaning into symbols that we then convey to another person or people, who in turn decode those symbols to try to understand our meaning. This process sounds straightforward, until you consider that individual and contextual differences introduce noise and lead to unique expectations, uses, and interpretations of symbols. People also vary in their knowledge of symbols.

Take, for example, the **Sapir-Worf Hypothesis**. According to this perspective, language determines what we know and how we see reality. Essentially, the symbols that we are taught to use direct our attention to focus on certain things, and also may cause us to overlook, or not even recognize, those things that we do not have symbols to explain.

Consider how we might interpret the following scenario: "He came into class, sat in the back, and was visibly upset." Chances are, you have a mental image of a guy sitting in the back of a classroom with a disgruntled posture and facial expression.

But, if we change the pronoun, our mental image changes: "She came into class, sat in the back, and was visibly upset." You are likely imagining a very different kind of "upset" from a female, maybe a more teary, sad expression.

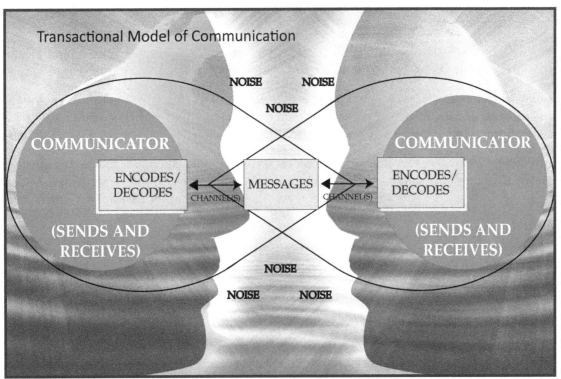

Thus, the symbols available to us in our language can direct our thoughts and impressions, which is why there is debate over whether and how to adjust our language to accommodate individual differences and reduce sterotyping and prejudice. What do you think: How would our impressions and interpretations change if there were no pronouns for "men" and "women" in the English language?

In addition to differences in the symbols we have to communicate, we also use and interpret symbols differently. Gender, traits, culture, and norms influence the meaning associated with verbal and nonverbal messages. Further, the unique contextual restraints and noise in a given situation makes **shared meaning**, or truly understanding each other's unique meanings, difficult to achieve.

Thinking about these elements of communication, we can start to see the types of things communication researchers might study:

- Encoding: How and why we use symbols to formulate messages the way we do; how our goals, traits, culture, norms, beliefs, and perceptions affect how we form messages.
- Messages: The types and use of symbols used to convey meaning; how best to convey meaning given the context, channel, and receivers.
- Channels: How and why we choose face-to-face or mediated options to relay a message and the implications of those choices.
- Decoding: How and why we interpret and respond the way we do to the symbols we receive; how our goals, traits, culture, norms, beliefs, and perceptions affect how we interpret messages.
- Context: The physical and social environment and relationship(s) among people interacting; how and why context affects encoding, message design, decoding, and noise.
- Noise: Anything in the physical environment and within people's emotional, physical, or psychological state that distracts us from sending and receiving messages, and how to overcome these barriers.

Based on this discussion of the transactional model and the use of symbols to communicate, for the purpose of this book, I offer the following tentative definition of communication:

Communication is a transactional process that occurs within a context and involves unique interactants who are formulating, sending, and interpreting verbal, written, and/or nonverbal symbolic messages via one or more channels.

In this book, we will be focusing on communication via new and emerging mediated channels in personal, professional, and mass media contexts. In particular, we will focus on **Web 2.0** channels. Web 2.0 includes *new technologies that provide opportunities for user activity, interaction, social connection, information storage, and mass dissemination.*

Insight into Innovation Activity: Read *PC Magazine*'s definition of "Web 2.0": http://www.pcmag. com/encyclopedia/term/56219/web-2-0. What Web 2.0 technologies do you use that fit with their definition? In what contexts do you use these Web 2.0 technologies: Do you use Web 2.0 to find and maintain your interpersonal relationships? Do you use them to build and maintain professional relationships? Have you used them for your education? Do you use them to make consumer purchases? Do you use them to find information? Do you use them for entertainment?

We will cover topics ranging from the presentation of self online, to changes in the wired workplace, to the challenges and opportunities for marketing and mass media online. To look more closely at the range of topics covered in this book, we'll take these definitions of communication as a discipline and Web 2.0 as a collection of communication channels and explore the fields of study in communication.

FIELDS OF STUDY: WHAT DO COMMUNICATION SCHOLARS RESEARCH?

Generally, the communication discipline is divided into **fields of study** that focus on different contexts. Looking over the divisions outlined by the National Communication Association (2014) can help us recognize the breadth of the fields of study in communication and start to see areas where Web 2.0 technologies are reshaping human communication processes.

Brief Overview of the National Communication Association's (2014) Fields of Study in the Discipline:

- **Communication Education:** Communication in the classroom
- **Electronic Media Content:** Study of media content on TV, online, etc.
- **Health Communication:** Health campaigns; communication between health professionals and patients; health information
- **International/Intercultural Communication:** Communication between cultures
- **Interpersonal Communication:** Communication between two people
- **Legal Communication:** Communication in legal settings
- **Mass Communication Effects:** Individual and social effects of media
- **Negotiation/Conflict Management:** Managing and resolving conflicts
- **Organizational Communication:** Communication in formal organizations
- **Political Communication:** Communication in political systems and political processes
- **Public Address:** Study of major public speeches
- **Public Relations:** Communication between organizations and their audiences
- **Rhetoric:** Analysis of communication artifacts, which include any existing communication
- **Semiotics:** Symbols and signs used to communicate
- **Group Communication:** Interactions and processes in groups
- **Speech:** Verbal and nonverbal speech making
- **Visual Communication:** Communication through visual artifacts

You can see the full list of areas of study in communication here: http://www.natcom.org/discipline/

Thinking critically about these fields of study, there are many areas of overlap: Public relations and organizational communication can be both national and international. Employees in organizations and members of groups develop interpersonal relationships. The negotiation of conflict happens in groups, organizations, interpersonal relationships, and in politics. Health, political, and legal communication include intercultural, interpersonal, group, organizational, and new and mass media communication. So, not only does it serve us all personally and professionally to be aware of the theory and research across the fields of study in communication because of the overlap among fields of study, but it is also useful for us as scholars to interact across these fields, particularly as new technologies require us to cut across traditional boundaries.

Insight into Innovation Example: To demonstrate the importance of looking at Web 2.0 technologies in each field of study, consider the following facts:

- **Communication Education:** Education is increasingly happening online. Over 5 million U.S. college students are taking online courses (U.S. Department of Education, 2014).

- **Electronic Media/Mass Communication:** Consumption of mass media has moved increasingly online. Over 1 billion people visit YouTube every month and watch over 6 billion hours of video (YouTube, 2014); the *Huffington Post* was valued at more than *The Washington Post* and *New York Times* combined as traditional news outlets have hemorrhaged readers.

- **Health Communication:** People go online to find and share health information. One-third of Americans go online for health information (Fox & Duggan, 2013).

- **International/Intercultural Communication:** Our online communities and many of our employers are international. 80 percent of YouTube users (YouTube, 2014) and 80 percent of Facebook users (Facebook, 2014) are outside the United States; almost 7 million Americans work overseas (U.S. Department of State, 2013).

- **Interpersonal Communication:** Interpersonal relationships are increasingly started and maintained through mediated channels. 38 percent of current singles looking for a partner have online dating profiles (Smith & Duggan, 2013); the average number of Facebook friends is 338 (Smith, 2014).

- **Legal Communication:** Even the practice of law is moving online. The American Bar Association recently partnered with Rocket Lawyer Inc. to help pair lawyers with online clients (J. Smith, 2014).

- **Organizational Communication:** Mediated channels are changing when, how much, and where we work. In 2012, nearly one-fourth of employed Americans reported telecommuting (Noonan & Glass, 2012); nearly 3 million employees work from home (Rapoza, 2013).

- **Public Address:** Even speeches are interactive, as people can tweet and post comments on formal forms of public address. There were 1.64 million tweets during President Obama's 2014 State of the Union (Hitlin & Vogt, 2014).

- **Public Relations:** According to the Bureau of Labor Statistics (2014), PR jobs are expected to grow by 12 percent through 2022 because of organizations' "increased use of social media," which will "create more work for public relations specialists as they try to appeal to consumers and the general public in new ways" (para. 2).

- **Rhetoric:** Old rhetorical artifacts are generating new interest online. The National Archives has a website with searchable archives, and Twitter, YouTube, Facebook, Pinterest, and Instagram accounts. On Facebook alone they average 6.9 million views per month (National Archives, 2013).

- **Semiotics:** Our symbols are changing quickly. In August 2013 alone, the Oxford English Dictionary added the words "selfie," "FOMO," "hackerspace," "Internet of things," and "srsly" to their online dictionary (Oxford Dictionaries Online, 2013).

- **Group Communication:** Groups have many new choices for meetings. Gotomeeting.com hosts over 34 million meetings each year (gotomeeting.com, 2014), and that's just one online meeting website!

- **Visual Communication:** Web 2.0 offers new opportunities for sharing opinions and information. 6 percent of Internet users use Reddit, which is known for viral memes (Duggan & Smith, 2013). On the information side of things, as of 2013, there were over 15 million slide presentations on Slideshare, and over 60 million people visit the site each month (Slideshare.net, 2014).

Clearly, each field in communication studies has been affected by new communication technologies.

PERSPECTIVES ON THEORY ACROSS FIELDS OF STUDY IN COMMUNICATION

Now that we've reviewed the discipline of communication, the fields of study, and how they relate to Web 2.0 technology, we move on to consider approaches to theorizing in the field. Craig (1999) argued that dividing communication into distinct fields of study wasn't productive, and we should instead think of communication theory from different *perspectives*, or, in other words, think about the different approaches to communication theory.

Craig (1999) outlined seven perspectives on communication theory: rhetorical, semiotic, phenomenological, cybernetic, sociopsychological, sociocultural, and critical. In the **rhetorical** view, communication is an art form that can be critiqued and classified to explore the best ways to persuade people. The **semiotic** perspective is somewhat more narrow, as it focuses on how people use and interpret symbols to convey meaning. From a more person-centered view, **phenomenological** approaches to communication stress the subjective nature of communication: each of us uses and experiences communication differently and understanding and appreciating these differences can help us build close connections with others. **Cybernetics**, on the other hand, looks less as the subjective and emotional side of communication and focuses instead on people as rational information processors. The **sociopsychological** approach incorporates both emotion and information processing by looking for clear cause-effect relationships among individual traits, situations, and the emotional and cognitive effects of messages. Continuing with the systems metaphor, or the idea that humans and human relationships are interrelated systems, but taking a more critical view, the **sociocultural** approach considers how communication creates and recreates social order by establishing and reinforcing social, cultural, and group norms. The **critical** perspective builds on this view of communication as a source of social order, but is particularly concerned with how it reinforces existing power structures in society and therefore leaves some groups powerless.

In this book, we will cover theories from the fields of study in communication described on the following page, and you will find that each theory we discuss will align with one (or more) of the perspectives Craig (1999) outlined. Just like our fields of study overlap, there are similarities among the perspectives on communication theory, and each perspective helps us understand the complexity of communication processes and effects more fully.

Perspectives on Communication Theory (adapted from Craig, 1999)		
Perspective	**View of Communication**	**Approach to Theory**
Rhetoric	Communication is a *practical art.*	Analysis of public discourse; Classifying and critiquing strategies and tactics.
Semiotics	Communication is the use of common *signs and symbols.*	Analysis of the uses and different interpretations of symbols.
Phenomenological	Communication is *dialogue* with *subjective* meaning.	Investigating people's experiences to understand how to build authentic relationships.
Cybernetic	Communication is *information processing.*	Analysis of human systems, such as social networks, attention, distraction, and cognition.
Sociopsychological	Communication is a series of *cause and effect relationships.*	Investigation of how traits and states determine interactions and message effects.
Sociocultural	Communication is the production and reproduction of *social systems.*	Analysis of how power structures and norms are created and maintained through interactions.
Critical	Communication is a means of *social oppression* and *liberation.*	Analysis of how social values— patriarchy, racism, etc.—are perpetuated and can be overcome through communication.

You can read Craig's (1999) article here: http://econoca.unica.it/public/downloaddocenti/ARTICOLO_communication_theory_as_a_field.pdf

🗨 DEFINING "THEORY"

Each field of study has its own unique theories from one or more of the perspectives outlined above. A **theory** is, most generally, *a lens for understanding some aspect or type of communication.* More specifically, communication theories should *apply* to real world communication situations in our daily lives by *describing*, *predicting*, or *explaining* communication strategies, processes, and effects in a way that is *parsimonious* (simple) and *testable* or *observable*. Let's look more closely at each of these components of our working definition of theory.

The strength of our discipline and, by extension, our theories, is that it applies to people's everyday interactions. There is no one grand theory of communication that will explain all of our interactions. Rather, our theories tend to be focused on one *type* of communication (e.g., self-disclosure, advertising, social media messages, etc.) or communication in a particular *context* (i.e., mass, interpersonal, group, or organizational).

Theory is developed to describe, explain, and/or predict communication processes (Hocking, Stacks, & McDermott, 2003). Depending on the perspective, communication theory may be used to *describe* a type of communication or communication within a particular context by defining the relevant concepts. A **concept** is an abstract idea that theorists clearly define. For example, "attitude" is a concept that theorists have defined as people's evaluations that range from extremely positive to extremely negative. Theory may also *explain* why particular variables are related to each other. Continuing with our example of attitudes, theories explain that our friends' opinions are one thing that affects our attitudes (e.g., Festinger, 1957). Lastly, a theory may *predict* how variables are related. **Variables** are anything that can be different or be changed from person to person. So, in terms of attitudes, variables like our friends' beliefs and behaviors predict our attitudes under certain conditions.

Clearly, as we saw in the overview of the transactional model of communication, there are a lot of concepts and, therefore, potential variables that affect communication processes and effects. When we theorize, we have to be careful about what we include in our theories to avoid them becoming so grand and overwhelming that they are no longer practical. Though theories do not necessarily have to be quick rules of thumb, they do need to be simple, or *parsimonious* enough, that they can be tested or observed through research so we can determine whether or not they are accurate.

APPLYING COMMUNICATION CONCEPTS FROM THEORY

Each theory highlights concepts that we can use in our everyday communication. In this book, we will focus specifically on applications to Web 2.0 communication tools. Using theories that clearly describe concepts, explain how they are related, and predict outcomes, students should finish this book with a toolbox full of useful strategies to employ in their everyday lives. You will see this structure throughout the theory chapters: I will introduce each theory's key concepts, explanations of communication processes, and predictions about communication outcomes. I will go on to talk about the methods used to test the theory, so that we can critically consider each theory's accuracy and limitations. For the last half of each chapter, I review recent applications of concepts, explanations, and predictions from the theory to Web 2.0 technologies so that we have clear take-aways from the theory and research that we can incorporate in our everyday interactions.

The book is divided into three parts, or general areas of study within the discipline: the self, social and professional relationships, and society. In this way, our discussion of theories will start at the micro-level (what's going on inside each person) and move to the macro-level (what's going on in society). Within each major part of the text, there are units that cover the fields of study in communication: the mediated self, sending and interpreting messages, interpersonal relationships, groups and organizations, persuasion, and mass communication.

Now that we have covered the communication discipline, fields of study within the discipline, perspectives on theory, and elements of theory, in the next chapter we will briefly consider the history of communication studies and Web 2.0 technologies. After we understand the major developments in the discipline and technology, we then move on to discuss the research methods we use in the field to develop, test, and apply theories with particular attention to the historical roots of our research methods and the practical applications of methods in terms of interpreting theory and creating new knowledge.

ACTIVITIES AND ASSIGNMENTS

1. The book gives a clear definition of communication being the "transactional process of formulating, sending, and interpreting verbal, written, and/or nonverbal symbols via a channel among interactants who are constrained and influenced by the broader context." What would you add to this definition? What would you eliminate or change? Why?

2. Complete a personal inventory of the Web 2.0 technologies you use on a daily basis (i.e., Twitter, Facebook, online forums, YouTube, shopping websites, chat/IM, online courses, etc.). Then choose the two that you use most often. Compare and contrast the process of encoding and decoding for those two channels, how the messages are similar/different, how the contexts are similar/different, and how the noise on each channel is similar/different.

3. Develop a theory of communication that you would be interested in exploring by (a) specifying the context you are interested in researching, (b) identifying the most important Web 2.0 technology used in that context, and (c) specifying the concepts you think are important in terms of the uses and effects of that Web 2.0 technology.

REFERENCES

Bureau of Labor Statistics. (2014, January 8). Public relations specialists: Job outlook. *Occupational Outlook Handbook*. Retrieved from http://www.bls.gov/ooh/media-and-communication/public-relations-specialists.htm#tab-6

Craig, R. T. (1999). Communication theory as a field. *Communication Theory*, 9, 119–161.

Duggan, M., & Smith, A. (2013, July 3). *6% of online adults are Reddit users.* Pew Research Internet Project. Retrieved from http://www.pewinternet.org/2013/07/03/6-of-online-adults-are-reddit-users/

Facebook. (2014). Newsroom: Statistics. Retrieved from http://newsroom.fb.com/company-info/

Festinger, L. (1957). *A theory of cognitive dissonance.* Stanford, CA: Stanford University Press.

Fox, S., & Duggan, M. (2013, January 15). *Health online 2013.* Pew Research Internet Project. Retrieved from http://www.pewinternet.org/2013/01/15/health-online-2013/

Gotomeeting.com. (2014). Citrix Online. Retrieved from https://www1.gotomeeting.com/m/sf/g2m-sflp.tmpl

Hitlin, P., & Vogt, N. (2014, January 30). *On Twitter, criticism exceeds praise for Obama's speech.* Pew Research Center. Retrieved from http://www.pewresearch.org/fact-tank/2014/01/30/on-twitter-criticism-exceeds-praise-for-obamas-speech/

Hocking, J. E., Stacks, D. W., & McDermott, S. T. (2003). *Communication research methods* (3rd ed.). Boston, MA: Allyn & Bacon.

National Archives. (2013, October 21). *Social media statistics dashboard: FY 2013 Summary.* Retrieved from http://www.archives.gov/social-media/reports/social-media-stats-fy-2013-09.pdf

National Communication Association. (2014). *What is communication?* Retrieved from http://www.natcom.org/discipline/

Noonan, M. C., & Glass, J. L. (2012). The hard truth about telecommuting. *US Bureau of Labor Statistics Monthly Labor Review.* Retrieved from http://www.bls.gov/opub/mlr/2012/06/art3full.pdf

Oxford Dictionaries. (2013). Buzzworthy words added to Oxford Dictionaries Online—squee! Retrieved from http://blog.oxforddictionaries.com/2013/08/new-words-august-2013/

Schmitt, J. (2014, October 22). Communication studies rise to relevance. *The Huffington Post.* Retrieved from http://www.huffingtonpost.com/jason-schmitt/communication-studies-ris_b_6025038.html?utm_hp_ref=tw

Slideshare.net. (2014). What is Slideshare? *LinkedIn.* Retreived from http://www.slideshare.net/about

Smith, A. (2014, February 3). *6 new facts about Facebook.* Pew Research Center Fact Tank. Retrieved from http://www.pewresearch.org/fact-tank/2014/02/03/6-new-facts-about-facebook/

Smith, A., & Duggan, M. (2013, October 21). Online dating & relationships. *Pew Research Internet Project.* Retrieved from http://www.pewinternet.org/2013/10/21/online-dating-relationships/

Smith, J. (2014, August 11). Online Legal Services Company to team up with American Bar Association. *The Wall Street Journal Law Blog.* Retrieved from http://blogs.wsj.com/law/2014/08/11/online-legal-services-company-to-team-up-with-american-bar-association/

Rapoza, K. (2013, February 18). One in five Americans work from home, numbers seen rising over 60%. *Forbes.* Retrieved from http://www.forbes.com/sites/kenrapoza/2013/02/18/one-in-five-americans-work-from-home-numbers-seen-rising-over-60/

U.S. Department of Education. (2014). *Enrollment in distance education courses, by state: Fall 2012.* National Center for Education Statistics. Retrieved from http://nces.ed.gov/pubs2014/2014023.pdf

U.S. Department of State. (2013, January). *Who we are and what we do: Consular Affairs by the numbers.* Bureau of Consular Affairs. Retrieved from http://travel.state.gov/content/dam/ca_fact_sheet.pdf

YouTube. (2014). *Statistics: Viewership.* Retrieved from https://www.youtube.com/yt/press/statistics.html

CHAPTER 2

FROM ARISTOTLE TO APPLE'S IPHONE: THE HISTORY OF COMMUNICATION THEORY AND RESEARCH

OUTCOMES

- *Knowledge:* Learn the major turning points in the emergence of the communication discipline.
- *Skill:* Apply knowledge of our history to understand current theorizing and methods.

The study of communication, particularly public address, dates back to Aristotle and his teachings about public oratory in *The Rhetoric*. Interestingly, though theory and concepts in our discipline date as far back as Ancient Greece, communication studies departments and programs are relatively new in academics. In fact, in 2014 the National Communication Association (formerly the Speech Communication Association) celebrated its 100th anniversary.

THE CLASSICAL PERIOD

Littlejohn and Foss (2009) provide an insightful overview of historical developments that brought us to the modern discipline as we know it today, with clear but interrelated fields of study, perspectives, theories, and research methods. Beginning in the Classical Period with the study of oratory in Ancient Greece and Rome, Aristotle and Plato worked to classify types of rhetoric and rhetorical tactics. Cicero and Quintilian focused their studies on gestures, and Augustine wrote about interpretation. As we will see in the unit that covers influence and persuasion, concepts from these early studies of oratory and scripture still direct our theory and methods in modern rhetoric.

Beginning with Aristotle in the 4th century BCE, there was an effort to identify the types of discourse, understand the psychology of the audience, and explain the process of developing a speech (Bizzell & Herzberg, 2001). Classic concepts that we still teach in communication courses today are taken from Aristotle's teachings. For example, the concepts of **ethos** (the speaker's authority on the subject), **pathos** (emotional appeals), and **logos** (logical appeals) are still taught and applied in public speaking and rhetoric classes today. Similarly, the **canons of rhetoric**, which were refined by Roman scholars such as Cicero and Quintilian, are still the cornerstone of modern speech courses: invention of rational appeals, arrangement of ideas and evidence, style of verbal delivery, memory used to learn the speech, and nonverbal delivery of the speech to an audience.

13

The Classical Period in rhetoric is important for a couple of reasons. First, it was the foundation of some of the earliest scholarship in communication studies, as authors such as Wichelns (1925) advocated using Aristotle's concepts to analyze and critique public address. Second, though we use very little direct application of Aristotle's concepts in research today, we do see the influence of the Classical theorists on modern rhetoric. Current rhetorical theory and research still focuses on those elements outlined by the Ancient Greeks and Romans: "purpose, audience, composition, argumentation, organization, and style" (Bizzell & Herzberg, 2001, p. 7).

💬 MODERN HISTORY

Though the foundation of our early communication theory and scholarship was established in ancient times, speech and communication as an independent academic discipline didn't emerge until the early 1900s. In fact, speech wasn't a key component of the college curriculum until the 1800s, though we see the discipline slowly taking shape well before that time.

Disciplinary Roots: 1600–1900. During the **Enlightenment** of the 1600s, influential philosophers like Descartes, Rousseau, Kant, and Milton explored the extent to which people are rational, how we maintain order in society, and highlighted the issues of social justice and freedom of speech (Littlejohn & Foss, 2009). It wasn't until the early 1800s that we see the elements of the communication discipline as it is today begin to emerge in America, with the rise of elocutionists (Cohen, 1994). Early **elocutionists** studied oral and nonverbal delivery and public speaking. These studies sought to refine categories of verbal and nonverbal behaviors and provide guidance on the best ways to convey content and emotion.

By the end of the 1800s, colleges and universities incorporated writing and speaking courses in the English curriculum in addition to the traditional English courses in topics such as rhetoric (Cohen, 1994). These courses incorporated oral communication and composition. "Oral English" became a branch of English instruction, and specialized texts in public oratory were developed to accommodate modern American courses that incorporated ideas from ancient rhetoric, such as Aristotle's concepts, and from the Elocutionists who had focused on nonverbal delivery. Around the turn of the century, courses in rhetoric and argumentation focused exclusively on speech communication and highlighted concepts like ethos, pathos, and logos, elocution, delivery, and types of speeches.

Founding of the First Speech Associations: 1910–1915. The Speech Association of the Eastern States was founded in 1910, marking a shift in speech communication away from English and toward becoming its own discipline (Cohen, 1994). Today, that organization is the Eastern Communication Association. In 1911, at the second meeting of Eastern States, the organizers established *The Public Speaking Review*, which was published as a trade magazine for public speaking instructors (Wichelns, 1969). By 1914, instructors of oratory, argumentation, and public speaking broke away from The National Council of Teachers of English to form the National Association of Teachers of Public Speaking, which is known today as the National Communication Association. The first publication of the national association was *The Quarterly Journal of Public Speaking*, founded in 1915.

You can read Howard Cohen's (1994) review of the history of the discipline The History of the Speech Communication Association: The Emergence of a Discipline, 1914–1945.

This was by no means a "clean split" from English. Though public speaking departments existed across the country, many professors of oratory were still in English departments, and many public speaking professors wanted to maintain that affiliation (Cohen, 1994). There were also significant challenges to establishing the new discipline, particularly speech's focus on performance rather than scholarship and theory. To establish themselves as an academic discipline, these speech teachers needed to engage in scholarship. Cohen noted that "members of the profession had done no research, and it is not at all clear that they knew what research was or how to conduct it" (p. 36). The Research Committee of the National Association reported that many other disciplines that "bordered" public speaking, such as psychology, sociology, literature studies, and language studies, had established research methods. So, though public speaking was a "practical" subject, the Research Committee recommended that "many teachers of public speaking could easily take courses in the departments of physiology, psychology, sociology or literature" to learn techniques for research that they could adapt to public speaking (p. 37).

This was a very important turning point for our discipline. As we noted in the last chapter, communication is a broad and diverse discipline, and one of our strengths is our interdisciplinary and mixed methodological roots. The very thing that makes communication flexible and relevant in the new media society is the realization—back in 1915—that we could take this practical, applied field of instruction and apply research methods and ultimately theory from these diverse disciplines. In fact, several of the "communication theories" in this book are borrowed from the very disciplines that the 1915 Research Committee suggested we turn to for insight into scholarship: sociology, psychology, linguistics, and literature.

The Emergence of Fields of Study and Research Methods: 1915–1945. Looking at the topics for possible research proposed by the National Association's Research Committee in 1915, we see the beginnings of the more general, interdisciplinary, communication discipline taking form. The Committee suggested research topics such as (from Cohen, 1994, p. 40):

- The structure and function of experience
- The processes involved in studying and learning
- The methods of teaching and learning
- Methods of studying a book
- Interrelations between public speaking and literature
- The structure, functions, and development of audiences.

In terms of methods, the Committee recommended the study of voice and gesture, audience analysis, the "scientific" study of speaking and listening processes, experimental study of methods of delivery, the study of the genetics behind speaking, study of the "unconscious give-and-take" between speakers and audiences, interpretive study of public speeches, study of speakers' experiences, and the study of the history of instruction and practice of public speaking. As we will discuss in the next chapter on research methods, we see these diverse methodologies in communication research and theory to this day, and these methods are applied to many modes of communication including Web 2.0 technologies.

Given the interdisciplinary nature of the roots of communication scholarship, it is not surprising that major shifts in theory and research in psychology also led to major shifts in communication. In the 1920s, Freud's work inspired research on personality that began to influence public speaking instruction, and by the early 1940s, researchers were calling for more instruction focused on conversation and building relationships throughout the speech curriculum (Cohen, 1994). Speech teachers and scholars were using surveys of personality to explore traits related to effective public speaking. This was the foundation of the **social sciences tradition** in communication studies.

At the same time, carryover from the discipline's roots in English gave rise to a distinct branch of research and theory in communication: rhetorical criticism of public speeches. Wichelns' (1925) essay, "The Literary Criticism of Oratory," pointed out that criticism of public discourse was very different from literary criticism. Though the methods overlap, criticism of oratory was focused on the *effects* of speeches, including considering the speaker, audience, historical context, content, and delivery, which are very different elements compared to literary criticism. Rhetorical criticism typically employed concepts and classifications developed by Aristotle, and the research methods were critical and historical. These critical and historical methods are still the foundation of the **rhetorical criticism tradition** in communication studies.

In addition to the influence of other disciplines on communication studies, the discipline was also shaped by historical events, such as World War I and World War II. Following World War I, there was focus in the discipline on speech as a way to promote citizenship, social responsibility, and ethical standards for discourse (Cohen, 1994). During World War II, interest in using speech to explore and promote the war efforts emerged, and research was published that considered how speech instruction could promote discussion, the challenges of intercultural communication at war time, propaganda, and broadcasting. Here, we see the very early roots of the fields of study discussed in the previous chapter: interpersonal, mass, intercultural/international, and electronic communication.

Also during the World War II era in psychology, some of the earliest studies of traits and experimental studies of propaganda were occurring, including the Yale Communication and Attitude Change Program headed by Hovland. The **Yale Program** was a series of experiments that explored communicator, message, channel, and audience variables to develop models and theories of persuasive messages and media effects. These studies, among others, gave rise to the **limited effects perspective** in the 1960s, or the idea that mass persuasion, propaganda, and mass media effects were relatively limited.

You can preview Hovland's (1957) book, *Communication and Persuasion: Psychological Studies of Opinion Change*, here: http://books.google.com/books/about/Communication_and_persuasion.html?id=j_FoAAAAIAAJ

Lastly, group communication became a topic of scholarly interest during the World War I and II eras as well (Cohen, 1994). Researchers in communication borrowed from their understanding of argumentation and debate to explain group leadership, prescribe group processes, and outline best practices for group discussion. Eventually, as experimental research in social psychology in the 1950s advanced clear theories about group and organizational processes, the social sciences tradition took hold in this field as well.

At the close of his review of the history of the communication discipline, Cohen (1994) pointed out that the division between the social science tradition, rooted in sociology and psychology, and the rhetorical tradition, rooted in literary criticism and historical methods, persisted. Indeed, it persists to this day.

Communication Theory: 1945 to the 1990's. The outcome of the social science work during and post World War II, such as the Yale project and group research, and the World War I era research on personality, is a series of social scientific communication theories related to interpersonal relationships, group processes, organizational and managerial communication, persuasive campaigns, and media effects. In this regard, we moved away from focusing exclusively on speech to the more general study of human communication in its many forms and in diverse contexts.

Insight into Innovation Example: Reflecting the evolving nature of our discipline, consider the name changes our national organization has undergone in its 100-year history (National Communication Association, 2014, emphasis added):

1914–1922: The National Association of Academic *Teachers of Public Speaking*

1923–1945: The National Association of *Teachers of Speech*

1946–1969: The *Speech* Association of America

1970–1996: The *Speech Communication* Association

1997–Present: The National *Communication* Association

That is not to say that speech and our early roots in English departments as instructors of elocution and oratory are not an integral part of our current discipline. The outcome of the early applications of critical and historical methods in the rhetorical tradition has brought us to an era of well-developed rhetorical theory that informs our understanding of the types, features, tactics, and societal implications of public speech, public address, and mass communication.

Even in this brief history of communication studies, it is easy to see why we are a flexible, practical, applied discipline that also has a solid foundation in research and theory. Our roots as instructors of practical skills in elocution and oratory solidified our emphasis on practical application within the discipline, and we still see that emphasis on producing skilled communicators in our modern communication programs. Similarly, our alignment with fields like psychology, sociology, English, and history provided us with the methodological tools to build a body of theory that is both diverse and rich.

Classical Rhetorical Theory Ancient Greece and Rome

Ethics, rhetorical theory and epistemology emerge.

Public Speaking and Eloquence 1800s

Interest in eloquence, public speaking and gestures develop.

Psychology and Rhetoric 1920–1940

Early studies of mass media effects, propaganda, and individual traits are conducted; modern critical and rhetorical theory advances.

Limited Effects and Relationships 1960–1970

The limited effects perspective emerges; studies in persuasion focus on internal processes; social lives, socialization, and power dynamics in society become prominent.

The Enlightenment 1600–1700

Rationalism, social order, and freedom of speech emerge and guide Western thought.

Psychoanalysis and Phenomenology 1900–1920

Theories move away from rationalism and focus on collective action, human thought processes, individual experiences, and attitudes.

Social Psychology 1940–1960

Clear fields of study emerge and specialized methods are applied to explore relationships, organizations, groups, attitudes, and media effects.

Distinct Fields 1970–1990

Specific fields of study exist in mass, persuasive, organizational, group, interpersonal, gender, intercultural, critical, and rhetorical communication; clear methods, theories and concepts are developed and refined in each field.

Courtesy of Rebecca Curnalia.

Based on the overview provided by Littlejohn and Foss (2009) in the Encyclopedia of Communication Theory.

A Brief History of the Communication Discipline

FROM 1990 TO TODAY:
COMMUNICATION THEORY, RESEARCH, AND WEB 2.0

In the early 1990s, communication scholars were interested in the uses and effects of new communication technologies (Littlejohn & Foss, 2009). Research and theory began to emerge on issues such as online group discussion and decision making, and media scholars began to consider the looming technology revolution and its implications for society.

There are many unique challenges and opportunities in the communication discipline in the new media environment. Given our roots in teaching practical communication skills, our skills training must adapt to this new mediated approach to communicating.

Luckily, we have a broad range of theories related to people's careful presentation of the self; interpersonal attraction, relationship maintenance, and conflict; group and organizational communication processes; persuasive tactics; and media uses and effects. Communication research and theories will prove invaluable as we move into an era of self branding, online dating, social networking, text messaging, long distance relationships, online meetings and telecommuting, marketing through social networks and online sales, and with more options and user control than ever over media content. Communication studies provides a broad set of theories that suggest practical skills and tactics for Web 2.0 users. Further, we have diverse research tools at our disposal to explore new communication phenomena as they unfold, which, as the Web Timeline below highlights, happens very quickly in the new media environment.

The discipline of communication evolved very quickly, broadening the scope of what we study from speech communication to all forms of human communication in just 50 years. Further, our inclusiveness in terms of incorporating diverse perspectives on research from related disciplines has been a constant core value in our discipline, even if we don't always work across our philosophical divides. Our adaptability, inclusiveness, and the applied nature of our discipline helps make us responsive as the communication environment changes. As flexible, inclusive, and applied researchers, we are well situated to use our understanding of human communication processes and outcomes to explain the uses and effects of new and emerging technologies.

1989	1993	1995	1997	2001
World Wide Web and AOL Instant Messenger launched	First web browser, Mosaic, launched	Amazon.com, Craigslist, Match.com, eBay, and Internet Explorer launched	Netflix begins as a video by mail service; Google.com is registered; the first Weblog is published	Wikipedia is launched

1991	1994	1996	1999	2002
First webcam developed, used to watch a coffee pot	Yahoo! launched; First online purchase is a pizza from Pizza Hut	Hotmail launched; first viral video of a 3D dancing baby	Napster is launched; 41% of Americans are online	The first social network, Friendster, is launched

2003	2005	2007	2010	2012
iTunes, MySpace, WordPress, and LinkedIn are launched	YouTube and Reddit are launched	iPhones are released	Pinterest and Instagram launched	Facebook had 1 billion users; internet commerce surpassed $1 trillion

2004	2006	2008	2011	2013
thefacebook.com, Mozilla and World of Warcraft are launched	Twitter launched	Google Chrome, the Apple App Store, and Groupon launched	Google+ launched; Egyptians use Twitter to start Arab Spring	56% of Americans had smartphones

Based on Pew Research Internet Project's (2014) World Wide Web Timeline: http://www.pewinternet.org/2014/03/11/world-wide-web-timeline/#2014

A Timeline of Major Developments in Web Technology

CONCLUSION

The communication discipline, particularly our research and theories, are increasingly relevant in the Web 2.0 environment. Dating back to Aristotle, communication research and theory has clarified and offered practical insight into how people communicate in different contexts, for different reasons, and with varying degrees of success.

Given our interdisciplinary roots, we drawn on theory and research from fields as broad as psychology, sociology, English, and history, and these research traditions that bridge the humanities and social sciences offer communication scholars tremendous flexibility as we seek to explain the uses and effects of new technological advancements. That being said, the diversity of our discipline has also led to divisions, beginning with those scholars who wanted to stay in English departments versus those who wanted to branch off, and continuing today in the healthy tension between our critical and humanistic research traditions and our social sciences approaches. These divisions are highlighted in the research traditions discussed in the previous chapter, and we will clarify why these are such distinct approaches to research and theory in the next chapter, as we consider research methods in the discipline.

ACTIVITIES AND ASSIGNMENTS

1. Reflect on some of the people discussed in this chapter—Aristotle, Plato, Freud, Hovland, and so on. Design an interview, and explain what you would ask these influential scholars to get insight into Web 2.0 technologies.

2. Write a position paper on whether or not communication's interdisciplinary roots in English, psychology, history, and sociology are good or bad. Consider whether it has strengthened or weakened the discipline, and whether it has made it harder or easier for communication to change in response to new technologies.

REFERENCES

Bizzell, P., & Herzberg, B. (2001). *The rhetorical tradition: Readings from Classical Times to the present* (2nd ed.). Boston: Bedford St. Martin.

Cohen, H. (1994). *The history of speech communication: The emergence of a discipline, 1914–1945*. Washington, DC: Speech Communication Association. Retrieved from https://www.natcom.org/HistoricalPublications/

Littlejohn, S. W., & Foss, K. A. (2009). *Encyclopedia of communication theory*. Los Angeles: Sage.

Pew Research. (2014, March 11). World Wide Web timeline. *Pew Research Internet Project*. Retrieved from http://www.pewinternet.org/2014/03/11/world-wide-web-timeline/

Wichelns, H. A. (1925). The literary criticism of oratory. In A.M. Drummond (Ed.) *Studies in rhetoric and public speaking in honor of James Albert Winans*. New York: Oxford University Press.

Wichlens, H. A. (1969). A history of the Speech Association of the Eastern States, 1909–1959. *Today's Speech*, *17*(2), 3–22.

National Communication Association. (2014). A brief history of NCA. Retrieved from http://www.natcom.org/historyofNCA/

METHODS IN COMMUNICATION RESEARCH

In this chapter, we will move on from focusing on what communication is (Chapter 1) and our history as a discipline (Chapter 2) to explore the **methods** that are used to create new knowledge about and insight into communication. That being said, it is important to note that our distinct research approaches in communication emerged during our historical development as a field, as we borrowed and learned from English, history, sociology, and psychology. The **critical and historical** approaches had been established for many years before our discipline's founding, and our incorporation of those research methods are part of the communication discipline's heritage in English departments. While the communication discipline was emerging as a distinct academic discipline, there were diverse approaches to research being applied as well in the disciplines that we borrowed from, particularly the **interpretive** (i.e., phenomenological) approach and the objective, **scientific** (i.e., empirical) approach. We will review each of these three approaches in this chapter, but let's begin with a discussion of why we should care about research and research methods.

WHY METHODS MATTER: METHODOLOGICAL THINKING IN AN INFORMATION SATURATED WORLD

CRITICAL THINKING AND INFORMATION LITERACY

Research methods are one way to understand the world around us. They also help us make reasoned decisions in our everyday lives. **Methodological thinking**, or thinking of things critically, from different perspectives, *and* objectively can help us critically consume information, recognize trends,

and reach reasoned conclusions. Whether we're shopping online, reading about current events, interpreting data for our jobs, or considering the merits of academic theory and research, methodological thinking gives us an orientation that can guide our decision making.

Imagine that you want to find out what type of diet you should adopt to lose weight or maintain your current weight. If you go online, you will find Weight Watchers, Jenny Craig, Nutrisystem, Atkins, Wheat Belly, Whole Foods, Cave Man, Cabbage Soup, Grapefruit, Sugar Busters, Beverly Hills, South Beach, Volumetrics, and Mediterranean diets to name just a few. Which one is the best?

Methodological thinking can help us make a reasoned decision. We consider the data available on the diets, and whether the available data is valid, reliable, and generalizable.

At the heart of methodological thinking is understanding **data**. Data is *anything* that can be *analyzed* to make inferences and reach conclusions. In communication studies, data can take many forms: textual content, spoken words and gestures, website content, videos, images, people's responses to open or closed questions, and numbers generated from tracking clicks, views, and shares. The type of data we look at depends on the **variables** that we are studying. Variables can be *anything that varies or changes from person to person or situation to situation*. A methodological thinker considers whether the data being used is a good source of evidence:

- **Validity**: Did they look at the right data to justify their conclusions?
- **Reliability**: Would we find the same results over and over again?
- **Generalizability**: Is their data representative of the general population?

Validity. Validity is about being accurate; whether a study is actually analyzing what it needs to analyze to find out about the variables being studied. This gets at researchers asking the right questions in the correct way to get at what they want to study.

Validity begins with **conceptualization**, or *the process of carefully defining our concepts*. **Concepts** are abstract ideas that we want to explore in research, such as specific feelings, states of being, attitudes, behaviors, or message strategies. So, if we want to compare and contrast the information available on different diets to choose one, we begin by conceptualizing what we mean by "diet" and exactly what we mean by "effective." We have to consider all of the health outcomes associated with food choices: good versus bad cholesterol, blood pressure, blood sugar, weight loss or weight gain, body mass index (BMI), body fat, muscle development, pant size, and so on. Say, for example, we choose to focus exclusively on weight loss. The next step is to **operationalize** the concept, or *decide how to measure it*. We can measure weight loss in terms of pounds lost, changes in BMI, or even changes in pant size. To have a valid indicator of diet effectiveness, we have to choose the measures that most accurately reflect the outcome we are interested in.

Reliability. Next we consider whether or not the measure is reliable: whether or not we get the exact same results over and over again using the same measure. For example, men tend to lose weight faster than women. So, if we use pounds lost to determine diet effectiveness, the results may not be reliable. There will always be **outliers**, or *individual instances that are far above or far below the norm*. But the vast majority of cases should be close to the **mean**, or the average. Since men and women will lose weight at different rates, we may choose BMI as a more reliable indicator of diet effectiveness because BMI accounts for one's height-to-weight ratio.

Generalizability. Now that we have a good idea of what variables are and validity and reliability standards, we consider *how much data researchers need to look at to reach a conclusion*. This is **sampling**. Researchers generally cannot collect all of the relevant data to analyze and reach conclusions, so we have to take a sample. How we sample data is very important, since that will decide whether or not findings are generalizable, or *how well they generalize to everyone or everything in the population*.

If we wanted to know which of the many diets available works best, we could ask our friends, look at a person's personal blog to read a weight loss story, watch a show like *Biggest Loser* to see how a dozen people lost weight, or read a report on a large-scale study that tested a particular diet method. If we're thinking methodologically, we know that the first three options aren't good ones because they are not generalizable samples.

Asking our personal friends is a **convenience sample**, or *a sample of people that we have easy access to*. Even if we asked hundreds of our Facebook friends, they would not be representative of the whole population, so we cannot learn generalizable results from their experiences. A personal blog is a sample of one person, who certainly cannot represent the diversity of body types and circumstances of the general public, so their results will not generalize to many others. Similarly, *Biggest Loser* is a **purposive sample**, or *a sample that is put together for a reason*, through cast-

ing of people who are obese and morbidly obese, so their outcomes will not generalize to most people. Rather, we need to refer to a study that uses **random sampling**, or *a large-scale study where all members of the population have an equal chance of being included*. A true, random sample may include people of different genders, races, geographic regions, health backgrounds, and family histories. Because of the diversity of a random sample of a lot of people, we should be able to generalize the findings to many more people.

Insight into Innovation Activity: Check out this infographic that compares diets: http://greatist.com/health/great-diet-comparison. Are the points of comparison valid and reliable? Why or why not? Is there any indication that the results of the recommended diets are generalizable?

Using methodological thinking to consider evidence, whether it is practical information about what we should or should not do or evidence provided for a theory, can help us make reasoned decisions about what to believe and what we should be skeptical of. This is particularly useful when using the Internet to find out about our options, as we are in an era of information overload, and unfortunately a lot of the information we find may not be valid, reliable, or generalizable.

In the next two sections we consider more traditional, academic uses of research skills as they relate to our focus on communication theories. We discuss research used to generate new theories, test existing theories, and apply existing theories.

TYPES OF RESEARCH STUDIES: EXPLORATORY, CONFIRMATORY, AND APPLIED RESEARCH

GENERATING NEW THEORIES

Research and research methods are essential tools for generating new knowledge about communication. **Exploratory research**, or *research that seeks to answer a question that has never been asked before*, can uncover new insights into human responses, behaviors, and experiences. Exploratory research is a useful first step toward discovering relevant concepts and new theories (Babbie, 2013).

Exploratory studies are typically guided by open questions, referred to as **research questions**, which we do not know the answer to. Because Web 2.0 technologies are so new, we are seeing a resurgence in exploratory research that seeks to discover how and why people are using new technologies, how this is affecting human relationships, and how this is affecting society and culture. On the basis of the findings of exploratory studies, we see new theories emerge and new concepts being refined to help us understand the effects of new technology on our sense of self, our social relationships, and society.

We sometimes see issues with reliability in exploratory studies. When we are researching in unchartered territory, it can be difficult to clearly define what we are looking for. In the absence of a clear, upfront conceptualization, there's the potential for inconsistent application and, as a result, unreliable findings. That is why exploratory research is a first step in developing a theory, followed by confirmatory research to test the tenants of a theory and applied research to see whether the theory works in real life.

Though exploratory research is common, this is not to say that existing research and theory is obsolete. As we will discuss throughout this book, even very old theories are still tested in the Web 2.0 environment and applied to Web 2.0 technologies to better understand how these advances in technology are changing us and our world, but also fit with what we already know about communication processes and effects. In fact, some older theories have increased in popularity as a result of interest in new communication technologies.

TESTING AND APPLYING THEORY

Confirmatory research seeks to *confirm the assumptions of a theory* and is typically guided by hypotheses that are based on existing theory. A **hypothesis** is a *declarative statement about how two or more variables are expected to be related to each other*. Most of what we discuss in this book is confirmatory and applied research, though we do also cover the earlier exploratory studies that laid the foundation for subsequent research. One issue we have to be concerned with in confirmatory research is the potential for a **confirmation bias**, or the potential that, *by seeking to confirm what we already believe to be true, we may look for evidence to support that notion and overlook what's really going on*. This can undermine the validity of research studies. One way to check the validity of a theory is to apply it to real situations to see whether the theory fully and accurately explains what is happening.

Applied research is when we take a theory and apply it to a real-life scenario. Applied research is *guided by theory-based research questions that ask about how specific concepts and assumptions from a theory apply to or explain a specific situation or event*. This can be done through **observational** studies where *we observe people's behavior in a particular situation*, by applying a theory to a current event to see if things happen the way the theory predicts, or by careful analysis of **artifacts**, which are *any kind of communication record*, to see if the concepts derived from a theory are present in people's communication.

Applied research, because of its focus on a single event, person, or situation, can sometimes lack generalizability. We know that research should be based on a large, random sample to be generalizable. Because applied research often, but not always, focuses on a single event or single person, the findings may not be generalizable. That being said, applied research contributes to our assessment of theory and research, because, as we mentioned in the previous chapter, one of the important qualities of a communication theory is that it applies to people's lives. Applied research also helps validate confirmatory research and can confirm the reliability of exploratory research findings by confirming that the theories developed and tested actually explain communication in diverse scenarios.

Type of Research	Exploratory	Confirmatory	Applied
Approach and purpose	Guided by open questions to develop a theory	Guided by clear hypotheses based on existing theory	Guided by theory-based research questions
Relative strengths/ weakness	Valid due to being "open" to discovering what's going on, but may have issues with reliability	Reliable due to clear conceptualizations and operationalizations, may have validity issues	Valid and reliable insofar as it employs clear conceptualizations and operationalizations, but may lack generalizability

Methods in Communication Research   27

RESEARCH METHODS IN COMMUNICATION STUDIES: CRITICAL/HISTORICAL, INTERPRETIVE, AND SCIENTIFIC APPROACHES

One reason I use the broad categories of exploratory, confirmatory, and applied research to explain the uses of research is because it fits well with the three common types of research methods in communication studies: critical/historical, interpretive, and objective (Baxter & Babbie, 2004; Merrigan & Huston, 2015). As you may recall from our discussion of the discipline, communication has historical roots in the arts, humanities, and social sciences. Our research methods in communication reflect the diversity of these historical roots.

It is important to note that one of the long-standing divisions in communication studies, other than our fields of study, centers on our research methods. Research methods reflect more than just the topic and goal of the research project, but also reflect the position and philosophy of the researcher. Therefore, in our discussion of each approach to inquiry, we will first discuss the *orientation of the researcher* in the process of inquiry. We go on to discuss specific methods associated with each general type of research, and consider the practical, everyday applications of these research methods in our personal, professional, and academic lives.

 For more insight into communication research, check out Baxter and Babbie's (2004) *The Basics of Communication Research:* http://books.google.com/books?id=PTE9AAAAQBAJ&printsec=frontcover &source=gbs_ge_summary_r&cad=0#v=onepage&q&f=false

CRITICAL/HISTORICAL METHODS OF INQUIRY

We will begin by discussing critical approaches to scholarship since this is the historical foundation of the discipline. Even as the interpretive and objective approaches have increased in use in the discipline, critical approaches have continued to thrive in Web 2.0 research. Initially, rhetoric was a narrow field that focused on the analysis of persuasive tactics in public address. More recent critical scholarship has broadened to address numerous persuasive tactics used in nearly every type of **discourse**, or human communication. Modern critical approaches look closely at the use of symbols in discourse, and are critical of how symbols are related to power structures in society, used to influence, and used to maintain or challenge social order. It is an **inferential** method, meaning that critics infer the intentions, meanings, and implications of discourse.

The critical orientation: The questioning critic. Foss (1989) described the critical orientation that she hopes to instill in her students: critics should always be "asking [questions] about the nature and function of symbols" (p. 191). She focuses on three general types of questions critical scholars ask: How is rhetoric related to context? How does rhetoric "construct a reality" for the person who created it and the audience that receives it? And, lastly, what does a particular artifact tell us about the rhetor, or the person who created the artifact?

These questions lead us to consider the underlying meanings, implications, and motives that drive human communication. Critical researchers focus their attention on the historical and social context of communication because communication norms and values change as a result of context. The social and historical implications of communication includes considering the effects of rhetorical choices on the audience or receivers, whether discourse is supporting or challenging the status quo, and whether or not it was effective. Lastly, considering the motivations and perceptions of the communicator helps critical researchers consider why particular rhetorical tactics were used.

Types and forms of critical inquiry. There are several methods that critical scholars use to evaluate the context, implications, and motivations of discourse. Critical inquiry includes criticism through close textual analysis, discourse and conversation analysis, semiotics, narrative analysis, and dramatistic approaches (Baxter & Babbie, 2004). Each of these methods is an approach to help us better understand the types of discourse used to influence people.

Criticism is often conducted using **close textual analysis**, or the careful analysis of artifacts to look for evidence of specific rhetorical tactics or to discover new rhetorical tactics used in the artifact. It can include looking at the visual elements of a message, the persuasive tactics in spoken language, or the production features in video and images. In criticism, what is said or depicted is important, but what is *not* said or depicted—what was selectively excluded from the message—is equally important. By looking at what is addressed and what is ignored, we get a sense of the social "reality" being created in the artifact and, by extension, we get a sense of the communicator's perception of reality.

Discourse and conversation analysis are methods that focus on the topics discussed and omitted; who gets to speak and who doesn't; who dominates the conversation; and the tone, connotations, and implications of the language used in discourse (Fairclough, 1995). These rhetorical choices include, exclude, and frame people, events, and issues, and can affect how we perceive reality. Similarly, **semiotics** is the study of the signs and symbols we use to communicate and their associated meanings (Babbie, 2013). Semiotics and conversation analysis are interesting research methods, because they can be critical methods when they are used to critique how symbols and interactions are a source of division and collective action in society. On the other hand, the use of specific symbols, signs, and conversational turns can also be objectively observed (which we discuss later in this chapter).

Insight into Innovation Example: "Fat." As an example of critical application of semiotics, consider our use of the word "fat." Is the word, in and of itself, negative? In the most basic sense, fat is an adjective used to describe size (i.e., being "fat") or contents (i.e., containing "fat"). Socially, we have many negative associations with "fat" because we have used it in our interactions as a derogatory term to describe people and our dietary guidelines suggested that fats were unhealthy. What do you think: Is "fat" a bad word? How do you use it in your conversations? How do other people use it? How does our use of the word "fat" create a social reality?

Narrative and **dramatistic** analytic methods move away from focusing on speaking roles and the use of specific symbols and focus our attention on the use of sequencing and emphasis in discourse. Narrative analysis asks us to consider discourse as narration, or an *intentionally constructed telling of how things are, were, or should be*. It includes considering the characters involved and how they are framed, how the setting is described, the selective sequencing of events, and the lessons taught. Dramatism builds on this idea, and adds that there are elements of stories that are emphasized while other elements are downplayed, and that looking at what is included or excluded can give us insight into the motives and goals of the communicator.

Think of it this way: a Republican and a Democrat can look at the very same situation and have two completely divergent evaluations and interpretations of what happened, which will lead them to retell distinct narratives. We see this in their conflicting explanations of international conflicts.

When we began the Iraq War in 2002, Republicans explained it was President George Bush's response to a terrorist threat that emerged before he was president. They argued that Iraq had amassed and used chemical weapons and was a growing threat to the United States. Democrats explained it as a war that Bush wanted. When President Obama ordered missile strikes in Syria in 2013 in response to their use of chemical weapons, Republicans said Obama was being reactionary rather than proactive, and Democrats accepted that it was a just response to the mass murder of Syrian civilians. In both of these situations, we have a similar event (humanitarian crises within sovereign nations) that led to military intervention by the United States in response to those reported events. But the Republican versus Democratic narratives used during those conflicts were fundamentally different, depending on who the president was: their description of the main character (the president), the setting, and series of events shifted according to whether they were trying to support the president from their own party or challenge the president from the opposing party. Thus, a critical look at the narratives people use can reveal their underlying perspectives on reality, their ideologies, and their biases.

The practice of critical inquiry. The process of critical inquiry includes describing the artifact in context, outlining the specific method used to analyze the artifact, reviewing the results and implications of the analysis, and explaining the contribution being made to critical rhetorical theory (Foss, 2004). This gets back to the questions Foss (1989) outlined. Critical researchers describe what they are analyzing and its historical, cultural, and social significance and context. The critic then explains the method—close textual analysis, semiotic analysis, discourse or conversation analysis, narrative, or dramatistic analysis—and explains the critical theory guiding the analysis. The critic uses the method to apply the theory to the artifact, and describes then critiques the rhetorical strategies used. In the end, the critic infers the consequences of rhetorical choices, and reports what was learned about the people or person who created the artifact and how that fits with and contributes to rhetorical theory.

Practical uses of critical inquiry. Clearly, having a critical orientation and understanding the breadth of rhetorical tactics people employ is useful as we consume media content and public discourse. Critical methods challenge us to reflect on how context affects choices, how communication affects society by reinforcing existing power structures, and how messages are constructed in a way that challenges or reinforces existing social structures and beliefs. This orientation can help us detect skewed and inaccurate information as we consider what is emphasized versus what is omitted, and it can give us insight into the person who created the message as well as the larger social forces at work in a message. This can help us as we navigate our information-saturated world and make decisions about what to believe and what to disregard.

INTERPRETIVE METHODS OF INQUIRY

Interpretive methods, like critical methods, are also inferential. But, rather than being a critic who is observing and analyzing an artifact as an observer, an interpretive scholar is typically immersed, or part of, the data being collected and analyzed through direct observation, conducting interviews, focus groups, or analyzing transcripts or recordings. The goal of the interpretive scholar is not to judge or evaluate, but to describe communication as it occurs from the perspective of the people involved.

The interpretive orientation: The empathetic observer. I think of interpretive scholarship as being empathetic, that is, trying to see communication and contexts from the perspectives of others to better understand their subjective realities. Interpretive scholars interact directly with the people they are researching to more fully understand people's individual social realities or standpoints (Merrigan & Huston, 2015). Interpretive scholars argue that there is no one objective meaning or objective truth, but meanings are within people and created as a result of their personal experiences and context. We learn meanings through interactions, and each of us has had different interactions (Berg & Lune, 2012). Interpretive scholars, therefore, *describe* people's unique interpretations and experiences.

Types and forms of interpretive inquiry. Interpretive research methods include observation, interviewing, focus groups, and open content analysis (Baxter & Babbie, 2004; Berg & Lune, 2012). Observational studies, or **ethnographies**, are when researchers go in to a group, organization, or setting, observe people in that natural environment, and take extensive field notes to describe the communication habits, tactics, and processes within that situation among those people. In ethnographic research, the researcher is embedded in the group being studied so that they have a very close, personal view of what is going on in a particular situation.

Both **interviews** and **focus groups** involve asking people open questions about the communication phenomena being studied. Interviews are interpersonal sessions where the researcher asks a person open questions. Focus groups are similar, but they involve asking open questions of a group of people who can give insight into the phenomena being studied.

Insight into Innovation Example: Why do So Many People Fail Online Courses? In some online classes, up to 20 percent more students have failed compared to similar face-to-face classes (e.g., Rivard, 2013). Numbers can tell us what happened to an extent, such as who passed and who didn't and the characteristics of students and faculty. Can qualitative methods help us understand what's going wrong? Having faculty observers in a course (ethnography) throughout the term observe interactions, interview students and faculty involved, and conduct focus groups of students and faculty involved could give insight into their unique expectations, experiences, thoughts, feelings, and reactions. This type of rich description can offer useful critiques and advice for future course developers.

Central to interpretive methods is the concept of **coding**, or identifying the trends and themes in field notes, transcripts, or other recorded forms of communication. Interpretive coding involves closely examing the communication, discovering recurring or prominent elements in the data, then interpreting the patterns found to develop a theory about what is going on.

The practice of interpretive inquiry. Interpretive analysis begins with asking questions about a communication phenomena; choosing a method for collecting data through ethnographic observation, interviewing, focus groups, or other archival data; coding the data that was collected to discover themes; identifying key examples; and using the findings to develop a theory. From the interpretive perspective, we cannot know what to expect until we are immersed in data collection and seeing events from others' perspectives, so these studies are typically guided by an open question. To answer that question, interpretive researchers choose one or more methods to collect their data depending on the availability of people involved and the types of data they need to fully explore the phenomena in depth. Then researchers code the collected data, trying to discover patterns or categories. Once there are clear patterns or categories that have emerged from the data, interpretive researchers choose prime examples from their data—such as quotes or images—that serve as a basis for defining each trend or category. Lastly, they develop a theory about the types, processes, or trends in communication that they discovered through coding, using the prime examples as cases in point when writing up results.

Practical uses of interpretive inquiry. Much like critical orientations and methods challenge us to think about the societal implications of communication, interpretive orientations ask us to see things through other people's eyes to understand people's perspectives and experiences. In general, being empathetic to people's unique feelings and experiences is a desirable trait professionally and interpersonally. In terms of applying methods, such as ethnography, interviewing, focus groups, and coding, these methods can be very helpful to us personally and professionally as well. Focus groups are used widely in marketing, public relations, and product development to explore people's responses to campaign plans or products. If you think about it, the whole world is a focus group now, because you can find online product reviews, critiques of websites, campaigns, corporations, and people in blog posts, comment threads, and review websites like Yelp! and Angie's

List. Online listening strategies are a common method used by campaigns and companies to track online commentary about their product, discover issues or assets that come up repeatedly in online posts, and adjust their product or message.

Even ethnography has new horizons online, as we can go into online communities and read posts and threads to gain insight into the experiences of people with different illnesses, and emotional, psychological, or social circumstances. We can use this information for our own benefit if we are seeking insight into situations in our own lives, to help people we know who are in similar circumstances, or as practitioners to better understand clients' experiences and to help them.

OBJECTIVE METHODS OF INQUIRY

The final grouping of research methods we will look at in this chapter to frame our discussion of communication theory is objective approaches. Objective approaches are distinct from critical approaches that infer biases, social injustices, and power imbalances, and interpretive approaches that describe people's subjective realities; objective approaches assume that there is one objective truth. It is a detached, factual orientation, rather than a critical or empathetic approach to research.

The objective orientation: The fact-finder. Objective researchers are detached observers who look to reach generalizable, factual conclusions about the types, processes, and effects of communication. Objective researchers focus on controlled, planned, systematic analysis of communication. Rather than being immersed like an interpretive researcher would be, or being a skeptic like a critical researcher would be, objective researchers try to stay neutral when conducting research. This neutrality should make their findings more replicable, or reliable, than findings from interpretive or critical inquiry, but objective researchers have to be particularly careful about the validity of the measures and analytic schemes they use to conduct research. Surveys, experiments, and content analytic frameworks have to be carefully designed before data analysis can begin.

Types of objective inquiry. Surveys, experiments, and content analysis are common objective methods applied in communication studies (Baxter & Babbie, 2004). Though when we think of objective research we may be tempted to only include quantitative methods, responses to open questions, communication artifacts, and observations of human behavior can be objectively coded without necessarily being quantified. **Quantification** is the process of *assigning numerical values to data, which allows researchers to statistically analyze data.* **Qualitative** research, on the other hand, can include objective, theory directed coding of content or open, interpretive approaches to discovering trends and themes, as described in the previous section. For example, some rhetorical methods are not quantitative, but they are typically objectively applied coding frameworks used to analyze public discourse that can be replicated by other researchers (Merrigan & Huston, 2015).

Surveys are carefully designed questionnaires that ask open and/or closed questions related to the variables being studied. Responses can be collected electronically via survey software, by distributing on paper, or by having interviewers ask the questions and record responses. The most familiar types of surveys use **Likert items**, where people respond on a scale of "strongly agree" to "strongly disagree." But there are many other types of questions that can be asked via surveys depending on the type of data the researcher needs: people can rank listed options, choose among a series of listed options, indicate their feelings on a range of positive to negative, or people can even be asked open questions that are later coded by the researcher. Survey items have to be very carefully worded and planned in advance to be sure that they are valid measures of the variables being studied. This gets back to carefully conceptualizing and then operationalizing variables so that we're sure that the measures are reliable and valid. Even though they require a lot of planning, surveys are convenient ways to get a lot of data, particularly now that they can be distributed via e-mail, social networks, and websites to collect a wide variety of responses.

Unlike surveys, where the researcher cannot really control the environment or variables being studied, **experiments** allow for the careful control over variables being studied by creating an artificial situation or message, having people participate in the experiment, then carefully observing or collecting self-reported responses. Experiments also require a significant amount of pre-planning, including developing the experimental conditions, designing measures for the variables being studied, and pre-testing to make sure that the experiment seems realistic and the measures are reliable.

Experiments tend to involve smaller samples than surveys because experiments take more time for participants compared to completing surveys, but they tend to be a method that others can replicate and they can be used to support **causal** claims. Causal claims, as we'll see in the discussion of many theories in the book, are when theorists argue that one thing *causes* another. Causal claims cannot be verified using most survey data, because surveys only give you insight into what people are thinking and feeling in the moment, not necessarily what caused those thoughts, feelings, and behaviors. Experiments can be used to substantiate causal claims because the researchers intentionally manipulate a variable then record the changes that result.

Insight into Innovation: Facebook's Experiments on Getting out the Vote. Facebook rolled out an "I'm Voting" app for use on election days, and conducted a series of experiments to explore the uses and effects of the button. Their experiments included varying the wording, placement of the button for the app, and the availability of the app. Some of the preliminary findings indicate that this did affect voter turnout. But was it ethical? Check out Mother Jones' critique: http://www.motherjones.com/politics/2014/10/can-voting-facebook-button-improve-voter-turnout

Content analysis is the systematic, objective analysis of communication messages that looks for clearly defined types of communication. Content analysis can be used to code responses to open-ended questions asked in interviews or surveys, to code observations of human behavior, and to code communication artifacts like media messages. Content analysis is objective because it begins with clearly defining what is being coded for before the analysis begins, unlike interpretive analysis that begins without a coding framework to see what concepts are discovered. Merrigan and Huston (2015) pointed out that some lenses used to conduct rhetorical analyses also fit the objective research approach. Thinking back to our discussion of semiotics, discourse analysis, and conversation analysis, these can be used as content analytic frameworks for objectively analyzing messages. Theories are also useful starting points for developing objective content analytic schemes, because theories tell us what concepts to look for in different types of communication messages and give us clear definitions for concepts to guide our analysis of messages.

The practice of objective inquiry. Operationalizing, sampling, and testing are the three key steps in objective research (Baxter & Babbie, 2004). Operationalizing is the process of deciding how data will be collected and analyzed to explore the variables being studied. Researchers then choose a sampling method to collect data. Once all of the data is collected, objective researchers analyze the data. This sounds like a relatively straightforward process, and the intricacies of each of these steps is beyond the scope of this brief chapter. But is important to appreciate the amount of planning and careful, justified decision making that goes into the early stages of objective research. One wrong decision at the outset of the project when operationalizing or sampling can make a study's results invalid, unreliable, or not generalizable.

Practical uses of objective inquiry. Though it requires a lot of preplanning, objective approaches to research can be useful to us personally and professionally. First, the criteria for good objective research—valid and reliable operationalizations and generalizable samples—gives us clear criteria that can be used to evaluate the quality of information we find. We know, based on these criteria, that polls taken on websites aren't generalizable because of the sample, that some polls' results may be inaccurate because of question wording, and that a single survey's findings cannot prove or disprove anything. This should help our methodological thinking in everyday life as we are inundated with claims that are allegedly "backed by data." Now we know that data can be very faulty.

Beyond our personal lives, the ability to design quality surveys and even experiments are useful skill sets for business professionals. This is why many undergraduate programs require a research methods course. Customer and client service involves being able to objectively assess the strengths and weaknesses of business practices and products. Designing and implementing campaigns involves carefully testing messages and strategies and following up with post tests to ensure that the campaign is working. Even websites need to be objectively tested before they are launched, and people's use of features should be tracked and analyzed regularly, so that companies know how best to provide content to their users.

New technology offers many unique opportunities for objective research, such as the Facebook experiment described above. We have an unprecedented ability to track, code, ask people about, and tweak and test communication online. That being said, we have to do these things ethically, with the consent of the people being researched and in a way that protects the people participating in our research from harm, embarrassment, or ill effects. Regardless of the approach to research or specific method chosen, we have an obligation to protect the people involved, to be careful and fair in our analysis of data, and be honest in our reporting of results.

Overview of Research Approaches (Merrigan & Huston, 2015)			
	Critical	**Interpretive**	**Objective**
Goal	Reveals power imbalances	Describes people's realities	Reports facts
Role of researcher	Orientation toward understanding context and the role of discourse in creating and reinforcing social structures	Orientation toward seeing communication and events from individuals' unique perspectives	Orientation toward discovering factual truths about human communication
Methods	Close textual analysis, narrative and dramatistic analysis, semiotics, discourse/conversation analysis	Ethnographic observation, interviews, focus groups	Surveys, experiments, content analysis

In this chapter, we have discussed some general criteria for research, that it is reliable, valid, and generalizable. We went on to discuss the types of research studies we see in the development and ongoing testing of communication theory: exploratory, confirmatory, and applied. Lastly, we covered the types of research methods we use in communication studies to explore, confirm, and apply theories: critical, interpretive, and objective methods. As a mixed methodologist myself, I see each research method as a tool to build, critique, and strengthen communication theory. These methods work together to build a body of knowledge about communication; none of them is perfect or complete in-and-of itself, and all of them have at their core the goal of creating new knowledge about human communication processes and effects.

These methods work together. When faced with a new phenomenon, such as a new online social network, we may not have a clear idea of where to begin research, particularly if no theory or research exists on the topic. What, then, can we do? We can use critical, interpretive, and objective approaches together to explore what is going on, develop a theory, and then test it. **Triangulation** is when we use more than one approach to answer a research question. Indeed, almost any communication, including computer-mediated communication, can be explored critically, interpretively, *and* objectively. We see our research methods merging with the growth of triangulated case studies, use of qualitative content analysis by software, and use of online experiments and surveys with open questions in addition to tracking clicks, shares, time spent reading, and comments.

Research isn't perfect. No one study can prove or disprove a theory. Rather, we look at the *body of evidence*, which typically includes several types of studies that employ different methods and measures. News articles and blog posts that cite academic research as "proof" that we should do something or stop doing something are very misleading. Because of the nature of research, we generally only get a snapshot of what's going on with some people at one moment in time. People and circumstances change dramatically and sometimes very quickly, and people are very diverse, so it is simply not possible for any one study to *prove* something is true. Rather, we look for long-term, replicated and validated findings across a broad range of studies to reach tentative conclusions about human communication; these tentative conclusions are used to build theory.

Research must be ethical. All forms of research also come with ethical obligations: we do not exploit people, take advantage of them, or injure them when conducting research. **Institutional review boards** were put in place to protect the people who are asked to participate in research studies, and these committees review people's research projects before data can be collected from people to ensure that people are not being exploited or harmed. Unfortunately, this is only true of academic and government-funded research, and private companies do not have to go through the review process before conducting experiments (such as Facebook's experimentation with newsfeeds) or conducting surveys (such as customer satisfaction surveys that pop up on websites).

Research is essential to theory and society. Research that is conducted ethically and well has the potential to change people and society for the better. Critical research helps us see social injustices, interpretive research helps us understand others more fully, and objective research can help us understand general rules and principles to guide our communication behavior. Research methods are also helpful tools in our professional lives as they help us make better, socially responsible, and person-centered decisions. Even though no one study can definitively prove a causal relationship, the body of evidence collected using these diverse methods over time can help us build theories to understand ourselves, our relationships, and our society.

ACTIVITIES AND ASSIGNMENTS

1. Write a one-page position paper: a) choose a research orientation that fits your beliefs about research (critical, interpretive, or objective) and b) explain why the orientation of researchers, methods, goals, and practical applications of the chosen approach to methods fits your beliefs, personal interests, and professional goals.

2. Write a critique of a popular blog post that is advocating for a particular behavior (such as parenting, dieting, relationship, or professional advice), critique the causal claims in the blog post and the validity, reliability, and generalizability of the evidence provided.

3. Imagine your university wanted to change their marketing tactics to increase enrollment. Write a brief paper explaining how your school's marketing and communication staff could use critical, interpretive, *and* objective research methods to plan their new campaign.

REFERENCES

Babbie, E. (2013). *The practice of social research* (13th ed). Belmont, CA: Wadsworth.

Baxter, L. A., & Babbie, E. (2004). *The basics of communication research*. Belmont, CA: Thomson Wadsworth.

Berg, B. L., & Lune, H. (2012). *Qualitative research methods for the social sciences* (8th ed.). New York: Pearson.

Fairclough, N. (1995). *Media discourse*. New York: St. Martin's Press.

Foss, S. K. (2004). *Rhetorical criticism: Exploration & practice*. Long Grove, IL: Waveland Press.

Foss, S. K. (1989). Rhetorical criticism as the asking of questions. *Communication Education*, *38*(3), 191–196.

Merrigan, G., & Huston, C. L. (2015). *Communication research methods* (3rd ed.). New York: Oxford University Press.

Examples:

Rivard, R. (2013). Udacity project on 'pause.' Inside Higher Ed. Retrieved from https://www.insidehighered.com/news/2013/07/18/citing-disappointing-student-outcomes-san-jose-state-pauses-work-udacity

THE SELF

In this first unit, we will cover theories related to the self. We will look at how our sense of self is developed and shaped through interactions, how we attribute and understand our own and others' behaviors, and how we can use mindfulness and active listening to more fully understand our self and others. In any discussion of the self, there are several concepts to consider: our self-concept, self-esteem, and perception.

Self-concept is who we see ourselves as being and not being. It is a combination of our personality, skills, roles, and norms. As we will discuss in the first chapter in this unit, our self-concepts are formed through our interactions with others, and it affects our behavior, or performances, in different situations.

Self-esteem is also related to how we see ourselves. Self-esteem is whether or not we like who we are; whether we are comfortable with our self. Generally, we tend to think of ourselves differently than we think about others, which we will discuss in the chapter on attributions and cognitive complexity. When we make attributions, we tend to use external excuses for our own behavior but attribute others' behaviors to their character and personality. This is a way to protect our self-esteem and self-concept, but also leads us to fundamentally misunderstand other people.

This leads to the third key concept related to the self: perception. We will talk a lot about perception in this unit because perception is internal and unique to each of us. Perception is how we see, experience, and interpret the things around us. Each of us has our own unique perception of just about everything. We take in information differently, process it differently, and thus understand it in a unique way.

Take, for example, the viral color-changing dress from 2015. When some people looked at the picture of a dress they saw white and gold, others saw blue and black, still others saw the colors on the dress change from white and gold to blue and black. Of course, the internet blew up, debating about the "real" color of the color-changing dress. Indeed, even my husband and I looked at the same picture of the dress at the same time and saw two completely different color schemes. This is because of perception: our eyes were taking in the same information,

Copyright © buran_4ik/Shutterstock.com

39

but we were processing that information differently, thus leading us to see things differently. It is one of many examples where my husband and I looked at the same thing and saw it completely differently. What was shocking about the dress picture is that something we often assume is objectively "real"—color—was actually being interpreted and thus seen differently.

Hear a couple of color experts explain how lighting and human perception led to the internet debate over the color of a dress in 2015: https://www.youtube.com/watch?v=I0OPNOpU6SY.

The debate on the internet and subsequent news stories brought up an important point: what we see and hear is interpreted. The internet, and people in general, were so absorbed by this story because it is was a reminder about how things that we take for granted as being certain and objectively true, like the color of a dress, can still be perceived in different ways. People, their behavior, and the situations we find ourselves in are like that dress: it can all be seen in different ways by different people. It depends on the angle we see things at, how our brains interpret elements of what we're seeing, and what we focus on.

So in the last chapter in the unit on the self, we will consider a method of trying to see people and things differently by refocusing our attention on new details. We discuss mindfulness as a way of thinking of things in more flexible ways and active listening as a way to learn about other people's perceptions and feelings rather than staying fixated on our own perspective. Mindfulness challenges us to stop saying "it is what it is" and consider, instead, how things could be seen differently. When we are mindful, we consider things from different perspectives, or angles. Mindfulness can help us reshape our self concept by considering new ways of thinking of the elements of our self. Rethinking those elements can help self esteem and being mindful when interacting with others helps us understand different perspectives on ourselves and others.

Though mindfulness is a rather complex and abstract concept, we will will discuss more concrete and specific methods of improving the accuracy of our perceptions, particularly communication competence, sensitivity to individual differences, and active listening. In the chapter on attributions and constructivism, we consider how competent, skillful communicators think more analytically about people and contexts, considering demographics, personality, situations, and even perceptions of communication channels when they interact with others. In the chapter on mindfulness, we look at another dimension of competence: listening. Part of getting to know people so that we may respond to them effectively is listening to better understand their perceptions and feelings in an interaction. Active listening with an open, mindful orientation, can actually make us better at formulating messages because we will develop more person-centered, situation-appropriate messages.

Of course, all of this is easier said than done. It is all well and good to suggest that we need to reconsider our preconceived notions about ourselves and others, that we should stop stereotyping and start listening to each unique person we meet. But in our Web 2.0 lives, this is increasingly difficult. Not only do we have our own internal distractions (our thoughts, emotions, senses), but we also have technological distractions—the buzz of our phones, pings from our texts and emails, and constant availability of social media. This makes truly focusing on and fully understanding and learning about others uniquely challenging. It is worth the investment if we can force ourselves to pay attention. There are clear benefits to taking the time to listen and learn, particularly if we want to influence people, be seen as likable, and be socially attractive.

CHAPTER 4

SYMBOLIC INTERACTIONISM AND IMPRESSION MANAGEMENT

OUTCOMES

- *Knowledge:* Learn about Mead's symbolic interactionism and Goffman's concept of "self-presentation" as a dramatic act.

- *Skill:* Consider the many modes of self-presentation, such as social networks, and the consequences of your own and others' self-presentational choices.

💬 INTRODUCTION

The idea behind **symbolic interactionism** is that the meanings that we have for ourselves, other people, and objects are "a social product formed through activities of people *interacting*" (Blumer, 1969, p. 5, emphasis added). So, who we are in terms of our roles, values, and character is the result of our interactions with other people. From a **dramaturgical perspective**, we perform impression management to project a specific image of ourselves; we are like actors on a stage playing a specific part, in a setting, with an audience (Goffman, 1959). So, symbolic interactionism focuses on social interactions and the development of our self, such as how we think about ourselves and others. The dramaturgical perspective focuses on presentation of the self to others.

Both of these theories focus on the self. Broadly defined, the **self** is who you see yourself as being. Mead (1934), the intellectual parent of symbolic interactionism, argued that we learn about our "self" through social interaction: considering how other people perceive us (**looking-glass self**) and living up to the good and/or down to the bad expectations that others have for us (**Pygmalion effect**). We learn these aspects of the self through interactions with specific people who are important to us (**particular others**) and the general observations we make about norms within our community and social groups (**generalized others**).

Goffman (1959), on the other hand, focuses on how we present the self to others. He reasons that we are selective about how we present ourselves, but also discusses how we are constrained by existing stereotypes and norms for the role we are playing, the setting we are in, and the audience for which we are performing.

41

OVERVIEW OF THEORIES OF THE SELF

MAIN IDEA

Symbolic interactionism explains sources of meaning: in our *minds* we have meanings for symbols that we have learned through interactions; our sense of *self* is formed through interaction and we infer norms from broader *society* (Mead, 1934). The dramaturgical perspective explains that we have an idea of who we are and how we want to be perceived by others, and we manage our public image so that others see us in a particular way.

Insight into Innovation Activity: Reflect on Your "Self"

Self: Take out a piece of paper and describe yourself: *Who are you? What are your important roles in life?*

Mind: Now look at those things that you listed to describe yourself. *What meaning, or descriptions, do you assign to each role you listed?*

Society: Thinking about those descriptions, *where did your understanding of what people in your specific roles come from?* Did family and friends tell you/show you what was expected (particular others) or did you learn by observing how most people behave in those roles (generalized others)?

Presentation: Think about how you present yourself to others when you are performing each of those roles—how you dress, talk, behave nonverbally—is this an act that is in keeping with how you view your roles rather than a reflection of who you really are?

KEY ASSUMPTIONS OF SYMBOLIC INTERACTIONISM (BLUMER, 1969)

Here is a great video overviewing symbolic interactionism: http://youtu.be/jFQIIM8IRZU

- *People act toward things based on the meanings that they have for those things.* Chances are, one of the roles you see yourself as playing is that of "student." If I think "college students go to class and study," I will act toward students, and think about myself if I am a student, based on this internal meaning for that role. Other people have different internal meanings for being a "student," such as "college students are figuring out who they are," and this will change how they act toward students and how they would see themselves if they were a student.

- *People learn meanings through interaction.* I learn what students should be like by observing what other people expect of them, such as how other people talk about them and act toward them, which is a perception based on generalized others. I also learn what students should be like based on my interactions with other people who are close to me, such as my family and friends, who are particular others. Thinking about this in terms of social networks, observing how people in my social circle respond to posts by and about students will affect the meaning I have for that group, as will content from blogs, news outlets, and other general sources of social information in my social media feed.

- *People interpret meanings and apply them within contexts.* I interpret and apply the meanings I have for being a student differently as a professor. My meanings were different as an undergraduate student, graduate student, and even as a nontenured professor. Similarly, as you move through your education and you experience new contexts and have new interactions, your meanings will evolve and change as well. This will be reflected in how you respond to others and how you see yourself.

 Insight into Innovation Example: What should you do in your 20s? Before reading through this example, take out a piece of paper and write down what you think *people typically do* and *what people should do* when they are in their 20s.

Symbolic interactionism teaches that people live up or down to others' expectations of them, and we learn meanings about who we are through interactions. Given how we discuss people in their 20s, and how we act toward them in our society, chances are you were pretty lenient in your expectations.

In a popular Ted Talk from 2013, therapist Meg Jay explained that the repeated phrase, "30 is the new 20," may be doing more harm than good. As we repeat this phrase and its variations, we communicate meaning about what our 20s should be like. This message can affect how we see ourselves and others. Accepting the idea that what you do in your 20s doesn't matter (because you can "get it together" when you're in your 30s) may lead to people in their 20s wasting a decade of their lives. It implicitly gives permission for people in their 20s to make bad decisions or lack direction, condones short-term thinking and nonstrategic decision making, and can lead to lifelong repercussions for professional success, wealth, marriage, child-rearing, and intergenerational success.

In short, as symbolic interactionism explains, social messages from others—like hearing that "30 is the new 20," referring to college students as "kids," and calling 20-somethings "twixters"—will affect how people such as parents, professors, and employers act toward people in their 20s. How these particular others act toward people in their 20s creates a Pygmalion effect, and people may live down to this standard for behavior as a kind of self-fulfilling prophecy.

In her Ted Talk, Jay reframes the 20s as a "defining decade" because that is when people define who they are going to be regardless of whether or not they are intentionally choosing a path. Does referring to one's 20s as a "defining decade" make you think about what you will do, are doing, or could have done in a new way? Has this example changed or affected the meaning you have for this decade in human development? Jay said that she hopes that hearing this new message about the importance of your 20s will reshape how we think about and act toward this pivotal period in people's lives.

KEY ASSUMPTIONS OF SELF-PRESENTATION (GOFFMAN, 1959)

In Goffman's view, all human interaction is a drama as we all engage in impression management to try to influence other people.

- *We perform behaviors according to the image of self we want to project.* This is the **front** we put forward. Front is a combination of our appearance and our behavior. For many roles, there are specific norms to adhere to; but for other roles, we may choose from a variety of fronts that guide our appearance and behavior. Much like symbolic interactionism, Goffman explained that these fronts are **stereotypes**, or established social expectations, that we learn and integrate into our own behavior. Further, he adds that we are restrained by these roles because we are expected to maintain consistency between our front, appearance, and behavior. Online, we have much more control over self-presentation, and maintaining consistency in our self-presentation is somewhat easier since we can be selective about what we post. It is also a difficult environment in terms of self-presentation, since we have less control over the audience. Different roles call for different behaviors, such as being a college student *and* son/daughter *and* an employee *and* a friend, but things like our tweets and blog posts are available for audiences from each of these different areas of our lives and they can live on long after our roles have changed.

- *Our performance is affected by the **region** where we are performing.* Regions are the space where we perform. Our politeness, in terms of how we interact with people, and our decorum, or how we behave, are bound by the region in which we are performing. Goffman uses the example of "**make-work**" to illustrate this point. When we are at work, we are expected to *look* busy. In addition to looking busy, there are also standards for how we interact with others, such as avoiding inappropriate gestures, touching, and topics of conversation. We can take a break from performances when we are **backstage**, or someplace separate from the work-related performance, such as the break room, or in our private office with close colleagues. One concern with social media, which we will focus on in this chapter, is that the distinction between backstage and other regions where we perform different roles are blurred now. Though we could argue that places like Facebook are backstage, because we're among "friends," and LinkedIn is a professional context because it is focused on professional connections, the audience in these two seemingly different contexts is not as different as we might prefer. Online "backstages" are not private or protected.

- *Our region-specific behavior is careful, and our backstage behavior is strictly private, because there is information about ourselves and our groups that would undermine the public impression we are trying to create.* So, the distinction between the front and back stage is blurring as social media gives us a platform that seems to be a backstage where we can express ourselves among our circle of friends. But this seemingly backstage region is also visible to unintended audiences, like employers or future customers. Thus, what we post to our friends on Facebook today may end up destroying our career tomorrow.

EXAMPLE OF THEORY IN WEB 2.0: LIVES DESTROYED BY INAPPROPRIATE SOCIAL MEDIA POSTS

There are, of course, positives and negatives to thinking about ourselves as actors on a stage in the Web 2.0 environment. On the positive side, we have a fair amount of control over how people view us online: we can choose what to post and we can carefully edit and curate content. Thus, impression management is more controllable. On the negative side, this constrains our behavior in sometimes stressful ways and some people aren't careful enough about what they post. In other words, people don't recognize who their audience *could be* online and how that region is fundamentally different from talking among friends or coworkers.

A *New York Times* article recounted Justine Sacco's life-destroying tweet as an example of how one thoughtless social media post can cause irreparable damage to a person's public image (Ronson, 2015). In 2013, Sacco tweeted a series of jokes while traveling to Africa, including the tweet, "Going to Africa. Hope I don't get AIDS. Just kidding. I'm white!" While she was inflight, a twitter firestorm erupted. Sacco was a corporate communication professional, and twitter users called for her to be fired. She was.

Sacco is just one example of a social media post that led to serious repercussions. Lindsey Stone was fired for a Facebook post where she posed in front of the Tomb of the Unknowns "flipping the bird" and pretending to scream as part of her ongoing online gag where she posed in ways that disobeyed signs in public areas (Ronson, 2015). In 2015, @Cellla_ posted "Ew, I start this f*** a** job tomorrow" to which her new employer responded "And…no you don't start that FA job today! I just fired you!" (Earnheardt, 2015). There are also teachers who tweeted about getting stoned and servers who posted about urinating in food (Umansky, 2014).

In these examples, we see the unfortunate intersection of the front stage and backstage play out in destructive ways. Many of these cases are instances of people trying to be funny on social media, a behavior that may have been more appropriate for a private, backstage interaction among friends rather than the public stage of social media. But these social media posts are also seen by employers and coworkers, and thus are judged in relation to the expectations of one's professional roles and norms. As Goffman explains, we have to be aware of the setting and the audience. Via social media, the potential audience is *everyone everywhere forever*. Though we can manage our circle of Facebook friends and the privacy settings for who initially sees our social media posts, we have less control over what happens to content after we post. Research suggests that students do manage their circle of friends online and the public visibility of their profiles, but they are not as careful about the actual content they post via social media like Facebook (Tufecki, 2008). Unfortunately, as of right now, there are no clear protections offered for social network users against their "private" content being redistributed using sharing features and screen shots, and the policies of social media sites like Facebook and Instagram have evolved such that users forfeit a lot of control over who sees their social media content when they sign up for these accounts (Sanvenero, 2013).

METHODS OF RESEARCH ON THE SELF

Qualitative studies. Symbolic interactionism explains that meaning is internal and a product of interaction; therefore, meanings are unique to each individual and require a person-centered, phenomenological approach. Research in this tradition includes collecting data through observation, interviews, or open questions, then exploring the data collected to describe the human condition (Berg & Lune, 2012). It is typically qualitative. Goffman (1959) also conducted qualitative, observational research to develop his theory of self-presentation. For example, if I wanted to understand people's social media selves, I could observe a small sample of people's social media behavior and others' responses to their behavior, interview people about their posting habits and rationale, have a focus group where users described their experiences online, or even distribute a survey of open questions where people describe their social media experiences. The observations or responses are the data, and I could look to see what common trends there are in people's responses. Then I could use those trends to develop concepts that explain how social media interactions shape people's understanding of the channel and their own behavior.

Surveys and experiments. Over the past half century, research has evolved significantly. Concepts from both symbolic interactionism and self-presentation have been the focus of quantitative survey and experimental research to explore self-concept and impression management, particularly in online contexts.

Jones and Pittman (1982) created a **taxonomy**, or a system for classifying, impression management strategies that people use: **self-promotion** through highlighting one's accomplishments, **ingratiation** to others using flattery and favors, **intimidation** by accentuating one's ability to punish or have power over others, **supplication** to receive sympathy by highlighting one's struggles, and **exemplification** to exceed expectations and be seen as a hard worker. Clearly, we can use this typology to code behavior by counting the number of times we see people in a particular context using each of these strategies. Researchers have also used the taxonomy to develop scale measures that assess people's use of these tactics (Bolino & Turnley, 1999).

Consider, for example, the scale measure of impression management tactics that people use at work (adapted from Bolino & Turnley, 1999). We could complete this scale to measure our use of these tactics. We also could use this to code people's behavior in workplace settings to see whether they do these things. We could ask people open questions about the types of conversations they have at work, then code responses to see whether they reflect these strategies. In short, impression management is a flexible area of study, and even the existing research tools we have can be applied in multiple ways.

Strategy	Scale items
Self-Promotion	At work, do you often talk about: • your experience and education • your talents and qualifications • how you're valuable to the organization • your accomplishments
Ingratiating	At work, do you often find yourself: • complimenting colleagues so you seem likable • taking an interest in colleagues' lives so you seem friendly • praising colleagues' accomplishments so you seem nice • doing favors for people so you seem likable
Exemplification	At work, do you often: • go in early to seem dedicated to the job • try to look busy even if things are slow • stay late so you look like a hard worker • stay late in the evenings or go in on weekends to show your dedication

Intimidation	At work, do you often find yourself:
	• intimidating others so you can get your job done
	• telling others you can make things hard for them if they "push you too far"
	• being forceful with others when they make it hard to get your job done
	• being strong and aggressive with people who stand in your way
	• intimidating people to get them to behave appropriately
Supplication	At work, do you often:
	• act unsure so people will help you
	• try to gain sympathy by acting needy
	• act like you don't understand something so someone will help you
	• act like you need help so others will assist you
	• act like you don't know something so you can avoid a particular project

Insight into Innovation Activity: Code Your Facebook News Feed. Use Jones and Pittman's (1982) typology of impression management tactics to code the posts made by your Facebook friends. For each of your friends' posts in your feed over the past hour, count how many were self-promoting, ingratiating, intimidating, supplicating, exemplifying, or other. What kinds of trends do you observe? Are there types of people you are friends with that are likely to use supplication or intimidation? Who are the self-promoters or humble braggers?

Beyond surveys, both symbolic interactionism and self-presentation are also assessed through experiments. For example, the Pygmalion effect was manipulated in an experiment by telling teachers that certain students were likely to have an intellectual "growth spurt" indicating that they had significant academic potential. These positive labels were related to an increase in students' IQ scores after a year, particularly for younger students and minority students (Rosenthal & Jacobson, 1968). This supported the Pygmalion effect from symbolic interactionism: teachers acted toward students based on the meaning they had for those students, thus affecting student learning. This study sparked decades of research that continues to this day about the consequences of labeling in academic settings.

Significant changes in the communication environment and progress in terms of developing measures have also led to numerous investigations of impression management online. For example, Walther's (1996) experiments, where he compares face-to-face and computer-mediated interactions, have given a lot of insight into the unique impression-management opportunities that we have online. In a 2007 study, Walther observed and coded people's editing behaviors when they were communicating via CMC: deleting content, inserting content, and replacing content after it had been written. He found that gender and whether the receiver was the same, higher, or of undetermined status affected people's editing behavior. In short, through an experiment, he found that we tend to edit our online messages, likely for self-presentation reasons, when we want to make a good impression.

In the last decade, a wealth of research has emerged that includes in-depth qualitative analyses of people's social media posts, interviews, and case studies about impression management online. Similarly, quantitative content analyses of social media content, surveys, and even some experiments have also shed light on people's impression management and tendency to conform to people's expectations online.

🗨 SELECTIVE SELF-PRESENTATION ONLINE

Walther (1996, 2007) pointed out that computer-mediated communication offers certain "affordances" to users that help us manage our online self-presentation. We are able to a) use attributes of new channels to enhance other people's impressions of ourselves, b) create messages that promote a particular impression of ourselves, and c) have the opportunity to think about our messages before posting online. In short, we are able to use new technologies to manage others' impressions of us through careful self-presentation.

Social media profiles. Though there is more control over self-presentation online, participating in social media can also be stressful. The affordances of social media, such as the ability to select and edit content that we post, give us more control over the front that we project, but it is also a complex environment that blends audiences from different regions, breaks down the barrier between the front and the backstage, and is affected by people's feedback and our observations of others' online behavior. It may serve to escalate tensions between the performed self and the real self, and in many ways social media challenges us to be everything to everyone.

On the one hand, presenting our honest, real self online can make us feel better as a result of the social support we receive from our Facebook friends (Kim & Lee, 2011). Our profile can also make us feel better about our self-image because our profiles tend to focus on the positive aspects of our self (Toma, 2013).

On the flip side of that, we are also typically presenting our "best" front online, which can be stressful. What we post is an *idealized* version of who we really are in our daily lives (Toma & Carlson, 2015). Presenting our "real" self has risks, and whether or not our Facebook interactions are positive can determine the extent to which we feel comfortable posting about our real selves (Burke & Ruppel, 2015). Thus, social media sites can create anxiety and stress as we balance how we want to be seen with the complexity of the multiple audiences we are performing in front of and as we consider their likely responses. Posting online can be a time- and thought-consuming task, as we consider who we are linked to, observe and consider the posts made by other people in our social networks, judge other people's posts, and use this information to guide our own posting behavior (Karakayali & Kilic, 2013).

Further, what we post online via social media sites can affect our real sense of identity. When we post image-defining content online, we are publicly committing to an image of ourselves. Public commitments can, in turn, shape our actual self-concept; we begin to see ourselves in keeping with the image that we are creating (Gonzales & Hancock, 2008). So, in addition to carefully presenting ourselves online to portray a specific front and being influenced by the posting behavior of others, our perception of ourselves may also be affected by the content we post.

Posting pics. Posting pictures via social media is a way to promote a particular impression of ourselves, but those pics may also unintentionally reflect social norms for the roles that we play in society. For example, in a study of profile pictures on Facebook, researchers found that these images tend to reflect gender stereotypes (Rose et al., 2012). Men tended to have profile pictures that projected images of dominance, activity, and independence. Women, on the other hand, had profile pics that highlighted their attractiveness and dependence. Also in keeping with group norms, college-aged students tended to post pictures of social activities and pictures with same-sex friends, representing themselves as acting out typical college life on social media (Mendelsen & Papacharissi, 2010). They typically did not post images of themselves with family members.

In all, we seem to be performing impression management online that is in keeping with the norms that we have learned for our gender and for our social groups. Thinking back to the examples used earlier in this chapter about what it means to be a college student and 20 being an extension of one's teens, the images college-aged people project via social media seem to align with the socially learned meaning for this stage of life. We often talk about college being as much a social experience as it is an educational endeavor. Thus, we expect college students to project images of themselves fulfilling those expectations: having fun and hanging out with friends. This is also a time to establish independence; thus, we do not see pictures and posts about parents as often at this stage.

Insight into Innovation Example: Instagram, Photoshop, and the "Ideal Self" If anything has given us the tools for impression management and creating a carefully crafted exhibition of our "self," it is digital imaging and popular apps like Instagram and software like Photoshop. Most images posted online are posed and rarely spontaneous (Mendelsen & Papacharissi, 2010). Hogan (2010) refers to online photos as an *exhibition* because online images are a collection of artifacts that reflect our self-image, such as photos, that we curate for other people to browse through. Thus, our Facebook albums are like an online art exhibition where we are the central subject of the art that we have created.

Photoshop software that allows us to edit and "fix" images has been around for over 25 years. But only recently has editing, cropping, and adding filters to enhance digital images been common for people's everyday pictures. Given the proliferation of digital photography options—our smartphones, tablets, webcams, and digital cameras—our images are now predominantly digital and, as a result, very easy to manipulate. Now, in our selfie-obsessed social media culture, we have a new tool to visually present a managed image of our self via social media. Along with editing what we post to project a managed impression, we can now edit visuals to reinforce that managed impression and make it seem even more real to people in our social circle.

Read more about Photoshop on National Public Radio's (NPR) *All Tech Considered* blog:

http://www.npr.org/blogs/alltechconsidered/2015/02/21/387839022/adobe-photoshop-democratizing-photo-editing-for-25-years

Looking at symbolic interaction and impression management we can take away two lessons about our sense of self and others: We learn the categories people and things fit into and the meanings of those categories through interaction, and we also try to manage people's impressions of us through interaction. The research on social media posting behaviors explains that our self-concepts and our own posting behavior is affected by what we see others doing online, and that self-presentation is one of our concerns when we create social media profiles, write posts, and post pictures to social media. These posts can affect how we see and feel about ourselves and how people see and feel about themselves.

Research on these two theories will be particularly important as we consider how new, Web 2.0 environments affect people's self-concept, public image, and, ultimately, their self-esteem. From a symbolic interaction standpoint, people are learning the meanings of things through social interactions that occur increasingly online. Given that online content is edited and thus not entirely "real," this has repercussions for how people see themselves and others. From a self-presentation perspective, we have new tools to help us construct a particular front, though the audience for this performance is increasingly complex and difficult to adapt to.

ASSIGNMENTS

1. **Understanding your "self."** One method used to assess self-concept is the "Twenty Statements Test" (Berg & Lune, 2012).
   a. Take out a piece of paper, and number lines 1 through 20.
   b. Write down your responses to the question, "Who am I?"
   c. Look at each response: Label all of the social roles you listed as E for external. Label all of the internal traits and characteristics you listed as I for internal.
   d. Now, total the number of E and I responses. Is your self-concept more externally defined or internally defined? How might that affect your sense of self and how you present yourself to others?

2. **Describe a typology of professors.** A typology is a list of types.
   a. Thinking about professors, what are the stereotypical "types" of professors? List four or five common, stereotypical types of professors.
   b. For each professor type, describe how that stereotypical type would dress, teach, and interact with students.
   c. For each type of professor, describe what would be out of character for that type in terms of appearance, teaching, and interactions with students.
   d. Reflect on how people may be restrained by these existing norms for how professors behave. In particular, how might professors' social media behaviors be restrained or affected by the stereotypical "professor" roles and norms?

3. **Essay**: Is Facebook a front or backstage, as explained by Goffman's theory of self-presentation? Why?

REFERENCES

Seminal Texts:

Blumer, H. (1969). *Symbolic interactionism: Perspective and method*. Englewood Cliffs, NJ: Prentice Hall.

Goffman, E. (1959). *The presentation of self in everyday life*. New York: Anchor Books.

Mead, G. H. (1934). *Mind, self, & society*. Chicago: University of Chicago Press.

Academic Articles:

Berg, B. L., & Lune, H. (2012). *Qualitative research methods for the social sciences* (8th ed.). Boston: Pearson.

Bolino, M. C., & Turnley, W. H. (1999). Measuring impression management in organizations: A scale development based on the Jones and Pittman taxonomy. *Organizational Research Methods, 2*, 187–206.

Burke, T. J., & Ruppel, E. K. (2015). Facebook self-presentational motives: Daily effects on social anxiety and interaction success. *Communication Studies, 66*, 204–217.

Gonzales, A. L., & Hancock, J. T. (2008). Identity shift in computer-mediated environments. *Media Psychology, 11*, 167–185.

Hogan, B. (2010). The presentation of self in the age of social media: Distinguishing performances and exhibitions online. *Bulletin of Science, Technology & Society, 30*, 377–386.

Jones, E. E., & Pittman, T. S. (1982). Toward a general theory of strategic self-presentation. In J. Suls (Ed.), *Psychological perspectives on the self* (pp. 231–262). Hillsdale, NJ: Lawrence Erlbaum.

Karakayali, N., & Kilic, A. (2013). More network conscious than ever? Challenges, strategies, and analytic labor of users in the Facebook environment. *Journal of Computer-Mediated Communication, 18*, 61–79.

Kim, J., & Lee, J.-E. R. (2011). The Facebook paths to happiness: Effects of the number of Facebook friends and self-presentation on subjective well-being. *Cyberpsychology, Behavior, and Social Networking, 14*, 359–364.

Mendelson, A., & Papacharissi, Z. (2010). Look at us: Collective narcissism in college student Facebook photo galleries. In Z. Papacharissi (Ed.), *The networked self: Identity, community and culture on social network sites* (pp. 251–273). London, England: Routledge.

Rose, J., Mackey-Kallis, S., Shyles, L., Barry, K., Biagini, D., Hart, C., & Jack, L. (2012). Face it: The impact of gender on social media images. *Communication Quarterly, 60*, 588–607.

Rosenthal, R., & Jacobson, L. (1968). *Pygmalion in the classroom*. New York: Holt, Rinehart & Winston.

Sanvenero, R. (2013). Social media and our misconceptions of the realities. *Information & Communications Technology Law, 22*, 89–108.

Toma, C. L. (2013). Feeling better but doing worse: Effects of Facebook self-presentation on implicit self-esteem and cognitive task performance. *Media Psychology, 16*, 199–220.

Toma, C. L., & Carlson, C. L. (2015). How do Facebook users believe they come across in their profiles? A meta-perception approach to investigating Facebook self-presentation. *Communication Research Reports, 32*, 93–101.

Tufekci, Z. (2008). Can you see me now? Audience and disclosure regulation in online social network sites. *Bulletin of Science, Technology & Society, 28*, 20–36.

Walther, J. B. (1996). Computer-mediated communication: Impersonal, interpersonal, and hyperpersonal interaction. *Communication Research, 23*(1), 3–43.

Walther, J. B. (2007). Selective self-presentation in computer-mediated communication: Hyperpersonal dimensions of technology, language, and cognition. *Computers in Human Behavior, 23*, 2538–2557.

Examples:

Earnheardt, A. (2015, February 22). Young adults to employers: Please ignore our social media posts. *The Vindicator*. Retrieved from http://www.vindy.com/news/2015/feb/22/young-adults-to-employers-please-ignore-/

Jay, M. (2013, May). Why 30 is not the new 20. *TedX*. Retrieved from http://www.ted.com/talks/meg_jay_why_30_is_not_the_new_20/transcript?language=en#t-860106.

National Public Radio. (2015, February 21). Adobe Photoshop: "Democratizing" photo editing for 25 years. *All Tech Considered*. Retrieved from http://www.npr.org/blogs/alltechconsidered/2015/02/21/387839022/adobe-photoshop-democratizing-photo-editing-for-25-years

Ronson, J. (2015, February 12). How one stupid tweet blew up Justine Sacco's life. *The New York Times*. Retrieved from http://www.nytimes.com/2015/02/15/magazine/how-one-stupid-tweet-ruined-justine-saccos-life.html?_r=2

Umansky, N. (2014, February 21). 10 Outrageous tweets that got people fired. *Oddee*. Retrieved from http://www.oddee.com/item_98873.aspx.

Further Reading Online:

George Herbert Mead. (1934). Mind self and society from the standpoint of a social behaviorist. Retrieved from https://www.brocku.ca/MeadProject/Mead/pubs2/mindself/Mead_1934_toc.html

Carl Straumsheim. (2015, February 5). Connected or disconnected? *Inside Higher Ed*. Retrieved from https://www.insidehighered.com/news/2015/02/05/face-face-socializing-down-social-media-use-among-freshmen

Tania Lombrozo. (2015, February 2). Beware of the pseudoscience of the self. Retrieved from http://www.npr.org/blogs/13.7/2015/02/02/383219046/beware-of-the-pseudoscience-of-self

CHAPTER 5

ATTRIBUTIONS AND CONSTRUCTIVISM

OUTCOMES

- *Knowledge:* Learn the internal, cognitive processes that occur when interpreting people's behavior.
- *Skill:* Develop communication competence, including responsiveness to individual differences in personality and access to and uses of communication channels.

 # INTRODUCTION

Competent communication means that we have knowledge of ourselves and others, motivation to apply that knowledge, and the skills to adapt (Cupach & Canary, 2000). These last two chapters in the unit on the self are focused on the theory-based knowledge and specific skills we can apply to be more competent communicators. In this chapter, we focus on theories of perception and interpretation to explore how we can develop the knowledge of ourselves and others to better adapt our messages.

There are benefits to thinking about ourselves and other people in complex ways and adjusting our message to adapt to the person with whom we are interacting. For example, a recent study authored by Robb Willer (2015) at Stanford University suggested that winning arguments and influencing people is more effective when we address the values of the person we're trying to persuade. His research also demonstrated that people typically do not take this approach, and focus instead on their own values when formulating arguments.

Attributions are our explanations of our own and other people's behavior (Heider, 1958). We can explain behavior as being the result of **internal** traits and characteristics, or we can attribute behavior to **external** causes such as the situation or context. Our attributions are often guided by how we feel about the person whose behavior we are trying to explain.

Our attributions, then, are used to develop constructs that we store in memory for ourselves and others. **Constructivism** looks at the complexity of people's understanding of others. We have personal constructs, or the aspects of our self that we are aware of, and we have constructs for other people stored in memory. **Constructs** are the unique descriptions we have of people. The more aspects of a person we consider when interacting, the more person centered and effective our messages are.

Many of us are not particularly good at thinking about other people and their characteristics in complex ways, and instead attribute their behavior to one or two characteristics or traits that we infer. Thus we tend to overestimate the effects of one or two personality traits that we have assumed a person has, and underestimate the effects of situation and context on people's behavior. But, as we discussed in the previous chapter, regions and audiences can mandate particular behaviors. Therefore, in this chapter, we will broaden our understanding of personality characteristics and of the complexities in online contexts to help us form more accurate perceptions of others and ourselves. Having more accurate and complete perceptions of others should make us better able to adapt when we are sending and interpreting messages.

OVERVIEW OF ATTRIBUTION THEORY AND CONSTRUCTIVISM

MAIN IDEA

We make attributions to explain our own and other people's behaviors. When we are perceiving our own and others' behavior, we attribute that behavior to internal or external causes. To help make sense of ourselves and others, we store perceptions in memory such as inferred personality traits and characterizations that affect how we interact with people.

OVERVIEW OF ATTRIBUTIONS AND PERSONALITY (HEIDER, 1958)

1. *We make attributions about behavior as part of the process of perceiving.* When we interact with people, they are perceiving us and we are perceiving them. **Perception** is a process of observing and inferring. That is to say, we are taking in observable information like words, tone, appearance, and gestures and we are interpreting, evaluating, and explaining what we see. Heider explains that this is the process of attributing behaviors and events to specific *causes*: needs, emotions, goals, personality, character, and situation. If you think about it, one of the biggest challenges when communicating online is the absence of context. Without information about the context, situation, or environment in which someone is communicating, our attributions for their messages may be far off base. Similarly, they do not have contextual information about our situation, so their attributions of our behavior are going to be based on limited information as well. Much of what goes on when we interact online is unseen; this increases the potential for misattributions.

2. *Internal attributions* *are when we explain behaviors as being the result of personality, traits, and other internal characteristics.* *External attributions* *are when we explain behaviors as being the result of situation and context.* We often explain other people's behavior as being

the result of their internal traits: they're nice or mean, likable or not likable, outgoing or shy, intelligent or unintelligent, and so on. We infer specific traits based on the limited data that we observe. Heider points out that this is our way of classifying people and making sense of our interactions. We often explain the undesirable outcomes of our own behavior by blaming the *situation*. These are external attributions that help protect our self-image and self-esteem. On the other hand, when we experience positive outcomes, we tend to attribute those to our internal traits. We are similarly biased when the people we like do things that we don't like, and tend to blame external situations for those behaviors as well.

Insight into Innovation Activity: Consider Examples of Self-Serving Attributions in Our Web 2.0 Lives. For each outcome listed, brainstorm other reasonable and likely explanations for the example outcomes experienced.

External attributions for negative outcomes	Internal attributions for positive outcomes	Brainstorm other reasonable explanations
I didn't do well in my online course. I attribute this to my instructor's poor course design.	I did well in my online class. I attribute this to me being smart and diligent.	What other factors affect grades in online courses?
I bought a nonreturnable product online and I do not like it. I attribute this to the seller not representing the product accurately.	I got a good deal on a nice product online. I attribute this to me being a savvy shopper.	What else determines purchase satisfaction?
No one is liking me on Tinder. I attribute this to there not being enough people in my region.	I found matches on Tinder. I attribute this to my attractiveness.	What else explains the outcomes on dating websites?
No one is responding to my online applications. I attribute this to there being too many applicants.	An employer responded to my online job application. I attribute this to my marketable skills.	What else affects employers' interest in applicants?
No one liked my Facebook post. I attribute this to Facebook's algorithm for selectively showing posts.	I received a lot of likes on my Facebook post. I attribute this to my popularity.	What else affects the number of likes on social media posts?

3. *Attributions are often biased.* Once we have categorized someone and decided whether or not we like them, that judgment biases our attributions during future interactions. When we like someone, we give them the benefit of the doubt when they do something we don't like, and tend to explain their good behavior as being the result of their good characteristics. This is a **halo effect**. On the other hand, when we don't like someone we may experience a **horn effect**. The horn effect is when we interpret their bad behaviors as evidence of their negative characteristics and their good behaviors as the outcome of the situation or as something that is "out of character" for them to do. So, we may think of one of our close Facebook friends who posts cheery messages online everyday as being happy, likable,

friendly, and outgoing. This may be a halo effect influencing our perception of their posting behavior. If someone we dislike is among our Facebook friends and posts cheery messages every day, we may experience a horn effect and attribute their posts to boasting, them being manipulative, or them putting on a front.

4. *Attributions are often incorrect.* We make attributions based on insufficient information. That is to say, we cannot completely know a person's internal feelings, goals, motivations, and traits. Thus, we are making judgments based on things that we cannot see. The **fundamental attribution error** is the result of our biases and the limitations of our own perception: we tend to overestimate the internal and underestimate the external causes of others' behavior. As we will discuss throughout this book, communication is affected by many situational factors: our relationships with the people we're interacting with, norms for the context, how we are socialized to behave through interactions and media depictions, and how we interpret the situation we are in. Thus, our communication—and others' communication—is not completely *caused* by their personality, traits, and skills.

5. *Attributions are enduring.* Though they are often biased and incomplete, once we have made attributions we tend not to question them. We tend to see traits as stable and enduring, in keeping with the adage that "people don't change." For example, a person whom we believe to be shy as a result of an interaction is, in our perception, always going to be shy. As a result, we explain their subsequent behavior based on the conclusions that we already have stored in memory. This is a **confirmation bias**. Everything we see that person do and everything they say can be seen as confirmation of the other person's shyness. If they are quiet at a party, they are being shy; if they post a lot online, they are compensating for being shy; if they text us, it is because they are too shy to call. Virtually any behavior can be "explained" in a way that confirms what we already believe to be true. By the way, this helps explain why it is so hard to recover from bad first impressions and why it is so very hard to move past long-standing disagreements with people we don't like.

Overview of Constructivism (Delia, O'Keefe, & O'Keefe, 1982). Constructivism helps us understand the link between our perception, attributions, and how we then interact with people. Attributions are the basis of our understanding of people. The more developed our understanding of others is, the more able we are to adapt a message to each unique person.

1. *We have constructs for people that we learn through interaction.* **Constructs** are the ways that we classify people and events based on the similarities and differences that we perceive. We identify what something or someone is, then we place it or them into one classification or another. The constructs that we have for people, and for ourselves, include "behavior, roles, personality characteristics, habits, attitudes, values, intentions, beliefs, and emotions" (p. 160). In other words, we get a sense of what a person does, what he or she is like, his or her opinions and feelings, and use those impressions to form our sense of who they are. We go through an internal process of comparing and contrasting them with other people we know, including ourselves.

For example, I know people who are extremely extroverted and people who are extremely introverted. When I meet people, one of the dimensions I consider is whether they are more like my outgoing friends or more like my shy friends. On the basis of this initial impression, I start to build a construct for the new person I just met. For many people, we apply **implicit personality theories**, or our own ideas about how traits cluster together. So, I tend to associate being boisterous, enjoying other people, socializing, charisma, and confidence with being extroverted (even though these are not necessarily interrelated traits). Similarly, I associate being quiet, contemplative, reasoned, and a homebody with being introverted (though, again, these are not necessarily related). Thus, these are my internal personality theories. When I meet someone for the first time, I consider whether they are introverted or extroverted (an attribution), then develop a construct about them that applies these implicit personality theories I have learned.

2. *Our constructs affect the strategies we use when communicating.* It is helpful to think of the constructs and implicit personality theories we have for people as a roadmap that we use to figure out how to get to where we want to be in an interaction. If I think one of my students is shy, then when I interact with her to discuss her progress in my course, I will probably choose to talk to her one-on-one in my office or via a private, mediated channel like e-mail. This is because the constructs I am using—"shy" and "student"—lead me to use a particular script, or strategy, for the interaction. The constructs guiding my strategy are developed based on my interaction with that student and are an outcome of comparisons between the behavior and traits of that student to other students I've had in the past.

Thinking about this from a student's perspective, how you respond to your professor in this course is a combination of both who you think the professor is *and* other professors you have had in the past. Thus, how you interact with your professor will be affected by how he or she compares to other professors you have known.

3. *The quality and quantity of constructs we have in memory are related to the effectiveness of our communication.* A good map to help us get where we need to go is going to have *details*. So, too, a good interpersonal construct is going to have details. The more details—or the more complex our constructs are—the better able we are to choose an effective course of action. If we think of people along a single dimension, such as being open versus dogmatic, then we will build a communication strategy based on that single dimension. Our message, then, probably will not be well suited to the other person. On the other hand, if we think of the other person in a more complex way, perhaps they are dogmatic but also sociable and optimistic, we can choose a more person-centered message that appeals to these distinct traits. Hence, **cognitive complexity**, or the quality and quantity of constructs we have for people, is related to our ability to communicate effectively. People higher in cognitive complexity are better able to create person-centered messages and to understand others' perspectives, which is called **perspective taking**.

METHODS OF ATTRIBUTION AND CONSTRUCTIVISM RESEARCH

Experimenting with Attributions. Attribution theory was developed by Heider, a psychologist who cited experiments on human perception to build the theory. Attribution theory also lends itself to experimental methods today, particularly in our new media environment. In fact, attribution theory has been used to explore everything from first impressions to interpersonal conflicts to people's perceptions of news media (Bazarova & Hancock, 2010).

New media offers many new avenues for experimenting with attributions. Think about Facebook for a moment. There are numerous features available on Facebook that provide information that may help people make attributions for what is posted: we have a profile picture and cover photo that reflect some aspects of our "selves," there are emoji to reflect our feelings at the moment or to represent the events we are participating in, we can tag friends, we can tag our exact location, and write the actual post and post a picture or video. Experimenting with these

different elements can help us control the attribution process via social media: Using emoji may change people's attributions for a given post because they can communicate our feelings. Including the location with our posts and tagging the people we're with can change people's attributions because it adds context.

Through continued experimentation and assessment of what people think about when forming impressions, researchers have expanded on the assumptions of attribution theory. For example, researchers have found that people's perception of **intention** is important in the attribution process. If we are going to attribute a behavior to someone's internal traits, then they must *want* to do what they're doing, be *aware* that they are doing it, *choose* to do it, and have the *skills* to do it. Otherwise, the behavior is unintentional.

Constructivism and the Questionnaire Method. Constructivism is an interpretive theory of human perception, rooted in the symbolic interactionism perspective. It typically involves asking people open questions. Delia et al. (1982) argued that constructs are unique to each person, though there are general trends in constructs, such as quality and quantity of constructs, that are related to communication. Thus, they argue for using a combination of research methods appropriate to the research question, which may include scales, open questions, and/or experimental manipulations. The research used to develop and apply the constructivist approach has employed all of these methods. In particular, constructivists have advocated the use of "free response" measures, such as the role categories questionnaire (RCQ), to measure variables (Crockett, 1965; O'Keefe et al., 1982). This approach has elements of both qualitative research (collecting open responses) and quantitative research (coding responses to find statistical trends and relationships among variables). The RCQ asks people to describe others, then their descriptions are coded to explore how many (quantity) unique constructs (quality) they have for others. More unique constructs are an indication of higher cognitive complexity.

APPLYING RESEARCH ON ATTRIBUTIONS AND CONSTRUCTIVISM TO DEVELOP OUR COMMUNICATION COMPETENCE

I am covering these two typical interpersonal theories in a unit focused on the self for a couple of important reasons. First, we make attributions about our own behavior as well as other people's behavior, and this contributes to our understanding of our own "self." We sometimes judge others against the traits we see in ourselves as well. Also, we perceive ourselves and vary in how self-aware we are; or in other words, we vary in the complexity of our understanding of ourselves. Thus, considering attributions and the constructs we have stored in memory for ourselves should give us insight into who we are and how we might improve ourselves.

The second reason to cover these theories in the unit on the self is that by reflecting on these questions, we can become more competent communicators. Burleson (2007) used constructivism to explain **communication competence**, or why some people "communicate more skillfully" by recognizing what's going on in a situation, understanding what others mean, and responding to others in effective ways (p. 106). Essentially, communication competence comes down to our understanding of our self, the situation, and others by accurately perceiving, attributing, and responding:

1. Using language correctly to express oneself;
2. Understanding social rules for verbal and nonverbal communication in a given situation;
3. Accomplishing one's goals through
   - **social perception**: accurately perceiving the other person and the situation;
   - **message production**: producing verbal and nonverbal messages that accomplish goals given the person and the situation; and
   - **message reception**: listening to and processing other people's messages.

To help us build these competencies we will apply attribution theory and constructivism to help us become more competent, and therefore more effective, Web 2.0 communicators. We will focus on two specific areas in this chapter: 1. expanding our understanding of general personality characteristics to develop our ability to differentiate between people and build cognitive complexity and 2. exploring the elements of online contexts that should inform how we compose and interpret online messages.

Insight into Innovation Activity: Weird Al's songs have a long history of social critique, and he is particularly critical of people's use of new media. Essentially, he's criticizing our communication competence in his songs, such as *Stop Forwarding the Crap to Me*, *Word Crimes*, and *Tacky*. What criticisms of our self-perception, social perception, and communication competency can you find in these songs? What are the *online* communication competencies that Weird Al addresses in these songs?

- *Stop Forwarding that Crap to Me*: https://youtu.be/KCSA7kKNu2Y

- *Word Crimes*: https://youtu.be/8GvOH-vPoDc

- *Tacky*: https://youtu.be/zq7Eki5EZ8o

IMPROVING OUR SOCIAL PERCEPTION SKILLS: INDIVIDUAL DIFFERENCES AND CONTEXT

Individual differences are related to use of computer-mediated communication (CMC) channels, impressions of CMC contexts, and the lack of "real" context affects the process of perceiving others. The information gleaned from the research can help us in two ways: we can better understand how and why different people communicate the way they do online by understanding their unique traits and circumstances, and we can consider how we may be perceived by others based on what we communicate via different CMC channels.

Demographics. Demographics like age and gender affect how we develop and interpret mediated messages. For example, college-aged students use social networking sites to be entertained, to maintain their interpersonal relationships, express themselves, and manage impressions (Park & Lee, 2014). These uses are related to a more intense use of Facebook and experiencing more of a sense of belonging. Gender also affects how people present themselves via social media, such that we tend to present ourselves in gender stereotypical ways online (Rose et al., 2012). Men and women also use social networks differently. For example, men tend to use them to develop new relationships and women tend to use them to maintain existing relationships (Muscanell & Guadagno, 2012). In the next unit, we'll discuss more of the research about demographic characteristics like gender and culture and how those individual differences are related to perceptions and uses of CMC.

Personality and traits. Most people are familiar with the "**Big 5 Personality Types**": Extraversion, agreeableness, conscientiousness, neuroticism, and openness (McCornack, 2010). They are interrelated, though not always in the way our implicit personality theories may assume. We see ourselves along these dimensions and evaluate others based on these dimensions. McCornack put it well when he wrote, "We evaluate people based on how we feel about ourselves. We like in others the traits we like in ourselves, and we dislike in others the traits we dislike in ourselves" (p. 94). Therefore, learning more about personality traits can help us better ourselves as communicators and perceivers, and also may improve our social perception as these traits help us better differentiate among people. Decades of research on communication has explored the many ways that these traits affect channel use, message formulation, and message interpretation (for an excellent review of how the Big Five was developed and has been applied, see John & Srivastava, 1999).

Personality Type (broad categories of the types)	Description (traits related to general types)
Openness	curious, imaginative, enjoys arts/aesthetics, reflective
Conscientiousness	orderly, reliable, efficient, dependable
Extraversion	talkative, energetic, outgoing, enthusiastic, assertive
Agreeableness	unselfish, forgiving, trusting, kind, cooperative
Neuroticism	tense, depressed, worried, moody, nervous

John and Srivastava (1999) pointed out that the broad personality categories of the Big Five can be used to create the anagram, OCEAN. Like oceans, personality types are very broad and deep: there are many specific personality traits within each broader personality type. For example, the broad personality type, extraversion, includes individual traits that can vary from person to person such as being talkative, energetic, and assertive. A person can be extraverted and not be particularly assertive. On the other end of the spectrum, a person can be introverted and also be very assertive. Thus, it is important to consider both the broad types of personalities we encounter in ourselves and others, and also consider individual differences in the traits associated with those types.

Though traits are generally seen as stable and enduring internal characteristics, they can change as people's lives change (John & Srivastava, 1999). Also, two people with one personality characteristic in common may be somewhat similar to each other in that one way, but they will be distinct in other ways. Thus, we must also look for those things that distinguish people from one another—that make them unique—to improve our cognitive complexity and the ability to differentiate.

For example, personality characteristics from the Big Five have been linked to social media use (Correa et al., 2010). Extraverts, people high in neuroticism, and people higher in openness used social media more. But in keeping with the idea that we need complex constructs for others to interpret their communication, the relationship between personality traits and social media use was different between men and women and older versus younger users. Put another way, the differences in social media use were affected by a *combination* of several personality types, gender, *and* age, with both gender and age affecting the link between personality and social media use. No single individual difference determined social media use; several unique dimensions worked together. Thus, having a more complex view of others may help us understand differences that we observe in their behavior, including their online behavior.

Insight into Innovation Example: Are Parents Fostering Narcissistic Traits? In the previous chapter, we discussed how interactions with particular others shape the meanings that we have for ourselves, others, and our environment. Over a century of research on parenting has reiterated that very subtle differences in how we communicate with, about, and in front of our children can affect them throughout their lives: the attributions they have for their own and others' behavior and how other-centered they are later in life. This also goes along with the idea that personality can be shaped and changed over time.

A study out of The Ohio State University generated a lot of media buzz when they found that parents who tell their children that they're "special" are increasing the risk that their kids will be narcissists later in life. **Narcissism** is not a desirable trait because it includes believing that one's self is more valuable or important than others and lacking empathy for others. On the other hand, telling children that they are "loved" and that they have "done a good job" builds self-esteem. **Self-esteem** is a good thing because it means feeling comfortable with who you are.

On the surface, there is little difference in the *intended* meaning of saying "you're special" compared to "you've done especially well." Thinking about this from an attribution perspective, the subtle distinction between these two statements of praise is that the former labels the *child* as exceptional and the later labels the *behavior* as exceptional. Many successes are specific to a circumstance or situation and are not an indication of unique, "special" skills and abilities. Also, thinking about constructivism, if a parent thinks of his or her child as being "special" and "gifted," that may influence how the parent behaves toward the child and the parent may be more likely to indulge, praise, and reward the child even when it isn't warranted. Consider some of the indicators of narcissism: wanting to be admired, wanting attention, expecting special favors, and trying to achieve status and power (Jonason & Webster, 2010). It makes sense that these types of characteristics would describe a person who has been told that they are important, special, and deserving of admiration and praise throughout his or her childhood.

Narcissism has steadily increased since the 1970s. This trend could be different if parents embraced the idea of their child being "developmentally normal" or "typical." Arguably, increased cognitive complexity among parents and more careful attribution for successes and failures could help slow this trend.

You can listen to the NPR interview with Dr. Bushman about his study of parental communication and narcissism here: http://www.npr.org/blogs/health/2015/03/09/391874530/do-parents-nurture-narcissists-by-pouring-on-the-praise?

UNDERSTANDING CONTEXT: INDIVIDUAL DIFFERENCES IN ACCESS, MOTIVES, AND USES OF NEW MEDIA

In addition to considering the unique personalities of the people we are interacting with, and thoughtfully reflecting on our own personality as well, we also have to be sensitive to context. People tend to change their messages based on both the channel and their perception of the audience (Bazarova et al., 2013). When posting via social media, users report that they "imagine" who is among their audience, and this guides what they post (Marwick & Boyd, 2010). We may consider who we are, how we want to be perceived, and who the audience is before posting to Web 2.0 platforms like Twitter. This diverse, blended, "imagined" audience presents unique challenges to us as communicators and perceivers.

Two features of context: Perceptions of media and "real life" situation. There are two elements of context for us to consider when perceiving and sending mediated messages: how we and other people see the media channel we are using as a context and the actual physical context we and others are in when we interact via mediated channels. People view different mediated channels in unique ways, which may influence how messages are perceived. Also, we are influenced by our actual, real-life feelings, events, and situation, though no one online can see those things to develop more informed perceptions.

People's view of the technology itself can affect how they use it. Thus, our impression of the context when communicating via Web 2.0 technologies may be fundamentally different than another person's perception of that context. Specifically, we vary in how much affinity we have for different mediated channels. **Affinity** is our liking of a channel. Some of the things that people like about CMC channels include features related to "speed, control, efficiency and convenience, reduction of negative [feelings], meeting new people, directness, overcome[ing] distance, and small talk" (Kelly & Keaten, 2007, p. 354). On the other hand, people also dislike CMC for various, related reasons: it can be impersonal, deceptive, interactants are separated, messages can seem trivial, there is potential for misunderstanding, it requires technology access and skills, and it isn't always convenient. Our affinity for the channel itself may influence how we perceive messages received via that channel and, as a result, our attributions and constructs for the people we are interacting with.

We will get into different uses, or **motives**, for using Web 2.0 messages in our chapter on uses and gratifications in the final unit of the book. The different uses a media channel serves for us— functional, relational, interactive, diversionary, and so on—also affect how we use, think about, and respond to mediated messages. People with a more task-oriented approach to a channel will formulate and interpret messages via that channel differently than people who see a channel as appropriate for emotional expression, relationship building, or killing time.

Building on the idea of context, people are also in a physical environment, mood, and situation when they communicate via mediated channels, but none of these things are immediately apparent to, or necessarily taken into account by, the receivers of those messages. For example, the research we'll discuss throughout this book and in this chapter focuses on how we prefer positive messages via CMC. That being said, people also often turn to CMC and social media to vent their frustrations because it is therapeutic, particularly when other people validate one's feelings of frustration and anger (see Feltman's 2015 *WaPo* article on the topic Why complaining on the Internet makes us feel so good).

How well we know the other person affects how we make attributions for online posts. When we don't know the other person particularly well, attributions for online messages tend to be more critical and internal. We are typically more forgiving when making attributions of our friends' posts compared to our acquaintances' posts (DeAndrea & Walther, 2011). We also expect that our own posts are more positively perceived by our social media followers compared to others' posts (Toma & Carlson, 2015). Even prospective employers make attributions based on what applicants have posted online. People who posted positive work-related content were evaluated more positively in terms of being a good fit for employment and more employable, likely due to the attributions associated with the social media posts and the fact that the evaluators had little else to go on when evaluating people (Carr & Walther, 2014).

Research suggests that there are some things we can include in our social media posts that will help people form impressions of us that are more in keeping with how we see ourselves (Evans, Gosling, & Carroll, 2008). Some of these elements are ways of helping us create a context, such as posting about important moments, while others are ways that we can reveal our personality to others by discussing our beliefs and heroes.

Posting Content and Accuracy of Perception (Evans et al., 2008)		
Increased Accuracy	**Decreased Accuracy**	**Didn't Affect Accuracy**
Posts about: • Heroes • Proud moments • Embarrassing moments • Beliefs	Posts about: • Pictures of things other than people • Bad/disliked websites and people • Preferences in books	Posts about: • Favorite songs, movies, and foods • Political attitudes • Relationship status

We don't often think critically and with self-reflection about our use of something as ubiquitous and pervasive as e-mail. We quickly, and with little thought, shoot off emails from our computers, phones, and tablets. People tend to think of themselves as being pretty good at communicating via e-mail, but also tend to fail to see their emails from the perspective of the receiver unless prompted to do so (Kruger et al., 2005). This limited perspective-taking may be the result of **egocentrism**, or our focus on ourselves when communicating via e-mail rather than focusing on the other person. But if we think of e-mail as a form of communication that people will perceive, make attributions for, and use to form constructs for us, it is clear that even e-mail requires communication competence.

Context. Looking for and using cues about context is one way we might make more accurate attributions and develop better constructs via e-mail exchanges. For example, a common feature of smartphones and tablets is that they have an e-mail signature that includes "sent from" and information about the brand. On the surface, this is clearly brand advertising for smartphone manufacturers. But having that little statement at the bottom of an e-mail sent specifically from a phone or tablet can be helpful to people who receive that e-mail: it creates a context for interpreting the response, and may help them make more accurate attributions because there is more information to inform social perceptions. Thus, the constructs people develop for you based on an e-mail exchange, such as perceiving the sender's professionalism and dedication, may be more positive.

For example, if we send a one-sentence e-mail in response to a colleague's questions without a salutation or closing, they might infer that we're annoyed. On the other hand, if we send that same e-mail with the line "sent from my iPhone" they'll know that we're not at our desk, we're probably in the middle of doing something else, and we're typing on a tiny screen with limited functionality. Thus, they may attribute the short e-mail more accurately to the situation we are in (e.g., we are away from our desk) rather than our feelings (e.g., inferring that we are annoyed or bothered) or our personality (e.g., assuming we are terse or unfriendly). This, of course, guards against the emergence of negative or unflattering constructs of us in the minds of others.

Research suggests that the content of our emails, such as grammatical errors, can affect perceptions of our professionalism and credibility (Carr & Stefaniak, 2012). That being said, people also expect a relatively quick response to their emails. In fact, focus group research suggests that people respond in overwhelmingly negative ways when there is no response to their e-mail, and this negative view extends to perceptions of the person they sent the e-mail to (Easton & Bommelje, 2011).

So we should consider how we can create context via e-mail that protects our self-presentation while also meeting people's expectations (Carr & Stefaniak, 2012). For example, if you think the sender may be impatient for a response, sometimes an e-mail that says "I'm not at my computer at the moment, but I will get back to you when I'm in my office/home" is sufficient.

Message Design. Part of competency when responding to e-mail is understanding the function, or reason, for the e-mail and creating messages that are effective given your knowledge of the person and their goals. Common **e-mail functions**, or reasons for emailing, include completing a task, building a relationship, giving excuses, participating, and/or making a favorable impression (Young, Kelsey, & Lancaster, 2011). This can guide your decisions about when and how to respond. If someone is trying to complete a task, responding immediately and directly may be appropriate and appreciated. But if someone is trying to build a relationship or form a favorable impression, then responding appropriately may require more emotional content and less directness so taking time to develop a longer response may be in order.

Mediated messages, such as e-mail, can be polysemic. **Polysemy** is when something has multiple possible meanings (Boxman-Shabtai & Shifman, 2014). This is why things like sarcasm and humor can be difficult to discern via e-mail: sometimes the humor is not perceived by the recipient in the way it was meant to be perceived. There are some features of e-mail messages in particular that seem to be more concrete. For example, using all caps in emails reduces likability of the sender and using emoticons increases likability (Byron & Baldridge, 2007). These cues are arguably less polysemic as it is generally accepted that all caps is "yelling" and smiley emoticons are "happy." Thinking of ways to reduce polysemy, or at least recognizing the multiple ways that your mediated messages may be perceived by the receivers, can help you craft a person-centered response written with the other person's perspective in mind.

CONCLUSION

In this chapter, we have looked at cognitive complexity and attributions as two ways that people perceive us and ways that we perceive others. Complexity is how developed and differentiated our perceptions of others are, and attributions are the causal explanations we have for our own and

I have:

- personality traits
- roles and norms
- life experiences
- perceptions of myself, others, and the situation.

You have:

- personality traits
- roles and norms
- life experiences
- perceptions of yourself, others, and the situation.

Individually, we have different traits, goals, and perceptions. To be competent communicators together, I have to try to see things from your perspective and you have to try to see things from my perspective. This requires a complex, flexible understanding of each other: recognizing the basis and potential bias of our existing attributions, being open to new information about each other, and being aware of each other's perception of the context.

Courtesy of Rebecca Curnalia.

others' behaviors. We also learned about how one's limited cognitive complexity and errors in attributions can undermine the accuracy of perceptions and, as a result, the effectiveness of our communication.

We introduced the concept of communication competence, particularly focusing on the interplay of demographics, personality, context, and technology. Competent communicators, both face-to-face and via CMC, recognize how these unique features of the individual and the situation affect how we and others perceive and communicate. Competent communicators move away from a self-focused, egocentric approach to communicating and think instead about how others may perceive a polysemic message. Competent communicators adjust their messages accordingly, with mindful consideration of who they are interacting with, of themselves, and of the limitations and opportunities resulting from the channel used to communicate. In the next chapter, we will delve deeper into the idea of mindful communication, and also introduce active listening as a research-based approach to responding to others via CMC.

ASSIGNMENTS

1. **Complete the RCQ.** One example of the intersection of qualitative and quantitative methods used in constructivist research is the role categories questionnaire (RCQ). Complete the form below, then see how you scored. Write a self-reflection essay on how your RCQ score may affect your personal and professional success, and what you might do to improve your score.

   RCQ Directions: Choose two people, one person you like and one person you dislike. Think for a moment about these two people. Then, take a few moments to describe each person, thinking in particular about their mannerisms, habits, characteristics, beliefs, etc.

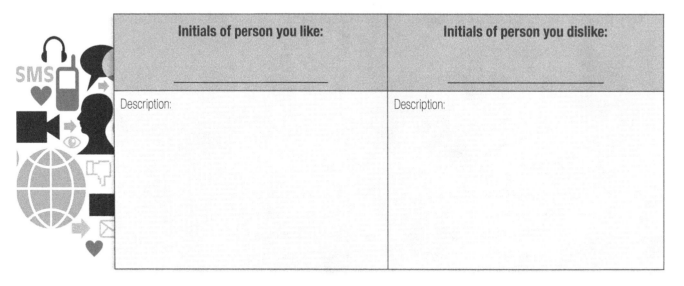

Initials of person you like:	Initials of person you dislike:
_____	_____
Description:	Description:

   To score the RCQ, give yourself one point for each unique term you use to describe the liked and the disliked person (no points for intensifiers or modifiers like "very" or "always"; no points for physical descriptions; no points for demographic descriptions like gender, race, or region). Add up the total number of characteristics to determine your personal construct differentiation score. The typical range of scores is between 3 and 45, with around 20 or 25 being average.

2. **Personal personality assessment.**
   - Begin by creating a bulleted list of the terms and phrases you would use to describe yourself.
   - Label each bullet point you listed using the following coding scheme:
     - **Write an O** next to statements that reflect whether or not you are open, creative, curious, and unique or original
     - **Write a C** next to statements that reflect whether or not you are organized, reliable, dependable, or disciplined
     - **Write an E** next to statements that reflect whether or not you are social, outgoing, friendly, talkative, or energetic/enthusiastic
     - **Write an A** next to statements that reflect whether or not you are sympathetic, forgiving, unselfish, and kind
     - **Write an N** next to statements that reflect whether or not you have feelings of depression, worry, moodiness, or nervousness.
   - What aspects of personality did you rely on the most when describing yourself (which letter appeared most frequently)? What does this tell you about the personality traits you feel are important?
   - What aspects of personality did you underemphasize or omit (which letter appeared least frequently or not at all)? What does this tell you about the personality traits you feel are important?
   - What aspects of your personality were not captured by the Big Five (which items did you list that had no corresponding letter)? What does this tell you about the limitations of this method?

3. **Take an online assessment of your Big Five personality traits** (such as http://www.outofservice.com/bigfive/). Look at your results for openness, conscientiousness, extraversion, agreeableness, and neuroticism and write a brief essay on the following:
   - Did you learn something about yourself that was not part of your personal constructs (i.e., that you didn't know about yourself or that you didn't think about before)? If so, what did you learn?
   - According to the results, what are your greatest strengths, or most positive traits?
   - According to the results, what are your weaknesses, or less desirable traits?
   - Thinking about personality as something dynamic and changeable, what from your results would you most like to change and how do you think you could go about changing it?

REFERENCES

Seminal Sources:

Crockett, W. H. (1965). Cognitive complexity and impression formation. In B. A. Maher II (eds.) *Progress in experimental personality research* (pp. 47–90). New York: Academic Press.

Delia, J. G., O'Keefe, B. J., & O'Keefe, D. J. (1982). The constructivist approach to communication. In Frank E. X. Dance (Ed.), *Human communication theory: Comparative essays* (pp. 147–191). New York: Harper & Row.

Heider, F. (1958). *The psychology of interpersonal relations.* Hillsdale, NJ: Lawrence Earlbaum.

Academic Sources:

Bazarova, N. N., Taft, J. G., Choi, Y. H., & Cosley, D. (2013). Managing impressions and relationships on Facebook: Self-presentational and relational concerns revealed through the analysis of language style. *Journal of Language & Social Psychology, 32*(2), 121–141.

Bazarova N. N., Hancock J. T.. (2010). From dispositional attributions to behavior motives: The folk-conceptual theory and implications for communication. In Salmon C. T. (ed.), *Communication yearbook 34* (pp. 63–91). New York: Routledge.

Boxman-Shabtai, L., & Shifman, L. (2014). Evasive targets: Deciphering polysemy in mediated humor. *Journal of Communication, 64*(5), 977–998.

Burleson, B. R. (2007). Constructivism: A general theory of communication skill. In B. B. Whaley & W. Samter (eds.), *Explaining communication: Contemporary theories and exemplars* (pp. 105–128). Mahwah, NJ: Lawrence Erlbaum.

Byron, K., & Baldridge, D. C. (2007). E-mail recipients' impressions of senders' likability: The interactive effect of nonverbal cues and recipients' personality. *International Journal of Business Communication, 38,* 70–100.

Carr, C. T., & Stefaniak, C. (2012). Sent from my iPhone: The medium and message as cues of sender professionalism in mobile telephony. *Journal of Applied Communication Research, 40,* 403–424.

Carr, C. T., & Walther, J. B. (2014). Increasing attributional certainty via social media: Learning about others one bit at a time. *Journal of Computer-Mediated Communication, 19,* 922–937.

Correa, T., Hinsley, A. W., de Zúñiga, H. G. (2010). Who interacts on the Web? The intersection of users' personality and social media use. *Computers in Human Behavior, 26,* 247–253.

Cupach, W. R., & Canary, D. J. (2000). *Competence in interpersonal conflict.* Long Grove, IL: Waveland.

DeAndrea, D. C., & Walther, J. B. (2011). Attributions for inconsistencies between online and offline self-presentations. *Communication Research, 38,* 805–825.

Easton, S. S., & Bommelje, R. K. (2011). Interpersonal communication consequences of e-mail non-response. *Florida Communication Journal, 39*(2), 45–63.

Evans, D. C., Gosling, S. D., & Carroll, A. (2008). What elements of an online social networking profile predict target-rater agreement in personality impressions? *Association for the Advancement of Artificial Intelligence.* Retrieved from http://www.aaai.org/Papers/ICWSM/2008/ICWSM08-013.pdf

John, O. P., & Srivastava, S. (1999). The big five trait taxonomy: History, measurement, and theoretical perspective. In L. A. Pervin & O. P. John (Eds.), *Handbook of personality: Theory and research* (2nd ed., pp. 114–158). New York: Guilford Press.

Jonason, P. K., & Webster, G. D. (2010). The dirty dozen: A concise measure of the dark triad. *Psychological Assessment, 22*, 420–432.

Kelly, L., & Keaten, J. A. (2007). Development of the affect for communication channels scale. *Journal of Communication, 57*, 349–365.

Kruger, J., Epley, N., Parker, J., & Ng, Z.-N. (2005). Egocentrism over e-mail: Can we communicate as well as we think? *Journal of Personality and Social Psychology, 89*(6), 925–936.

Marwick, A. E., & Boyd, D. (2010). I tweet honestly, I tweet passionately: Twitter users, context collapse, and the imagined audience. *New Media & Society, 13*(1), 114–133.

McCormack, S. (2010). Reflect and relate: An introduction to interpersonal communication (3rd ed.). Macmillan.

Muscanell, N. L., & Guagadno, R. E. (2012). Make new friends or keep the old: Gender and personality differences in social networking use. *Computers in Human Behavior, 28*, 107–112.

Park, N., & Lee, S. (2014). College students' motivations for Facebook use and psychological outcomes. *Journal of Broadcasting & Electronic Media, 58*, 601–620.

O'Keefe, D. J., Shepherd, G. J., Streeter, T. (1982). Role category questionnaire measures of cognitive complexity: Reliability and comparability of alternative forms. *Central States Speech Journal, 33*, 333–338.

Rose, J., Mackey-Kallis, S., Shyles, L., Barry, K., Biangini, D., Hart, C., & Jack, L. (2012). Face it: The impact of gender on social media images. *Communication Quarterly, 60*(5), 588–607.

Toma, C. L., & Carlson, C. L. (2015). How do Facebook users believe they come across in their profiles? A meta-perception approach to investigating Facebook self-presentation. *Communication Research Reports, 32*(1), 93–101.

Young, S., Kelsey, D., & Lancaster, A. (2011). Predicted outcome value of e-mail communication: Factors that foster professional relational development between students and teachers. *Communication Education, 60*(4), 371–388.

MINDFULNESS

INTRODUCTION

According to Ellen Langer's theory of mindfulness, events themselves have no meaning; how we think about events means everything. In the first two chapters of this unit on the self, we talked about how we learn meanings about ourselves and others through interaction, about our own cognitive complexity, and how we make attributions. In this chapter, we will expand on that discussion and explore how we can be more mindful. **Mindlessness** leads us to behave automatically rather than thoughtfully, such that we rely too much on previous attributions and meanings in our everyday lives and fail to notice new things about people and situations. **Mindfulness**, on the other hand, is choosing to be more aware of one's self, others, and the context: "noticing new things" in our everyday lives. We will focus on listening as a way to improve our own self-awareness and our awareness of others and to overcome the pitfalls of misattributions that we discussed in the previous chapter. Active and empathic **listening** in particular, whereby we pay attention to the other person and try to understand the other person's thoughts, feelings, and what they are implying, is one way to be more mindful in our distracted world.

The research and theory behind mindlessness, and the suggestions for mindfulness that are important as we move through theories of human communication. Many of the theories we will discuss throughout this book highlight the pitfalls of mindless communication and technology use. Nearly every theory in this book teaches us a way to be more mindful in our personal, professional, or mass mediated lives and also explains the repercussions when we aren't thoughtful. Mindlessly muddling through life is certainly easier, but it has consequences for the quality of our lives, our personal and professional relationships, and our participation in society.

MAIN IDEA

We tend to go through much of life mindlessly following routines without noticing new details and subtle differences. This limits our perspective, our behavioral choices, and our ability to interact effectively with others. To be mindful, we should think of things in more conditional ways, consider different perspectives, and take in new information that helps us see things more completely.

 Insight into Innovation Example: Watch Dr. Langer discuss how we are trapped by categories we have learned: https://youtu.be/4XQUJR4uIGM. She argues that our emphasis on "certainty" undermines our learning and that most things are only "true" in certain contexts. Instead, we should be actively looking for new details and trying to "notice new things." In what ways can learning different theories make us more mindful?

KEY ASSUMPTIONS OF MINDFULNESS (LANGER, 1989)

1. **We are trapped by the categories we have learned.** In the first chapter, we discussed how we have a role in a specific region. We see other people in their respective roles as well. We all perform and respond according to the expectations for the roles being played. In many ways, we are trapped by the categories we put people and things into because those categories define those people and things for us. Sometimes the categories include stereotypes and presumptions about what people are like, such as when we focus on a person's age (e.g., "old people are slow"), region (e.g., "New Yorkers are rude"), race (e.g., "Asians are smart"), gender (e.g., "women are nurturing"), income (e.g., "poor people are lazy"), or occupation (e.g., "politicians are dishonest"), or any other similar categories. We do the same thing with events and situations: they will be easy or hard, fun or boring, worthwhile or a waste of time, and so on.

Langer (1997) applies mindfulness to explore different approaches to learning, so we will use education examples throughout this chapter.

Consider how you have *categorized* the new media theory course you are currently taking and everything that you associate with that *type* of course:

- Is it upper or lower division?
- Is it a major or elective or general education course?

Copyright © microvector/Shutterstock.com

Now consider your expectations:

- How hard is this class going to be?
- Are you going to enjoy this class?
- How much will you learn in this class?

Chances are, the expectations you listed relate directly back to those typical categories used for college courses.

2. **We behave and respond automatically, without thinking, and this limits our response options.** When we mindlessly rely on categories, we respond to people and things based on our preexisting notions about how things are, rather than who people really are or what the situation is really like. Relying on familiar categories makes life easier for us, but it also leads to ineffective communication and limited understanding. Effective communication is person centered and responsive to contexts.

So, continuing with the previous example, if this is a lower division, general education course, you likely would expect it to be somewhat easier with less writing and more multiple choice–type tests. If this is an upper division course for your major, on the other hand, you would probably expect a more difficult class that involves some writing and maybe essay tests. If we have low expectations for the course, we'll probably follow a familiar pattern of behavior in keeping with that category: skimming the book, writing down what's on the PowerPoint slides during class, reading through notes before an exam, and that's about it. Similarly, we have a script we follow for harder classes, which may involve reading more closely, taking more detailed notes, and perhaps studying in more depth before an exam. In essence, the category that the class fits—the label put on the class by the university such as "upper" versus "lower" division—dictates our behavior in the class.

Now imagine another scenario: You sign up for a class that has no course number, no assigned instructor, called "Communication Seminar." When you show up on the first day of that class, what would you expect? For a vague course that didn't have any clear existing category, you would probably show up on the first day of class ready for just about anything and thus prepared to do whatever needed to be done. You would have more options for your own behavior in the new, uncertain situation rather than there being a clear script for you to follow. In the unlabeled course, you would likely also be more alert, attentive, and take in more information because of your uncertainty in that situation.

3. **We tend to think of things from a single perspective.** Having a sense of certainty as a result of relying on preexisting categories, stereotypes, and attributions makes life easier for us because it doesn't require intense thought. We prefer certainty and to view things in a unidimensional way rather than looking at things from multiple angles. In terms of interpreting and responding to people, our tendency is to judge things by the standard "what would I do" or to make an attribution such as "this person is this way." This blinds us to the reasons people have for the things that they do. Langer (1989) argues that, even when people do things that are negative, chances are they did it for a good (or at least reasonable) reason, but we cannot see other people's motivations. Considering people's motivations, the context, and reasoning gives us more options for how to respond; it makes us more empathetic. Also, when we consider our own motivations, it can help us reframe our problem behaviors in ways that promote personal change and growth.

So, thinking again about this class, you probably are coming into it with a set of expectations about *what it should be and what it should not be.* When the professor went over the syllabus, chances are that your judgment was based on that notion of what the class should be based on the type of class it is. Was there anything in the syllabus that surprised you or that you disagreed with? Try to think of the syllabus mindfully: Why would your professor use *those* assignments in *this* particular class? Are there features of the context, such as the delivery method for the course, or requirements imposed by the department or university, that may have required your professor to include some of the work in this class?

4. **We should be more mindful in our daily lives.** Langer (1989) provides advice on how to be more mindful. Specifically, she outlines "key qualities of a mindful state of being: 1) creation of new categories; 2) openness to new information; and 3) awareness of more than one perspective" (p. 62).

   Increasing discrimination is one way to overcome mindless reliance on categories and associated meanings. Typically, we **discriminate**, or tell the difference between things, based on just one or two attributes. You are unique, complex, and constrained by the situation you are in; there is more to you than what meets the eye. The same is true of every person that you interact with. Thus, we try to discriminate more, or discover more unique attributes for other people and for the situations we experience. When we are mindless, we put people in categories—male or female, young or old, educated or uneducated, black or white or brown, and so on—without really thinking about *who* a person *is*. Worse, we then judge and act toward others based on the categories they are placed in rather than the persons that they really are.

   Increasing discrimination, which is similar to high cognitive complexity from the previous chapter, requires taking in new information about people, reframing the information we have, and moving away from judging people on single dimensions such as a single trait, or their gender, race, age, or social class.

Insight into Innovation Example: RateMyProfessor.com's Hot Profs and Bossy Lady Professors. We often think of people in different professions as being a specific "type" of person with specific characteristics. Perceptions of professional people's behavior are also guided by whether they are male or female, attractive or unattractive, young or old, and so on. Once we label a professional, such as a professor, then our expectations and responses to their behavior are determined by what we associate with that "type" rather than our knowledge of them as a person. These categories, or types, then affect how we interact with and perceive people. Consider the dimensions for evaluating professors on ratemyprofessor.com (RMP): hotness, easiness, and clarity.

Professors who are "hot" according to student reviewers on RMP tend to get more positive comments overall, and professors who are "not hot" receive more comments about the actual content of their courses (Silva et al., 2008). We tend to associate a lot of positive characteristics with physical attractiveness. Thus, we tend to perceive people's characteristics, such as likeability, friendliness, and even expertise, based on whether or not they are attractive. What students write on sites like RMP are important, because those comments also set expectations for students entering our classes.

Copyright © Altana/Shutterstock.com

Reading RMP reviews affects students' sense of control, attitude toward the class, and expectations about grades before they ever interact with the professor (Kowai-Bell et al., 2011).

Gender Bias in Evaluation. Women are particularly susceptible to being judged based on their attractiveness and are also judged more harshly for certain behaviors. Though gender bias is not as apparent in the quantitative measures on sites like RMP (Stuber et al., 2009), we see that how people *describe* female professors in the comments may be fundamentally different. For example, an interactive tool created by Ben Schmidt in 2015 used data from RMP reviews to explore how reviewers described men versus women. The interactive tool and findings were highlighted in the *New York Times*: "Male professors are brilliant, awesome and knowledgeable. Women are bossy and annoying, and beautiful or ugly" (para. 1). The *Times* article also points out that these findings generalize to many other professions as well. Female CEOs, women in tech fields, and women in other leadership and managerial positions are often described in more negative ways for the exact same behaviors that garner praise for men.

Copyright © Kopytin Georgy/Shutterstock.com

The differences in people's reactions based on attractiveness and gender may be because people mindlessly use gender-specific categories and associated expectations to judge others' behavior. Thus, a male professor being assertive and direct is mindlessly perceived as a confident expert. A female professor being assertive and direct is mindlessly perceived as bossy.

Insight into Innovation Activity: Check out some of the details on Dr. Schmidt's analysis of RMP reviews, and try the tool yourself using some words that you would use to describe a professor, like "brilliant" or "bossy." It is available on his blog: http://benschmidt.org/2015/02/06/rate-my-professor/

What do the differences between descriptions of male versus female professors tell us about students' perceptions? How might predefined gender categories explain these results? Could mindfulness help us move away from gender-based evaluations and improve student learning?

People who increase discrimination and take in new information are also better at thinking of things from multiple perspectives. In communication research, we refer to this as **perspective taking**. We discussed perspective taking in more detail in the previous chapter when we reviewed constructivism and attributions. We tend to think of our own behavior in more positive and flattering ways but think of another's behavior in less flattering ways. We do this because of our perspective on ourselves versus others: we have a lot more information about the effects of context on our own decisions and thus better understand why we behave the way we do. Say, for example, a student is regularly late to class. The student may describe the behavior as evidence that he or she is "very busy" because of other classes, work, and obligations. On the other hand, the professor may describe the behavior as "irresponsible" because he or she sees the situation from the perspective of a student having signed up for a specific class at a specific time and then not following through on that obligation. Both perspectives have some merit: clearly the student is busy *and* did not plan well. Perspective taking means that we consider these different perspectives on the situation rather than simply being committed to our own perspective.

Perspective taking can help immensely when managing disagreements, even when you are committed to your position in the conflict. Being able to understand how the other person sees the situation can help you explain how and why your perspective is different and, maybe, change his or her mind. Also, while thinking of your own behavior from different perspectives, you may realize that something that you have always thought of in one way could be seen in another way. This realization can promote positive personal changes.

To see things from different perspectives and get new information, there are a couple of specific things we can do (Langer, 1989, 1997):

- Being willing to hear and consider new information, also called **openness**, is essential to increasing discrimination and perspective taking. Without curiosity and a desire to find out more, we cannot get the information necessary to look at things from a fresh perspective.
- **Changing contexts**, or intentionally changing things up, makes us more alert and more aware. Sometimes it is the repetition of the routine that leads us into mindlessness. Breaking up the routine can make us more alert, mindful, and thus more productive, particularly at work and in school.
- **Reframing** behaviors and contexts can also change our perceptions. Reframing is considering something in a new way. For example, try to think of things that we have framed as a negative attribute in a positive way: a class isn't "hard," it is instead "challenging." A person isn't "mean," they are instead "being assertive."
- Asking questions is also part of being mindful, particularly mindful learning. Langer (1997) concludes her text on mindful learning: "How can we know if we do not ask? Why should we ask if we are certain we know? All answers come out of a question" (p. 139). Questioning and embracing uncertainty rather than seeking certainty opens us up to new perspectives and signals our openness to new information and approaches.
- Lastly, having a **process orientation** is when we think about how and why things happen rather than focusing on a specific outcome. Often, when we approach a person or situation, we are focused on the outcomes we want rather than considering the process of doing something: We set a goal then go for it. This is an **outcome orientation**. Process orientations are empowering, and they open our minds to the possibilities of a situation.

So, instead of an outcome orientation, we try to think of the process of doing something. Langer (1989) points out that every behavior is a choice. When advising students, I often find myself saying, "you will get out of a class what you put into it." Put another way, you choose how you think about a class, how you behave in a class, how you study, and how you approach projects in a course. That is a very empowering position to be in!

Mindlessness is characterized by:	Mindfulness is characterized by:
• Relying on attributions, stereotypes, and categories • Routines • Certainty • Having a single perspective • Focusing on outcomes	• Looking for new things; noticing differences • Thinking from multiple perspectives • Considering different frames • Asking questions • Considering processes

 Insight into Innovation Activity: Focus on Options. Imagine that you are told to "write a 10-page paper summarizing mindfulness as an approach to communication." What questions might you ask yourself before you start? How could you *frame* this assignment in a positive way? How could you change the *context* for writing this paper compared to how you've approached other papers in the past? What are some of the choices you can make throughout the *process* of completing the paper? Do you think taking this more mindful approach to writing would result in a better paper? Why or why not?

METHODS IN MINDFULNESS RESEARCH

Langer's research is drawn both from her clinical experience in psychology and also from her field experiments. In her studies, participants are usually in one of two groups: given a task or new way to think about something (treatment group) or no intervention (control group). For example, in her book *The Power of Mindful Learning*, Langer (1997) describes an experiment where she tested the extent to which using conditional language affects students' learning. She took a textbook excerpt and modified the language to be more conditional and less certain, such as replacing "is" with "usually is" or "could be." Some students read the conditional version and other students read the original version. The students who read the modified, conditional version of the textbook

were able to list more details when answering an open question about the material. This experiment is one example of how moving away from certainty and talking about, teaching, and thinking about things in more open and flexible ways can actually help people learn more.

Since Langer's initial book on mindfulness was published over 25 years ago, numerous studies in education, health, and social work have been conducted that test the tenants of mindfulness and applications of mindfulness training. Mindfulness is a vague concept, and it is a broad theory about "how to think." Thus, tests of mindfulness as a way of life are very difficult to conduct. Mindfulness is an internal process that is hard to completely and accurately observe, and the outcomes of mindfulness apply to every aspect of our personal, professional, and even physical lives, which makes its effects difficult to measure. That being said, ongoing research programs have begun to explore the extent of mindfulness training needed to experience the benefits of this approach to thinking about one's self and others, with very promising results.

Insight into Innovation Example: "9 Ways to Be Mindful" Summarizes 25 years of Mindfulness Research. To celebrate the 25th anniversary of *Mindfulness*, Langer republished her seminal text and also did a tour of interviews to discuss her recent research into mindfulness. You can listen to Dr. Langer's interview on Boston Radio, or read the summary of the interview here: http://radioboston. wbur.org/2014/10/15/mindfulness-langer. During the interview, Langer describes the power of reframing "housework" as "exercise" in one of her more recent experiments, and she also describes the "houseplant experiment" that was one of the foundational studies upon which she built the theory of mindfulness.

APPLIED RESEARCH: LEARNING TO LISTEN AND UNDERSTAND

In *The Power of Mindful Learning*, Langer (1997) argued that mindful attention and asking questions are essential for learning. This is particularly difficult to do when we are focused intently on technology and not actively noticing and thinking about the people around us and the context. Thus, for the remainder of this chapter, we will discuss active listening. We can actively listen when we are engaged in mediated interactions or when we are interacting face-to-face. But that may mean that we have to focus on one interaction at a time.

Active listening involves being attentive and responsive (Bodie et al., 2013). Thus, it is both cognitive (what we think about) and behavioral (what we do):

- Cognitive:
  - Trying to understand what the other person is saying, implying, and feeling
  - Remembering what they say.
- Behavioral:
  - Summarizing what's been said
  - Asking questions
  - Verbally and nonverbally signaling that you are listening and receptive.

Listening is an essential skill. Listening to others helps us better understand other people, understand ourselves, build relationships, remember conversations, and interpret messages more accurately (Bodie, 2011). When we are listening for information and emotions, and considering what is being implied, we are better able to understand and respond to other people. These benefits apply to our personal, professional, and educational success.

There is evidence that we are engaging in less interpersonal listening than before because our attention is divided between technology and face-to-face interactions. For example, Emanuel et al. (2008) found that college students are spending more time listening to media and less time listening to other people than students in the 1980s. We are also spending less time interacting interpersonally overall. According to research from UCLA's Higher Education Institute, today's college students spend less time with friends and family than ever before and they spend more time online (Eagan et al., 2014). If we don't interact with and listen to people, we may become more internally focused and more mindless about our professional and interpersonal connections with others.

 "We're Losing Our Listening," Practice RASA to Reclaim it: https://www.youtube.com/watch?v=cSohjlYQI2A

In this Ted Talk, Julian Treasure offers RASA as a method of listening to make us more attentive. RASA stands for receive, appreciate, summarize, and ask. Be receptive to what people are saying, show people that you are listening, summarize what you have heard, and ask questions. These are elements of active, mindful listening: we are taking in new information, checking to see if our perceptions are shared with the other people we interact with, and we are expressing our openness. This is a process approach to listening: rather than listening to confirm what needs to be done or to confirm what we believe, we are engaging in a process of seeking mutual understanding. How do you think we can practice RASA in our mediated communication? Can we signal reception and appreciation, summarize, and ask questions via e-mails, Facebook comments, or retweets? Are we more or less likely to actively listen online?

As all elements of our lives gradually merge to one medium, we have more opportunities for mindful interaction, but there are also more demands on our attention that can undermine our mindful awareness of ourselves and others. How difficult is it for you to turn off technology and really, genuinely focus on a conversation in class, at work, or even at home? If you're like me, it is very, very difficult to ignore technology and focus your thoughts and attention on what's happening in the moment you are in right now. But, in our professional and personal lives, actively listening is an essential skill so that we are competent at what we do, form good impressions in the minds of other people, and build meaningful and satisfying relationships.

Active listening and communication professionals. To demonstrate the importance of listening and critical thinking for professional success, a communication professor had his students conduct a survey of professionals to explore the communication skills needed in people interested in pursuing public relations careers (McCleneghan, 2006). Communication professionals at Fortune 500 companies ranked "active listening" in the top five most needed skills, and the respondents were also critical of recent graduates' ability to listen, think critically, and communicate effectively in face-to-face interactions. In terms of any communication-focused career, from teaching to public relations and sales, listening to the people you serve is essential. Understanding how students, customers, and clients feel and perceive things can help you respond to them more effectively and better meet their needs.

Active listening and interpersonal relationships. Becoming more aware of ourselves and others through participating in active listening and considering what is said, implied, and felt can benefit us in our social lives as well. For example, engaging in active listening in the form of asking questions and summarizing what people said made people in initial interactions feel more *understood, satisfied*, and led to the active listener being perceived as more socially *attractive* (Weger et al., 2014). Thus, when interacting with people in both personal and professional contexts, actively listening can help us understand them more fully and they will feel better about the interaction and about us. Active listening is also a form of *emotional and social support* in interactions that can help people cope with stressful situations (Jones, 2011). It is person-centered and signals involvement, which offers people emotional support when they face personal challenges such as the loss of a loved one. Being supportive builds stronger relationships and is helpful to the people we are interacting with.

Insight into Innovation Example: Mindlessness, Listening, and Multitasking. In the age of mobile technology and social media, our attention is divided between our mediated interactions and our face-to-face lives. Rather than choose between the two, we often multitask. **Multitasking** is when we are doing two or more things at once, such as working on a project and texting, or working on multiple projects at once. Sometimes we do this without even knowing, such as when we're in the middle of doing something and our phone buzzes with a new message or notification and we automatically (and mindlessly!) look at it.

Research suggests that multitasking during interactions, such as doing something while we text or talk on the phone with others, affects people's comfort, satisfaction, and how well we remember both what we are doing and the content of the conversation (Bowman & Pace, 2014). Thus, texting or talking on the phone while doing other things may undermine the relational outcomes of the interaction.

Multitasking with social and interactive media has implications for how well we perform tasks and how much we learn. Students who used IM and browsed Facebook during a lecture, for example, performed worse on multiple-choice tests about the lecture material (Wood et al., 2011). Even with practiced multitasking, the difference in exam scores persisted between students who focused on taking notes versus students using IM and Facebook. Thus, we may not actually get better at multitasking. This is reflected in education outcomes. Students who report using social media and texting while working on homework also had lower overall GPAs (Junco & Cotten, 2012).

One explanation of the poor relational and task outcomes associated with communication technology multitasking is that we have limitations to our cognitive load (Lee, Lin, & Robertson, 2011). **Cognitive load** is how much we can think about at any one time. The more tasks we introduce, the more our cognitive load is divided among the tasks; our cognitive capacity does not necessarily increase or expand to accommodate the additional tasks. Thus, when something is just in the background while we are working, such as a TV in the background, our cognitive load is not necessarily divided because we aren't really thinking about what's on the TV. Communication technologies are different, though, because to respond to social media and instant messages we have to think and this divides our cognitive load, taking away from the primary task.

Turner and Reinsch (2007) termed our interactions via multiple channels at one time **multicommunicating**. Multicommunicating is unique because:

- we have many different means of communicating at once (chat, IM, texting, e-mail, etc.),
- it allows us to compartmentalize interactions that are going on at the same time,
- we are able to control the pace of the interactions,
- it is interactive and thus requires us to attend and adapt, and
- we still must consider both the content of what we are communicating and the relationship dimensions of what's being communicated.

Thus, people tend to choose whether or not to multicommunicate based on their sense of certainty. When people feel uncertain, they tend to multicommunicate less so that they can focus on one interaction. This brings us back to mindfulness and active listening.

Being mindless tends to occur in circumstances where we feel certain, comfortable, and when we're in a routine. In lectures, when we're doing familiar tasks, or when we feel comfortable with and certain about the person(s) we're interacting with, we allow our attention to be divided. Unfortunately, since our cognitive load may be limited, our interactions are less satisfying as a result, we recall less, and our performance on the primary task tends to be diminished. In short, our sense of certainty and our comfort leads us to listen less actively, leading to interpersonally, professionally, and educationally less positive outcomes. But, as mindfulness theory explains, this is a choice we make. Turner and Reinsch explain that we are "presence allocators"; we choose how to allocate our attention when we are multicommunicating. Though we may see multicommunicating as a good thing for us socially and professionally to "balance" work, school, and our personal lives, we also have to consider the extent to which our divided attention may undermine our performance in those three domains. In all, we should each be more mindful, allocate more presence, and expend more focused cognitive effort when we interact.

CONCLUSION

In this chapter we reviewed the tenants of mindfulness, a theory about awareness that can be used to help us notice new things about people, places, and situations in our everyday lives. I included mindfulness as the final theory in the unit on the self because, though mindfulness is a theory that helps us better understand and respond to others, it also challenges us to be introspective. Being introspective, or thinking about who we are and how we feel, is how our sense of self evolves. There are many benefits to mindful living, such as reduced stress, increased empowerment and choice, and more satisfying interactions. And mindfulness sounds very easy: notice and think about the people and things you encounter. We know, of course, that we live in a distracted world where our attention is often divided. Consciously choosing to be active listeners can help us overcome the challenges associated with our divided attention.

When we practice active listening as part of our mindfulness, we go even further and make the people we interact with feel appreciated, understood, and satisfied. Because we look to other people for information about ourselves, mindfulness and active listening can also help us reflect on how other people see us and why they see us the way they do. When we think of ourselves from multiple perspectives, reframe attributes we see in ourselves, and listen actively to the feedback about ourselves that we get from others, we can grow as individuals.

It is of course interesting that research about and popular media coverage of mindfulness have grown even as the distractions in our daily lives have made paying attention to details, introspection, and contemplation much more difficult. We live in a culture and a media age that embraces multitasking. Multitasking divides our attention, making cognitively effortful tasks like active listening, questioning, and perspective-taking more difficult and, arguably, unlikely. What do you think: Has technology made mindfulness impossible? Unlikely? Maybe mindfulness is more likely now with us having more control over our interactions?

ASSIGNMENTS

1. Compare ways of thinking about "work–life balance." Langer criticizes notions of "work–life balance" as being a mindless approach to life that forces us to rely on roles: either we are in a work role or in a home role. Let's consider some other ways of thinking about this to see if mindfully considering other perspectives, examining information, and reframing this area of stress can help us rethink work–life balance and find new ways to feel more comfortable and fulfilled:

   What would "work–life *integration*" look like?

   - Are we the same person, or a different person at work versus at home? Why?
   - What things do we do at home that we should do more of at work?
   - What things do we do at work that we should do more of at home?
   - In what ways do we create stress by trying to maintain barriers between work and home life?

2. Complete the Listening Style Inventory, tabulate your results, and write a self-reflection essay on three things you could do to be a more mindful listener.
   Listening Style Inventory
   http://www.nova.edu/yoursuccess/forms/listening_inventory.pdf

REFERENCES

Seminal Texts:

Langer, E. J. (1989). *Mindfulness.* Reading, MA: Addison-Wesley.

Langer, E. J. (1997). *The power of mindful learning.* Cambridge, MA: Perseus Books.

Academic Articles:

Bodie, G. D. (2011). The active-empathic listening scale (AELS): Conceptualization and evidence of validity within the interpersonal domain. *Communication Quarterly, 59*(3), 277–295.

Bodie, G. D., Gearhart, C. G., Denham, J. P., & Vickery, A. J. (2013). The temporal stability and situational contingency of active-empathic listening. *Western Journal of Communication, 77,* 113–138.

Bowman, J. M., & Pace, R. C. (2014). Dual-tasking effects on outcomes of mobile communication technologies. *Communication Research Reports, 31,* 221–231.

Eagan, K., Stolzenberg, E. B., Ramirez, J. J., Aragon, M. C., Ramirez Suchard, M., & Hurtado, S. (2014). The American freshman: National norms Fall 2014. *Cooperative Institutional Research Program at the Higher Education Institute of UCLA.* Retrieved from http://www.heri.ucla.edu/monographs/TheAmericanFreshman2014.pdf

Emanuel, R., Adams, J., Baker, K., Daufin, E. K., Ellington, C., Fitts, E., Himsel, J., Holladay, L. & Okeowo, D. (2008). How college students spent their time communication. *International Journal of Listening, 22,* 13–28.

Jones, S. M. (2011). Supportive listening. *The International Journal of Listening, 25,* 85–103.

Junco, R., & Cotton, S. R. (2012). No A 4 U: The relationship between multitasjing and academic performance. *Computers & Education, 59,* 505–514.

Kowai-Bell, N., Guagagno, R. E., Little, T., Priess, N., & Hensley, R. (2011). Rate my expectations: How online evaluations of professors impact students' perceived control. *Computers in Human Behavior, 27*(5), 1862–1867.

Lee, J., Lin, L., & Robertson, T. (2011). The impact of media multitasking on learning. *Learning, Media and Technology, 37,* 94–104.

McClenghan, J. S. (2006). PR executives rank 11 communication skills. *Public Relations Quarterly, 51,* 42–46.

Silva, K. M, Silva, F. J., Quinn, M. A., Draper, J. N. et al. (2008). Rate My Professor: Online evaluations of psychology instructors. *Teaching of Psychology, 35,* 71–80.

Stuber, J. M., Watson, A., Carle, A., & Staggs, K. (2009). Gender expectations and on-line evaluations of teaching: Evidence from ratemyprofessors.com. *Teaching in Higher Education, 14,* 387–399.

Turner, J. W., & Reinsch, N. L., Jr. (2007). The business communicator as presence allocator: Multicommunicating, equivocality, and status at work. *Journal of Business Communication, 44*(1), 36–58.

Weger, H., Jr., Castle Bell, G., Minei, E. M., & Robinson, M. C. (2014). The relative effectiveness of active listening in initial interactions. *The International Journal of Listening, 28*(1), 13–31.

Wood, E., Zivcakova, L., Gentile, P., Archer, K., De Pasquale, D., & Nosko, A. (2011). Examining the impact of off-task multi-tasking with technology on real-time classroom learning. *Computers & Education*, *58*(1), 365–374.

Examples:

The New York Times. (2015, February 6). Is the professor bossy or brilliant? Much depends on gender. The Upshot. Retrieved from http://www.nytimes.com/2015/02/07/upshot/is-the-professor-bossy-or-brilliant-much-depends-on-gender.html?abt=0002&abg=1

SENDING AND INTER-PRETING MEDIATED MESSAGES: CULTURE, GENDER, AND CONTEXT

In Unit 1 we focused on the self, including self-presentation, attributions, constructs, and becoming more mindful communicators. Theories related to the self help us understand the limitations of our own perceptions and build competencies such as creating person-centered messages and actively listening to others to develop more complex, differentiated constructs. In this unit on sending and interpreting messages, we will look at more general expectations we may have of others, and the social norms that we may unintentionally conform to, by focusing on cultures, gender, and context.

The lessons learned in the first unit about how we are all constrained by roles, often flawed in our attributions, limited by our constructs for other people, and tend to interact mindlessly should also help us understand the theories related to culture, gender, and context that we will discuss in this unit. The limitations of our perspective and perception lead to problems when we interact with people from other cultures and backgrounds, like overaccommodation and impoliteness. Similarly, our mindless reliance on categories such as gender set expectations for others' behavior that may restrict our own communication and lead us to unfairly judge or inaccurately perceive others' communication.

Communication accommodation theory teaches us that there is a fine line between person-centered messages that adapt to others' communication styles versus adapting to *perceived* differences between ourselves and others. The theory warns against accommodating others too much based on perception of their limitations, their culture, or demographic group. In interactions with people who are different from us, whether the differences are based on age, gender, race, or disability, we need to work on having a more complex understanding of who people are as unique individuals, much like we discussed in the chapter on attributions and constructs.

We will also discuss theories that describe "polite" message structures, again focusing on how perceptions of politeness vary based on individual differences. These perceptions of what constitutes "polite" versus "impolite" communication lead us to create and interpret messages differently, particularly in negotiations and conflicts. Often these different perceptions escalate conflicts and prolong negotiations that could otherwise be resolved amicably if the people involved moved away from their self-focus to an issue-focus.

How we accommodate others' communication styles and whether we perceive their communication as polite or impolite is affected by gender-based expectations. For example, we may expect women to be more emotional and men to be more rational. Based on that gender stereotype, we may change how we would typically communicate based on the gender of the person we are interacting with by being more indirect and descriptive with women and more direct with men. We may also judge women who are very direct and factual in their messages as being impolite because they are failing to conform to our gender-based expectations.

Theories of accommodation, politeness, and gender communication styles all help us understand the important role of *expectations* in interactions. People expect certain behavior from certain types of people in certain circumstances. Violating expectations can lead to dislike and conflict. Expectancy violations theory explains the link between expectations, contextual norms, individual differences, and reactions. Through self-awareness, sensitivity to context, and awareness of individual differences we can learn how to approach different situations to minimize misunderstanding.

In sum, in this unit, we will consider how culture and gender affect how we create and react to verbal and nonverbal communication. Our expectations and evaluations can create misunderstanding, increase dislike among people, and escalate conflict. On the other hand, learning about these intercultural and gender communication processes and applying concepts like differentiation and mindfulness from the previous unit, we can become more competent, flexible, and responsive communicators who understand how to increase liking and closeness, and deescalate conflict.

These skills are particularly important in the Web 2.0 environment. In ways that were inconceivable just decades ago, we can communicate instantaneously with people from across the globe. Though these new technologies are amazing opportunities to build international communities, they can also highlight and exacerbate tensions and differences that drive us further apart. People have access to, and use, many new options for punishing people online who violate norms, such as doxing, spoofing, hacking, and flaming. People may be dishonest online, or become trolls who shut down meaningful discussion and debate. Arguably, new media may be exacerbating rather than relieving cultural and gender divisions and silencing people rather than helping us embrace differences.

CHAPTER 7

COMMUNICATION ACCOMMODATION AND POLITENESS THEORY

INTRODUCTION

We are in a global economy and this means we will be interacting with people from across the world as part of our professional lives (Ting-Toomey, 1999). With the continued expansion of social media and teleworking, people are interacting with more diverse people as a routine part of their personal lives and careers. Even in education, the growth of online education has led to diverse online classrooms that include nontraditional students with full-time jobs, soldiers stationed overseas, students from other states and other countries, in addition to traditional students living on or near campus. Thus, considering how culture affects the messages we formulate and how those messages may be received by people from different cultural backgrounds and life circumstances is important for both our personal and our professional success.

Both communication accommodation theory and politeness theory help us understand individual differences, particularly cultural differences, in formulating and interpreting messages. Generally, **culture** refers to values shared by a group of people (Gudykunst & Lee, 2003). But, as constructivism and mindfulness researchers point out, even within a culture there are individual differences in identity, demographics, and personality that we should recognize and adjust to when communicating. Mindfulness is essential for successful intercultural interactions.

MAIN IDEA

Both accommodation theory and politeness theory focus on formulating messages and offer insight into how culture and perceptions of cultural differences affect the messages we create. Accommodation theory teaches us to adjust our messages to the person we are interacting with but to avoid accommodating based on uninformed stereotypes. Politeness theory teaches us specific strategies that are perceived as polite or impolite based on whether or not we protect our own or other people's face in an interaction.

KEY CONCEPTS FROM ACCOMMODATION THEORY (GILES, COUPLAND, & COUPLAND, 1991)

We each have a communication style that is influenced by group norms, the region we're from, and our traits. **Communication style** includes how long we speak, our rate of speech, use of pauses, use of voice, how long we take to respond, disclosure of personal details, use of jokes, gestures, facial expressions, and our posture. When we are in interactions with people who have different communication styles, we may consciously or unconsciously change how we communicate in response to their style.

1. *People often accommodate others' communication styles.* **Accommodation** is when we adjust our messages in reaction to others' communication styles. We can accommodate by moving toward the style of the other person, maintaining our unique style, or moving away from their communication style. **Convergence** is when we seek to match others' styles. **Divergence**, on the other hand, is when we accentuate differences. In computer mediated communication (CMC), accommodation may include adjusting the length of messages, use of emoticons, punctuations, word choice, and the tone of the messages to converge with or diverge from others. Think of it this way: if someone sends you an e-mail that includes smiley faces and exclamation points, you may match their e-mail style by using punctuation and emoticons even if that isn't how you typically write (convergence); you may write how you typically write; or you may choose to be even more formal than usual and send a short, factual reply (divergence).

2. *Our decision to converge or diverge is influenced by power and needs.* We tend to converge when we are in interactions with people who have more social or political power than we do. We maintain our communication style or diverge when we interact with people who have less power. So, if it was your boss who sent you an e-mail with exclamation points and smiley faces, you may be more inclined to converge to match his or her style and promote liking. On the other hand, if a subordinate sent you that kind of e-mail, you may choose to maintain

your style or diverge to maintain the social distance between yourself and the sender. In terms of needs, converging with the other person signals our need to be socially integrated with the other person's group. Thus, we if we feel a strong need to be liked and be part of the social group of the person we're interacting with, we will converge to fulfill that social need.

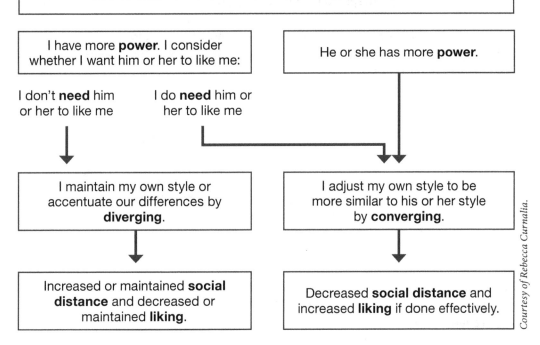

Communication Accommodation Theory:

In an interaction with someone from a different social group or region, I choose whether to adjust my communication to his or her style, how much to adjust, and whether to move toward his or her style or away from it.

I have more **power**. I consider whether I want him or her to like me:

He or she has more **power**.

I don't **need** him or her to like me

I do **need** him or her to like me

I maintain my own style or accentuate our differences by **diverging**.

I adjust my own style to be more similar to his or her style by **converging**.

Increased or maintained **social distance** and decreased or maintained **liking**.

Decreased **social distance** and increased **liking** if done effectively.

Courtesy of Rebecca Curnalia.

3. *Person-centered accommodation, particularly convergence, can be helpful in interactions and lead to positive outcomes.* We've discussed person-centered communication in previous chapters, but it bears repeating that convergence is a good thing if it is done mindfully, drawing upon a complex understanding of the other person. When accommodation is focused on people—that is to say, we accommodate based on their feelings, personality, and circumstances rather than our stereotypes—we can improve understanding, increase our own social attractiveness, increase liking, and increase mutual satisfaction in our interactions.

4. *Sometimes people overaccommodate based on stereotypes or perceptions of others' limitations and this hurts interactions.* **Overaccommodation** is when we perceive that the other person has some limitation or stereotypical characteristic and we mindlessly change our communication based on that perception. For example, people often do this with people who are older, disabled, or underprivileged. People may assume that older people

are easily confused, people with visible disabilities are less capable, or people from less privileged backgrounds are less knowledgeable, and accommodate by unintentionally "talking down" to them. No one likes condescending messages, but one reason people condescend to others is because of some perceived limitation. This is where the advice from the first unit can be very helpful: increasing discrimination between people and developing complex constructs by being an observant interactant can help us avoid overaccommodation.

KEY CONCEPTS FROM POLITENESS THEORY (BROWN & LEVINSON, 1987)

Chances are, when we are accommodating others, we are trying to be polite. But overaccommodating can make us seem impolite. When we overaccommodate we may damage other people's **face**. Face is a concept from Goffman, whose work we discussed in the unit on the self: people want to have and to project positive images of themselves. Recall from that chapter that we get feedback about our self from others, such as how they talk to us and how they talk about us. When talking to us, if someone overaccommodates in a way that makes us feel small or less capable, this can damage our face.

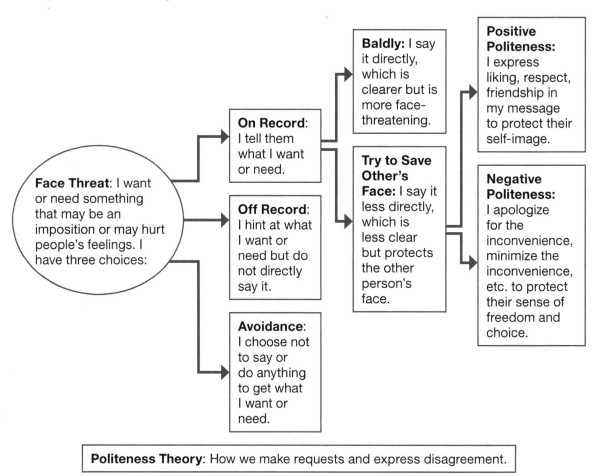

Face Threat: I want or need something that may be an imposition or may hurt people's feelings. I have three choices:

On Record: I tell them what I want or need.

Off Record: I hint at what I want or need but do not directly say it.

Avoidance: I choose not to say or do anything to get what I want or need.

Baldly: I say it directly, which is clearer but is more face-threatening.

Try to Save Other's Face: I say it less directly, which is less clear but protects the other person's face.

Positive Politeness: I express liking, respect, friendship in my message to protect their self-image.

Negative Politeness: I apologize for the inconvenience, minimize the inconvenience, etc. to protect their sense of freedom and choice.

Politeness Theory: How we make requests and express disagreement.

Thus, we will look at politeness theory as a lens for considering our message options when we are interacting with people who are different from ourselves. Though this theory, like communication accommodation, is often applied to intercultural interactions, the implications of the theoretical concepts, processes, and effects generalize to individual differences in identity.

1. *People have positive and negative face needs* and these are related to culture. **Positive face** is our need for others to like and respect us. **Negative face** is our need for freedom, choice, and autonomy. If you think about it from the position of an instructor in a class, for example, we want to be liked and respected by our students (positive face). On the other hand, we want our class to follow the process and schedule that we laid out in the syllabus (negative face). Of course, students also have positive face needs, such as wanting to be liked and validated by their instructors. And students have negative face needs, such as having autonomy and choices even within the structure of the class. Thus, when we interact, we should consider each other's positive and negative face needs as well as our own face needs.

2. *Some types of messages are inherently face-threatening to receivers.* **Face threats** are when we communicate a message that could injure either positive or negative face. When we give orders to others, make requests of other people, offer advice, remind people to do something, and the like, these threaten negative face because they are a challenge to the autonomy of other people. If we express disappointment, disapproval, or criticism, we are threatening positive face. Think about this in the context of the classroom: if your instructor tells you to turn in an assignment on a specific date in a specific format, it is a threat to your autonomy because you do not have a choice in the matter. When the instructor returns the assignment, if it is heavily marked up with corrections and critiques, this is a threat to positive face because it can be perceived as the instructor criticizing or being disapproving of your work.

3. *Some types of messages are face-threatening to the speaker.* When we express or accept thanks and apologies, we are potentially damaging our own negative face. When we embarrass ourselves, admit or confess our guilt, or express emotions that we would prefer to control or hide, we are potentially damaging our own positive face. If an instructor says, "thank you for turning in your assignment early," he or she is acknowledging the limits of his or her control in that situation. Thus, saying "thank you" can damage a speaker's negative face. When we admit that we made a mistake, such as fumbling a lecture or having errors in the syllabus, this can damage our positive face by making us less likable or competent in the eyes of our students.

4. *We choose whether or not to deliver face-threatening messages and how to deliver face-threatening messages.* For many things, we can simply choose not to do a face-threatening act by not asking people for things, not engaging in disagreement, and avoiding criticizing others. Sometimes, though, we do not have a choice and have to do a face-threatening act as part of our personal or professional obligations. When we must communicate a face-threatening message, we can go **off record**, which is communicating what we want or need indirectly. On the other hand, we can be very clear and direct, which is communicating **baldly**. So, when collecting assignments in class, I could say "turn in your work now," which would be a bald tactic. Or, I could say "I'm collecting assignments," which would be a less direct, off-record tactic. Though communicating baldly may sound like a bad approach, we should be careful not to confuse being direct with verbal aggression or bullying. **Verbal aggression** is when people intentionally attack another's face by verbally or nonverbally threatening,

insulting, attacking, or demeaning him or her. One can communicate baldly by not protecting the face of the other person without necessarily being aggressive. Indeed, there may be instances when communicating baldly is the best option.

 Learn about the causes, types, symptoms, and ways to respond to aggression here: http://www.skillsyouneed.com/ps/dealing-with-aggression2.html

5. *When delivering a face-threatening message, we can use different types of politeness to protect the other person's face.* **Positive politeness** protects the positive face, or self-image, of the person with whom we're communicating. For example, I can deliver criticism by saying that a student's paper "is a good start, but needs some work." Saying that it is a "good start" is positive politeness. **Negative politeness** is what we include in messages to protect other people's negative face. So, we may say "I can tell you invested a lot of time and thought in this paper, but there are a few revisions that could make it stronger." Including sentiments such as "you invested a lot of time and thought" and the word "could" addresses the student's freedom of choice.

6. *We balance our own and others' face needs in interactions based on our culture and self-identity.* This is called **facework**. According to face negotiation theory, our cultural values that emphasize either the individual or the collective, as well as our own identity and personal values, affect the directness of the messages we send. **Individualistic cultural values**, like we have in the US, tend to value autonomy, independence, and personal success. Thus, we tend to be more direct in individualistic cultures. On the other hand, **collectivist cultural values**, such as Asian cultures, tend to focus on the collective: building, maintaining, and protecting relationships. In those cultures, people may be more indirect in an effort to preserve the relationship and face of the other person.

METHODS IN ACCOMMODATION AND POLITENESS RESEARCH

Linguistics. Both communication accommodation and politeness research closely examine variations in people's messages. Both theories are built upon research in **linguistics**. Linguistics is a research method that looks closely at people's language use to consider things like taking turns in a conversation, the length of turns, topic shifts, the phrasing of what is said, and the types of words used in interactions. Accommodation theory research also looks at speech rate, use of gestures, posture, and other forms of nonverbal communication. This is done by observing people's interactions, either in real life or in experimental settings, and **coding** what they say and do. We can code for politeness, for example, by determining whether or not a single statement is bald, off-record, positive politeness, or negative politeness. We can code for accommodation by measuring people's speech rates when they are interacting, or coding other types of verbal and nonverbal behavior, and determining if people converge or diverge over the course of an interaction.

Experiments. Accommodation theory is often tested using experiments. For example, researchers may have one group of people interact with a higher power person and another group of people interact with a lower power person. They would then code the people's verbal and nonverbal behavior to determine whether the power differences affected accommodation. Many of the studies we will review in our discussion of Netiquette in the remainder of this chapter are experiments where people are placed in a particular context, asked to interact via a mediated channel, and then their behavior is observed and coded. These studies have helped us understand how and when people converge or diverge in online interactions.

Observation. Politeness theory is a useful framework for analyzing observed interactions to determine the types of politeness strategies used, who uses which strategies to accomplish which types of tasks, and how people respond to different strategies. Both accommodation and politeness can be observed in online posts and interactions to help us understand messages strategies and reactions to messages via many new media technologies such as e-mail, social networks, instant messaging (IM), and comments sections. For example, we could collect emails from students who were unhappy with their grades and determine the types of politeness strategies used and whether those strategies varied by the type of class (lower division versus upper division) and type of professor (adjunct, assistant, associate, and full) and compare the effectiveness of each strategy.

APPLYING ACCOMMODATION AND POLITENESS: NETIQUETTE

Some of the rules of netiquette can help us apply what we've learned from communication accommodation theory and politeness theory to our online interactions. **Netiquette** is online etiquette, or guidelines for behaving appropriately in online contexts (http://www.albion.com/netiquette/corerules.html). Netiquette challenges us to 1) think about the people we are communicating with and how best to accommodate them; 2) make ethical choices when sending online messages; 3) adapt to the context, whether it is personal or professional; 4) be selective about who receives messages, while understanding that we no longer control the message once it is sent; and 5) integrate, or balance, our own face needs with the needs of others.

Practicing netiquette is one way to create an online environment that fosters understanding and the exchange of ideas by encouraging us to be thoughtful, considerate, honest, and open in our interactions. Teaching netiquette can also decrease **cyberbullying**, which is the repeated use of aggressive tactics online to hurt someone whom is seen as having less power. (Park, Na, & Kim, 2014). On the other hand, the rules of netiquette may also be seen as a way to standardize human communication (Marcoccia, 2012).

Insight into Innovation Activity: Take Shea's (1994) Netiquette Quiz. You can take a quiz testing your netiquette skills at http://www.albion.com/netiquette/netiquiz.html. After you take the quiz, reflect on your netiquette: Do you consider the gender, culture, and norms of the people you interact with online? Are you ethical and sensitive in your online interactions to both your own and other people's face needs?

1. **Remember that you are communicating with people.** On the other side of your computer or smartphone screen are people reading, watching, or hearing your mediated messages. Sometimes, when we cannot see them, we forget they're there. This can make us less civil and less sensitive to our receivers and their unique characteristics such as their personality and culture. Numerous studies point to the "disinhibiting" effect of interacting online, such that people are more aggressive, hostile, face threatening, and more likely to cyberbully online compared to face-to-face. As we will discuss for the remainder of this chapter, aggressive and hostile behavior is not productive in general, and it is likely to escalate problems online.

   It is exceedingly difficult to accommodate others online because of this disconnect, but we should still be person-centered in our message construction in that we think about the person on the receiving end of what we post. Similarly, we should consider the face—the public image—of the people we are interacting with online. Not only are we affecting our own public image by what we post, but we may also be attacking or supporting the public image of the people we communicate with and the people we communicate about.

   There are simple ways of incorporating face-saving into our online interactions, even when we don't personally know the people we are interacting with. For example, writing e-mails that include polite phrases such as "please" and "thank you" lead people to converge in politeness when responding (Bunz & Campbell, 2004). Taking time with e-mail, rather than shooting off knee-jerk reactions, gives us the opportunity to think about the person we are corresponding with, temper our own feelings, and consider the permanence of the messages we are sending (Sloboda, 1999).

   It also promotes politeness if people are identifiable in an interaction. In comparisons of online comments sections, researchers found that Facebook comments sections were more civil compared to anonymous comments on a website because people were less likely to

   directly threaten the face of other people via Facebook (Rowe, 2015). This may be because technologies like Facebook, where we can see the names and sometimes pictures of people we are responding to, is humanizing and reminds us that we are interacting with real people online. On anonymous message boards where there is no name or picture associated with the other people, we may lose this sense of humanity and, thus, default to less polite messages. And messages posted online to social media can damage people's face (Masullo & Abedin, 2014). Face-damaging messages such as rejections and criticisms can incite aggression in people as they try to protect their public image. There are relatively simple things we can do to humanize our online interactions, such as having pictures of ourselves in our e-mail and social network accounts.

2. **Maintain your "real life" ethical and legal standards when you are communicating online.** One way to choose how best to interact with people online and avoid antisocial behavior is to adhere to clear ethical standards for *all* of our interactions. Ethical communication involves being open to individual differences, protecting other people's face needs, and avoiding personal attacks. The National Communication Association has outlined

ethical communication principles* (Copyright © National Communication Association. Reprinted by permission.) that should guide all of our interactions (http://www.natcom. org/ethicalstatements/):

- practicing "truthfulness, accuracy, honesty, and reason" in interactions;
- seeking to "understand and respect other communicators before evaluating and responding";
- promoting "access to communication resources and opportunities" for the betterment of others;
- promoting "communication climates" that encourage "caring and mutual understanding" of other people's needs and characteristics;
- condemning communication that "degrades individuals and humanity through distortion, intimidation, coercion, and violence, and through the expression of intolerance and hatred";
- being committed to the "courageous expression of personal convictions in pursuit of fairness and justice";
- balancing the rights to share "information, opinions, and feelings when facing significant choices" with our obligation to respect others' privacy;
- accepting responsibility for the consequences of our communication choices.

In other words, we should be honest, mindful, and respectful of others and their rights, open to disagreement, willing to thoughtfully express ourselves, and own the outcomes of our choices. If we apply these standards for ethical communication, we should not be hostile or cyberbullies. Rather, these guidelines suggest that we should express our own interests, needs, and goals thoughtfully and with concern for the other people involved in the interaction. Thus, we should be sensitive to the context, audience, and our own interests in interactions.

3. **Consider the context and norms before posting.** People tend to converge in social settings, particularly when they are interacting via CMC among friends or as part of an online community. Convergence is also a key strategy to get what we want in contexts where our goal is to persuade others.

Different contexts (IM, chat, social networks, and e-mail), people (people we know versus strangers), and interaction goals (whether we have a task or social goal) lead to different message strategies. Looking at the length of IMs and the time between IMs, Riordin et al. (2012) found that people converge more when they interact online with *friends*, and diverge more when interacting with *strangers*. People also tended to converge more when trying to accomplish a *task*, such as persuading others, compared to when they were just socializing. People also tended to converge less when engaged in disagreements online. Similar results have been found in studies of Twitter communities and in online chat forums. Twitter users who are part of an online community converge with their group's language use (Tamburrini et al., 2015). In online chat forums where people interact to build relationships, they tend to converge on important CMC features, such as the use of emoticons (Fullwood, Orchard, & Floyd, 2013).

Thus, when we are building relationships online, we tend to converge. This is perfectly natural, because convergence should build interpersonal liking and trust. On the other hand, when we interact with strangers and when we are in negative situations, like conflicts, we tend not to converge and sometimes we diverge. Divergence can lead to greater perceived differences between ourselves and others.

4. **Manage your audience: Consider who should receive (and not receive) online messages.** Clearly, based on the discussion above, we should carefully consider our audience and, when possible, manage the audience for our online messages. We should consider our relationship with the other person and their expectations when posting and interacting online: How formal or informal should we be given the power differences? What is our relationship—personal, professional, acquaintances, or strangers? How has our interaction evolved over time? What do we both expect out of this interaction? This understanding of our receivers should inform our online etiquette (Lewin-Jones & Mason, 2014).

Generally, different audiences require different message strategies. We can manage who receives our posts and messages by managing our privacy settings on posts and carefully selecting who we reply to in emails, such as whether or not everyone should receive your reply or whether just one or two people in an online conversation should receive your reply. "Reply all" and "public" messages are not appropriate in many personal and professional interactions.

At the same time, when we send or post something online, we must be aware that we are creating a permanent record that the other person can disseminate to others. So, we should send messages with our relationship to the specific receivers in mind, and also craft them in such a way that they will not damage our public image or other relationships if they somehow get out.

5. **Manage people's impression of you in your online messages.** Considering and accommodating other people's unique characteristics and communication styles and needs doesn't mean that we should ignore our own unique characteristics and goals. Avoidance of differences is generally not a satisfying approach. Rather, think of interactions as an opportunity to **integrate** your wants and needs with the wants and needs of others. Integrative tactics consider your own and other people's needs, including face needs, to reach solutions or resolutions that are mutually satisfying.

Integration may be more difficult online. One unfortunate outcome of the lack of human connection during online interactions is that we are more likely to be impolite, or face-threatening, to others online. This tendency leads to less positive outcomes for us when we negotiate. Research suggests that the inclination toward being hostile during online negotiations, such as being dishonest, threatening, or insulting, is actually linked to less favorable outcomes (Stuhlmacher & Citera, 2005). In other words, when we negotiate online and use more direct, aggressive tactics, we are actually less likely to get what we want. People who negotiated online tended to be more hostile, and negotiations resulted in less profit when they were conducted online versus face-to-face. One explanation of the hostility and the negative outcomes associated with online negotiations is a lack of trust among interactants

(Naquin & Paulson, 2003). If we think critically about it, it makes sense that we would have less trust in the people we are interacting with online: we cannot see them, making it very difficult to determine their individual characteristics and needs and so we would be less able to accommodate.

We can consciously choose to use negotiation tactics that build up other people's face, even in online interactions, and this may lead to more positive outcomes. Specifically, a more effective approach to collaboration online may be to build up each other's positive face, such as focusing on common ground, offering reciprocation, and expressing willingness to cooperate (Vinagre, 2008). These are characteristics of collectivist cultural values. Indeed, collectivist cultures appear to negotiate more productively online and reach more integrative, mutually beneficial outcomes via mediated negotiations compared to individualists (Potter & Balthazard, 2000).

💬 CONCLUSION

Both politeness theory and accommodation theory discuss communication strategies that can help us become better online communicators and warn us against strategies that may undermine the effectiveness of our interactions. In general, person-centered convergence can be used strategically to build liking. Similarly, politeness strategies can be used to protect the face of other people in interactions, even when we disagree or are in a negotiation. Both politeness theory and accommodation theory have been applied in the general, practical discussion of netiquette.

Though politeness, accommodation, and netiquette research has been criticized for being too narrow and not addressing the breadth of communication choices in interactions, they are a good starting point for considering our own and others' culture, personality, and communication style. Being aware of variations in politeness behaviors and the many dimensions of communication that we can converge on in our online interactions should encourage us to mindfully consider our message strategies online, and help us better interpret other people's mediated messages. Thus, we should be more flexible, adaptable online communicators and promote an internet environment that encourages, rather than silences, free and open discourse across cultural and ideological divides.

ASSIGNMENTS

1. Consider the following scenario, and evaluate your response options:

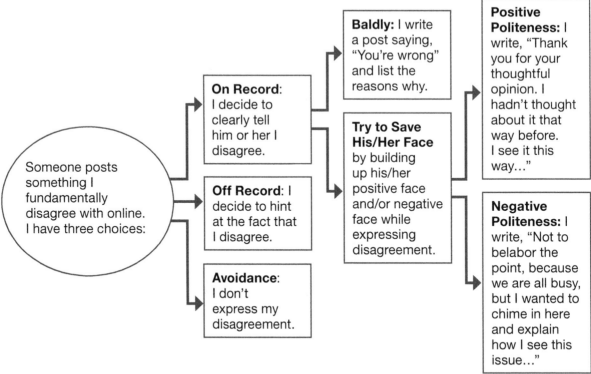

Courtesy of Rebecca Curnalia.

Politeness Theory/Netiquette Activity:
Of the options here, which responses are most ethical according to NCA's principles?
Which options fail to live up to NCA's ethical principles?
Which options fit the standards for Netiquette?
Which options seem more integrative?
How would you respond in this situation?

2. Reflect on the guidelines for netiquette. What would you add to or change about the netiquette guidelines? Write a 5-item guide to netiquette that incorporates concepts from both accommodation theory and politeness theory.

REFERENCES

Seminal Works:

Brown, P., & Levinson, S. C. (1987). *Politeness: Some universals in language usage* (Studies in interactional sociolinguistics). Cambridge: Cambridge University Press.

Giles, H., Coupland, N., & Coupland, J. (1991). Accommodation theory: Communication, context, and consequence. In H. Giles, J. Coupland, & N. Coupland (eds.), *Concepts of accommodation: developments in applied socio-linguistics.* Cambridge: Cambridge University Press.

Academic Sources:

Bunz, U., & Campbell, S. W. (2004). Politeness accommodation in electronic mail. *Communication Research Reports, 21*(1), 11–25.

Fullwood, C., Orchard, L. J., & Floyd, S. A. (2013). Emoticon convergence in Internet chat rooms. *Social Semiotics, 23*(5), 648–662. doi:10.1080/10350330.2012.739000

Gudykunst, W. B. (2003). Intercultural communication theories. In W. B. Gudykunst (ed.), *Cross-cultural and intercultural communication* (pp. 167–190). Thousand Oaks, CA: Sage.

Gudykunst, W. B., & Lee, C. M. (2003). Cross-cultural communication theories. In W. B. Gudykunst (ed.), *Cross-cultural and intercultural communication* (pp. 7–34). Thousand Oaks, CA: Sage.

Lewin-Jones, J., & Mason, V. (2014) Understanding style, language and etiquette in email communication in higher education : A survey. *Research in Post-Compulsory Education, 19,* 75–90.

Marcoccia, M. (2012). The Internet, intercultural communication and cultural variation. *Language & Intercultural Communication, 12*(4), 353–368. doi:10.1080/14708477.2012.722101

Masullo Chen, G., & Abedin, Z. (2014). Exploring differences in how men and women respond to threats to positive face on social media. *Computers in Human Behavior, 38,* 118–126. doi:10.1016/j.chb.2014.05.029

Naquin, C. E., & Paulson, G. D. (2003). Online bargaining and interpersonal trust. *The Journal of Applied Psychology, 88*(1), 113–120. doi:10.1037/0021-9010.88.1.113

Park, S., Na, E., & Kim, E. (2014). The relationship between online activities, netiquette and cyberbullying. *Children & Youth Services Review, 42,* 74–81. doi:10.1016/j.childyouth.2014.04.002

Potter, R. E., & Balthazard, P. A. (2000). Supporting integrative negotiation via computer mediated communication technologies an empirical example with geographically dispersed Chinese and American negotiators. *Journal of International Consumer Marketing, 12*(4), 7–32.

Riordan, M. A., Markman, K. M., & Stewart, C. O. (2012). Communication accommodation in instant messaging: An examination of temporal convergence. *Journal of Language & Social Psychology, 32*(1), 84–95. doi:10.1177/0261927X12462695

Rowe, I. (2015). Civility 2.0: A comparative analysis of incivility in online political discussion. *Information, Communication & Society, 18*(2), 121–138. doi:10.1080/13691 18X.2014.940365

Stuhlmacher, A., & Citera, M. (2005). Hostile behavior and profit in virtual negotiation: A meta-analysis. *Journal of Business & Psychology, 20*(1), 69–93. doi:10.1007/ s10869-005-6984-y

Sloboda, B. (1999). "Netiquette"—New rules and policies for the Information Age. *Management Quarterly, 40*(4), 9–35.

Tamburrini, N., Cinnirella, M., Jansen, V. A., & Bryden, J. (2015). Twitter users change word usage according to conversation-partner social identity. *Social Networks, 40*, 84–89. doi:10.1016/j.socnet.2014.07.004

Ting-Toomey, S. (1999). *Communicating across cultures*. New York: Guilford Press.

Vinagre, M. (2008). Politeness strategies in collaborative e-mail exchanges. *Computers & Education, 50*(3), 1022–1036. doi:10.1016/j.compedu.2006.10.002

CHAPTER 8

GENDERLECT STYLES, MUTING, AND STANDPOINT THEORY

OUTCOMES

- *Knowledge:* Learn how we are socialized into gender norms that influence how we perceive and respond to gender.

- *Skill:* Recognize your own gendered style, learn to capitalize on gender differences to improve corporate outcomes, and be flexible in interactions to accomplish tasks.

🗨 INTRODUCTION

Gender and women's studies may sound like a topic more appropriate for a book from your parents' era, particularly since many people believe that we have made great strides in gender equality. Unfortunately, research suggests that technology has provided a new channel for and means of participating in harassment and exclusion rather than helping give a voice to traditionally silenced members of the population. We are socialized into gender norms, much like we are socialized into a culture. This socialization begins for many people in infancy, as baby girls are given baby dolls and baby boys are given trucks and superhero toys. From these early developmental stages, girls are socialized to be nurturing and boys are socialized to seek power.

People from racial minority groups, women, and members of the LGBTQ community have historically been silenced by socialized norms and institutionalized policies. This silencing was perpetuated through denying people voting rights, restricting access to participation in public debate, and limiting access to professions. Through hard-won legal and social battles, these forms of institutionalized silencing have been curbed, though we still see social norms restricting people's access to careers and participation in public discourse. We see evidence of this ongoing exclusion in fields like technology and computer science, where women and other minorities are underrepresented. Many social norms and stereotypes have persisted due to how people perceive, communicate with, and communicate about women.

In this chapter, we will look at three interrelated explanations of why and how women are silenced in our modern, Web 2.0 society: genderlect styles of communication that men and women are socialized into, muting of women and other minority groups as a result of the power structure of society, and the unique standpoint that results from women's position in society.

OVERVIEW OF GENDERLECT AND MUTED GROUP

MAIN IDEA

Genderlect research describes gendered communication styles as culture types: masculine culture is more task-oriented and the feminine culture is more relationship-oriented. The values associated with each gender affect how we communicate and interpret messages. Due to our social norms, according to muted group theory, masculine communication is valued in our society, thus **muting** minority voices, or excluding diverse voices from our public discourse. To understand each other, we have to consider our own and others' values and our unique **standpoints**, or the positions we occupy in society and how that affects what we know.

Genderlect communication styles explain the gender-specific ways in which we communicate as a result of how we are socialized. In turn, these gendered ways of communicating are similar to cultural differences. **Muting** is the process whereby minority voices are silenced through direct and indirect coercion and harassment, and one method of muting is privileging male communication styles over female styles. Lastly, **standpoints** are the unique perspectives of people from minority groups. One aspect of our standpoints is gender, but our standpoint also includes social class, sexuality, culture, and race, all of which affect what we know. In all, these theories help us understand how socialization, norms, and standpoints make having a truly equal society very difficult, even in a society with the technological resources to make great strides in equal representation and participation.

KEY CONCEPTS FROM GENDERLECT THEORY (TANNEN, 1990)

Copyright © FMStox/Shutterstock.com

Gender as Culture. In the previous chapter, we defined culture as values shared among a group of people. Though we often think of culture being the values and behaviors in a specific geographic region or in a cultural group, Tannen argued that gender is like culture. Each gender has values and needs that are expressed through communication, so we have different **genderlects**, or distinct ways of communicating that are similar to a dialect. Thus, to understand each other, we must understand the genderlect styles being used by others and ourselves.

We should avoid the temptation to assume that all men have a masculine genderlect and all women have a feminine genderlect. **Gender** is a social construct—something we have created and defined through social interaction—and it exists on a range from very feminine to very masculine.

Biological sex, on the other hand, is how we are born. Think of it this way: when a baby is born, the doctor confirms the baby's sex with a physical examination, then the nurse wraps the baby in either blue or pink thus beginning socialization into a gender.

Messages and Metamessages. One key to understanding genderlect styles is the difference between messages and metamessages. Tannen argues that the masculine genderlect includes a focus on **messages**: what is actually said or done. The feminine genderlect tends to focus on the **metamessage**, or the underlying relational meaning of what is said or done. Metamessages are a frame for understanding what is being discussed, such as the nature of the relationship between the people interacting, status, and power differences between interactants.

Insight into Innovation Activity: Watch Deborah Tannen Explain Rapport Talk vs. Report Talk. What do you think about her contention that neither genderlect is "good or bad" or "better" than the other? Are there situations when one or the other may be desirable or more effective? Why or why not?

Rapport versus Report Talk. Tannen explains that feminine communication seeks to build **rapport**, or personal connection. The more masculine **report** style focuses on tasks and relaying information. These genderlects lead us to approach interactions differently and to communicate both verbally and nonverbally in different ways.

Feminine: Desire for intimacy	Masculine: Desire for independence
• Focus on understanding, intimacy, relationships	• Focus on fixing things, power, independence
• Ask more questions to build connection and understanding	• Ask few questions to avoid losing power and status
• Express sympathy, empathy, and similarities	• Fix, minimize, or dismiss people's problems
• Seek understanding from others	• Give advice
• Talk more in the home	• Talk more in public
• Focus more on personal details	• Focus on information
• Tend to avoid conflict	• Engage conflict
• Tend to listen with confirming nonverbals	• Tend to interrupt more
• More direct and intimate nonverbals, such as eye contact and posture	• Indirect when discussing personal problems
	• Indirect nonverbals

We may see these two communication styles as fundamentally different and, thus, conflicting. Indeed, interactions between people with a feminine genderlect and people with a masculine genderlect can lead to misunderstanding and conflict. On the other hand, recognizing and adapting to these distinct styles when we interact with others can help us better understand others.

Tannen argues that we don't necessarily need to adopt a more masculine or feminine style in interactions, but understanding these styles will help us interpret and respond to people's communication more effectively. When someone with a masculine style is direct or seems dismissive when I express my feelings, for example, I may interpret the metamessage as being a lack of caring. If I consider the masculine style though, I can reframe the metamessage as "this person is trying to help me get over this" rather than "this person doesn't care about me." The reverse is also true. If someone with a masculine style is interacting with me and I use a lot of personal anecdotes in my explanation, rather than seeing it as me talking too much or using anecdotal evidence to make my point, the other person can interpret it as me trying to build a connection and share my perspective.

KEY CONCEPTS FROM MUTED GROUP THEORY (ARDENER, 1975)

Tannen's genderlect theory looks at why people communicate the way they do and how they enact and interpret gendered communication styles. Genderlect focuses on conversations. Muted group theory and standpoint theory, on the other hand, focus on issues of power and control in society, particularly how women are disadvantaged and excluded in the public realm.

Hierarchy of Power: Dominant and Muted Groups. Ardener (1975) argues that there are **dominant groups** that hold power and control discourse in society and **muted groups** who are defined by *and* excluded from public discourse. We can think of this in terms of business: 4.8 percent of Fortune 500 CEOs in 2014 were women, which was a "historical high" (Fairchild, 2014). The statistics in American politics are somewhat better: 19.4 percent of the 2015 U.S. Congress were women (Center for American Women and Politics, 2015a) and women represented 24.2 percent of state legislators in 2015 (Center for American Women and Politics, 2015b), but there were only three female governors at the time (Center for American Women and Politics, 2015c). Thus, men hold major positions of power in society, such as running our largest corporations and our elected government, and as a result, women are excluded from important discussions that have a direct bearing on their lives and on society. This leads to three assumptions about women as a muted group in society:

1. *Men and women have different experiences, which leads to different perspectives on the world.* From the muted group perspective, men are born into positions of power and women are born into positions of subordination, thus directing our experiences throughout our lives.

2. *Women's perspectives, ideas, and experiences are ignored in public discourse.* Given that men still hold most of the positions of power in society, their perspectives and, perhaps more importantly, their definitions of people and events dominate our lives and direct how we see the world.

3. *Women who want to participate in public discourse must "translate" their ideas and experiences into language created by and for men.* Ardener observed that women often seem inarticulate and attributes that to the difficulty women face when trying to translate their unique experiences into a male-dominated language.

These three interrelated assumptions help us understand why women's standpoints are often not fully understood and also why it is important to explore the standpoints of women and other minority groups. In keeping with the gender communication approach of this chapter, let me use myself as an example. One reason I wanted to write a theory book is because I have been teaching communication theory for over a decade and most of the theory books I have reviewed and the ones I have taught from didn't seem to fit my personal standpoint. As a late Gen X/early Millennial, female faculty member from a middle class background, I occupy a particular social position. I have a unique standpoint. I have achieved intergenerational upward mobility; I embrace the advancement of technology, but am skeptical of how it is used; I believe in gender equity in hiring, promotion, and pay because I am a working mother with two daughters. Why is my standpoint valuable? Because I see society, higher education—and yes, even theory—through the lens of those experiences. You also see these things through the lens of your unique standpoint as well.

To fully understand a theory, political issue, social group, or business environment, we have to explore those contexts from the unique standpoints of the people involved. It is also worthwhile to consider how our own standpoint limits our understanding of others' circumstances, and in some cases, our unique standpoint may help us see things more clearly than other people are able to see those things. This is referred to as **situated knowledge**. Hartsock (1983) offered **feminist standpoint theory**, which explains that gender divisions in society are the result of the dominant, powerful position of men in our social structure. Much of feminist standpoint theory is rooted in Marxist theorizing about social structure and domination of one class or group over a lower class or less powerful group.

Direct and Indirect Muting. Women's ability to express their unique standpoints is limited by muting. There are sometimes very obvious and direct ways that women may be muted, such as ridicule and harassment. Women who use too feminine a style of communication or too masculine a style of communication are often ridiculed, for example. And women who try to break into a typically male-dominated industry are sometimes harassed, as we'll discuss later in this chapter when reviewing #gamergate.

Some women try to conform to the masculine standards of the group they want to join, but even conforming can incite ridicule. If a woman is too "girly," she cannot be taken seriously, and if she's too masculine she is not feminine enough. Just think for a minute about all of the derogatory terms we have for women who are too direct, demanding, powerful, strategic, or aggressive. Then think about all the condescending ways we describe women who are emotional, expressive, and nurturing. This is often called a **double-bind**, or a lose–lose situation, where either option leads to ridicule.

EXAMPLE OF THEORY IN WEB 2.0: #GAMERGATE

To see how female voices are often drowned out, we can look at the case of #gamergate that erupted in 2013. Male video game developers used threats, harassment via social media like Twitter, and doxing (publishing people's personal information online) to silence female video game developers.

Dewey (2014) provides a helpful summary: Zoe Quinn, an independent, female video game developer, created an artistic game that tells a woman's narrative of her depression. Traditional gamers didn't see it as a real video game, though some users and critics really liked the game. Then it came out that Zoe may have had a sexual relationship with a video game critic, and gamers took to social media to protest the perceived ethical breach. That "protest" morphed into a sustained social media campaign targeting female gamers and critics who voiced their concerns about male domination in the video game industry. The campaign included direct threats to the lives and families of women, posting women's addresses online, and eventually forcing women to leave their homes out of fear for their safety.

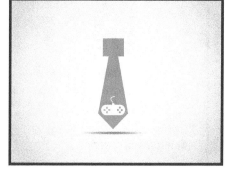

Frank (2014) outlined how the dominant male voices tried to mute female game developers and critics: They alienated women and ignored the games women produced. They focused instead on women's personal lives rather their professional products. They attacked men and women who vocalized support for females in the game industry. They created the title "social justice warriors," or SJWs, to organize their efforts and define their critics, framed their attacks as an effort to promote transparency and ethics, and used their financial resources to fund their campaign. Frank observed, "In fostering this culture of terror, you can ensure the majority is silent—that it *won't* speak out against the harm you are doing" (italics original; para. 14).

In this example, we see several of the themes from genderlect, muted group, and standpoint theories at work in a very real, recent controversy. The game that started the controversy, Depression Quest, was developed by a woman and clearly has a more feminine approach in that it focuses on an emotional, personal story. Thus, it did not fit with the more power-focused, aggressive, masculine video game genre. Arguably, the game may have been an expression of the developer's standpoint, a standpoint that traditional male gamers may not have recognized, appreciated, or even wanted to be aware of. The reaction to the expression of this standpoint, and others' support of this standpoint, was harassment and threats, in an effort to mute the voices of people, predominantly women, who sought to broaden the definition of "video game" and argued for inclusion of the female perspective in game development.

This might all sound trivial, particularly if you don't care about video games. But this event is one indicator of a larger social and political issue with social media, the internet, and gender equality: sometimes a powerful, vocal minority can use these new media tools to move gender equality efforts backward by drowning out the voices of women and minorities, controlling public discourse and defining other groups, and ultimately harassing and threatening women and minority groups into silence. In general, in online environments, women may be particularly susceptible to muting. In a Pew Research report, Duggan (2014) revealed that women are more likely to be sexually harassed and stalked online compared to men, much like the female game developers and bloggers were stalked and harassed online during the Gamergate controversy.

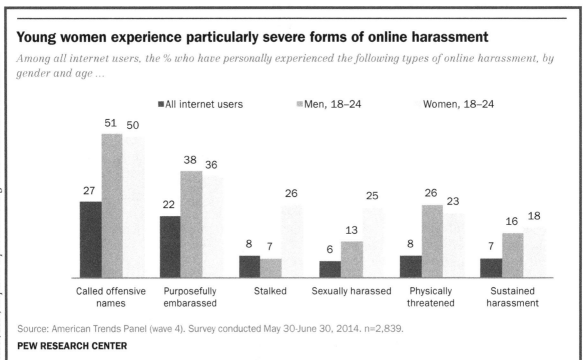

Young women experience particularly severe forms of online harassment

Among all internet users, the % who have personally experienced the following types of online harassment, by gender and age …

■ All internet users   ▥ Men, 18–24   Women, 18–24

	Called offensive names	Purposefully embarassed	Stalked	Sexually harassed	Physically threatened	Sustained harassment
All internet users	27	22	8	6	8	7
Men, 18–24	51	38	7	13	26	16
Women, 18–24	50	36	26	25	23	18

Source: American Trends Panel (wave 4). Survey conducted May 30-June 30, 2014. n=2,839.

PEW RESEARCH CENTER

Much like this example of Gamergate, the research on gender communication employs close observations, analyses, and critiques of people's communication and our social structure. Genderlect was developed by Tannen using the **linguistics** approach, or the close, qualitative study of the messages people use in real-life situations. By closely studying how men and women formulated messages, interpreted each other's messages, and responded to each other's messages, she was able to see trends and themes in people's communication styles and their reactions to messages. Linguistics looks at both what is said and done, or the message, and the implications and interpretations of what is said and done, or the metamessage. Thus, using this method, Tannen found that men often responded to messages and women responded to metamessages.

Linguistics and discourse analysis explore the structure of messages, meaning of messages, interaction management techniques, and the social meanings associated with verbal and nonverbal messages both face-to-face and online (Herring, 2013):

Level of Analysis	What We Look For	Implications
Structural Features	Organization of thoughts, syntax, formatting, and punctuation (online)	Insight into communication styles
Meaning/Metamessage	Intended meaning, interpretations of meaning	Insight into effects and effectiveness
Interaction Management Strategies	How we take turns, interactaction length and sequences	Insight into how we react and respond
Social Organization	Expression of one's power and status, one's own/other's face	Insight into power dynamics and culture

Adapted from Herring (2013, p. 5)

Muted group is from the **anthropological** research tradition, which looks at communication and rituals within cultural groups. The anthropological approach looks closely at messages as well, and also considers how power dynamics and social structures are created and reinforced within social groups through social norms and rituals. Much of the research on standpoints, for example, is based on Marxist theorizing about oppression of minority groups through domination of public discourse by a small powerful class of people. If we think about it, social norms within our society may help explain why there are fewer women in politics and comparatively few female CEOs: Our government and our corporations were created by men, who then defined what the government and corporations are, what they do, and how they do it. Thus, this position of power over the structure and meaning in our society excludes the feminine style and the female standpoint.

APPLIED RESEARCH: LEANING IN AND GENDER INTELLIGENCE

Sheryl Sandberg

Two popular texts have come out recently to address gender in the workplace: *Lean In* and *Work With Me*. *Lean In* was written by Sheryl Sandberg, COO of Facebook. Interestingly, Sandberg takes more of an anthropological approach as she describes her own experiences working her way up to powerful positions in technology corporations. Annis and Gray look more closely at how men and women interact and interpret and misinterpret each other's behaviors in the workplace, thus taking a more linguistic approach. These different approaches lead to very different suggestions for how to correct the imbalance between men and women in the workplace.

Encouraging Women to Lean In *to their Careers.* Sandberg (2013) argues that women have to learn to face their fears and keep moving forward in their careers by seeking leadership opportunities, advancement, and inclusion. In other words, women need to lean in to their careers. In her viral Ted Talk, Sandberg (2010) explains that "women are dropping out" of the workforce, and we need to change the messages we send women at work about work. *In essence, she is advocating women adopting some characteristics of masculine, task orientation*: Women should participate more and take credit for their accomplishments, men and women in relationships need to work together and share household and childrearing responsibilities, and women should move forward in their careers rather than "leaning back" because they are planning to have families.

Sandberg wants women to be encouraged to sit at the table during meetings and to contribute, both literally and figuratively. Women, she reasons, underestimate their abilities and attribute their success to external factors, whereas men tend not to have these crises of confidence and attribute their success to internal factors. Women, therefore, second guess themselves and fail to fully participate, which undermines their chances of getting ahead.

Similarly, Sandberg advocates encouraging and being supportive of men who take on more household responsibilities and participate in raising their children. Just as women are not fully integrated into the workplace, men tend not to be fully integrated at home. In the home, even in the homes of women who work full time, most of the responsibility for domestic labor falls to the women.

Lastly, she said women tend to "lean back" when they consider having children. Put another way, when women are thinking about their careers, they think earlier and more often about their family plans—even when they don't have children yet—and they often lean back and choose not to push forward in their careers because of their plans for having families.

Gender Intelligence. *Work With Me*, on the other hand, was written by Barbara Annis and John Gray and advocates changes to corporate culture and organizational dynamics to capitalize on women's standpoints and the feminine genderlect. *Annis and Gray reason that men and women need to work at understanding each other's gender communication styles and the needs unique to each gendered style to capitalize on the strengths of each perspective. They refer to this as **gender intelligence**. This, in turn, will* help everyone involved overcome negative perceptions of the opposite gender: women feeling excluded by men, men being afraid of upsetting women, men accusing women of asking too many questions, women accusing men of not listening, men and women not recognizing each others' expression of emotions, and both men and women being generally insensitive to each other's unique communication styles.

John Gray

Insight into Innovation Activity: Embracing Gender Differences to Improve Corporate Outcomes. In his speech on 8 Common Blindspots Between Men & Women in Business, John Gray explains that business was "built by men for men and not for women" and if we can fix that we can realize 100 percent of our potential as a country (6:30). Gray advocates "gender intelligence," which means awareness and "interpreting the differences between men and women in a positive way." He argues that we have "blind spots" that we have to address to capitalize on the potential of women in the workplace. Blind spots are those things we cannot see, but need to be able to see, to take advantage of the unique skills and perspectives women have to offer. For example, Gray discusses the ability of women to notice what could be improved and make companies work better. He also suggests that the female perspective can help promote work–life balance in companies. Thinking about this presentation in terms of the theories discussed in this chapter:

- What evidence does Dr. Gray offer that fits the ideas outlined in Tannen's genderlect theory about report and rapport talk?

- How does Dr. Gray's description of American corporate history and culture fit with muted group theory? What is the effect of this muting on corporate outcomes?

- Lastly, how does he suggest we capitalize on the feminine genderlect and women's standpoints to improve corporate outcomes?

You can read a summary of the 8 blindspots Gray outlines in this *Forbes* article: http://www.forbes.com/sites/susanadams/2013/04/26/8-blind-spots-between-the-sexes-at-work/

Adapting Conversation Rituals. Though both *Lean In* and *Work With Me* are clearly popular press books, the claims of both texts fit well with what we have talked about in this chapter. Deborah Tannen (1994) also wrote a book about gender in the workplace: *Talking From 9 to 5*. Tannen attributes many of the issues that Sandberg and Annis and Gray discuss to the gendered conversation styles outlined in genderlect theory. She reasons that conversations are rituals, and we have rituals that we follow in everyday interactions that align with gendered styles. Women, for example, apologize frequently, even for things that are not their fault. Women also tend to ask a lot of questions, even when they know the answer to those questions. This is part of their ritual for interactions.

Tannen advocates more flexibility on the part of men and women to know when to *adapt their conversational style and to be sensitive to differences in conversational rituals.* There are situations where the feminine conversational style is helpful, when we should ask for help, apologize, ask questions, and balance our own wants and needs with others' wants and needs. There are also times when the masculine approach is appropriate, when we should negotiate for our interests, advocate for ourselves, make decisions, and verbally and nonverbally express confidence and directness. It is not necessary, or even desirable, for women to try to be more like men or vice versa, as trying to have a style different from your own may make you uncomfortable, undermine your credibility, or even silence you. Rather, we should adjust to the person and the context when we interact, and choose the communication style most likely to help us achieve our task or goal.

There is, of course, a downside to this type of **code switching**, or moving between gendered styles. Tannen acknowledges that men and women face ridicule when they adopt a style that is not in keeping with social norms. These pitfalls should be weighed against the repercussions for not using the style appropriate to the organizational culture and the task. For example, Tannen argues that one reason for pay inequity is that women are held back by their feminine communication style when they interview for jobs, negotiate salaries, and ask for raises and promotions.

 You can read more about *Talking 9 to 5* here: http://faculty.georgetown.edu/tannend/sandbox.htm

So we are left with three slightly different approaches to gendered styles in the workplace: one that advocates adopting a more masculine approach, one that advocates gender sensitivity, and another that advocates flexibility. All three acknowledge that organizations were created by men for men and typically have a more masculine culture. All three also acknowledge that there are double-binds that women face in the workplace, particularly trying to move into male-dominated fields and professional positions, such as breaking into computing and information technology.

WOMEN IN COMPUTING AND TECHNOLOGY

Lack of Women in Computing and Tech. Thinking about the #gamergate example and the challenges women face in the workplace in general, we see just how hostile and aggressive people can be when women break into a male-dominated profession and express the feminine genderlect in a typically masculine culture. This explains some of the statistics surrounding women in information technology and computing fields. In 2006, 41 percent of science, engineering, and technology professionals entering the workforce were women (Hewlett et al., 2008). On the other hand, women dropped out of those careers at alarming rates: 52 percent of women quit in those fields, largely due to the culture of those organizations. Specifically, they cite "hostile macho cultures" where over 60 percent of women report being sexually harassed. Women in these fields also reported feeling isolated, uncertain of their career path, that the culture of rewarding taking risks worked against them, and that the work pressures were too extreme.

To a certain extent, it would benefit women to adopt some characteristics of the masculine style when the situation calls for it, such as participating, interviewing, and negotiating for salary. On the other hand, if organizations like video game development companies and software development companies want women as customers and clients then it is in their best interest to have women's standpoints represented at all levels of the organization. This requires both gender intelligence on the part of organizations to recognize what each gendered perspective has to offer and adjusting cultures to be inclusive. This also may require flexibility on the part of individual employees to communicate effectively. Tannen points out that there is no one golden rule for communicating at work. Rather, we have to be flexible, adaptable, and mindful of individual differences.

A Perception-Based Explanation of Why Women Drop Out. People's perceptions of women in the workplace are another issue, and may also explain why women are not pursuing careers in technology. For example, people tend to attribute the underrepresentation of women in technology fields to the characteristics of women themselves, such as their personalities, confidence, and expertise (Eckert & Steiner, 2013). Thus, there may be a perception that women are not suited to work in tech fields.

Unfortunately, as both Sandberg and Tannen pointed out in their books, just having a man's name rather than a woman's name changes people's perceptions of likability. People judge professional accomplishments of men and women similarly, but successful people with male names were judged as more likable than successful people with female names. So, even when women are accomplished in their profession and people recognize those accomplishments, there are repercussions in terms of their perceived likability.

A recent study pointed out that even teleworking and working after hours in the modern, 24/7 workplace has not helped people's perceptions of professional women. When women leave work early, it may be assumed to be family related, whereas when men leave early it may be assumed to be for work-related reasons (Paquette, 2015). These misperceptions can result in women not being promoted, particularly in demanding careers.

Societal Implications of Excluding Women. Beyond the personal and social repercussions for the women who are excluded from IT through organizational cultural and social norms, there are also broader societal implications for women's exclusion. Specifically, feminist approaches to technology studies include considering how "specific technologies are shaped by gender and in turn have consequences for gender relations" (Cunningham, 2015). If we think about technology as a cultural product and a means of "cultural production" then the absence of the feminine standpoint in technological development has broad and important social repercussions. Technology is typically created by men (product) and may then privilege the masculine style and standpoint (cultural production). Imagine, for example, if Twitter had been designed by a woman. How might that technology be different?

As we've discussed throughout this chapter, the feminine standpoint and style is different than the masculine standpoint and style. Thus, the technologies likely to emerge from feminine developers versus masculine developers would likely be very different, such as Zoe's video game that triggered Gamergate. Thinking about this from a societal perspective, male domination in IT fields has implications for the types of technology we have available and how we use that technology. Arguably, the exclusion of the feminine standpoint from technology development disadvantages half of our population and reduces our potential for continued innovation. Particularly in a social media world, it seems to me that the feminine style, with its focus on social connection and responsiveness, would be particularly beneficial to advancing these products.

Gender shares of employment, computer and information technology occupations (2013 annual averages)

	Women	Men
Computer and information research scientists	26.1%	73.9%
Computer and information systems managers	28.6%	71.4%
Computer network architects	7.5%	92.5%
Computer occupations, all other	22.8%	77.2%
Computer programmers	23.0%	77.0%
All occupations	47.0%	53.0%
Computer support specialists	29.0%	71.0%
Computer systems analysts	34.9%	65.1%
Database administrators	37.4%	62.6%
Network and computer systems administrators	17.3%	82.7%
Software developers, applications and systems software	19.7%	80.3%
Web developers	39.5%	60.5%

0%   20%   40%   60%   80%   100%

Note: Gender shares of employment are 2013 annual averages for all people employed (includes part-time and self-employed)

Source: Bureau of Labor Statistics, Current Population Survey (CPS)/ Graph by the Women's Bureau, U.S. Department of Labor

http://www.dol.gov/wb/stats/Computer-information-technology.htm

Insight into Innovation Example: Women in Tech Fields. Take a look at some recent stats from the United States Department of Labor (2013), presented in the chart above. Consider how we might improve the statistics for women in tech fields. Do you think calling on women to lean in when entering the tech industry, promoting gender intelligence among tech companies, and/or learning to be sensitive to and adapt to gendered conversational styles could help improve the share of women in these occupations? Why or why not? What are some repercussions for women being underrepresented in fields like software development and application development for women's careers and for women who use technology in general?

CONCLUSION

Coincidentally, when I wrote the first draft of this chapter, my two young daughters were home with me during their break from school. I was also teaching online classes and directing the graduate program in my department. I was, at once, *leaning in* by accepting the graduate program directorship and continuing work on this book, performing both gender typical roles as a mother and less typical roles as an author, researcher, and distance education professor. This, of course, comes at a cost: the book was done later than scheduled, and my kids' summer wasn't full of dance classes, soccer teams, and as much practice reading and writing as I'd hoped. So this also fits with Gray's contention that we cannot really have it all, at least not all at the same time. It also follows Tannen's advice that we be flexible and adaptable. I have plans for how and when things will be done, but I adjust as needed.

People may perceive me as being less productive because I'm not around the office much as a result of my schedule. So even as I balance these competing demands, and I do tend to accomplish most of what I set out to accomplish professionally, there is nonetheless the potential that this will hurt my career. What do you think? Is the answer to lean in and forge on? Is the answer to promote gender intelligence in the workplace? Or is there some other answer to the ongoing gender divisions in the home and at work?

ASSIGNMENTS

1. **Everyday Sexism.** Watch Laura Bates' Ted Talk, Everyday Sexism, and read some of the comments on YouTube.

   a. How do the statistics cited by Bates about parliament, the judiciary, the arts, and the news media in Britain relate to the representation of women's standpoints in society?

   b. What are the societal repercussions for the underrepresentation of women in public positions?

   c. What comments on Bates' YouTube video could be evidence of muting? How so?

2. **#DistractinglySexy.** In 2015, Nobel Prize winner Sir Tim Hunt said that "girls" can be a problem in laboratory settings because "Three things happen when they are in the lab; you fall in love with them, they fall in love with you and when you criticize them, they cry" (para. 2). In response, women posted pictures of themselves conducting scientific research with the hashtag #DistractinglySexy. Read more on CNN.

   a. From a genderlect theory perspective, what was the metamessage in Tim Hunt's comments?

   b. How could comments like this explain the number of women who drop out of fields such as scientific research?

   c. Do you see comments such as Tim Hunt's as having a potential muting effect? Why or why not?

REFERENCES

Seminal Texts:

Ardener, S. (1975). *Perceiving women*. London: Malaby Press.

Hartsock, N. C. M. (1983). *Money, sex, and power: Toward a feminist historical materialism*. New York: Longman.

Tannen, D. (1990). *You just don't understand: Women and men in conversation.* New York: William Morrow.

Academic Sources and Books:

Annis, B., & Gray, J. (2013). *Work with Me: The 8 blind spots between men and women in business.* New York: Palgrave Macmillan.

Cunninham, C. M. (2015). "Men are like Bluetooth, women are like WiFi": What feminist technology studies can add to the study of information and communication technologies. *The Northwest Journal of Communication, 43,* 7–21.

Eckert, S., & Steiner, L. (2013). (Re)triggering backlash: Responses to news about Wikipedia's gender gap. *Journal of Communication Inquiry, 37*(4), 284–303.

Herring, S. C. (2013). Discourse in Web 2.0: Familiar, reconfigured, and emergent. In D. Tannen & A. M. Tester (Eds), *Discourse 2.0: Language and new media* (pp. 1–26). Washington, DC: Georgetown University Press.

Hewlett, S. A., Luce, C. B., Servon, L. J., Sherbin, L., Shiller, P., Sosnovich, E., & Sumberg, K. (2008). The Athena factor: Reversing the brain drain in science, engineering, and technology. Harvard Business Review. Retrieved online from http://documents.library.nsf.gov/edocs/HD6060-.A84-2008-PDF-Athena-factor-Reversing-the-brain-drain-in-science,-engineering,-and-technology.pdf

Sandberg, S. (2010). *Lean in: Women, work, and the will to lead.* New York: Knopf.

Tannen, D. (1994). *Talking from 9 to 5: Women and men at work.* New York: Harper.

Examples:

Adams, S. (2013, April 26). 8 blind spots between the sexes at work. *Forbes.* Retrieved from http://www.forbes.com/sites/susanadams/2013/04/26/8-blind-spots-between-the-sexes-at-work/

Center for American Women and Politics. (2015a). Women in the U.S. Congress. *Eagleton Institute of Politics.* Retrieved from http://www.cawp.rutgers.edu/fast_facts/levels_of_office/documents/cong.pdf

Center for American Women and Politics. (2015b). Women in state legislatures 2015. *Eagleton Institute of Politics.* Retrieved from http://www.cawp.rutgers.edu/fast_facts/levels_of_office/documents/stleg.pdf

Center for American Women and Politics. (2015c). Statewide elective executive women 2015. *Eagleton Institute of Politics.* Retrieved from http://www.cawp.rutgers.edu/fast_facts/levels_of_office/documents/stwide.pdf

Duggan, M. (2014, October 22). Online harassment. *Pew Research Center: Internet, Science & Tech.* Retrieved online from http://www.pewinternet.org/2014/10/22/online-harassment/

Dewey, C. (2014, October 14). The only guide to Gamergate you will ever need to read. Washington Post. Retrieved from http://www.washingtonpost.com/news/the-intersect/wp/2014/10/14/the-only-guide-to-gamergate-you-will-ever-need-to-read/

Fairchild, C. (2014, June 3). Number of Fortune 500 women CEOs reaches historic high. Forbes. Retrieved online from http://fortune.com/2014/06/03/number-of-fortune-500-women-ceos-reaches-historic-high/

Frank, J. (2014). How to attack a woman who works in video gaming. *The Guardian*. Retrieved from http://www.theguardian.com/technology/2014/sep/01/how-to-attack-a-woman-who-works-in-video-games

Paquette, D. (2015). Why women are judged far more harshly than men for leaving work early. *The Washington Post*. Retrieved from https://www.washingtonpost.com/news/wonk/wp/2015/06/10/why-women-are-judged-far-more-harshly-than-men-for-leaving-work-early/

United States Department of Labor. (2013). *Computer and Information Technology Occupations*. Retrieved from http://www.dol.gov/wb/stats/Computer-information-technology.htm

CHAPTER 9

EXPECTANCY VIOLATIONS THEORY

OUTCOMES

- *Knowledge:* Learn about the sources of our verbal and nonverbal expectations.
- *Skill:* Recognize and respond to norms in new media environments.

INTRODUCTION

We've seen in the previous chapters how being socialized into a culture and gender shape our values and communication styles. In this chapter, we move on to discuss theory and research that focuses on **nonverbal communication:** the use of gestures, movement, eye contact, personal space, facial expression, and touch in face-to-face interactions. Nonverbal messages in text-based mediated interactions are somewhat different, and include use of punctuation, font, emoticons, and emoji.

Both culture and gender influence our nonverbals and also affect our expectations of others' nonverbal behaviors. As we'll see throughout this chapter, context is also an important determinant of appropriate and effective nonverbal behavior. Expectancy violation theory (EVT) is one theory that explains how the expectations we are socialized to have set the standards for what behavior we expect from others and how perceptions of the context, the behavior, and the other person are related to our response to others' verbal and nonverbal messages. EVT is a particularly interesting theory to consider in the context of social media and our Web 2.0 lives because of both the potential for careful, selective nonverbal self-presentation online *and* the ambiguity of some online contexts that lead people to violate norms.

MAIN IDEA

Copyright © shipfactory/Shutterstock.com

EVT was initially developed to explain violations of people's personal space. **Personal space** is our "preferred distance from others" (Burgoon, 1978, p. 130). There is **normative distance**, or the socially acceptable distance between two people given the context and the culture of the people involved in the interaction. When people stand closer or further than expected, this is a **violation** of our expectations. In later research, EVT has been applied to many different types of **nonverbal behaviors** including eye contact, movement, use of touch, gestures, facial expressions, posture, and body movement.

How we respond to a violation depends on our **threat threshold**, or our own unique threshold for what makes us feel uncomfortable. Some violations are **positively valenced**, such as nonverbal messages that signal confirmation, liking, and interest. On the other hand, some violations are **negatively valenced** because they signal disconfirmation such as disapproval, dislike, and disinterest. In addition to considering whether the violation itself is positive or negative, we also consider whether the person who committed the violation is rewarding or punishing. **Rewarding** people are those who offer a more positively valenced interaction overall and who we hold in higher regard. **Punishing** people, on the other hand, tend to communicate more negatively valenced messages overall and tend to be people that we hold in lower regard.

EVT is an empirical theory from the social scientific tradition, and thus it has specific predictions about how our expectations are formed, what we consider when there is a violation of our expectations, and how we respond to those violations. Burgoon (1978) outlined 11 assumptions:

People use nonverbals to achieve closeness or distance.

1. People have *needs* in an interaction that influence their nonverbal behaviors. Needs for closeness lead us to use affiliative, friendly nonverbal behaviors; needs for personal space lead to less affiliative behavior.

2. The *rewards* that we stand to receive from a particular interaction affect our need for closeness in that interaction.

3. When the reward value is high in an interaction (i.e., when we think we might gain something important to us) we have an increased need for closeness and so we use nonverbals to achieve *closeness*. When the reward value is low, we may avoid the interaction or use nonverbal *distancing*.

4. People can *perceive* others' nonverbal closeness and distancing.

Nonverbal behaviors are affected by the situation and individual characteristics.

5. People's patterns of nonverbals in interactions are also affected by the *norms* for the group in which they are interacting.

6. Individuals also have *idiosyncrasies*, or their own unique patterns for nonverbal interactions.

7. Thus, in a given situation, people's individual characteristics (needs, personality, culture, gender, etc.), the type of interaction (personal, professional, familial, romantic, etc.), *and* the environment (context, arrangement of the physical space) in which the interaction occurs, determine what would be considered "normal" nonverbal behavior for that interaction.

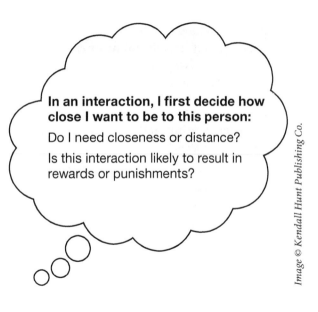

In an interaction, I first decide how close I want to be to this person:

Do I need closeness or distance?

Is this interaction likely to result in rewards or punishments?

Image © Kendall Hunt Publishing Co.

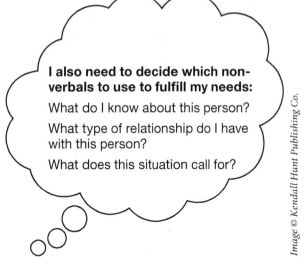

I also need to decide which nonverbals to use to fulfill my needs:

What do I know about this person?

What type of relationship do I have with this person?

What does this situation call for?

Image © Kendall Hunt Publishing Co.

People have expectations for how others will behave nonverbally in an interaction, and violations of expectations can be evaluated as positive or negative.

8. Our perception of the other person, our relationship, and the environment set our *expectations.*

9. Violations of our expectations *arouse* our interest and attention in the interaction.

10. We *evaluate* people.

11. Our evaluations of others' nonverbals are positive when that person and the nonverbal message are positive, but when someone who is rewarding sends a negative message it is viewed as punishing. When a negatively valued person sends a positive nonverbal message, it is seen as negative, but when a negatively valued person sends the expected negative message, it is rewarding. Think of it this way: if someone you like signals closeness, you probably like it. If someone you don't like signals closeness to you, you probably won't like it.

> **This person violated my expectations!**
>
> Do I feel it's threatening?
>
> Do they have reward value?
>
> Is it a positive or negative nonverbal message?

Image © Kendall Hunt Publishing Co.

Copyright © gpointstudio/Shutterstock.com

Let's consider an example: You meet a person on an online dating site, and make plans to meet face-to-face after a few weeks of texting each other. You seem to have a lot in common and you feel like you have a sense of his or her personality and background. So you meet for coffee at a small coffee shop to see if you two click. You see the person for the first time, and he or she is well dressed, attractive, and seems friendly. As you sit down and start to talk, he or she keeps texting with someone else. You decide that this is not going to work out because this person is obviously not that into you.

EVT helps us understand this scenario. You may have gone into this interaction with a *need* for closeness, met in an *environment* that encourages closeness, had a sense of the other person's *characteristics*, and may have seen this person as potentially very *rewarding* in terms of fulfilling that need for closeness. But when that rewarding person *violates expectations* by sending a *distancing* nonverbal message, it is *perceived* negatively. On the other hand, if you had met this person and immediately thought there was no way you'd ever want to be close to him or her, the other person continually texting throughout the date may actually have been a good thing.

Notice that EVT doesn't tell us whether or not our reactions to violations are correct or incorrect. Indeed, that person in our example who seemed disinterested may have been texting someone to tell him or her how awesome the date was going. Rather than focusing on the accuracy of our interpretations, EVT explains the factors that predict our expectations and reactions to others' nonverbals.

Thus, EVT has a lot of practical value in terms of informing our nonverbal communication behaviors. Assuming we are mindful in our interactions and actively listening to and observing the people we are interacting with, we can get a sense of their perception of our reward value and be aware of their nonverbal signals for closeness versus distance. If we get the sense that they see us and the interaction as rewarding, we can increase closeness through eye contact and more intimate gestures. This may lead to a more positive interaction outcome and make us even more likable. On the other hand, if we get the sense that we are perceived as low in reward value or that the interaction isn't perceived as potentially rewarding, we can be more conservative. This advice can inform our nonverbal behaviors in dating relationships, as described in this example, and also in our professional interactions and online interactions.

APPLYING EVT: NONVERBAL EXPECTATIONS AND LANDING A JOB

Understandably, EVT and nonverbal communication have been applied to professional contexts, particularly job seeking and interviewing. Research has explored employers' expectations in face-to-face (FtF) contexts and via computer-mediated communication (CMC), interviewees' nonverbal behaviors, and what happens when norms and expectations are violated.

Perhaps not surprisingly, how people behave nonverbally in an initial interaction, including a job interview, can affect the attributions people make about the interviewee's personality (De Groot & Gooty, 2009). In particular, indicators of conscientiousness and extraversion can be useful indicators of the kind of employees people will be: Will they do their work in full and on time? Will they get along well with others? Are they management material? Interestingly, in survey studies of employers' decisions about hiring recent college grads, results indicated that how interviewees presented themselves nonverbally in terms of sociability, image, appearance, nonverbal delivery, and verbal style, were almost as important as the written credentials submitted to the employer (Ugbah & Evuleocha, 1992). Unstructured interviews are particularly susceptible to the biasing effects of nonverbals (Barrick, Shaffer, & DeGrassi, 2009).

Insight into Innovation Example: Body Language as the Key to Success? One way to get ready for an interview is to practice confident nonverbals. Check out Dr. Amy Cuddy's Ted Talk on body language: http://www.ted.com/speakers/amy_cuddy. Not only are other people influenced by our nonverbals in terms of making judgments about whether or not we are likable, credible, and powerful, nonverbal expressions of power can also influence how we see ourselves. What do you think, can we change how other people see us and how we see ourselves by managing our nonverbals?

In terms of concrete, practical advice to inform our interview behavior, let's take a look at several nonverbal behaviors that can influence prospective employers' perceptions of you as a job candidate: eye contact, facial expression, use of touch, posture, and use of time to communicate.

- In FtF interviews, qualified candidates who met or exceeded expectations for **eye gaze**, or maintaining eye contact with the interviewer, were evaluated as more competent, sociable, and composed compared to people who did not maintain much eye contact (Burgoon, Manusov, Mineo, & Hale, 1985). Maintaining normal or more than normal eye contact also increased perceptions of the interviewee's attractiveness.

- **Facial expressions**, such as smiling, may seem like an open-and-shut case when it comes to interview situations: smiling signals friendliness and may make us more likable. On the other hand, there are interview contexts where smiling actually decreases interviewers' ratings of applicants, such as professions where the employee is expected to be serious (Ruben, Hall, & Schmid Mast, 2015).

- **Tactile** communication, or the use of touch to communicate, is also important in interviews. Generally, touching is frowned upon in professional contexts, with one exception: the handshake. The handshake is widely known to be an important aspect of nonverbal interaction during an interview. It includes using a full grip of the other person's hand, the strength of the grip, duration of the handshake, vigor, and maintaining eye contact while shaking hands (Stewart, Dustin, Barrick, & Darnold, 2008). Having a solid handshake was particularly beneficial to interviewees, and male interviewees tended to have better handshakes compared to women.

- **Posture** is how we position our bodies. When we orient ourselves toward the person we are interacting with, we are signaling engagement. Thus, posture, along with facial expression, gestures, eye contact, and use of voice influences judgments of future job performance (DeGroot & Motowidlo, 1999).

- **Chronemics**, or how we use time to communicate, is also an important nonverbal. We communicate how important someone or something is by the amount of time we set aside and by managing our response time. Taking too long to answer an e-mail from a prospective employer is a negative expectancy violation that reduces the employer's evaluation (Kalman & Rafaeli, 2010). There was a particularly pronounced negative effect on evaluations for job candidates whom were otherwise perceived as high reward value.

Most of the advice listed above is relevant to FtF interviews, but a lot is changing—and will continue to change—in terms of job hunting. Take, for example, Skype and video interviewing. Skype is a video chat website, and employers are increasingly turning to Skype and other video chat websites to conduct interviews. Much like what we've covered for nonverbals in FtF interviews, interviewees who are skyping should (Kiviat, 2009):

- Make eye contact with the camera like you would a person.
- Sit up and orient yourself toward the camera, but not directly *at* the camera (i.e., avoid a mugshot pose).
- Have the video recorder at a comfortable distance from you so that the interviewers see more than just your face, but not so far away that you seem distant.
- Dress like you would for a regular FtF interview by wearing professional attire. Also be sure that your attire doesn't blend into the background. While you're at it, make sure the background is free of backlighting, distractions, or other clutter.

In terms of Dr. Cuddy's advice for practicing a power posture, video interviews give you the unique opportunity to practice before the interview. Set your webcam up where you plan to have the interview and have a dress rehearsal of what you will say and how you will say it. This will give you the opportunity to reflect on your nonverbal presentation and check the video quality and environment so that you are fully prepared for the interview ahead of time.

EVT RESEARCH METHODS

Experiments. EVT is typically tested using experiments. EVT defines specific independent variables (knowledge of the other person, relationship context, environment, and how the other person behaves) that researchers can manipulate to test the effects of those variables on people's responses. So, in Burgoon's (1978) first test of EVT assumptions, trained interviewers were either nonverbally friendly or unfriendly. The more positive the nonverbals of the interviewer, the more favorable people's impressions were of their attractiveness, likability, competence, and composure. Thus, friendly nonverbals increased the perceived reward value of people in an initial interaction. In terms of distance, friendly interviewers who sat at closer distances were evaluated more positively, whereas unfriendly interviewers who sat less close, but still closer than the normal distance, were evaluated more positively. In other words, when people are nonverbally nice, we want to be closer to them than when people are not nonverbally nice.

The process of experimenting to test the assumptions of EVT has moved out of the lab and now also includes online experiments. In these studies, researchers manipulate the content of chat, IM, and social network posts to test the effects of different types of expectancy violations on people's responses and impressions of others.

Self reports. EVT can also be used to interpret people's self-reports of what they expect and how they respond via CMC. As you will see in the next section, EVT has been used as a framework for interpreting focus group results. Given the clear definitions for the variables involved in forming expectations and responding to expectation violations, EVT is ideal to use as a framework for coding people's explanations of the nonverbals they use in different contexts and how they respond when their expectations are violated by people in different contexts. EVT has also been used to construct questionnaires and surveys about how people interpret expectancy violations online since many of the variables in EVT, such as desired closeness/distance, expected nonverbals, and people's responses to nonverbals, can be measured using scale items.

 Insight into Innovation Activity: Code for violations and responses. Corporations can violate expectations just like individual people, particularly via social media. Check out this ad for the Honeymade "This is Wholesome" campaign: https://youtu.be/2xeanX6xnRU. Watching the ad, what do you see that violates your expectations for a national product ad? Next, look at the (sometimes offensive) comments on the video: How many are confirming and suggest increased closeness due to the violation? How many comments are disconfirming and suggest distancing due to the violation? Overall, was this expectancy violation effective or ineffective? Why?

NONVERBALS VIA CMC ;)

Though EVT is a theory of nonverbal communication, and CMC is often perceived as lacking nonverbal cues, EVT predictions help explain interactions via CMC in a way that is similar to what Burgoon (1978) found in her early experiments (Tong & Walther, 2015). When we go into an interaction with another person via CMC, we take what we know about their personality and situation and form expectations. Those expectations guide our behavioral choices and our interpretation of their messages. If we expect someone to be in a bad mood, for example, but he or she interacts with us in a way that's unexpectedly positive, we form a more favorable impression of him or her. Thus, interacting via CMC may actually help us improve people's perceptions of us because we are able to control the messages we send and increase others' liking of us by positively violating their expectations.

Social Media as Connection/Privacy Paradox. One thing to keep in mind when using social media is that there are norms for behavior on social media, and thus there are expectations for how one should and should not behave (Hooper & Kalidas, 2012). The view of what is appropriate or inappropriate on social media depends on who we are interacting with online and the specific context, and we learn these rules for appropriate behavior by participating and observing others online.

Even companies that use social media are subject to the norms and expectations we have for social behavior online (Sung & Kim, 2014). People tend to like corporations that have social, interactive social media posts but tend to dislike promotional messages, probably because promotional messages violate norms for social media use, that is, forming and maintaining social connections. This, of course, may be a paradox related to social media use: Professionals in fields like journalism who are more interactive and personal on social media are more liked, but are also seen as less professional and their reporting is taken less seriously compared to less interactive journalists on social media (Lee, 2015). In the initial discussion of EVT, Burgoon (1978) pointed out that the needs people have—to be close to others, but also to have personal space—are **paradoxical**, or stand in direct opposition to each other. Social media complicates this paradox, as we join social networks to make connections and be closer to people, but we also want to carefully manage our presentation and keep things private.

Norms on social media. These paradoxical needs are reflected in the norms we have for social media: we expect people to post, but not post too much. We expect our privacy and face to be protected, but we forfeit a lot of our control over what's posted about us when we join. We want to get to know others, but we don't want them posting about the mundane details of their days or their personal drama. This may be why social media can actually be a significant source of stress for people, as we are expected to be on social networks to maintain contact with people, but it often annoys us, makes us feel badly about ourselves, or damages our face to be on those networks (Fox & Moreland, 2015).

McLaughlin and Vitak (2012) conducted focus groups and found that norms are often implicit, or implied, and inferred rules for behavior that we learn through observation. These observed rules change over time, and people adjust their behavior accordingly. Some Facebook norms include:

- posting content, such as posts and images, that is appropriate given the types of relationships with Facebook friends (close friends, family, colleagues, *and* acquaintances),
- accepting friend requests from people you know,
- only deleting the most unlikable friends,
- using chat/message features for sharing information that is not of general interest,
- protecting other people's public image and privacy in posts and images.

Violations of norms and expectations on social media. Thus, overposting status updates, posting overly emotional status updates, fighting and arguing, and posting and tagging other people in unflattering pictures are considered violations of the current norms. In keeping with EVT predictions, how we react to norm violations depends on the type of relationship we have with the person who violated our unspoken rules and how serious the violation was:

- When the violation is seen as very serious, the violator is unfriended
- When the violation is moderate, the violator is hidden/unfollowed

Being unfriended, or defriended, on Facebook is often an expectancy violation for the person who was deleted (Bevan, Ang, & Fearns, 2014). In keeping with the predictions of EVT, when people reported having close ties with the person who unfriended them, the violation was seen as important and very negative. This is likely because unfriending someone is a distancing tactic. If you think about it, we use social networks to connect with people, and sending a friend request is a way of nonverbally signaling closeness with someone. When we send friend requests and they are rejected, or accepted and then terminated later, someone we were seeking closeness with is nonverbally distancing himself or herself from us.

DISHONESTY IN ONLINE PROFILES AND CMC

Violations of norms are an important aspect of EVT, and violations of contextual norms are often interpreted as indicators of deception (Levine et al., 2000). Levine et al. found that people who violate norms, regardless of the expectations of the people involved, were perceived as less honest. If you think about it in the context of FtF interactions, when someone seems to distance themselves from us too much, pauses more than is normal, breaks eye contact too often, or fidgets too much, all of these norm violations could be *perceived* as an indication that people are lying, even if we expect them to be less than competent verbal and nonverbal communicators. For the record, *these violations of norms are not necessarily indicators of deception.*

FACE-TO-FACE DECEPTION

Interpersonal deception theory is an extension of the research on EVT that focuses specifically on behaviors that people engage in when they are deceiving others: information management, behavior management, and image management (Buller & Burgoon, 1996). **Information management** is when we knowingly manipulate the information we give others. **Behavior management** is when we control our nonverbal behaviors so that the other person won't recognize that we're being deceptive. Lastly, **impression management** is what we include in a deceptive message to protect our own face (public image) if we get caught being deceptive. In terms of FtF interactions, we tend to have a **truth bias**. That is to say, we generally expect people to be honest.

Engaging in informational, behavioral, and impression management to formulate and sustain deceit requires a lot of cognitive effort, or requires a lot more active thinking. Thus, there is **nonverbal leakage**, or unintended nonverbal signals, that are signs of deceit when we interact FtF, such as those discussed in the *How to Spot a Liar* Ted Talk. But, when we are actually in interactions with people, it can be very difficult to detect deceit, particularly when we are interacting with people we don't know. Further complicating detecting lies is that our truth bias is more pronounced when we're interacting with people we care about and trust.

Burgoon and Buller's (2004) research has yielded some insight into deceit in FtF interactions:

- Deceivers feel anxious before an interaction.
- Initially, deceivers are brief, vague, and nonspecific in their responses and they are nonverbally less immediate, or, put another way, deceivers are nonverbally distant.
- As deceivers become comfortable during an interaction there are fewer verbal and nonverbal indicators of deceit. The nonverbal differences between people being truthful versus dishonest become *indistinguishable* as the interaction progresses.
- People who are being deceptive manage their behaviors to appear to be truthful and carefully watch the people they are interacting with to adjust their behavior if they feel like their receivers are catching on.
- There are different levels of deception: **fabrication**, which is directly providing false information; **equivocation**, which is being intentionally unclear; and **concealment**, which is intentionally hiding information.
- Unexpected nonverbal behaviors from others, such as vagueness, nervousness, reduced eye contact, and increased distance, lead to increased suspicion.
- But, because deceivers are adjusting based on the feedback received from their receivers, people's suspicions tend to subside over the course of the interaction.

DECEPTION VIA CMC

So, knowing that we are bad at detecting lies and people are good at lying when we are interacting, what does this mean for mediated deception? It should be much easier to deceive via CMC after all, because we can carefully craft and edit our messages. And it should be more difficult to detect lies because there is less potential for leakage. That being said, many of our online interactions are with people we know or people we may wish to meet, and online messages have a permanence to them that discourages deception. So even though there are unique features of CMC that make deceit easier to carry out, the potential for meeting in real life, or for being found out later, is present online.

Interestingly, research suggests that we are not necessarily more prone to lie via CMC, but rather that some conditions make it more or less likely that we will be deceitful (Whitty, 2007). In particular, we are less likely to deceive when we are identifiable, when we know or are likely to know the interactants face-to-face, and when we are creating a permanent record of our communication (such as via e-mail).

Deceit versus Selective Self-Presentation. Online, there is a fine, but blurry line between selective, careful "self-presentation" and "deceit." Some research suggests that people do not intend to be deceptive per se, but they are trying to put their best face forward and project the best possible image of themselves (Zytko, Grandhi, & Jones, 2014). In CMC interactions, such as dating profiles, people report being careful about how much they embellish their profiles because of the potential for meeting face-to-face (Ellison, Hancock, & Toma, 2011). On the other hand, they also admit that they hide socially undesirable aspects of their identities (such as bad habits) and use equivocation to avoid openly revealing things that are potentially unattractive (such as physical characteristics). For example, people may embellish what they do for a living, slightly misrepresent their age, use euphemisms to describe their physical appearance, and conceal bad habits like smoking and drinking.

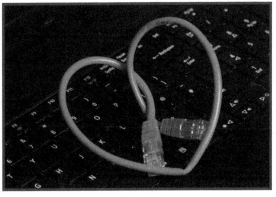

People also have the opportunity online to experiment with different presentations of the self, and sometimes try out different self-presentations when creating profiles online (Whitty, 2007). This can be a liberating and fun experience for users.

People who are familiar with these *norms* on dating sites are aware of these typical, modest embellishments and read profiles with that in mind: they *expect* some minor misrepresentations. Indeed, though online profiles are perceived as offering valuable insight about people, and posts can help us understand another person's personality traits, people are skeptical of user-generated self-presentations (Hall, Pennington, & Lueders, 2013). It seems like we expect some equivocation online and some concealment, but we still tend to reject complete fabrication because it violates the norms of our mediated communities. If the self-presentations we carefully construct online are too different from who we are in real life, it is seen as deceptive and undermines receivers' perceptions of the deceiver's character (Whitty, 2007).

Insight into Innovation Example: Internet Trolls. An interesting exception to the tendency to be honest in our online self-presentation is trolling. If you read the comments sections on websites and news stories, chances are that you have encountered the phrase "don't feed the troll!" Internet trolls are people who intentionally disrupt discussions by saying inflammatory or insulting things with the goal of starting a fight. Interestingly, being an internet troll has been seen as a type of online self-identity for particular internet users (Donath, 1998). There are several dimensions of troll posts (Hardacker, 2010):

- *Deception*, which may go unnoticed, as the troll establishes his or her fake identity within the group. It is difficult to distinguish between truly naive posters who are not competent users and trolls who are posting content to goad people into fights.

- *Aggression* is often labeled trolling online, such as when people insult and flame others.

- *Disruption* is also a common trolling behavior, such as getting an entire group discussion off topic or shutting down a discussion with irrelevant posts.

The success of trolling depends on getting people to believe their deceit. So, when online users recognize a trolling post, thwart trolls' efforts to hijack discussions, or trolls' comments fail to incite a conflict or emotions, it is a trolling failure.

Check out *This American Life*'s segment covering a woman's story about being the target of internet trolls and her interaction with a particularly malicious troll (vulgar language): http://www.thisamericanlife.org/radio-archives/episode/545/if-you-dont-have-anything-nice-to-say-say-it-in-all-caps?act=1

Detecting Online Deceit. We look for indicators of deceit in online profiles, such as whether people seem to be open versus "uptight" in their profiles, to determine whether or not they are trustworthy (Venus & Martin, 2015). That being said, highly motivated deceivers still tend to be less detectable via mediated channels (Hancock, Woodworth, & Goorha, 2010). This may be because the verbal disfluencies and nonverbal tenseness related to deception are more easily managed by online deceivers and more difficult for online receivers to notice. Though it seems that we expect a modest amount of deception through concealment and equivocation online and adjust our interpretations of strangers' mediated self-presentations accordingly, there is evidence that there is still a truth bias when interacting via CMC with people we know (Boyle, Kacmar, & George, 2010). So the cards are stacked against us in terms of detecting online deception.

CONCLUSION

In this chapter, we reviewed expectancy violations theory, then applied it to a variety of contexts, including social networks, online dating, interviewing, and online community norms and communication. In general, we seem to expect people to be honest, but accept a modest amount of embellishment, and we look for nonverbal indicators of deceit in online interactions. In this chapter, I have taken a largely neutral stance on norms, expectations, and deception. You may expect that researchers believe that deception is unethical. But this is not always true. Sometimes deceit is selfish or malicious and damages relationships, such as trolling, but sometimes it is done to protect the face of the people we interact with (Afifi, Caughlin, & Afifi, 2007) or simply to manage self-presentation (Whitty, 2007).

Indeed, one key aspect of a person's social and task attractiveness is his or her use of nonverbals, as evidenced in Dr. Cuddy's Ted Talk and in the advice gleaned from studies of nonverbal behaviors in interview situations. It makes intuitive sense that we look for nonverbal indicators of immediacy and confidence, such as eye contact, facial expressions, and posture, since we often seek closeness in our interactions and we tend to interpret less immediate behaviors as an indicator of dishonesty. This appears to be the case across contexts, such as online dating, social networks, and online interviews: we look for written and nonverbal cues that a person is being open and honest. We make attributions about people's honesty and their personality by how they behave, and they make similar attributions about us based on our nonverbal behavior.

ASSIGNMENTS

1. **Google Hangout Interview.** Use Google Hangouts to have a professional interview with a classmate. First, prepare four open, interview-like questions that are professional (not personal) and focus on his or her academic background and career plans. Second, arrange a time to meet via Google Hangouts. Third, take turns interviewing each other while you record the interaction. Lastly, submit the link to the recorded interview to your instructor and complete the self-assessment questions:

   a. Self-assessment: Looking at your own verbal and nonverbal behavior, consider your strengths and weaknesses in each of the following areas:

      i. Did you use eye contact well? Why or why not?

      ii. Was your facial expression appropriate? Why or why not?

iii. Was your posture appropriate? Why or why not?

iv. Did you use time and space effectively in the interview? Why or why not?

v. What did you learn about your verbal and nonverbal behaviors by watching yourself respond to interview questions?

vi. What is one thing you would like to improve about your verbal and nonverbal responses?

vii. What is one thing that you were happy with in terms of your verbal and nonverbal responses?

viii. Overall, do you think you failed to meet, met, or exceeded the expectations of the person who interviewed you? Why do you think this?

REFERENCES

Seminal Articles:

Burgoon, J. K. (1978). A communication model of personal space violations: Explication and an initial test. *Human Communication Research, 4,* 129–142.

Buller, D. B. and Burgoon, J. K. (1996). Interpersonal deception theory. *Communication Theory, 6*(3), 203–242.

Academic Articles:

Afifi, Caughline, & Afifi, (2007). The dark side (and light side) of topic avoidance and secrets. In. In B. H. Spitzer & W. R. Cupach (Eds.) *The dark side of interpersonal communication* (pp. 61–92). Mahwah, NJ: Lawrence Erlbaum.

Barrick, M. R., Shaffer, J. A., & DeGrassi, S. W. (2009). What you see may not be what you get: Relationships among self-presentation tactics and ratings of interview and job performance. *Journal of Applied Psychology, 94*(6), 1394–1411.

Bevan, J. L., Ang, P.-C., & Fearns, J. B. (2014). Being unfriended on Facebook: An application of expectancy violation theory. *Computers in Human Behavior, 33,* 171–178.

Boyle, R. J., Kacmar, C. J., & George, J. F. (2010). Electronic Deception: How Proximity, Computer-Mediation, and the Truth Bias May Influence Deceptive Messages. In N. Kock (Ed.), *Interdisciplinary Perspectives on E-Collaboration: Emerging Trends and Applications* (pp. 312–337). Hershey, PA: Information Science Reference.

Burgoon, J. K., & Buller, D. B. (2004). Interpersonal deception theory. In J. S. Seiter & R. H. Gass (Eds.) Perspectives on persuasion, social influence, and compliance gaining (pp. 239–264). Boston: Allyn & Bacon.

Burgoon, J. K., Manusov, V., Mineo, P., & Hale, J. L. (1985). Effects of gaze on hiring, credibility, attraction and relational message interpretation. *Journal of Nonverbal Behavior, 9*(3), 133–146.

DeGroot, T., & Gooty, J. (2009). Can nonverbal cues be used to make meaningful personality attributions in employment interviews? *Journal of Business and Psychology, 24*(2), 179–192.

DeGroot, T., & Motowidlo, S. J. (1999). Why visual and vocal interview cues can affect interviewer's' judgment and predict job performance. *Journal of Applied Psychology, 84*, 986–993.

Donath, J. S. (1998). *Identity and deception in the virtual community.* In M. A. Smith & P. Kollock (Eds.), *Communities in cyberspace.* London: Routledge.

Ellison, N. B., Hancock, J. B., & Toma, C. L. (2011). Profile as promise: A framework for conceptualizing veracity in online dating self-presentations. *New Media & Society, 14*(1), 45–62.

Fox, J., & Moreland, J. J. (2015). The dark side of social networking sites: An exploration of relational and psychological stressors associated with Facebook use and affordances. *Computers in Human Behavior, 45*, 168–176.

Hancock, J. T., Woodworth, M. T., & Goorha, S. (2010) See no evil: The effect of communication medium and motivation on deception detection. *Group Decision and Negotiation, 19*, 327–343.

Hall, J. A., Pennington, N., & Lueders, A. (2013). Impression management and formation on Facebook: A lens model approach. *New Media & Society, 16*, 258–282.

Hardaker, C. (2010). Trolling in asynchronous computer-mediated communication: From user discussions to academic definitions. *Journal of Politeness Research, 6*, 215–242.

Hooper, V., & Kalidas, T. (2012). Acceptable and unacceptable behaviour on social networking sites: A Study of the behavioural norms of youth on Facebook. *The Electronic Journal Information Systems Evaluation, 15*, 259–268.

Lee, J. (2015). The double-edged sword: The effects of journalists' social media activities on audience perceptions of journalists and their news products. *Journal of Computer-Mediated Communication, 20*(3), 312–329.

Kalman, Y. M., & Rafaeli, S. (2010). Online pauses and silence: Chronemic expectancy violations in written computer-mediated communication. *Communication Research, 38*, 54–69.

Kiviat, B. (2009, October 20). How Skype Is Changing the Job Interview. Retrieved from http://content.time.com/time/magazine/article/0,9171,1933214,00.html

Levine, T. R., Anders, L. N., Banas, J., Baum, K. L. Endo, K., Hu, A. D. S., & Wong, C. H. (2010). Norms, expectations, and deception: A norm violation model of veracity judgments. *Communication Monographs, 67*, 123–137.

McLaughlin, C., & Vitak, J. (2012). Norm evolution and violation on Facebook. *New Media & Society, 14*, 299–315.

Ruben, M. A., Hall, J. A., & Schmid Mast, M. (2015). Smiling in a Job Interview: When Less Is More. *The Journal of Social Psychology, 155*(2), 107–126.

Stewart, G. L., Dustin, S. L., Barrick, M. R., & Darnold, T. C. (2008). Exploring the handshake in employment interviews. *Journal of Applied Psychology, 93*(5), 1139–1146.

Sung, K.-H., & Kim, S. (2014). I want to be your friend: The effects of organizations' interpersonal approaches on social networking sites. *Journal of Public Relations Research, 26*, 235–255.

Tong, S. T., & Walther, J. B. (2015). Confirmation and disconfirmation of expectancies in computer-mediated communication. *Communication Research, 42*, 186–212.

Ugbah, S. D., & Evuleocha, S. U. (1992). The importance of written, verbal, and nonverbal communication factors in employment interview decisions. *Journal of Employment Counseling, 29*(3), 128–137.

Venus, J. S., & Martin, C. (2015). "A Match Made…Online?" The effects of user-generated online dater profile types (free-spirited versus uptight) on other users' perception of trustworthiness, interpersonal attraction, and personality. *Cyberpsychology, Behavior and Social Networking, 18*(6), 320–327.

Whitty, M. T. (2007). Manipulation of self in cyberspace. In B. H. Spitzer & W. R. Cupach (Eds.), *The dark side of interpersonal communication* (pp. 93–120). Mahwah, NJ: Lawrence Erlbaum.

Zytko, D., Grandhi, S. A., & Jones, Q. G. (2014). *Impression management through communication in online dating.* In Proceedings of the companion publication of the 17th ACM conference on Computer supported cooperative work & social computing, ACM, New York, NY, 277–280.

Examples:

http://content.time.com/time/video/player/0,32068,46937715001_1933401,00.html

UNIT 3

INTERPERSONAL RELATIONSHIPS ONLINE

In the previous two units, we looked inward and reflected on how we see ourselves and others (Unit 1) and how we formulate and interpret verbal and nonverbal messages (Unit 2). We covered some specific competencies that can help us better understand and more mindfully respond to our own and others' unique characteristics and circumstances. In Unit 3, we begin to look at our relationships. We cover theories related to our interpersonal relationships first—those dyadic relationships between us and our friends, romantic partners, family members, and even coworkers.

In a recent report by The Cooperative Institutional Research Program at the Higher Education Research Institute at UCLA (Eagan et al., 2015), it was evident that our interpersonal relationships are clearly and consistently moving away from face-to-face interactions to online interactions:

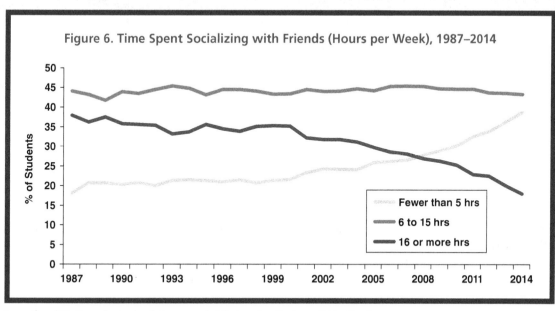

Figure 6. Time Spent Socializing with Friends (Hours per Week), 1987–2014

Source: Eagan, et. al., The American Freshman: National Norms Fall 2014. UCLA: 2014, p. 11.

Image from http://www.heri.ucla.edu/monographs/TheAmericanFreshman2014.pdf, p. 8.

133

The theories covered in this unit help us understand the benefits and the drawbacks of making and maintaining interpersonal connections via mediated channels. We look first at attraction, and consider the different things that attract us to our friends and dating partners. In addition to physical attraction, we also consider things like social attractiveness and whether we are a socially valuable asset to others. We also look at how attraction is different in online contexts, where things like our social capital become important in terms of attracting new online connections. We also consider how online dating and social networks are changing attraction, and how some channels highlight physical attractiveness, such as Tinder, while other channels highlight social attractiveness, such as Twitter.

We then move on to discuss how the process of relationship formation is changing in online environments. We reduce uncertainty and learn about other people online through Google and creeping on their social media profiles, which is fundamentally different than the information seeking used in face-to-face relationships. Similarly, other people learn about us as we disclose more online, but we are also more selective about what we disclose, which has repercussions for how rapidly our relationships form. The move to online dating gives us more control, and perhaps an intensified, hyperpersonal sense of certainty and closeness, compared to meeting and dating face-to-face. On the other hand, it can also make us more susceptible to being deceived and lead us to disclose more than we should disclose. Much of this relates to the affordances of technology, or the ability to project the best, most attractive aspects of ourselves and the disinhibition we may feel when we use mediated channels that *feel* anonymous (even though they aren't).

Insight into Innovation Example: The Ashley Madison Hack. In 2015, the Ashley Madison website, which is used to help married people find hookups and have affairs, was hacked. The names, e-mail addresses, and personal details that users had posted on the website were made public. Though it may be difficult to think of prospective "cheaters" as "victims," this case actually points to the very serious dangers of using the Internet for interpersonal relationships. Interpersonal relationship are close, intimate connections where we share otherwise very guarded aspects of who we are with people that we trust. When we share that information via a mediated channel—whether it is our darkest fear or most personal fantasy—it is being conveyed via a vulnerable, public medium. Thus, in the wake of the Ashley Madison hack, people's professional and personal lives were destroyed by what should have been a very private indiscretion. Though I certainly cannot condone websites like Ashley Madison, we should appreciate the vulnerability we all have as potential victims of such an attack—whether it is a dating website profile, social media account, or our bank account.

Read more about the privacy concerns raised by the Ashley Madison hack here: http://www.cnn.com/2015/08/27/opinions/yang-ashley-madison-hack/index.html

Beyond online dating, technology has impacted our stable, face-to-face relationships as well. When we think about the uses and effects of technology in our face-to-face relationships, the first consideration is the potential for conflicts, or dialectical tensions. Dialectical theory helps us think more deeply about our own needs and the needs of others, as well as the layers of meanings in the relational messages we send. With new technologies connecting us to other people and to work, there is a new opportunity to stay closely connected to those people we care about throughout the day, but there is also the potential for technology to interfere in our relationships when we lack clear boundaries or rules. So, though we can text our romantic partners anytime and that may make us feel closer, we may also find ourselves distracted at home—and from those very people we want to be closest to—by texts or emails from work.

Lastly, we look at rewarding and equitable relationships by considering social exchange processes in relationships. We consider whether people weigh costs and rewards in relationships, and how we use mediated communication to maintain, withdraw from, and sometimes terminate relationships when we feel that the relationship is inequitable, when we aren't getting as much out of a relationship as we are putting into it, or when the relationship just isn't as rewarding as we need it to be.

The chapters in this unit give us a lot to think about in terms of our interpersonal relationships: what attracts us to others and others to us, how we communicate to build closeness, how we can recognize and manage conflicting needs, and how we weigh the rewards and costs as we consider whether or not to continue investing in a relationship. Technology has been both a way to help us find and build close connections to others through online dating and social networks, but also creates new tensions and needs in relationships that can pull us away from the people we care about. Taken together, these theories can help us better understand our own role and satisfaction in our relationships, and also consider our relationships through the eyes of our interpersonal partners. We may better understand relationships that have faltered or failed in the past, and should also learn how to build rewarding, lasting relationships.

REFERENCES

Eagan, K. Stolzenber, E. B., Ramirex, J. J., Aragon, M. C., Suchard, M. R., & Hurtado, S. (2015). The American freshman: National norms Fall 2014. Retrieved from http://www.heri.ucla.edu/monographs/TheAmericanFreshman2014.pdf

CHAPTER 10

INTERPERSONAL ATTRACTION

OUTCOMES

- *Knowledge:* Learn about the types of attraction.
- *Skill:* Use social networks to build your social capital.

There is not a single, unified theory of interpersonal attraction. You may wonder why, if there is no specific theory, we should cover attraction in a theory book. Let me explain: attraction leads us to communicate more with people, which is the essential first step to forming an interpersonal relationship, including a romantic relationship, friendship, or even being involved in a group. Thus, the later chapters on how relationships evolve and dissolve and on group processes would be missing a key piece of the interpersonal puzzle if we didn't discuss what attracts us to people in the first place.

Also, there are some common misconceptions about attraction. We often think of attraction as deciding whether or not someone is good-looking: a pleasant face, appealing body type, and so on. But attraction is **multidimensional**, which means that it has several different aspects (McCroskey & McCain, 1974). Put another way, we are attracted to others for several reasons, not just their physical appearance. If you think about someone you are close friends with, for example, chances are there are many reasons you're friends: they are fun, they understand you, you enjoy doing things together, maybe they help you out when you need them, and so on. On the flip side of that, we can all probably think of times that we interacted with someone who was physically attractive but not likable for one or more reasons.

It is, in many ways, unseemly to talk and write about attraction and attractiveness because it divides people into categories, like "desirables" or "undesirables." But take heart, because there are numerous ways a person can be attractive, and some of these are things that we can work on and improve upon. As with most theories and related competencies we discuss in this book, attractiveness is something we can work toward if we understand the types of attraction, sources of attraction, and if we are self-aware and reflective about personal strengths and weaknesses.

MAIN IDEA

There are different types of attraction: physical, social, and task attraction. Judgments of physical attraction are almost instantaneous. Other elements of attractiveness are less immediately obvious, but through initial interactions that are positive, confirming, and competent, people can improve perceptions of their attractiveness.

Attraction has several dimensions including, but not necessarily limited to, social, physical, and task attraction (McCroskey & McCain, 1974).

1. **Physical attraction** includes seeing someone as sexy, good-looking, handsome, and/or pretty. It can include the beauty/attractiveness of a person's face and other physical attributes such a height, body shape, and athleticism. We do make very quick initial appraisals of other people when we meet them. For example, lab studies have found that we can assess physical attractiveness in as little as 100 milliseconds and that those determinations can trigger the physical attractiveness stereotype and related, positive attributions (Locher et al., 1993).

   Beauty may be "in the eye of the beholder" and "only skin deep" but we associate many positive traits, such as sociability and competence, with being physically attractive as well. This is referred to as the *"beauty-is-good" effect* or the *physical attractiveness stereotype* and it has been confirmed in numerous academic studies (Eagly, Ashmore, Makhijani, & Longo, 1991). Indeed, both children and adults who are attractive are evaluated more positively by people, treated better by others, and demonstrate more positive traits (Langlois et al., 2000). Also, in keeping with conventional wisdom, men place more importance on physical attractiveness compared with women (Feingold, 1990).

   Though research suggests that there are specific facial characteristics that people find attractive, such as youthfulness and facial symmetry with large eyes, high cheekbones, and a small nose, we also modify our appearance to make ourselves more attractive to others (Regan, 2011). For example, when women expect to meet someone who is physically attractive, they tend to wear more makeup. Also, when women are looking for a partner, they tend to wear particular types of clothing, such as more sheer, tighter, or more revealing clothing (Grammer, Renninger, & Fischer, 2004).

   Whether or not intentionally modifying one's attractiveness is "deceptive" there are particular affordances online that people seem to take advantage of. For example, less attractive online daters tended to choose pictures of themselves for their profiles that are more attractive than they are in real life and they describe their physical attributes less honestly (Toma & Hancock, 2010).

2. **Social attraction** includes being someone that people would like to talk to, socialize with, and is fun or pleasant to be around. We see evidence of the importance of social attractiveness in online profiles where people describe themselves as "outgoing" and "fun-loving." Social attraction also explains why extraversion is such a desirable trait, as extraverts tend to be sociable, outgoing, and have a wide circle of friends.

3. **Task attraction** includes whether or not people will help us get what we want, such as being reliable, dependable, and someone we would be able to work with. This is most often associated with workplace relationships and group relationships, but there is also a task element to some friendships and romantic relationships as well.

Finkel and Eastwick (2015) proposed an **instrumentality principle** in interpersonal attraction. They argued that we are attracted to people who help us fulfill our needs and achieve our goals, particularly if those needs and goals are a high priority. Further clarifying how needs and goals are at the heart of attraction, Montoya and Horton (2013) explained that we tend to seek relationship partners who are both *capable* of helping us achieve our goals and *willing* to help us. Think of it this way, if I want a successful career, it would be essential for me to find a partner a) that had the resources to help me pursue that career and b) who was willing to share those resources. The same can be true of any goal or need we have—wanting marriage, children, financial security and/or wealth, to live a certain lifestyle, to have particular freedoms, and so on—the partners we choose will either help or hinder us in achieving those important life goals.

McCroskey and McCain's (1974) measures of interpersonal attraction (summarized):	
Social Attraction	• This person could be a friend • I could have a friendly chat with this person • This person would fit into my social circles • This person would be difficult to meet and talk to* • I could not have a personal friendship with this person* • This person is pleasant to be around
Physical Attraction	• This person is very handsome or pretty • This person is somewhat ugly* • This person is sexy • This person is attractive physically • I like the way this person looks • This person isn't good-looking
Task Attraction	• This person goofs off when they have a job to do* • I can count on this person getting the job done • I am confident that this person is able to get the job done • I could depend on this person if I wanted to get things done • I could not accomplish anything with this person • This person would not be good for me to work with

* denotes a reverse coded item.

1. **Communication:** *People's conversational style, communication competence, and nonverbal immediacy behaviors affect social, physical, and task attraction.*

   Conversational style, such as being animated, relaxed, and attentive during interactions, is related to increased perceptions of social and task attraction (Brandt, 1979). **Communication competence**, which we've discussed in previous chapters, also increases perceptions of social, task, and physical attractiveness, but the most pronounced effects of competence are on social and task attractiveness (Duran & Kelly, 1988). We tend to like interactions where the other person is empathic (responsive to the feelings of others), shows affinity toward us (nonverbal signals of liking), communicates supportively, and seems to be relaxed (Wiemann, 1977).

   Thus, nonverbal immediacy may be important for increasing attraction (Houser, Horan, & Furler, 2008). **Immediacy** are those behaviors that bring us psychologically closer to someone, such as making eye contact, nodding our head in agreement, smiling, having an open and relaxed posture, and communicating in a positive, friendly, inclusive way. In sum, it involves seeming comfortable with and interested in the other person. Using verbal and nonverbal immediacy behaviors increase perceptions of a person's **perceived outcome value**, which is the perception of the rewards we could get from a prospective relationship.

Immediacy Behaviors that Promote Closeness (Anderson, 2009):	
Verbal:	**Nonverbal:**
• Plural pronouns (we, us) • Use of nicknames • Open communication • Positive statements about the person/relationship • Compliments	• Eye contact • Leaning in/moving closer • Smiling • Appropriate interpersonal touch

2. **Propinquity:** *Physical and social proximity increase interpersonal attraction. We can increase propinquity through communication.*

   Propinquity is closeness or similarity. It can include things like being close to someone physically (i.e., living on the same floor, or in the same neighborhood), but it also includes having similar goals and aspirations, similar socioeconomic status, and similar social circles.

   There is evidence that links similarity and physical attractiveness, commonly known as the matching hypothesis. The **matching hypothesis** assumes that people select partners that are similar to themselves in terms of social and physical attractiveness (Walster et al., 1966). More recent research into online dating clarifies that people *try* to initiate relationships online with people who are more attractive than themselves but typically only get responses from people who are similarly physically attractive ([Taylor, Fiore, Mendelsohn, & Cheshire, 2011](#)). Also, in terms of matching partners' popularity, people who were very popular connected with other people who were very popular, and unpopular people tended to connect with each other.

Insight into Innovation Activity: Check out this summary of Taylor et al.'s research on the matching hypothesis: http://datascience.berkeley.edu/dating-matching-hypothesis/. What do you think? Do people "match" others in terms of physical attractiveness and popularity? What other factors (or variables) may explain whether or not someone responds to an online profile?

Thus, **similarity** is a very early determinant of attraction. Some evidence suggests that when we perceive that we are *generally* similar to another person (i.e., when you perceive that you "have a lot in common" and that you "have similar personalities"), it can lead to romantic attraction. Interestingly, *actual* personality similarity is not necessarily related to attraction ([Tidwell, Eastwick, & Finkel, 2013](#)). Further, as relationships progress, similarity decreases in importance to the point that being similar to your long-term friends and romantic partners may not be important later in the relationship ([Sunnafrank, 1985](#)). Rather, as we will discuss in later chapters, how you and your partner navigate your differences over time is more important than your differences.

Physical proximity is how close a person is to you, and it is a slower, longer-term source of attraction. When you can see and interact with another person more often, you tend to gradually find him or her more attractive. Think about it this way, it is difficult to know if a person might be socially attractive or be instrumentally important if you don't get to know them. The best way to get to know someone is to see and interact with him or her often. Thus, over time, you may find that someone is more attractive than your initial appraisal of their physical attractiveness. Also, if a person is close to you—in the same classes you take, in the same neighborhood or social circle, and so on—then you probably have a lot in common, which can lead to attraction. Absence does not make the heart grow fonder, at least not in terms of attraction.

METHODS IN ATTRACTION RESEARCH

Attraction research is typically quantitative and employs surveys, experiments and, increasingly, big data collected from people's online activities. In my experience teaching attraction research, people are often skeptical that statistics can be used to describe and predict attraction, and are even more skeptical that we can use it to describe and predict love. Though feelings are intuitively qualitative because they seem like they should be unique to each one of us, there are testable and observable patterns in human interactions that can help us understand how and why people choose romantic partners and friends.

For example, the dimensions of attraction at the beginning of the chapter are based on McCroskey and McCain's (1974) work developing a scale measure of attraction. Based on the literature, they contended that there were more dimensions to attraction than just physical attraction, which had, up to that point, been the dominant focus of research. Their development of the attractiveness scale provided a convenient, useful pretest and posttest for experiments that manipulate variables like sociability, immediacy, disclosure, and physical attractiveness to see how those changes affect perceived attractiveness.

If we think of this in terms of a field experiment, we can also see how those measures can be (and have been) very useful. For example, researchers can use those scale items to assess people's perceptions of individuals in online dating profiles, or people who met during a speed dating event, to explore how different types of attraction vary based on the communication that occurs between people and the extent that different types of attraction are related to seeking a second date. Even in terms of social networks, understanding the types of attraction that draw people together could be informative in terms of predicting which friend requests we send out, which people we unfriend as we get to know them, and how our perceptions of their attractiveness may change.

Insight into Innovation Example: Using Math to Explain Romantic Attraction. Mathematician Hannah Fry uses data from dating websites to explore interpersonal relationships. After analysis of the profiles that people responded to, she concludes that physical attractiveness doesn't predict popularity on dating websites. Rather, being perceived as attractive by some people but *not everybody* makes it more likely that people will respond to an online dating profile. You can watch Hannah Fry's Ted Talk on using math to find and maintain romantic relationships here: https://www.ted.com/talks/hannah_fry_the_mathematics_of_love?language=en

Can finding love boil down to finding optimal mathematical patterns? What do big data research projects such as hers teach us about the usefulness of research in our personal lives?

In addition to scale items that can help us understand people's attraction to prospective friends and romantic partners, we can also observe initial interactions in new ways online. By looking at the most and least popular profiles on social networks and dating sites as indicated by likes, shares, comments, and responses, we can collect data on the people who are most and least attractive: What types of images do they use? What type of language do they use? To what extent are they interactive? Immediate? We can use big data to confirm or to update our understanding of the most effective communication styles, immediacy behaviors, and self-presentation tactics in social and romantic profiles.

BECOMING ATTRACTIVE: ELECTRONIC PROPINQUITY

Electronic propinquity theory has been proposed to explain how mediated channels can be used to make us feel closer to people. In general, it proposes that mediated channels can create a sense of closeness between people when those channels 1) create a sense of *presence* between interactants, 2) allow for sharing and *interacting*, and are 3) used *competently* by interactants (Korzenny, 1978). On the other hand, closeness is reduced by the presence of *complex* information, *rules*, and feeling like one has too many channel *options*.

Walther and Bazarova (2008) pointed out that this particular theory hasn't been widely researched, which is unfortunate since it seems like it would apply well to Web 2.0 technologies such as social networks and dating sites. Walther and Bazarova confirmed some of the assumptions of the theory in an experiment. They found that communication competence did increase propinquity, particularly in situations where the channels limited interactants, though even highly skilled communicators were not able to overcome the hurdles of a highly complex task via a low-quality channel. Also, the introduction of more communication channels decreased a sense of closeness.

So, what does this tell us about interpersonal attraction and Web 2.0 technologies? Creating a feeling of closeness with people through mediated channels may not be as straightforward as simply being a competent and immediate communicator, though that does help. Interpersonal attraction may also be affected by the features of the specific channel or software we use.

Online Dating. Pew (2015) reported that almost 60 percent of American adults have positive attitudes toward using online dating to meet people.

Take, for example, Tinder. According to comScore (2014), 35 to 40 million people use online dating technologies, with mobile and social media apps like Tinder leading the pack. Taking what we know about attraction and electronic propinquity and applying it to dating in the Web 2.0 environment, we can get useful insight into the popular-

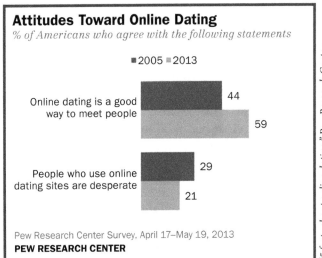

Attitudes Toward Online Dating
% of Americans who agree with the following statements

■ 2005 ■ 2013

Online dating is a good way to meet people — 44 / 59

People who use online dating sites are desperate — 29 / 21

Pew Research Center Survey, April 17–May 19, 2013
PEW RESEARCH CENTER

ity of Tinder. Users are shown a picture of a potential match and a brief bio, and immediately swipe left for people they aren't interested in and swipe right for people they like. The interface is simple and a surprisingly intuitive design; thus electronic propinquity theory suggests that it would be ideal for increasing closeness. In addition, prospective matches on Tinder are geographically close, which may increase propinquity. If two people both swipe right on each other's profiles, it is a "match" and they can message each other through the Tinder app. This early interaction can help two people determine if they might have a lot in common, such as similar goals, interests, and needs.

Learn more about why we "swipe right" to indicate liking and "swipe left" to indicate less liking in this interesting post from cognitive scientist, Jim Davies: http://nautil.us/blog/why-tinder-charmers-and-movie-heroes-move-the-same-way

🗨 FRIENDSHIP: SOCIAL CAPITAL (AND ATTRACTIVENESS) ON FACEBOOK AND TWITTER

We can think about social networking sites as large, online *communities* where people's interactions follow a general pattern, they engage in social rituals, they form a sense of belonging, and they see the network as a community (Parks, 2011). There is evidence that propinquity is the primary determinant of who we friend and maintain friendships with via social networks, further supporting the notion that social networks are a type of community where we maintain ties with people who are similar to ourselves (Lewis, Gonzalez, & Kaufman, 2012).

As a community, social networks are a way for people to build **social capital**. Social capital is the number and strength of a person's social connections within a community (Putnam, 2000). Social capital benefits *both* the person who has the connection via a social network and the people closely connected to that person. Thus, people who have a lot of social capital via social networks like Twitter and Facebook tend to be attractive to us: they can help us build our own social networks and capital (social attractiveness) and be useful to us in terms of professional networking and helping us find useful resources (task attractiveness).

Social capital is affected by social network features in several ways (Tong et al., 2008). First, our own profile pictures and posts can enhance perceptions of our social and physical attractiveness. Also, the connections we make via social networks can enhance perceptions of our attractiveness. Having physically attractive friends on social networks can improve people's assessments of our own physical attractiveness. And, lastly, having a lot of friends, but not too many friends, also increases perceptions of our social attractiveness.

Social attraction leads to increased disclosure which, as we will discuss in the next chapter, is a key aspect of building close interpersonal relationships (Sheldon, 2009). Disclosure and ongoing online interactions then build *more* social attraction (Antheunis, Valkenburg, & Peter, 2010). In all, building social capital through online communities like social networks can make us more attractive to other people, which will lead to more close ties and the expansion of social networks, and thus build our social capital and attractiveness even more.

Insight into Innovation Example: Are Your Facebook Friends More Socially Attractive Than You Are? The **friendship paradox** is the finding that, on average, your friends have more friends than you do (MIT Technology Review, 2014). So, if you went to Facebook and looked at the number of friends you have, then calculated the average number of friends among your friends, your Facebook friends would have more friends than you do.

There's an interesting mathematical explanation of why our Facebook friends are more popular (i.e., socially attractive) than we are. Facebook users who have a lot of friends on social networks a) are more likely to be your friend because they're friends with so many people; therefore, b) your popular friends increase the overall average of number friends among your connections. So, yes, your friends are on average more socially attractive than you are, and the research also suggests that they are happier and wealthier too. Thus, your friends have more social capital than you do, but being connected to those popular people also builds your own social capital via social networks.

CONCLUSION

Though there is no one unified theory of attractiveness, we have gone over several well-established concepts from psychology, sociology, and communication studies. Taken together, these fields of research do point to specific types of attraction, predictors of attraction, and outcomes associated with attractiveness.

Specifically, people vary in physical, social, and task attractiveness. Judgments of physical attractiveness are almost instantaneous, but through face-to-face and/or online communication, we can promote perceptions of our social and task attractiveness. These types of attraction require a certain amount of propinquity—geographic proximity, overlapping social networks, or mediated means of becoming close—so that we can meet and interact. Through these initial interactions, we can communicate immediacy, similarity, and demonstrate our value as a friend or romantic partner. These connections that we make may then lead to even more connections and increased attractiveness.

There is, of course, a lot more to be done in terms of research and theorizing about interpersonal attraction. In some ways, the explanations of attractiveness discussed here are offering conflicting advice: physical attractiveness research suggests that beauty is essential, the instrumentality principle suggests that social or material rewards are essential, and propinquity research contends that closeness and similarity are essential. Overall, I take this to mean that we can enhance our attractiveness by being valuable to others (i.e., through social capital and resources) and increasing our closeness to others (i.e., by finding points of similarity, communicating closeness, and using technologies that enable closeness). This makes some intuitive sense as we look at the popular social media sites and dating apps: popular and attractive people on social networks are valuable connections to have and maintain, technology helps us find points of similarity, makes us feel closer to people, and it is easy to use social networks to maintain those connections. Subsequent research on attraction, particularly how attraction changes as we interact via social network sites and dating apps, could help us move toward a clearer theory about how and why we are attracted to others (or not) online.

ASSIGNMENTS

1. **Compare and contrast dating websites/apps.** Look at the features of two competing dating websites or apps. Compare and contrast the features of the websites/apps in terms of the types of attraction emphasized and deemphasized by the features of app and the types of profile content permitted:

   a. Does the website or app link people together based on *similarity*? How?

   b. Does the website or app link people together based on *proximity*? How?

   c. Does the website or app focus on users' *physical attractiveness*? How?

   d. Does the website or app allow users to demonstrate their *communication competence* and create *immediacy*? How?

   e. Overall, which website or app best meets the criteria for *electronic propinquity*? How so?

2. **Evaluate social capital on Twitter.** Check out the Twitter pages for some of the most popular celebrities (i.e., Katy Perry, Justin Bieber, Taylor Swift, Lady Gaga, etc.).

   a. Looking at their posts, how did they develop their social capital? For example, do their posts highlight their physical attractiveness, express similarity to followers, seem immediate and conversational, highlight their instrumentality to followers, and so on?

   b. What can we learn about building and maintaining social capital by looking at how they use Twitter?

REFERENCES

Seminal Work:

McCroskey, J. C., & McCain, T. A. (1974). The measurement of interpersonal attraction. *Speech Monographs, 41*, 261–266.

Academic Sources:

Brandt, D. R. (1979). On linking social performance with social competence: Some relations between communicative style and attributions of interpersonal attractiveness. *Human Communication Research, 5*(3), 223–237.

Duran, R. L., & Kelly, L. (1988). The influence of communicative competence on perceived task, social, and physical attraction. *Communication Quarterly, 36*(1), 41–49.

Eagly, A. H., Ashmore, R. D., Makhijani, M. G., & Longo, L. C. (1991). What is beautiful is good, but…: A meta-analytic review of research on the physical attractiveness stereotype. *Psychological Bulletin, 110*, 109–128.

Eli Goodman. (2014, September 8). Tinder Sparks Renewed Interest in Online Dating Category. Retrieved from http://www.comscore.com/Insights/Blog/Tinder-Sparks-Renewed-Interest-in-Online-Dating-Category.

Feingold, A. (1990). Gender differences in effects of physical attractiveness on romantic attraction: A comparison across five research paradigms. *Journal of Personality & Social Psychology, 59*, 981–993.

Finkel, E. J., & Eastwick, P. E. (2015). Interpersonal attraction: In search of a theoretical Rosetta Stone. In J. A. Simpson & J. F. Dovidio (Eds.), *Handbook of personality and social psychology: Interpersonal relations and group processes.* Washington, DC: American Psychological Association.

Grammer, K., Renninger, L., & Fischer, B. (2004). Disco clothing, female sexual motivation, and relationship status: Is she dressed to impress? *The Journal of Sex Research, 41*, 66–74.

Houser, M. L., Horan, S. M., & Furler, L. A. (2008). Dating in the fast lane: How communication predicts speed-dating success. *Journal of Personal & Social Relationships, 25*, 749–768.

Locher, P., Unger, R., Sociedade, P, & Wahl, J. (1993). At first glance: Accessibility of the physical attractiveness stereotype. *Sex Roles, 11*, 729–743.

Sheldon, P. (2009). "I'll poke you. You'll poke me!" Self-disclosure, social attraction, predictability and trust as important predictors of Facebook relationships. *Cyberpsychology: Journal of Psychosocial Research on Cyberspace, 3*(2). Retrieved from http://cyberpsychology.eu/view.php?cisloclanku=2009111101&article=(search in Issues)

Sunnafrank, M. (1985). Attitude similarity and interpersonal attraction during early communicative relationships: A research note on the generalizability of findings to opposite-sex relationships. *Western Journal of Speech Communication, 49*, 73–80.

Tidwell, N. D., Eastwick, P. W., & Finkel, E. J. (2013). Perceived, not actual, similarity predicts initial attraction in a live romantic context: Evidence from the speed-dating paradigm. *Personal Relationships*, *20*, 199–215.

Tong, S. T., Van Der Heide, B., Langwell, L., & Walther, J. B. (2008). Too much of a good thing? The relationship between the number of friends on Facebook and interpersonal impressions. *Journal of Computer-Mediated Communication*, *13*, 531–549.

Langlois, J. W., Kalakanis, L., Rubenstein, A. J., Larson, A., Hallam, M., & Smoot, M. (2000). Maxims or myths of beauty? A meta-analytic and theoretical review. *Psychological Bulletin*, *126*(3), 390–423.

Lewis, K., Gonzalez, M., & Kaufman, J. (2012). Social selection and peer influence in an online social network. *Proceedings of the National Academy of Sciences*, *109*(1): 68–72.

Montoya, R. M., & Horton, R. S. (2013). A two-dimensional model for the study of interpersonal attraction. *Personality and Social Psychology Review*, *18*(1), 59–86.

Parks, M. R. (2011). Social network sites as virtual communities. In Z. Papacharissi (Ed.) *A networked self: Identity, community and culture on social networks* (pp. 105–123). New York: Routledge.

Putnam, R. D. (2000). *Bowling alone: The collapse and revival of American community*. New York: Simon & Schuster.

Regan, P. C. (2011). Cinderella revisited: Women's appearance modification as a function of target audience sex and attractiveness. *Social Behavior & Personality: An International Journal*, *39*(4), 563–576.

Toma, C. L., & Hancock, J. T. (2010). Looks and lies: The role of physical attractiveness in online dating self-presentation and deception. *Communication Research*, *37*(3), 335–351.

Walther, J. B., & Bazarova, N. N. (2008). Validation and application of electronic propinquity theory to computer-mediated communication in groups. *Communication Research*, *35*(5), 622–645.

Wiemann, J. M. (1977). Explication and test of a model of communicative competence. *Human Communication Research*, *3*, 195–213.

CHAPTER 11

HYPERPERSONAL SOCIAL PENETRATION AND UNCERTAINTY REDUCTION

OUTCOMES

- *Knowledge:* Learn about typical thoughts and feelings in initial interactions and how they affect communication.
- *Skill:* Balance privacy needs in online relationships with the need for information, closeness, and support online.

INTRODUCTION

In the last chapter, we covered research on what attracts us to people in initial interactions, including physical attraction, social attraction, and task attraction. In this chapter, we look at the next stage: relationship development. Relationship development varies greatly among couples and friends, and doesn't always follow a timeframe or step-by-step pattern. For example, I'm sure you know people who believe in love at first sight, people who believe that real love takes time, and still others who spend a lifetime in an on-again, off-again relationship.

As with most human communication, it comes down to the reality that we have different traits, characteristics, and needs in our interactions and relationships, and those differences lead us to perceptions, expectations, and behaviors that are distinct. Thus, in this chapter, we will look at **relationship development** as a dynamic, interactive process between two people that occurs in a context that may enhance or hinder bonding, depending on how people communicate, perceive each other based on that communication, and develop a feeling of closeness.

To explore relationship development, we will look at three theories that are interrelated but, at their core, focus on learning about the other person and feelings of closeness that develop through interaction.

- Uncertainty reduction theory explains that how we communicate and what we learn through interactions in a relationship will lead to increases or decreases in liking depending on whether those interactions make us feel more or less certainty about the other person.

149

- Social penetration theory explains that we reveal personal information gradually, over time, and that the rewards we get out of the relationship are weighed against the costs of being in the relationship to determine whether or not we want to become closer.
- Hyperpersonal communication incorporates concepts from uncertainty reduction theory and social penetration theory, and explains that we disclose more via computer-mediated communication (CMC) compared to face-to-face interactions (FtF), and we are also more selective in our self-presentation, thus leading to an increased sense of certainty, liking, and intimacy.

Thus, online relationship development is different from face-to-face relationship formation for several reasons, and so we will ground our discussion of mediated relationship development in the **hyperpersonal communication** perspective. Hyperpersonal communication is marked by being more personal earlier in relationship formation and developing an increased sense of closeness compared to face-to-face relationship development.

💬 OVERVIEW OF RELATIONSHIP DEVELOPMENT THEORIES

MAIN IDEA

Uncertainty reduction theory focuses on initial interactions and explains that we feel a lot of uncertainty in our first encounters with people and so we communicate to try to reduce our feelings of uncertainty. **Social penetration theory** takes a longer view of relationship development, and asserts that relationships become closer and more personal through gradually increasing self-disclosure. **Self-disclosure** is when we reveal personal information about ourselves to other people. Hyperpersonal communication brings together some concepts and tenants from these theories by explaining that some of the features of mediated communication, such as the ability to carefully edit what we say and manage how we present ourselves, may make us disclose more personal information earlier in the relationship and feel closer to the other person more quickly when we form relationships online.

KEY ASSUMPTIONS OF UNCERTAINTY REDUCTION THEORY
(BERGER & CALABRESE, 1975)

Uncertainty reduction theory is a somewhat controversial theory because it is **axiomatic**, which means that it has very clear and specific axioms, or assumptions, about causes and effects (see the table below summarizing the axioms). Berger and Calabrese argued that feelings of uncertainty are a primary *motivation* for communication behavior in initial interactions.

- Interactions follow developmental stages, from a norm-driven **entry** phase where we tend to be more guarded and controlled by social conventions, to the **personal** phase wherein we exchange our feelings and attitudes more spontaneously, and ending at an **exit** phase, where we indicate to each other whether or not we would like to meet again and perhaps make plans to do so.
- People want to reduce uncertainty in interactions because they want to be able to *explain* and *predict* other people's behaviors. Recall from attribution theory that we make internal

and external attributions and that those explanations of our own and others' behaviors then affect how we interact. Berger and Calabrese reasoned that attributional certainty helps us understand people, thus we should be more comfortable interacting with them when we feel certain about their attributes.

- Because we don't have a basis for expectations of the other person early on, we tend to **reciprocate** their verbal and nonverbal behaviors. Put another way, we tend to mimic people's verbal and nonverbal cues when we are uncertain.

- We use **information seeking** to learn about the other person. There are three types of information seeking: interactive, active, and passive information seeking. **Interactive strategies** are when we converse with the person so as to learn about him or her. **Active strategies** are when we talk to others about a person so that we can learn about him or her. Passive strategies, which are especially easy online, include observing how a person interacts with others to learn about him or her.

- As we get to know another person, we may discover that we have a lot in common, share social networks, or find that he or she is nonverbally very open and welcoming. Similarities, overlapping networks, and verbal and nonverbal affiliativeness can help reduce uncertainty and increase liking.

Summary of the Axioms of Uncertainty Reduction Theory:	
Initial Feelings and Behaviors	**Effects**
Feeling uncertain	Decreases the intimacy of self-disclosure
	Decreases liking of the other person
	Increases information seeking
	Increases reliance on reciprocity
Verbal communication	Decreases uncertainty, which increases verbal communication
Nonverbal closeness/warmth	Decreases uncertainty, which increases nonverbal closeness
Discover similarities	Decreases uncertainty
Discover shared social networks	Decreases uncertainty

Thinking back to our discussion of attraction, we see some intersections between uncertainty reduction theory and the research on attraction and propinquity. Recall, for example, that there is some evidence to support the importance of perceived similarity and matching in initial attraction. Also, we discussed how nonverbal immediacy can increase attractiveness. Thus, some of the assumptions of uncertainty reduction theory fit well with the research on initial attraction.

Though some aspects of uncertainty reduction theory fit well with what we have discussed so far in this book in terms of our tendency to make attributions and form expectations in situations and the types of things that attract people to others, the theory does have some detractors. Social penetration theory focuses on the stages of relationship development and focuses on rewards and costs as determinants of closeness.

1. *Relationships develop through stages of self-disclosure.* During these stages, self-disclosure becomes more intimate.
   a. Orientation: We begin by disclosing peripheral, or basic details about ourselves.
   b. Exploratory: We slowly disclose more personal information about ourselves.
   c. Affect Exchange: We disclose our personal feelings, beliefs, and attitudes.
   d. Stable Exchange: We disclose intimate details about ourselves that are central to our sense of self.
   e. Depenetration: This occurs when we move backward in the relationship stages, or when we terminate a relationship.

2. *Self-disclosure varies in depth.* **Disclosure depth** refers to how personal, or intimate, the details are that we self-disclose. Notice in the stages discussed above that the intimacy of the disclosure gradually increases. This is an increase in disclosure depth over the course of relationship development.

3. *Self-disclosure varies in breadth.* **Disclosure breadth** refers to the number of topics we cover in our disclosures. Initially, in the orientation and exploratory phases, we disclose information on a broad range of topics (e.g., age, where we are from, occupation, some personal history, attitudes about a range of topics, etc.). As disclosure becomes more personal (i.e., increases in depth), the range of topics we disclose about decreases (i.e., decreases in breadth).

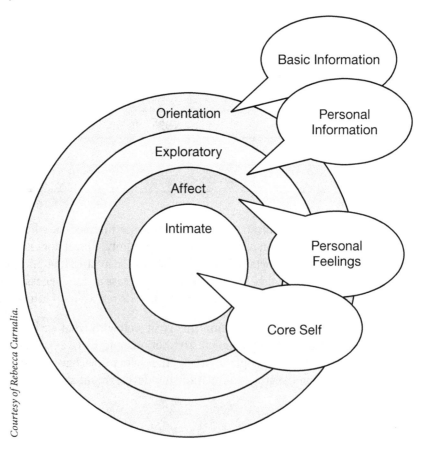

Courtesy of Rebecca Curnalia.

Think of social penetration as gradually revealing layers of yourself to people: we start by disclosing *a lot* of *basic* information, then move on to disclose *many* personal details, then reveal *some* of our personal feelings, and, in our most intimate relationships, reveal a *few* of our most intimate details.

4. *Self-disclosure is reciprocal in depth and breadth.* Generally, our expectation is that people will reciprocate the depth (how personal) and breadth (range of topics) of our self-disclosure. So if I disclose how I feel on a topic, I expect the other person to also disclose how he or she feels on that topic or a similarly personal topic.

5. *Self-disclosure is based on assessment of rewards and costs.* One thing that influences how likely we are to become more intimate in a relationship, and thus disclose more to promote closeness, is the rewards versus costs of that relationship. **Rewards** are those benefits, or needs that are fulfilled, in a relationship. **Costs** are the drawbacks, sacrifices, and investments required for a relationship. We will discuss rewards and costs more in the next chapter. Notice, though, that rewards and costs are a recurring theme in theories of message interpretation (like expectancy violation theory), attraction (such as the instrumentality principle and social and task attraction), and now again in theories of relationship development.

 Insight into Innovation Activity: Self-Check the Breadth and Depth of your Disclosure. Look at IMs, texts, or private mediated messages you have recently exchanged with a close friend. Code those messages for breadth (the number of topics covered) and depth (how personal the topics are: basic demographic details, personal details, insight into attitudes and feeling, insight into your core self). What does this tell you about how close you are with this person? Did you think that the disclosures were different via CMC compared to what you would have disclosed FtF? How so and why?

UNCERTAINTY REDUCTION AND SOCIAL PENETRATION ONLINE: HYPERPERSONAL COMMUNICATION (WALTHER, 1996)

So uncertainty reduction may be one motivation for information-seeking, and rewards and costs may be a motivation for seeking closeness through self-disclosure. Do these motivations and communication patterns fit with what we have observed in mediated relationship development? In general, both information-seeking and disclosure appear to be more rapid via CMC compared to FTF. Also, features of technology, like **asynchronicity** (the fact that CMC allows for delays in responses) and the absence of nonverbal cues, can make people feel more certain and closer via mediated interactions.

CMC interactions are hyperpersonal. Hyperpersonal communication is the idea that CMC is more "socially desirable" compared to similar FtF interactions. This happens for four reasons:

1. *The receiver forms an idealized perception of the other.*
2. *The sender optimizes his or her self-presentation using the affordances of CMC.* The reduced nonverbal and visual cues via CMC give us more control over others' impressions of us. We are able to more carefully construct our messages via CMC, which can make us seem more attractive and rewarding than we really are, or at least allows us to present the best possible impression of ourselves.
3. *Asynchronous channels have affordances that promote idealized perceptions and allow for selective self-presentation.* CMC allows us to interact and respond in our own time, thus

diminishing the time constraints and demands on our attention that are common in relationships. Because of these reduced time constraints, we have more control over CMC interactions and can respond more thoughtfully.

4. *The combination of idealized perceptions, selective self-presentation, and channel affordances create an intensification loop* that leads to mediated relationships that feel more intimate and more intense than FtF relationships. Intensification loops happen when we a) form an impression of a person, b) communicate with him/her according to that perception, which in turn c) affects how he/she communicates, and thus d) we receive messages confirming our perceptions.

I am covering uncertainty reduction, social penetration, and hyperpersonal communication in one chapter because uncertainty reduction and social penetration both informed the development of the hyperpersonal explanation of interpersonal CMC. If we are forming idealized perceptions of the other person via CMC, and the other person confirms these idealized perceptions, then that person will seem rewarding and our uncertainty should be reduced. Both uncertainty reduction theory and social penetration theory, therefore, predict that we would like that person more and communicate more intimately with him or her. CMC also reduces the costs of a relationship because it occurs on our own time, and thus we invest less in the initial relationship.

This is not to say that these three theories are the same. There are some key differences between these theories, particularly in terms of the motivations that drive communication early in relationship development and the specific type of communication described by the theory. Hyperpersonal, for example, doesn't speak directly to our motivation for closeness, though selective and careful self-presentation can be interpreted as a motivation (we want to be attractive to others). But, hyperpersonal does incorporate elements of both uncertainty reduction (i.e., information-seeking and feelings of intimacy and closeness) and uncertainty reduction theory (i.e., breadth and depth of self-disclosure).

Theory	Motivation for Communication	How to Achieve Intimacy
Uncertainty Reduction	We want to reduce uncertainty; Predict and explain others' behavior	Information seeking; nonverbal warmth/closeness
Social Penetration Theory	We want to maximize rewards and reduce costs; Manage privacy needs	Increasingly intimate self-disclosure
Hyperpersonal Communication	Selective self-presentation	Selective self-disclosure and careful message construction due to channel affordances

The hyperpersonal model for CMC relationships also has implications for both uncertainty reduction (Ramirez et al., 2002) and for social penetration processes (Walther, 1996). Specifically, "CMC liberates communicators to seek information in new and unique ways" (Ramirez et al., 2002, p. 219). People also tend to disclose more via interpersonal CMC compared to FtF. For example, in an experiment where people interacted with strangers either FtF or via CMC, Tidwell and Walther (2002) found that strangers who met for the first time via CMC:

- asked more questions (direct strategies for uncertainty reduction)
- self-disclosed more (interactive strategies for uncertainty reduction leading to deeper social penetration)
- were seen as more effective when they asked questions
- asked each other more intimate, or personal questions
- reported feeling more impaired by the setting
- overcame uncertainty in their attributions for the other person so that, in the end, confidence in their attributions were similar to the FtF interactants

Courtesy of Rebecca Curnalia.

The Hyperpersonal Intensification Loop

EXAMPLE OF THEORY IN WEB 2.0: ONLINE RELATIONSHIP TRAJECTORY FROM SWIPING RIGHT, TO IMING, CALLING, AND MEETING FTF

Looking at the research that has been conducted on self-disclosure via CMC versus FtF, there seems to be support for the idea that people disclose more frequently via CMC (Nguyen, Bin, & Campbell, 2012). This increased frequency helps people overcome the limitations of mediated channels, so that ultimately they end up with a similar sense of certainty as FtF interactants. On the other hand, disclosure depth (how personal the self-disclosures are) seems to depend on whether or not we know the person in real life, and we seem to be more willing to disclose more personal details with people that we have known for longer periods of time and we may prefer to disclose more intimate information FtF. Thus, the rapid nature of hyperpersonal communication via CMC may be most evident in new relationships where disclosures are less personal and intimate.

If we take a step back from the research, it makes sense that online interactions would require more disclosure early in a relationship. We get a lot of information about people from their nonverbals, as expectancy violations theory explained. When we meet someone in person, we see his or her height, body type, and other physical characteristics, and we can infer his or her status, wealth, and even social capital from his or her appearance and mannerisms. Thus, via mediated channels where there are not as many nonverbal cues to observe and learn from, we have to convey those details to the other person through information-seeking and self-disclosure. So rather than seeing that a person is in his or her mid-forties and middle class, we would ask his or her age, occupation, and so on, and he or she would probably disclose information that reveals social class. As a result, those early stages of relationship development via CMC require a lot of questions and disclosures to convey information that would otherwise be quickly inferred during an FtF chat.

Insight into Innovation Activity: Compare Meeting FtF versus Online. Take a look at the two images below and imagine you were meeting this man for the first time. If you picked him up at his place, as in the picture on the left, what would you infer about him? Now look at the hypothetical online profile on the right. What would you have to ask him via text or IM to get the same information that you would get visually by meeting face-to-face?

Meeting Face to Face (FtF)

Copyright © Elena Elisseeva/Shutterstock.com

CMC Profile

JD, 45

About JD:

I'm John Doe, but go by JD. I'm starting a business and looking for someone who wants to be part of that adventure! Must love dogs, outdoors, and sports.

Copyright © Elena Elisseeva/Shutterstock.com

METHODS FOR STUDYING INTERPERSONAL RELATIONSHIP DEVELOPMENT

Experiments. Hyperpersonal communication, much like uncertainty reduction and social penetration, is typically explored using experiments. Researchers may compare FtF and CMC interactions between strangers, such as Tidwell and Walther's (2002) study. This is in keeping with the lab studies conducted to test the assumptions of social penetration theory where people would interact with either someone they knew well or someone they didn't know. Both experimental methods involve two groups of people being observed when they interact (acquainted/unacquainted or FtF/Mediated). Researchers then code interactions by counting messages such as the number of self-disclosures, the depth of self-disclosures, the number of questions asked, and the types of questions asked. They will also often manipulate attractiveness through the use of photos, researcher confederates (i.e., people trained to covertly participate in the experiment), and avatars, or measure attractiveness using scales such as McCroskey's attractiveness scale (see the previous chapter). The researchers then look for differences in disclosure and information-seeking between the two experimental groups, and differences in liking, closeness, attributional certainty, or attraction to determine if they interacted differently and what the effects of those differences are in terms of relationship development.

Experiments allow researchers to control for factors like how well people know each other and the specific affordances of mediated channels. For example, if we wanted to see how the introduction of more nonverbal cues increases or decreases self-disclosure and attraction, we could design an experiment where people either interacted for the first time via FtF, FaceTime (video chat), iMessage (texting with images, emoticons, and video attachments), or just text messages. We could record their interactions, code for the breadth and depth of disclosure and information-seeking, then ask them about their sense of physical, social, and task attraction toward the other person. By comparing groups' interactions and attraction, we could see whether adding affordances to mediated channels confirms the assumptions of hyperpersonal communication.

Surveys. Surveys are also used to assess people's uncertainty and disclosure via CMC. In surveys, people self-report their use of CMC and answer questions about how much they disclose and how personal their disclosures are. In a review of research on self-disclosure that compared CMC to FtF disclosure, Nguyen, Bin, and Campbell (2012) found that surveys and experiments tended to support the hyperpersonal perspective: people disclosed about more topics via CMC. On the other hand, the findings about the depth, or intimacy of self-disclosure, were mixed. Experiments tended to suggest more depth via CMC; surveys tended to find no difference in disclosure depth between CMC and FtF.

APPLIED RESEARCH: THE ONLINE SELF-DISCLOSURE/PRIVACY PARADOX

Taken together, these theories suggest that learning information about another person through information-seeking and self-disclosure drives certainty and closeness, and people are compelled to self-disclose more online via social network posts, blogs, chat/IM, and in virtual groups. But this comes with some dangers as well. Disclosure via CMC, whether it is a photo on Instagram, a private text message, or a check-in on Foursquare, can make people vulnerable to stalking, predators, and cyberbullies. Thus, we need to balance our needs for closeness *and* privacy online.

Trust is central to self-disclosure and interpersonal closeness. Consider, for example, the following indicators of interpersonal solidarity, or interpersonal closeness, adapted from Wheeless' (1976) work on disclosure and trust:

1. Feeling very close to each other
2. Him/her having an influence on my behaviors
3. Completely trusting him/her
4. Feeling similar about most things
5. Disclosing both good and bad information to him/her
6. Understanding each other
7. He/she discloses both good and bad information
8. Not distrusting of him/her
9. Liking him/her more than most other people I know
10. Frequently interacting with him/her
11. Feeling love for him/her
12. Understanding who he/she really is
13. Interacting more with him/her than with other people
14. Feeling close to him/her
15. Having a lot in common with him/her
16. Doing helpful things for each other
17. Having a private way of communicating with each other
18. Feeling very close to him/her

Notice that the indicators of closeness include open disclosure, understanding, similarity, and trust. When we disclose to others, whether FtF or online, we are *trusting* them with our personal information.

It seems counterintuitive that people would be more trusting of other people online, and therefore disclose more via CMC. Some features of CMC make it *less risky* to disclose information online, such as anonymity and the "**passing stranger**" phenomenon that suggests that people will disclose more to people they are unlikely to ever see again (Gibbs, Ellison, & Heino, 2006). This sense of anonymity may have a disinhibiting effect, leading people to disclose more information earlier in a relationship. As we disclose more, we may feel more similar and more certain about the other person, and therefore trust him or her more when we interact via CMC. This is a benefit of CMC, as we can develop close relationships, feel liked, be validated, and receive social support from others. On the other hand, this can also be a drawback, as our sense of trust in the other person may be misplaced.

THE DARK SIDE OF CMC RELATIONSHIPS: OVER-DISCLOSURE, SEXTING, AND SCAMS

Though the threat of online predators may be exaggerated in mass media (see, for example, the chapter on cultivation theory), it is also dangerous to make certain personal information public by sharing videos and pictures, creating social network profiles containing personal information, and even texting and IMing personal information and pictures. On the other hand, as uncertainty reduction and social penetration theory suggest, using CMC to interact with friends does improve the quality of teenagers' friendships as teens feel more comfortable self-disclosing via mediated channels (Valkenburg & Peter, 2009). Thus, teens need to learn to balance their privacy needs with their needs for closeness to use CMC for relationship development.

Over-Disclosure. A content analysis of teenagers' blogs suggests that they are revealing too much information about themselves that makes them potential targets for online sexual predators and cyberbullies (Huffaker, 2006). More than half of teenage bloggers revealed their first name, age, location, and contact information on their blogs. Almost half of teenage bloggers also discuss their romantic lives, such as crushes, relationships, and sexual experiences. If we think of these findings as whole, teens are identifiable via their blogs and they are posting personal feelings via their blogs. This can make them targets for predators who would know their vulnerabilities and how to find them. This also has implications for cyberbullies, who can exploit the self-disclosures that teen bloggers make online.

Copyright © Lighthunter/Shutterstock.com

Some of the over-disclosure of personal information online appears to be a response to online norms for teens' behaviors (Mesch & Beker, 2010). Teens who use the internet more, are older, and who report social norms supportive of online disclosure tend to disclose more personal information, create online profiles, and share photos online. Teens apparently notice these different norms for self-disclosure and uncertainty reduction online, and respond to them as they use mediated channels to form and express their identities, find and maintain friendships, and interact with potential dating partners.

Adults aren't immune to the potential disinhibiting effect leading to self-disclosure via blogs. Though adult bloggers who provided personally identifying information tended to disclose less, Hollenbaugh and Everett (2013) found that bloggers who posted pictures of themselves tended to disclose more personal information.

Sexting. One example of the effects of social norms on teens CMC disclosure is sexting. **Sexting** is when people send sexually explicit photos and messages to other people via text messaging. Pew (2015) found that 17 percent of teenagers aged 12 to 17 years have received a nude, or nearly nude, photo via text message (read the report here: http://www.pewinternet.org/2009/12/15/teens-and-sexting/).

Norms for sexting are clearly very different compared to norms for sexual expression and intimacy in FtF contexts. As you might expect, the need to be liked and to be popular may be key motivations for sexting. Teenagers who have a more intense need for popularity tend to be more likely to sext (Vanden Abeele et al., 2014). Also, for girls, sexting was related to one's popularity with boys but *not* with one's popularity among other girls. This may be because boys tend to pressure girls to participate in sexting, and girls tend to be judged harshly for participating whereas boys are not (Lippman & Campbell, 2014). Thus, there are norms and pressures to engage in sexting, but serious social risks for doing so. Girls, in particular, experienced a double-bind in terms of sexting because they were seen as prudish if they did not participate, but were seen as "slutty" if they did participate.

Eliminating teenage sexting and over-disclosure may be increasingly difficult, but it is also increasingly important. Teens who sext have been charged with possession of child pornography (Galonos, 2009). And sext messages can easily be shared with other people and posted on the Internet.

Though conventional wisdom may suggest that being a protective parent will prevent teenagers from engaging in risky mediated behaviors like sexting, research suggests that direct control over teenagers' phone use doesn't reduce sexting behavior (Campbell & Park, 2014). Rather, the more effective strategy for reducing sexting behaviors appears to be parents using mobile technology to connect with teenagers.

Romance Scams. The tendency to disclose too much, the dangers of excessive disclosure, and a hyperpersonal sense of closeness and intimacy extends to adults as well. For example, the *New York Times* (2015) reported that online scammers were using dating websites to find victims, typically women over age 50. The pattern outlined in the article is in keeping with what the theories in this chapter suggest: people meet on a dating website like Match.com, then shift their interactions to e-mail or IM where they build a sense of trust, and those who were swindled via online love connections felt "a bond that may not be physical but that is intense and enveloping" (para. 5). The connections we build through self-disclosure are intimate, personal, and very real, even when they begin and develop online. Indeed, we may find ourselves feeling a sense of certainty about our online friends and romantic partners that can make us vulnerable in many ways.

THE BRIGHT SIDE OF CMC RELATIONSHIPS: INFORMATION, CLOSENESS, AND SOCIAL SUPPORT

Though use of CMC to seek and establish interpersonal relationships does have some potential dangers such as vulnerability to predators, dangerous sexual behaviors, and vulnerability to scammers, there are also some unique benefits of using CMC in the formation of relationships. There are many tools we can use to learn about others online, and thereby reduce our uncertainty. Also, the disinhibiting effects of mediated channels may increase feelings of closeness.

Reducing uncertainty online. The features of social networking sites provide numerous opportunities to reduce uncertainty (Antheunis, Valkenburg, & Peter, 2010). For example, we can use passive strategies to observe the people we friend or follow. We can also use features of the sites to interact with people in our social network, which is an effective way to reduce uncertainty. When we meet someone via a dating site, we often use both interactive and passive uncertainty reduction strategies, particularly when we have privacy concerns or are skeptical about people representing themselves honestly (Gibbs, Ellison, & Lai, 2011). We look for **warranting information**, or information that we find online that is not generated by the person we are trying to find out about. For example, a post on someone's Facebook timeline by their real-life friend or family member would have high warranting value because it is information from someone who knows them and it is not something that he or she strategically disclosed.

As we find out information about our social connections through interactions, creeping on their profiles, and taking in warranting information, we can begin to feel more certain and thus closer to him or her. This sense of closeness can help us reduce uncertainty, increase liking, and promote increased self-disclosure to bring us even closer to others.

Disclosing information via private CMC: Fulfilling needs for closeness. People use private messages when disclosing more intimate details, and they do this to build close personal relationships with others (Bazarova & Choi, 2014). Experimental research studies suggest that people tend to reciprocate the intimacy of self-disclosures in CMC interactions (Jiang, Bazarova, & Hancock, 2013). In other words, people tend to match their interaction partners in terms of the depth of self-disclosure when they are IMing or texting. Importantly, via CMC, people *perceived* disclosures as more intense, or intimate, compared to those same disclosures via FtF interactions. Thus, based on that *perception* of intimacy, people tended to disclose more intimate details. The amount of self-disclosure and being intentional when disclosing online are related to successful online dating experiences, such as achieving online dating goals and being optimistic about meeting someone online (Gibbs, Ellison, & Heino, 2006). Thus, disclosure via private mediated channels seems to help people fulfill needs for interpersonal closeness through reciprocal, intimate self-disclosure.

Disclosing information via public CMC: Fulfilling social validation needs. People also disclose information publicly, though the reasons for doing so and the resulting disclosures are different from more private mediated channels (Bazarova & Choi, 2014). People disclose less intimate information in status updates, and use them as a way to achieve social validation when other people like their statuses and offer positive comments, and for self-expression or to relieve "pent-up feelings" (p.645). As people feel more validated and closer to others via these types of disclosures, it encourages them to the disclose even more over time (Trepte & Reinecke, 2013). Research suggests that the larger a person's audience via social networks, the more he or she is likely to disclose (Vitak, 2012). On the other hand, as people's social network followers diversify to include friends, family members, work associates, and acquaintances, the more they use the privacy features to control who sees those disclosures. These targeted, but still public, self-disclosures were more honest and intimate, much like private messages sent via CMC. Arguably, though, they may be less validating than public self-disclosures that can garner hundreds of likes.

CONCLUSION

We have covered social penetration theory and its predictions about self-disclosure processes, uncertainty reduction theory and its predictions about uncertainty reduction strategies and closeness, and hyperpersonal communication, which brings together the previous two theories to explain how relationships progress via mediated channels. Taken together, we see that fundamental communication concepts such as self-disclosure breadth and depth and uncertainty reduction are still essential elements of relationship development online. On the other hand, new communication channels have changed how people disclose information about themselves, perceive disclosures, and reduce uncertainty. The affordances of new technologies make it both easier to disclose and reduce uncertainty earlier in relationships, but as we discussed, it also introduces new dangers as people may over disclose or be exploited as a result of a sense of hyperpersonal closeness via CMC.

Thus, on one hand, using CMC to find and develop relationships has so much promise, because we can invest less time upfront in a relationship, manage our self-presentation, and let our guard down. It is also a unique opportunity to build social connections that make us feel validated. But then, on the other hand, it makes us vulnerable as well, as we develop heightened feelings of closeness and trust with others online, and may end up trusting people we should not trust or disclosing too much online, which could make us vulnerable to predators and scammers.

Clearly, research on relationship development via CMC has many new avenues to explore and the stakes are relatively high for real people who are increasingly moving to mediated interpersonal relationships. For example, though there are new ways to reduce uncertainty online, such as Googling someone or checking out their social media profiles for warranting information, these options for building trust and closeness depend on other people providing complete and accurate basic information when we meet them online. But, as we went over in the discussion of over-disclosure, providing information that makes us personally identifiable also makes us potential targets for predators. Thus, it is inadvisable to provide identifying information early in a relationship or in a public forum, and yet that very information is essential to help people reduce their uncertainty.

When forming relationships online, then, a healthy amount of skepticism and realism may be in order. Hyperpersonal communication is as much a description of CMC relationship development as it is a warning about relying too much on perceptions and attributions: we increase attributional certainty through information-seeking and reciprocal self-disclosure, but people are responding to those very attributions and, thus, our perception of them may be more favorable, and our feelings of closeness more intense, as a result of our own feelings and behaviors.

ASSIGNMENTS

1. **Are we facing a "dating apocalypse"?** Read Sales' (2015) *Vanity Fair* article, "Tinder and the Dawn of the Dating Apocalypse": http://www.vanityfair.com/culture/2015/08/tinder-hook-up-culture-end-of-dating. Please be aware the article discusses sexual culture and contains profanity.
   a. Does the dating culture as described by Sales support or challenge the assumptions of uncertainty reduction theory? How so?
   b. Does the dating culture as described by Sales fit with social penetration theory's assumptions of how relationships progress? Why or why not?
   c. Could hyperpersonal communication explain the rise of the "hook up culture" via online dating sites and apps? Why or why not?
   d. Thinking about these three theories, how well does communication theory explain modern relationship processes? What should be done to study and explain the changing nature of romantic relationships?

2. **Myths about Online Dating.** Take a look at Rudder's "5 Myths About Online Dating" from *Washington Post*'s Business Insider: http://www.businessinsider.com/here-are-the-5-myths-about-online-dating-2015-10. In particular, consider his review of "Love is Blind Day" on OkCupid (Myth 5).
   a. Use uncertainty reduction theory to explain why users may have been upset when OKCupid removed all profile pictures.
      i. How are profile pictures related to uncertainty?
      ii. In the absence of profile pictures, what other options do users have for reducing uncertainty?
   b. Rudder explained that, when the pictures were removed from profiles, people's conversations changed.
      i. In terms of social penetration theory, how might the absence of pictures on profiles change people's self-disclosure during initial interactions?
      ii. Would removing profile pictures be better for daters or worse? Why?

REFERENCES

Seminal Texts:

Altman, I., & Taylor, D. A. (1973). Social penetration: The development of interpersonal relationships. New York: Holt, Rinehart, and Winston.

Berger, C. R., & Calabrese, R. J. (1975). Some explorations in initial interaction and beyond: Toward a developmental theory of interpersonal communication. *Human Communication Research, 1,* 99–112.

Walther, J. B. (1996). Computer-mediated communication: Impersonal, interpersonal, and hyperpersonal interaction. *Communication Research, 23*(1), 3–43.

Academic Articles:

Bazarova, N. N., & Choi, Y. H. (2014). Self-disclosure in social media: Extending the functional approach to disclosure motivations and characteristics on social network sites [An earlier]. *Journal Of Communication, 64*(4), 635–657.

Campbell, S. W., & Park, Y. J. (2014). Predictors of mobile sexting among teens: Toward a new explanatory framework. *Mobile Media & Communication, 2*(1), 20–39.

Gibbs, J. L., Ellison, N. B., & Heino, R. D. (2006). Self-presentation in online personals: The role of anticipated future interaction, self-disclosure, and perceived success in Internet dating. *Communication Research, 33*(2), 152–177.

Gibbs, J. L., Ellison, N. B., & Lai, C. (2011). First comes love, then comes Google: An investigation of uncertainty reduction strategies and self-disclosure in online dating. *Communication Research, 38*(1), 70–100.

Hollenbaugh, E. E., & Everett, M. K. (2013). The effects of anonymity on self-disclosure in blogs: An application of the online disinhibition effect. *Journal of Computer-Mediated Communication, 18*(3), 283–302.

Jiang, L. C., Bazarova, N. N., & Hancock, J. T. (2013). From perception to behavior: Disclosure reciprocity and the intensification of intimacy in computer-mediated communication. *Communication Research, 40*(1), 125–143.

Kang, T., & Hoffman, L. H. (2011). Why would you decide to use an online dating site? Factors that lead to online dating. *Communication Research Reports, 28*(3), 205–213.

Lippman, J. R., & Campbell, S. W. (2014). Damned if you do, damned if you don't…if you're a girl: Relational and normative contexts of adolescent sexting in the United States. *Journal of Children & Media, 8*(4), 371–386.

Mesch, G. S., & Beker, G. (2010). Are norms of disclosure of online and offline personal information associated with the disclosure of personal information online? *Human Communication Research, 36*(4), 570–592.

Nguyen, M., Bin, Y. S. B., Campbell, A. (2012). Comparing online and offline self-disclosure: A systematic review. *Cyberpsychology, Behavior, and Social Networking, 15*, 103–111.

Ramirez, A. Jr., Walther, J. B., Burgoon, J. K., & Sunnafrank, M. (2002). Information seeking strategies, uncertainty, and computer-mediated communication: Towards a conceptual model. *Human Communication Research, 28*, 213–228.

Tidwell, L. C., & Walther, J. B. (2002). Computer-mediated communication effects on disclosure, impressions, and interpersonal evaluations: Getting to know one another a bit at a time. *Human Communication Research, 28*, 317–348.

Trepte, S., & Reinecke, L. (2013). The reciprocal effects of social network site use and the disposition for self-disclosure: A longitudinal study. *Computers in Human Behavior, 29*, 1102–1112.

Valkenburg, P. M., & Peter, J. (2009). The effects of instant messaging on the quality of adolescents' existing friendships: A longitudinal study. *Journal of Communication, 59*, 79–97.

Vanden Abeele, M., Campbell, S. W., Eggermont, S., & Roe, K. (2014). Sexting, mobile porn use, and peer group dynamics: Boys' and girls' self-perceived popularity, need for popularity, and perceived peer pressure. *Media Psychology, 17*(1), 6–33.

Vitak, J. (2012). The impact of context collapse and privacy on social network site disclosures. *Journal of Broadcasting & Electronic Media, 56*(4), 451–470.

RELATIONSHIP DIALECTICS

🗨 INTRODUCTION

It goes without saying that even those relationships that make it through the early stages of formation can be difficult to manage and maintain. There is, for example, a "Cost of Caring" (Pew, 2015). That is to say, maintaining relationships, including maintaining relationships via social networks and computer-mediated communication (CMC), can introduce stress into our lives. So why, then, do we still maintain relationships? Because we want social connection! So, we may want to be free from the burdens and stress of relationships, but at the same time, we crave the close personal relationships with other people even though those relationships bring with them challenges and obligations.

According to relationship dialectics, we all face tensions, such as wanting connection to others and wanting autonomy, and wanting to be open with others while also wanting privacy. One aspect of maintaining interpersonal relationships is managing these dialectical tensions, or these contradictory needs we all have. These tensions are present in all types of long-term interpersonal relationships, including dating, marriage, families, and friendships.

MAIN IDEA

Relationship dialects focuses on the *conflicting needs* we have in relationship: the need to be close to others, yet maintain our individuality; the need to have stability in our lives, but also the need for excitement and change; and the need to be open with others, but also protect our privacy. These competing needs are evidenced in **dialectics**, or interpersonal communication within a relationship.

OVERVIEW OF RELATIONSHIP DIALECTICS THEORY
(BAXTER & MONTGOMERY, 1996)

Dialectics theory focuses on discourses, or how people communicate in a way that reveals the tensions and contradictions we all feel. Put another way, real life and real love is messy, and sometimes we want two things at once and those two things are inconsistent with each other. Baxter and Montgomery proposed that "a healthy relationship is one in which the parties manage to satisfy both oppositional demands" (p. 6). There are four things we look at when exploring the discourses in a relationship to understand tensions and relationship changes that result:

1. *Contradictions are central to personal relationships.* These oppositional demands, or **contradictions**, are central to human relationships and are revealed in people's communication. Contradictions are opposite, or opposing wants and needs. These opposite wants and needs are **interdependent**. That is to say, we understand the need for certainty, in part, based on our understanding of uncertainty. Having contradictory wants and needs leads to **tension**, where relationship partners continually try to balance contradictory needs.

2. *Tensions lead to ongoing changes in relationships.* These changes can occur within a relationship in an ongoing cycle, referred to as a **spiral**. In spirals, we manage contradictory needs which brings up new contradictions. We then manage those tensions but this brings up still more tensions, and so on.

3. *We affect and are affected by these changes in our relationships.* This is referred to as **praxis** in the theory, or the idea that we are actors as we make communication choices, but we are, in turn, affected by those choices as they change our relationships.

4. *Thus, we must look at relationships as a whole, or in totality, to observe contradictions.* People don't always recognize tensions as they arise, but there is evidence of tensions in people's communication. Thus, we look at relationships as a complicated system of inter-related people and, thus interrelated contradictions. These contradictions are both internal (within the relationship) and external (with the larger social environment).

For example, say you're getting close to graduating from college and have to start applying for jobs. This can bring up all kinds of dialectical tensions: you may feel the need to stay close to family, friends, and a romantic partner, but may also feel the need to travel to new places and meet

new people. Thus, you may apply for jobs that are far away, but then, feeling guilty, may not pursue those jobs and instead focus your job search on a specific region near your family. But then, when you take a job in that region, you may still feel wanderlust and look at jobs elsewhere because you still feel that need for change and independence. Perhaps you decide to take an offer somewhere else and move there with your significant other. This can then lead to pressure to travel home for holidays and special events, or may lead to resentment from your partner who may not be happy about the move. It can create tensions within your relationship and between you as a couple and your family or friends.

Copyright © ImageFlow/Shutterstock.com

This is the experience of contradictory needs, wanting closeness and independence, stability and security, but also change and new experiences. It is also a spiral, because making one change brings up tensions that lead to another change and so on. Lastly, this is also praxis, because as you make decisions you are, in turn, affected by those decisions. To observe this spiral and the interplay of contradicting wants and needs that is creating the spiral, we have to look at the relationship as a whole, and see the conflict between the two people in the interpersonal relationship, and also the tension between the couple and the people they are connected to.

There are three broad types of internal and external contradictions, or dialectical tensions, in interpersonal relationships that Baxter and Montgomery observed in their research:

1. **We want stability *and* change.**
   a. *Internal to the relationship:* This manifests itself in many ways, such as wanting people to be dependable, but also getting bored in a relationship; wanting certainty in a relationship, but also wanting to be surprised, and so on.
   b. *External from the relationship:* We may, for example, want stable employment, but become bored with how the routine affects our lives; enjoy participating in family or group rituals (like annual holiday celebrations), but at the same time want to try something new and so on.
2. **We want openness *and* closedness.**
   a. *Internal to the relationship:* This often occurs in our self-disclosure. For example, we may disclose to someone because we want to be open with them and feel closer to them, but at the same time we may want privacy and to protect our deep, dark secrets.
   b. *External from the relationship:* Just as we want to protect our personal privacy, we also want to maintain the privacy of our intimate relationships. For example, we may want to disclose problems or events in our romantic relationship to friends or family members, but at the same time want our relationship to be private.
3. **We want closeness *and* independence.**
   a. *Internal to the relationship:* We want to be interpersonally close to other people, but that means that we give up our autonomy in terms of making decisions and doing certain things. For example, we may value a person and want to be close to him or her, but not want him or her interfering with work and school decisions.
   b. *External from the relationship:* Similarly, we want to be close to our family, friends, and coworkers, but at the same time want our interpersonal relationships to be independent from the influence of others. So, for example, we may feel a sense of obligation to stay close to home during or after college, but at the same time may we may also want the freedom to move away to live someplace we've always dreamed of living or to pursue a career in another region.

MANAGING DIALECTICS

The process of managing dialectics is ongoing. There are several strategies that people use to manage dialectical tensions as they arise in interpersonal relationships. These management tactics can occur and reoccur during the ongoing cycle of managing tensions.

- **Alternation** is prioritizing one need over the other. When deciding where to move after graduation, we may prioritize staying close to a significant other over our independent ambitions, or vice versa. This is prioritizing one side of the dialectic over the other.

- **Denial** is denying that there is tension. This is when we carry on like nothing is wrong, even though we feel tension. So, we may take whatever job we're offered, wherever it is, and deny that there is any tension between work and family.

- **Segmentation** is focusing on a tension in one context, but not another. Thus, we may decide that there is an independence/closeness tension surrounding holidays and deal with that one context, but not recognize or deal with the independence/closeness tension surrounding where we buy a home. This is dealing with one context (holidays) but not another (daily life).

- **Disorientation** is when we become overwhelmed, and may include leaving the relationship. In this scenario, we may have fights, withdraw from others, or even walk away from the relationship. Here too, in the tension about whether to stay at home or move away, the choice may be so overwhelming that we withdraw from family, and may even sever ties with the people who are "holding us back."

- **Balance** is compromising. So, maybe you don't move across the country, but you may decide to stay "within driving distance" of extended family and have a job search within a few hundred miles' radius. This balances the need to move, and the need to be close to family.

- **Reaffirmation** is accepting the tension. We choose to do one thing or another, and accept that tension does and will continue to exist. I think of this as the "it is what it is" approach to handling tensions. Maybe you decide to move (or to stay) and just accept that it will never be perfect.

- **Recalibration** is when we reframe the tension to change how we think about it. We can, for example, make moving away to pursue a career more acceptable to ourselves and others by *reframing* the tension: we may call ourselves a "professional couple" to reframe the issue.

- **Integration** is arguably rare, and it involves meeting both party's needs without having to compromise. For example, you may decide to move away but visit home every couple of months, which keeps you close to family while also allowing for your individualism. Or you may decide to stay close to home, but travel extensively in your free time or take a job that involves a lot of travel to meet your needs for closeness and independence.

💬 METHODS IN RELATIONSHIP DIALECTICS RESEARCH

Relationship dialectics is a *descriptive* theory because it "describes a small set of conceptual assumptions" rather than offering axioms or testable propositions (Baxter & Montgomery, 1996, p. 6). We cannot take RDT and predict whether a relationship will thrive or fail, for example. Baxter and Montgomery were clear in their explanation of the theory that interpersonal relationships are messy, complicated, and constantly changing. Also, something as complex as wanting two conflicting elements is difficult to capture with scale measures and other, quantitative social scientific methods. Rather, they recommend a dialectic approach.

The dialectic approach looks at people's messages and descriptions of their relationships for evidence of tensions and management techniques. People would not typically say, "I want stability and change." Rather, they might say something like, "I appreciate knowing she'll always be there for me" and then, later, say something like "sometimes it gets boring." This implies tension between desires for certainty and spontaneity. Thus, relationship dialectics theory researchers often employ qualitative research methods, particularly interviews where people describe their relationships and researchers analyze transcripts for evidence of internal and external tensions (Baxter & Braithwaite, 2010). Less often, researchers analyze focus group discussions of relationships or recorded interactions between relationship partners. In interviews, researchers often ask people about their "ideal" relationship and about their "real" relationship with others. Then they closely analyze people's discussions for a) the discourses, or meanings people have for their relationships; b) competing or conflicting discourses about the relationship; and c) the meaning of those competing discourses.

Insight into Innovation Activity: Recognize your Dialectical Tensions. Answer the following questions about an interpersonal friendship:

1. What is an "ideal" friendship like? What does "being friends" mean to you?

2. Describe a specific, close friendship that you have. What is it like? What do you enjoy doing together? What makes it unique? What challenges does the friendship face?

3. Compare the "ideal" friendship to your "real" friendship. How are the two different? What tensions, or contradictions, are revealed in your description of an ideal friendship versus your real friendship?

Though relationship dialectics theory does outline clear, useful concepts that we can apply to our real-life relationships, some have argued that it isn't a real theory because it isn't testable (for a review, see Halliwell, 2015). On the other hand, its usefulness is evident in how it can be applied to understand the individual needs and tensions in relationships and how people handle those tensions. It can also be applied to many types of messages, not just interview transcripts. For example, we can look at people's personal blogs, social media posts about their relationships, and online support group posts to see the tensions at play in people's interpersonal relationships. Also, it has been applied to many types of interpersonal relationships and contexts: coworker relationships, social support and bereavement, friendships, family relationships, marriages, dating relationships, blended family relationships, and so on.

APPLYING DIALECTICS: WORK–LIFE BALANCE IN A TELEWORKING WORLD

There are many applications of relationship dialectics, such as explaining the tensions that occur when blending two families through remarriage, the tensions associated with major turning points in relationships such as moving in together or having children, and the tensions associated with close friendships over the course of a lifetime. We will focus here on something that all of us will at one time or another experience, and that you may be experiencing now as you take college courses: the competing needs for career success and personal relationship success.

Yoshimura (2013) describes the demands of family and of work as "functional opposites." That is to say, one interferes with the other in many ways, as one can distract attention and time away from the other. Further complicating work-life tensions, work can also be a place where we make friends and those friendships have their own unique tensions.

Friends at work. Workplace relationships are complex, because there are unique dialectical tensions associated with coworker relationships (Bridge & Baxter, 1992). If you think about it, the role of an "employee" and the role of a "friend" can come with two very distinct sets of expectations, one with a task orientation and the other with a social orientation.

- *Instrumentality—Affection.* Coworker friends offer us access to information, help with work, and provide emotional support at work. Thus, they can be instrumental in our professional success. Also, given the fact that we see them often and bond with them, we also develop affection for our coworker friends.

- *Impartiality—Favoritism.* Of course, there are also some challenges associated with having friendships at work. For example, we expect impartiality in the workplace, but at the same time being "friends" comes with an expectation of favoritism. For example, if you are good friends with your boss, it may be particularly hurtful if he or she honestly reviews your job performance. On the other hand, he or she should not show partiality to you, because that would not be fitting with the expectations of the role.

- *Judgment—Acceptance.* We expect our friends to accept us as we are and to like us for who we are, but at the same time being an employee means that you will be evaluated and judged. Nearly every profession has some form of "annual review" which can bring up tensions between judgment and acceptance among coworker friends.

Because of the potential for unique tensions in workplace relationships, coworker friends use dialectical management techniques like segmentation to focus on one side of the dialectic in one context, and a different end of the dialectic in another context. For example, coworker friends may go out for lunch or to happy hour, and in that context focus on acceptance and expressing liking. On the other hand, in meetings, their focus may be on instrumentality and impartiality. Coworker friends also use integration, particularly when there are fewer tensions experienced.

Though coworker friendships face unique tensions, they are important to people's satisfaction at work. Even people who telework are more committed to their jobs and more satisfied in their jobs when they have social connections with the people at work (Fay & Kline, 2011). In teleworking situations, informal interactions with one's coworkers include being sociable, giving and receiving support, disclosing about one's self, and commiserating about work (Fay, 2011).

Insight into Innovation Example: Working from Home. Check out this research brief about Gajendran et al.'s study here: http://news.illinois.edu/news/14/0918telecommuting_RaviGajendran.html

In what ways do you think teleworking might help us manage dialectical tensions associated with work-life balance?

In what ways might teleworking introduce new dialectical tensions associated with work-life balance?

Using CMC to collaborate with coworker friends is one way to balance coworker tensions. For example, CMC allows for people to connect and collaborate while also maintaining their autonomy. CMC helps people balance the need to complete a task via a more functional channel like e-mail, with their socioemotional needs to stay connected with coworkers (Thompson-Hayes et al., 2009). When we work on a team project via CMC, we can often do our part on our own time, which helps fulfill our need for independence. At the same time, we are working with people that we can interact with socially as well, which can help us fulfill our need for connection.

Research suggests that teleworkers also want to maintain ties with their coworkers, and may actually do more work for the organization because they don't want their coworkers or bosses to feel that they are "taking advantage" of the arrangement (Gajendran, Harrison, & Delaney-Klinger, 2015). When worker–boss relationships are strained, teleworking can actually help improve that relationship. Also, people who telework improve their helpfulness toward and cooperation with workers.

This is not to say that workplace friendships are easy to manage, even via CMC, and not all friendships prove to last indefinitely. Indeed, in terms of workplace friendships that were terminated, several important themes emerged (Sias et al., 2004):

- Coworker friends may have a *personality trait or characteristic that is undesirable* or *disliked*.
- Coworker friends also may have *life events*, such as new relationships beginning or old relationships ending, that divert their attention to or need for the coworker relationship.
- Coworker friends also experience *complications at work* that affect the friendship, such as negative evaluations, reviews, or failure to support each others' opinions or positions.

Work as a distraction from home and family (and vice versa). Much like dialectics theory asserts, work-life balance is an *internal tension* that can occur within a couple, as they negotiate who does what at home, whose career will take the lead, and how they will balance competition for time and attention at work and at home. Also, there is tension between professional couples and their workplaces, which is an *external* tension, as workplace policies and procedures may conflict with the couple's wants, needs, and negotiated roles.

Looking at the role of communication in work-life issues, Kirby and Buzzanell (2014) explained that there are five interrelated sources of work-life tension: policies, norms, ideals, identities, and routines.

Policies are developed by the government or an organization to help employees in their personal lives. For example, the United States has the Family Medical Leave Act, which guarantees full-time employees at large organizations unpaid leave to help care for newly born, adopted, or sick family members. Organizations also develop policies that can help ease the tensions of work-life balance, such as offering flextime and teleworking.

Norms, however, are more difficult to address because they are implicitly communicated within society and within organizations. There are social and organizational norms that can either support work-life balance or undermine it. Things such as how we talk about work-life balance at work and the presence of workplace friendships that offer support can create norms that help us negotiate work-life tensions.

Ideals surrounding workers—how we define an ideal employee—also affect the experience of work-life tension. Recall from the discussion of dialectics theory methods that we consider the "ideal" and then the "real" relationship to discover tensions. This is true at work as well: our perception of an "ideal" employee versus who we are as a "real" employee may reveal conflicting needs. Ideals such as financial success, professionalism, and holding powerful positions at work may lead people to work more. Thus, being an "ideal worker" and an "ideal family member" becomes increasingly impossible.

We learn these ideals, as symbolic interactionism teaches us, through interactions over the course of our lifetimes. American parents talk to and in front of their children about work, mass media promotes a narrow definition of professional success, and even organizational rhetoric and websites communicate expectations for an "ideal worker" who works long hours, values work over personal life, and is personally responsible for work-life balance (Kirby & Buzzanell, 2014, p. 359).

Insight Into Innovation Example: Work-Life Balance and Parental Leave Policies. It may be tempting to think of work-life balance as something of particular concern to women, but research suggests that men feel the need to be both good fathers and provide financial security to their families through work (Duckworth & Buzzanell, 2009). Men described struggles much like women have, such as choosing jobs that allowed them to be with their families more and putting aside personal activities to instead spend time with their families when they were not at work. Also, men reported having a "web of responsibilities," including obligations to their partners, to their children, and within their communities (p. 566).

Indeed, in an article in the *Harvard Business Review*, Josh Levs (2015) explained that new fathers face particularly difficult competing demands from work, home, and norms. Using examples of men who had been professionally punished and even fired for taking time off for their families, Levs points out that it is a combination of workplace norms, cultural norms, business practices, and national laws that exacerbate work-life tensions for men. Specifically, our laws do not guarantee

paid paternity leave. Even employers who do offer leave sometimes punish men who use parental leave by holding them back in their careers. Thus, Levs contends that we have a vicious cycle where men don't always have leave available, may be punished if they take leave, and so the men who do not focus on their families rise to the top and continue the hard line against men's family leave.

For large, successful companies trying to attract top talent, this trend may be changing (Levs, 2015). In 2015, Johnson & Johnson, Virgin, Goldman Sachs, Netflix, and Microsoft (to name a few) announced expanded parental leave policies. Thus, in an era of dual-career couples, companies may be realizing that it is good for the bottom line to offer leave in an effort to attract the best employees. What do you think? What kinds of policies can be enacted to help fathers better balance work and home demands?

People's identities, therefore, are shaped by their work and cultural norms based on gender. For example, working mothers face "identity tensions in navigating the expectations of being (ideal) workers and caregivers" (Kirby & Buzzanell, 2014, p. 361). Indeed, women's professional careers are sometimes framed as a "choice," unlike men's careers, which are an expectation. Thus, professional women often delay getting married and having children, and when they do have children they will sometimes downplay caregiving obligations at work and intentionally prioritize work.

Routines then emerge in families and dual-career couples trying to manage tensions between work obligations and home obligations. Dual-career couples often develop a daily routine to complete tasks, improvise when there are extenuating circumstances, and restructure their routines as life events occur. As we'll discuss in the next chapter, equity can be a major tension, even in dual-career relationships where the couples have a set routine. In particular, women tend to take on more domestic responsibility, even when they have a career. In keeping with the assumption of relationship dialectics, couples can and do modify their routines when tensions arise. They may choose to renegotiate who does what, or try to adjust their expectations for completing tasks to accommodate their partners.

Insight into Innovation Example: "The Mommy Wars" on Battleground Web 2.0. http://ti.me/1tEPlwB

We see the tensions resulting from conflicting ideals, identities, and routines in the "Mommy Wars." Briefly, the Mommy wars is a phenomenon where women, implicitly and explicitly, post on blogs, social media, and websites about "who has it worse" and "who does it better" when comparing stay-at-home moms (SAHM) and moms who work outside the home. Initially, these tensions were expressed dialectically in interactions among and with women who had families. Thompson (1998) put it well in her piece for *The Washington Post*: "behind the scenes,

stay-at-home mothers often criticize office-going moms for neglecting their kids, and working mothers often disparage their at-home counterparts for getting some sort of retro free ride" (para. 12). An article in *Psychology Today* pointed out that a lot of this (real and imagined) tension comes from competing ideals: "Stay-at-home mothers fulfill society's ideals of motherhood but are found lacking when measured against the world of work" and "Mothers with jobs are touchy, too, because to the extent that they fulfill ideals at work, they fail to fulfill ideals of motherhood" (Williams, 2012, para. 4–5).

The Mommy Wars, of course, spilled over into social media. From Pinterest to personal blogs, opinions about what a "good mom" should do, judgments and evaluations of other people's parenting, and ideas for everything from healthy, kid-friendly meals to educational activities and projects are posted everywhere. Though social media, such as Facebook and blogs, could serve as a guide to help parents handle the dialectical tensions inherent in having children, they can also set an impossibly high standard for modern parents.

One movement in 2012 sought to empower parents and relieve the cycle of judgment and social pressure that women face: The Campaign for Judgement-Free Motherhood (http://ctworkingmoms.com/campaign-for-judgement-free-motherhood/). This campaign used blogs, Twitter, and was picked up by other new media such as Upworthy, to share images of mothers who had made very different choices happily coexisting. Essentially, this campaign is modeling prosocial, supportive, nonjudgmental behavior for other mothers and working to stop at least one source of external pressure for modern families: societal and cultural demands for perfection.

Do you think campaigns like this may also help parents manage the internal tension between being a "productive citizen" and being a "good parent"? What else could be done via social media to help people manage the competing demands of work and home?

On one hand, relationship dialectics is an interesting alternative to theories like social penetration theory, which outlines relationship stages. Most of us recognize that relationships are not perfectly linear—that is, they do not move predictably from one stage to the next and then the next—relationship dialectics highlights the reality that relationships change drastically over time, moving forward, backward, and even stagnating in a pattern that is unique to that specific relationship. So, though dialectics does not give us a roadmap to relationship development per se, it does help us understand why relationships can be so difficult and why they fluctuate as they do.

Importantly, as the research bears out, dialectics theory helps us understand tensions and fluctuations in all types of relationships, including dating, marriage, friendship, family, and coworker relationships. We have focused in this chapter on friendship and families, particularly the tensions between work and our personal life. If we start to think about the stressful things in our lives as tensions—us being caught between two opposing needs, both of which are important to us personally—we can recognize the source of that stress and more mindfully navigate those difficulties both internally and externally. We may even be able to think of new, integrative ways to handle those tensions so that conflicting needs are managed, or satisfied at work and at home.

ASSIGNMENTS

1. **Dialectical tensions of college students.** Consider your experience as a college student.
   a. What is an "ideal" college student like?
   b. What are you like as a student? Describe your experience being a student.
   c. What are the key differences between the "ideal" student and yourself as a "real" student?
   d. Which of the dialectical tensions (stability/change, openness/closedness, closeness/independence) do you see evidence of in your comparison of the "ideal" student you described and yourself as a "real" student?
   e. Do you think having friends at school would help you manage your competing needs? Why or why not?
   f. Do you think taking online, distance education courses would help (or has helped) you manage your competing needs as a student? Why or why not?

2. **New dialectics and dialectical management via CMC.** Thinking critically about the types of dialectical tensions we experience in relationships (stability/change, openness/closedness, closeness/independence) and the ways we manage dialectical tensions (alternation, denial, segmentation, disorientation, balance, reaffirmation, recalibration, or integration), how might mediated communication (such as texting) affect the tensions we experience in our relationships?
   a. When we text to stay connected to our partners, which specific dialectical tensions might be brought up? Why?
   b. When we text to stay connected to our partners, which specific dialectical tensions might be resolved, or made easier to manage? Why?
   c. When we text our partners to manage our dialectical tensions, which management strategies do you think we are most likely to use? Why?

REFERENCES

Seminal Texts:

Baxter, L. A., & Montgomery, B. M. (1996). *Relating: Dialogues and dialectics*. New York: Guilford Press.

Academic Articles:

Baxter, L. A., & Braithwaite, D. O. (2010). Relational dialectics theory, applied. In S. W. Smith & S. R. Wilson (Eds.), *New directions in interpersonal communication research* (pp. 48–66). Los Angeles, CA: Sage.

Bridge, K., & Baxter, L. A. (1992). Blended relationships: Friends as work associates. *Western Journal of Communication, 56*(3), 200–225.

Duckworth, J. D., & Buzzanell, P. M. (2009). Constructing work-life balance and fatherhood: Men's framing of the meanings of both work and family. *Communication Studies, 60*(5), 558–573.

Fay, M. J. (2011). Informal communication of co-workers: A thematic analysis of messages. *Qualitative Research in Organizations and Management: An International Journal, 6*, 212–229.

Fay, M. J., & Kline, S. L. (2011). Coworker relationships and informal communication in high-intensity telecommuting. *Journal of Applied Communication Research, 39*(2), 144–163.

Gajendran, R. S., Harrison, D. A., & Delaney-Klinger, K. (2015). Are telecommuters remotely good citizens? Unpacking telecommuting's effects on performance via I-deals and job resources. *Personnel Psychology, 68*(2), 353–393.

Halliwell, D. (2015). Extending relational dialectics theory: Exploring new avenues of research. *Communication Yearbook, 39*, 67–95.

Kirby, E. L., & Buzzanell, P. M. (2014). Communicating work-life issues. In L. L. Putnam & D. K. Mumby (Eds.) *The Sage handbook of organizational communication: Advances in theory, research, and methods* (pp. 351–374). Thousand Oaks, CA: Sage.

Sias, P. M., Heath, R. G., Perry, T., Silva, D., et al. (2004). Narratives of workplace friendship deterioration. *Journal of Social & Personal Relationships, 21*(3), 321–340.

Thompson-Hayes, M., Gibson, D. M., Scott, A. T., & Webb, L. M. (2009). Professorial collaborations via CMC: Interactional dialectics. *Computers in Human Behavior, 25*, 208–216.

Yoshimura, C. G. (2013). A dialectic approach to work-family conflict. *Northwest Journal of Communication, 41*(1), 7–40.

Examples:

Hampton, K., Raine, L., Lu, W., Shin, I., et al. (2015, January 15). The cost of caring. *Pew Research Center: Internet, Science, & Tech*. Retrieved from http://www.pewinternet.org/2015/01/15/the-cost-of-caring/

Levs, J. (2015, May 14). Stop punishing the family man. *Harvard Business Review*. Retrieved online from https://hbr.org/2015/05/stop-punishing-the-family-man

Levs, J. (2015, August 5). What Netflix's parental leave means for all parents. *Time*. Retrieved from http://time.com/3986582/netflix-leave-parental-family-leave/

Thompson, T. (1998, February 15). A war inside your head. *Washington Post Magazine*. Retrieved online from http://www.washingtonpost.com/wp-srv/national/longterm/mommywars/mommy.htm

Williams, J. C. (2012, April 15). Will there ever be a truce in the Mommy Wars? What to do about the ongoing conflict between working and stay-at-home mothers. Psychology Today. Retrieved from https://www.psychologytoday.com/blog/family-friendly/201204/will-there-ever-be-truce-in-the-mommy-wars?collection=101067

SOCIAL EXCHANGE THEORY

INTRODUCTION

An article in *The New York Times* reported that

> By observing singles pursuing one another at online dating sites and in speed-dating experiments, researchers have found that people tend to end up with those of similar mate value. That pattern also occurs in married couples: Attractive, well-educated, high-earning people tend to marry people like themselves (Tierney, 2015, para. 8–9, emphasis added).

Importantly, mate value can change over time as we get to know people. As we reduce uncertainty and participate in self-disclosure, we get a clearer sense of how we can benefit from some relationships and whether or not we benefit enough from a relationship to justify staying in the relationship.

So-called "mate value" has been a recurring theme in these chapters on relationship development. Consider the concepts of social and task attraction from the first chapter in this unit: we are attracted to people with social capital who can help us get what we want. Also recall, from social penetration theory, that the reward value of the person whom we are considering as an interpersonal relationship partner determines the extent to which we confide in them through self-disclosure to move the relationship forward. Baxter and Montgomery (1996) are clear that relationship dialectics is not about *material* rewards. Rather, their theory focuses on our needs for different things, and how we manage those opposing needs in relationships. Nonetheless, the tensions described in the previous chapter can be seen as a very real cost of relationships. Social exchange sees relationships as an exchange of resources—both real resources and intangible resources—and also acknowledges that relationships come at a cost. In this chapter, we look at mate value in a slightly different way: relationships as a way of exchanging rewards and costs, and managing competing needs.

This view of relationships is similar to the idea of **return on investment**: When we invest in something, be it time or other resources, we expect sufficient returns on that investment. Also, given the importance of mate value in attraction and early relationship progress, it shouldn't be surprising that the rewards that we get from a relationship are weighed against the cost of the relationship in long-term relationships.

MAIN IDEA

Social exchange theory (SET) explains that we seek relationships that maximize our **rewards**, or our benefits in terms of need fulfillment, and that we also avoid or try to minimize **costs**, which are anything that eliminates benefits or costs us resources. Further, we invest in those relationships that offer us the greatest return on our investment and abandon relationships that do not yield sufficient rewards or when we find a new relationship that offers more rewards.

💬 OVERVIEW OF SET (THIBAUT & KELLEY, 1959)

KEY CONCEPTS IN SET

- *Rewards* are "pleasures, satisfactions, gratifications" and the needs fulfilled through interaction (p. 12). Rewards can include *similarity* in preferences and things you enjoy doing together. They can also include dissimilarities or *differences*, or things that you see in the other person that are different from yourself but are rewarding. For a reward to be achieved, the other person has to be *willing* to share that reward. For example, we may seek someone who is similar to us in terms of values and behaviors because those interactions would be rewarding.

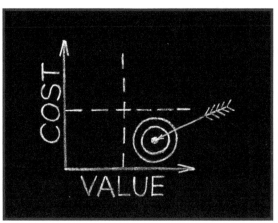

On the other hand, we may also seek someone who is dissimilar in terms of power and status, so that we may benefit from that status if he or she is willing to share that power with us.

- *Costs* are the effort, negative emotions, and conflicts in interactions. In relationships, a person can bring costs, or can help us reduce our costs. One reason that dissimilarity in values and behaviors can be a cost, for example, is because it may make us uncomfortable. That discomfort is a cost, because it is a negative feeling.

- *Outcomes* are the consequences of interaction in terms of the rewards we received and the costs incurred. For example, rejection occurs because a person or relationship incurs too many costs and/or does not offer sufficient rewards.

KEY PREDICTIONS OF SET

1. *People are rational and seek to maximize rewards and minimize costs.* What we perceive as a reward versus a cost is unique to each of us based on our own "values, needs, skills, tools, and predispositions" (p. 14). But we recognize what we are putting into a relationship, what we are getting out of a relationship, and whether our outcomes are a good return on our investment. Getting back to that idea of mate value, what I see as comparably valuable to my own career and education, for example, may be different compared to what you would see as valuable. I may want and need someone of equal education and earning potential; you may prefer someone who is able to support your career, or vice versa.

2. *We compare what we are getting out of relationships with our minimal standards and with other potential relationships.* **Comparison level** is the minimum threshold for rewards. Put another way, there is "a *standard* by which the person evaluates the rewards and costs of a given relationship" and that standard is what a person thinks he or she "deserves" (p. 21) in terms of relationship outcomes. When a relationship fails to meet our minimum standard, or falls below our minimum standard, we exit the relationship.

   In addition to the minimum standards we have for a relationship, we also compare our relationships with other potential relationships and choose the one that will provide the best outcomes. **Comparison level of alternatives** is when we compare relationships to other potential relationships and pursue the relationships that are most rewarding. We will also leave relationships when the outcomes fall below our comparison level of alternatives. That is to say, we each have an idea of what type of romantic partner or friend we might

Should I Stay or Should I Go?

Rewards – Costs = Outcomes:
What am I going to have to put into the relationship?
What might I get out of the relationship?
Is what I put in worth less than what I'll get out of it?
Comparison Level:
Am I getting what I deserve?
Do I have more rewarding alternatives?

Image © Kendall Hunt Publishing Co.

attract. Thus, prospective romantic partners and friends are compared to this potential alternative partner. In all, it may not be sufficient for a prospective partner to *match* our wants and needs, they also have to *surpass* other prospective partners.

3. *Relationships are an interdependent exchange of costs and rewards.* In many ways, we depend on our interpersonal relationship partners to help us get what we want, or to facilitate fulfillment of our needs, and they depend on us. Thus, partners are **interdependent**. We can stand between people and the rewards they seek (*interference*), or we can help them achieve those rewards (*facilitation*). **Interference** includes habits, behaviors, and tendencies in the other person that leads to us not getting the response or outcome we want. On the other hand, **facilitation** occurs when one relationship partner helps the other reap some kind of reward. We can exchange rewards *directly* (i.e., saying "I'll give you this if you give me that") or *indirectly* (i.e., "I'll do this, which will affect you in that way"). I can, for example, either facilitate my partner's career aspirations by helping toward professional goals, or I can interfere with my partner's career by withdrawing my support. I can do this directly, by saying "I will only do this if you do that" or I can do this indirectly by reducing my facilitative behavior or increasing my interference behavior.

4. *This exchange speaks to our **power**, or our ability to influence people in the relationship.* Power in the relationship comes from interdependence, or others' reliance on us for rewards. People who depend *less* on the relationship for outcomes have more power. We exert power in relationships by affecting each other's outcomes:

   - **Fate control** is when you change your behavior in a relationship to affect someone else's outcomes. So, if I know that someone depends on me to do something, I can stop doing that to reduce my partner's rewards.
   - **Behavior control** is when you change your behavior, which motivates a change in your partner's behavior. I may choose to do something to benefit my partner in the hope that my partner will then be motivated to contribute more to the relationship.

5. Exchange patterns are also affected by norms and roles. Though people in relationships often negotiate costs and rewards, *most relationships have implicit rules for trading resources and we also experience norms for who does what in relationships.* **Norms** are stable "rules about behavior" based upon "agreement and consensus" within the broader society and within the relationship (p. 134–135). Thus, we infer norms from broader social groups, and those norms control and constrain what we do within our relationship. We see norms affecting the division of labor in relationships, or "who does what." Norms also affect the behavioral sequences people use in relationships, or how we negotiate to get what we want. Importantly, norms also help determine our **roles** in a relationship, or what exactly we are expected to do.

AN IMPORTANT EXTENSION TO SET: EQUITY THEORY

Adams (1965) added the concept of **equity** to social exchange, explaining that *we recognize unequal outcomes in relationships and can perceive when someone is getting more out of or putting less into a relationship than we are.* In short, we want our inputs and outcomes to be roughly equal.

In any given relationship, we may find that we are **over-benefitted**, or receiving more out of the relationship than our partner, and feel guilty. Or we may find that we are **under-benefitted**, or receiving less out of the relationship than our partner, and feel angry. Either way—whether we are over- or under-benefited, we are dissatisfied in the relationship when we perceive that there is inequity. **Equity theory** asserts that, when we perceive that there is inequity in a relationship:

- We try to *maximize* our positive outcomes.
- We try to *minimize* costly investments in relationships, particularly investments or changes that injure our self-concept or self-esteem.
- We may *rethink* our own or our partner's costs and outcomes to handle feelings of inequity.
- We *withdraw* from a relationship when there is modest inequity, and we will leave when we perceive a lot of inequity that we cannot or do not want to correct.

Should I Stay or Should I Go?

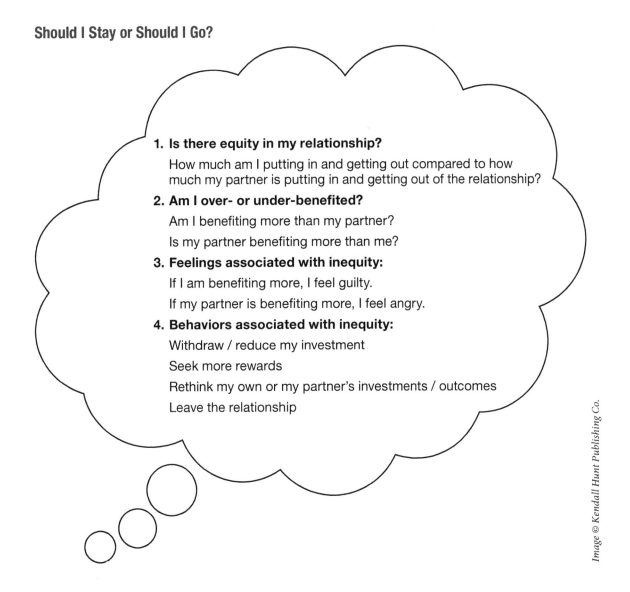

1. **Is there equity in my relationship?**

   How much am I putting in and getting out compared to how much my partner is putting in and getting out of the relationship?

2. **Am I over- or under-benefited?**

   Am I benefiting more than my partner?

   Is my partner benefiting more than me?

3. **Feelings associated with inequity:**

   If I am benefiting more, I feel guilty.

   If my partner is benefiting more, I feel angry.

4. **Behaviors associated with inequity:**

   Withdraw / reduce my investment

   Seek more rewards

   Rethink my own or my partner's investments / outcomes

   Leave the relationship

EXAMPLE OF SOCIAL EXCHANGE AND EQUITY: WOMEN IN DUAL-CAREER COUPLES

Copyright © Monkey Business Images/ Shutterstock.com

Historically, women have been under-benefited in dual-career couples, because even as they increasingly work outside the home, women have typically performed more of the household chores as well. Slowly, this trend is shifting, as we discussed in the previous chapters with examples such as *Lean In* and the new trend in major corporations toward paid leave for fathers. Women have reported numerous ways that they restore a sense of equity in their relationships (Canary & Stafford, 2011):

1. Decreasing investments in either one's home or work;
2. Improving outcomes by finding time for themselves;
3. Getting partners to invest more in the home;
4. Comparing themselves to other women, who may be more under-benefited, rather than to their partners;
5. Perhaps the least effective is women reenvisioning themselves as "super women" who can do it all.

Since the trend toward equity in dual-career couples is shifting, why focus on women? Research suggests that women typically *invest* more in relationships (Canary & Wahba, 2006). For example, they tend to be more sensitive to relationship changes and inequity, are more likely to try to resolve conflicts, more often take on the role of promoting new relationships, and invest more in maintaining relationships. In short, "women are more *relationally responsive*; that is, women (vs. men) tend to engage in thoughts and actions that protect and promote their personal involvements" (p. 342, emphasis original). This gets back to some of the issues we talked about in the unit on gender, where we considered how women are socialized to be more relationship-focused.

We see this pattern of women investing more time and being more responsive via social media as well. For example, *The Washington Post* declared that "Moms won the internet" (Dewey, 2015) because some of the most popular pushers of viral online content, like Upworthy and Viral Nova, focus on stories and images that middle class moms are likely to enjoy and share. In fact, women, in general, tend to be most active Facebook users: they have more friends, share more, and interact more. Women, more so than men, are users of Facebook, Pinterest, and Instagram and are roughly equal users of LinkedIn compared to men (Duggan, Ellison, Lampe, Lenhart, & Madden, 2014). Moreover, women seem to use social networks more for maintaining relationships, compared to men who use them for entertainment (Chan, Cheung, Shi, & Lee, 2015).

Taken together, it *may* be that social media use is a way for women to make and maintain relationships that are personal, professional, and domestic, and may even be a way for women to establish a sense of equity. Social media use and consuming viral Internet content may be a way for women to find time for themselves, compare themselves to others so that they (may sometimes) feel better about themselves, and even fulfill their relationship-orientated roles with friends, family, and coworkers at a lower cost. What do you think? Are social networks a way to find equity in a relationship? Or are they a distraction from "real" relationships?

Insight into Innovation Example: Check out this YouTube video that describes social exchange and equity in interpersonal relationships: https://youtu.be/uZDmb9FaNy0

METHODS IN SOCIAL EXCHANGE RESEARCH

Quantitative surveys. Clearly, when we talk about "rewards minus costs equaling outcomes" we are applying an equation to predict relationship outcomes. Indeed, both SET and equity theory are typically quantitatively measured, either through quantitatively coding people's responses to open questions about their relationships or through quantitative survey items.

Surveys can be done over time, called **longitudinal** studies, to get a sense of how people's rewards and costs change and how relationship outcomes change, such as whether people stay in a relationship, for how long, and how happy they are in their relationships.

This research has provided a lot of insight into the importance of rewards and costs, particularly in terms of equity, in almost every imaginable type of relationship. Researchers have surveyed coworkers, employees and their bosses, married couples, dating couples, family members, and friends to explore the exchange of costs and rewards and perceptions of equity.

Insight into Innovation Activity: Are you over-benefited or under-benefited in your relationship?
A common survey measure of equity is the answer to one survey question (Canary & Stafford, 2011):

Thinking about "what you put into a relationship versus what you get out of it, and what your partner puts into the relationship compared to what he or she gets out of it," respond on a scale of 1 (you get a better deal) to 7 (he or she gets a better deal):

1	2	3	4	5	6	7
"I am getting a much better deal than my partner."			"We get a roughly equal deal."			"My partner is getting a much better deal."

Lower scores (1, 2, and 3) indicate that you are over-benefited, and higher scores (5, 6, 7) indicate that you are under-benefited.

Reliance on survey items, of course, can lead to some challenges. For example, how would you define "satisfaction" in a relationship? What would you ask if you wanted to know whether people were satisfied in a relationship? One common scale measure of satisfaction is Hendrick's (1988) **relationship assessment scale**, which is measured on a scale of 1 (low) to 7 (high):

1. Does your partner meet your needs?

2. Are you satisfied in your relationship?

3. Is your relationship good compared to other relationships?

4. Do you often wish you had never gotten into this relationship?

5. Does your current relationship meet the expectations you had at the outset?

6. Do you love your partner?

7. Do you have a lot of problems in your relationship?

Looking critically at these summarized scale items, they include elements of SET, such as one's needs and expectations being met, comparison level, and feelings (which can be a cost if they are negative or a reward if they are positive). But the scale doesn't speak to equity in costs, rewards, or outcomes. What other elements might you add to a scale like this? Are there items in this scale that you think might not fit well? Though many scales are developed by having people respond to open questions then using those responses to form scale items, there is still the potential that important elements of what we are measuring may be missed. That being said, Google Scholar reports over 1,000 citations for this particular measure, so it is widely used in research.

APPLYING SOCIAL EXCHANGE AND EQUITY: MAINTAINING, WITHDRAWING, AND ENDING RELATIONSHIPS IN A WEB 2.0 WORLD

One of the unique contributions of SET and equity theory is that it gives some fairly clear indications of when we will maintain a relationship, withdraw from a relationship, and end a relationship.

Relationship Maintenance. **Relationship maintenance** is an ongoing investment in a relationship, and includes things that we do in a relationship to keep relationships at the desired level of intimacy. Canary, Stafford, Hause, and Wallace (1993) outline several types of relationship maintenance behaviors that people report in relationships they want to sustain:

Maintenance Behavior	Definition
Positivity	Being polite and expressing happiness with each other
Openness	Talking about thoughts, feelings, love, commitment
Social networks	Having mutual friends and spending time with them
Sharing tasks	Equal and fair division of chores
Joint activities	Spending time together doing activities
Mediated communication	Using e-mail and cell phones to stay in touch

Relationship maintenance behaviors are important for several reasons (Canary & Stafford, 2011). They are how we stay "close" to partners. Maintenance behaviors are also an input, or in SET terms, they are a cost or investment in the relationship. Thus, maintenance behaviors are motivated or demotivated by whether the cost/reward exchange in a relationship is perceived as equitable.

One reason that social media, texting, and IMing may be valuable for maintaining relationships is because they are a low cost, easy way to maintain relationships. For example, one of the primary reasons that young people report for using instant messaging (IM) is for relationship maintenance (Quan-Haase, & Young, 2010). Also, people have reported that relationship maintenance needs drive their photo messaging (Hunt, Lin, & Atkin, 2014). Indeed, couples use texts, IMs, and e-mails to interact throughout the day, and these messages include talking about what they're up to, making observations, coordinating tasks, seeing what the other person is up to, and sharing media (Laliker & Lunnutti, 2014). There are unique benefits to using CMC, particularly texts and IMs, such as the ability to be in regular contact and the sense of privacy that comes with text messaging (Pettigrew, 2009).

It is important to point out that, in several of these studies, ease of using the technology was a key determinant of fulfilling relationship maintenance needs via CMC. Thus, we may use CMC as part of our relationship maintenance when it is relatively easy for us to do so. Research suggests that we use CMC for maintenance because of a desire to communicate with our partners, when our attitudes about the ease of technology use are favorable, and because of the affordances of technology such as it fitting into our schedules (Hales, 2012). Further, people reported that using CMC for relationship maintenance was related to higher relationship quality, stability, and satisfaction.

That being said, CMC can be too much of a good thing in a relationship. Just as SET suggests, the emergence of rules and norms within a relationship are important. This extends to use of technology in the relationship as well. Research suggests that rules such as having rules about the content of cell phone use, can help people feel satisfied in a relationship (Miller-Ott, Kelly, & Duran, 2012). Content rules are things such as not starting fights or trying to have serious conversations via cell phones.

Insight into Innovation Activity: What Rules Would You Suggest for CMC in Relationships?
Technology can be an interference in couples' and families' lives (McDaniel, 2015). McDaniel recommends asking yourself a few questions when you are considering whether technology may be interrupting, rather than helping to maintain, your relationships:

1. How often are you using technology throughout the day?

2. How much of this technology use throughout the day is truly necessary?

3. What needs are you trying to fulfill with technology and might you be using technology to avoid others rather than to engage them?

4. What are some of the negative consequences of your technology use in terms of how you feel and your personal relationships?

5. Do you sometimes use technology to replace things in your "real life" that were good before?

After considering your use of technology, consider how you might use it for the benefit of the relationship without distracting from the relationship. What relationship rules do you think would improve relationship equity and outcomes but also minimize interference?

Termination. Though CMC can be useful for maintaining relationships, it can also move relationship partners further apart and is sometimes used for terminating relationships. Though CMC provides some important affordances for relationship maintenance, the messages we send via texts can also have a distancing effect (Jin, 2013). We infer the intent of messages sent via text, and when we perceive that the intent of the message is to be hurtful it can make us feel more distant. This is particularly true in relationships where satisfaction is already low.

For example, there are indicators in our face-to-face and mediated communication when a relationship is likely to end, such as the **Four Horsemen of the Apocalypse** (Gottman, 1994; see also www.gottman.com). The four horsemen are negative ways of communicating in a relationship, and using these types of messages *frequently* in a relationship signals that the relationship may be near its end:

- **Criticisms** are personal attacks on our partner.
- **Contempt** is when we express disdain for the other person.
- **Defensive** messages are when we complain and blame the other person.
- **Stonewalling** is avoiding or withdrawing from interactions.

When we compare the four horsemen with the maintenance behaviors in equitable, satisfying relationships, we can see how communication shifts dramatically when we are dissatisfied. Communication shifts from maintenance strategies such as positivity, openness, and doing things together to distancing messages such as negativity toward the other person, pushing the other person away, and withdrawing.

Indeed, both SET and equity theory explain that when we are not getting what we think we deserve out of a relationship, we will end that relationship. Terminating is sometimes a slow process of withdrawal. On the other hand, there are also sudden or indirect strategies, such as texting, changing your relationship status on Facebook, or ghosting.

Insight into Innovation Example: Ghosting and the Modern Breakup. *The New York Times* reported that Charlize Theron was "ghosting" her boyfriend, Sean Penn. They explain this method of relationship termination as "ending a romantic relationship by cutting off all contact and ignoring the former partner's attempts to reach out" (Safronova, 2015, para. 2). In other words, ghosting is ignoring someone's calls, texts, and other messages. On the other hand, preliminary survey research suggests that many people may have experienced a direct breakup message via CMC, particularly text messages (Weisskirch & Delevi, 2012). What do you think: What is the most effective, competent, and ethical way to end a relationship based on the material we've covered so far in this book?

Social exchange theory, to some, is a cynical explanation of love and relationships. Some may argue, for example, that it is difficult to explain lifelong love as an internal list of pros versus cons. On the other hand, SET has clearly generated a significant amount of research, including influencing several theories in this book (e.g., social penetration theory has an assumption about rewards vs. costs, expectancy violations theory has predictions based on the rewardingness of others, and attraction theory looks at social and task rewards to explain attraction).

Further, both SET and equity theory have been used to explain dating relationships, marriages, family relationships, coworker relationships, employee satisfaction and productivity, and social media use. Thus, it has been both heuristic (i.e., it has generated a lot of research) and applies to many communication contexts. Indeed, it has even been used to explain brand loyalty, and could probably also be applied to predict voting behavior, following/unfollowing people via social media, and a myriad of other social behaviors. So, even if SET and equity theory seem a little too focused on rational choice in seemingly irrational contexts such as love and familial bonds, it still seems to have a strong record of empirical support.

Importantly, we can also consider technology through the lens of SET and equity theory. Technology can be a low-investment maintenance strategy for a relationship, such as texting friends periodically to stay in touch or messaging romantic partners throughout the day. It may also help us build our sense of equity in relationships by giving us time to ourselves and helping us consider our relationships compared to other relationships described in social media posts and blog posts. But we have to be careful, because technology can also distract us from our relationships. CMC can involve taking time away from our partners, friends, and families, and may cause us to send distancing messages to people in our face-to-face interactions, such signaling withdrawal as we stare into our phones or tablets.

ASSIGNMENTS

1. **Consider a current friendship.** Think about a friend you have on campus or at work.
   a. What are the rewards associated with that friendship?
   b. What are the costs associated with that friendship?
   c. What do you do to maintain that friendship?
   d. Do the rewards, when compared to the costs, help explain the number and types of investments (i.e., relationship maintenance behaviors) you use? Why or why not?

2. **Explaining declining marriage rates.** Marriage is a major investment. Research from Pew Social Trends (2014) suggests that fewer people are getting married, and they suggest that this is because women are seeking men with a steady job who also have similar plans for children, whereas the number of employed unmarried men has decreased. How might social exchange theory (SET) explain the decline in marriage? Read the report and answer the following questions:
   a. Thinking about SET, do modern marriageable men seem to meet modern women's comparison level? Why or why not?

b. Given that research suggests that we seek people of similar "mate value," what do the demographic changes in education and marriage among men and women tell us is likely to happen to marriage rates in the future?

c. Pew projects that by 2030, up to 47 percent of men and women aged 25 to 34 years will not be married.

    i. What are the costs associated with not being married at this age?

    ii. What are the benefits of not being married at this age?

    iii. In your estimation, is marriage worth the investment for people aged 25 to 34? Why or why not?

REFERENCES

Seminal Texts:

Thibaut, J. W., & Kelly, H. H. (1959). *The social psychology of groups*. New York: Wiley. Retrieved from https://archive.org/details/socialpsychology00thib

Adams, J. S. (1965). Inequity in social exchange. In L. Berkowitz (Ed.) *Advances in experimental psychology: Volume 2* (pp. 267–299). New York: Academic Press.

Academic Articles:

Canary, D. J., & Stafford, L. (2011). Equity in the preservation of personal relationships. In J. Harvey & A. Wenzel (Eds.) *Close romantic relationships: Maintenance and enhancement* (pp. 133–152). Mahwah, NJ: Lawrence Erlbaum Associates.

Canary, D. J., Stafford, L., Hause, K. , & Wallace, L. (1993). An inductive analysis of relational maintenance strategies: A comparison among lovers, relatives, friends, and others. *Communication Research Reports, 10*, 514.

Canary, D. J., & Wahba, J. (2006). Do women work harder than men at maintaining relationships? In D. J. Canary (Ed.) *Sex differences and similarities in communication* (pp. 342–359). Mahwah, NJ: Lawrence Erlbaum Associates.

Chan, T. K., Cheung, C. M., Shi, N., & Lee, M. K. (2015). Gender differences in satisfaction with Facebook users. *Industrial Management & Data Systems, 115*(1), 182–206.

Duggan, M., Ellison, N. B., Lampe, C., et al. (2015, January 9). Demographics of Key Social Networking Platforms. *Pew Research Center.* Retrieved from http://www.pewinternet.org/2015/01/09/demographics-of-key-social-networking-platforms-2/

Gottman, J. M. (1994). *What predicts divorce? The relationship between marital processes and marital outcomes.* Mahwah, NJ: Lawrence Erlbaum Associates.

Hales, K. D. (2012). Multimedia use for relational maintenance in romantic couples. Paper presented at the Annual Conference of the International Communication Association. Retrieved online from Ebscohost.

Hendrick, S. S. (1988). A generic measure of relationship satisfaction. *Journal of Marriage & the Family*, *50*(1), 93–98.

Hunt, D. S., Lin, C. A., & Atkin, D. J. (2014). Communicating social relationships via the use of photo-messaging. *Journal of Broadcasting & Electronic Media*, *58*(2), 234–252.

Jin, B. (2013). Hurtful texting in friendships: Satisfaction buffers the distancing effects of intention. *Communication Research Reports*, *30*(2), 148–156.

Laliker, M. K., & Lannutti, P. J. (2014). Remapping the topography of couples' daily interactions: Electronic messages. *Communication Research Reports*, *31*(3), 262–271.

McDaniel, B. T. (2015). "Technoference": Everyday intrusions and interruptions of technology in couple and family relationships. In C. J. Bruess (Ed.) *Family communication in the age of digital and social media*. New York: Peter Lang.

Miller-Ott, A. E., Kelly, L., & Duran, R. L. (2012). The effects of cell phone usage rules on satisfaction in romantic relationships. *Communication Quarterly*, *60*(1), 17–34.

Pettigrew, J. (2009). Text messages and connectedness within close interpersonal relationships. *Marriage & Family Review*, *45*, 697–716.

Quan-Haase, A., & Young, A. L. (2010). Uses and gratifications of social media: A comparison of Facebook and Instant Messaging. *Bulletin of Science, Technology & Society*, *30*(5), 350–361.

Weisskirch, R. S., & Delevi, R. (2012). Its ovr b/n u n me: Technology use, attachment styles, and gender roles in relationship dissolution. *Cyberpsychology, Behavior & Social Networking*, *15*(9), 486–490.

Examples:

Dewey, C. (2015, July 16). How moms won the Internet—and what that means for the rest of us. *The Washington* Post. Retrieved from https://www.washingtonpost.com/news/the-intersect/wp/2015/07/16/how-moms-won-the-internet-and-what-that-means-for-the-rest-of-us/

Safronova, V. (2015, June 26). Exes explain ghosting, the ultimate silent treatment. *The New York Times*. Retrieved from http://www.nytimes.com/2015/06/26/fashion/exes-explain-ghosting-the-ultimate-silent-treatment.html?_r=0

Tierney, J. (2015, June 29). For couples, time can upend the laws of attraction. *The New York Times*. Retrieved from http://www.nytimes.com/2015/06/30/science/for-couples-time-can-upend-the-laws-of-attraction.html?_r=0

Further Reading Online:

Read more about the 4 horseman of the apocolypse here: Bradberry, T. (2012, July 24). Retrieved from http://www.forbes.com/sites/travisbradberry/2012/07/24/four-signs-a-relationship-is-failing/2/

Read more about the good and bad of texting in relationships here: DiDonato, E.T. (2014, March 21). Retrieved from https://www.psychologytoday.com/blog/meet-catch-and-keep/201403/is-constant-texting-good-or-bad-your-relationship

GROUPS AND ORGANIZATIONS IN ONLINE ENVIRONMENTS

In the final unit looking at personal and professional relationships, we focus on communication in groups and organizations. As we discussed in the previous unit on interpersonal relationships, friendships among coworkers are essential to our acclimation and commitment to the workplace. So, we know that interpersonal, group, and organizational communication overlap considerably.

In the unit on groups and organizations, we delve further into the complex relationships we have with coworkers and within groups and organizations. We begin by discussing groups comprised of three or more people to accomplish some task or outcome. Though friendships can promote group bonding, groupthink warns us that being too cohesive in a group can undermine critical thinking and lead to faulty decisions in groups. Not all close relationships among group members will necessarily lead to groupthink, but rather groupthink among bonded participants is likely in times of stress when there seem to be few good options available to the group and the morale is low.

We also discuss some ways to improve our group interactions, such as mindfully building work groups and teams based on how well they will work together and the knowledge and skills that each member can contribute to the task. Similarly, we discuss group functions as the essential things that we can do when we work in groups to avoid groupthink and promote critical thinking and problem solving. We end that chapter with pointers for how to manage virtual teams, including training and monitoring interactions and progress.

Groups and teams exist within a larger system, typically an organization, and they are affected by the resources in that broader system and the organization's culture. We move on in the second chapter in this unit to look at organizational cultures—what they are, how they are studied, and the effects of culture on people within the organization. We also consider how each of us affects and is affected by organizational culture, and discuss some things that might influence whether or not we "fit" in an organization. We cover some things that we should reflect on when considering organizational fit, such as our boundary preferences between work and home and the leadership styles and organizational processes that we are more likely to feel comfortable with.

Feeling a sense of "fit," or organizational cultural identification, is not just good for you in terms of making work a more comfortable place to spend 40 or more hours each week. Organizational "fit" can also affect commitment to your job and ultimately your productivity. Thus, organizational culture, climate, and individual fit in that environment are important to a company's bottom line, even in modern, wired workplaces. There seem to be two extremes in modern workplaces: the flexible, supportive companies such as Google, and the structured, demanding companies such as Amazon. Clearly, both of these tech giants have managed to be profitable and innovative, even though their companies are very distinct cultures. Thus, organizational cultures challenge us to consider what works best for our specific company's goals *and* our specific employees' work styles, communication styles, and boundary preferences.

As with interpersonal relationships, the work that we do can be rewarding in many ways, and we weigh the costs of a particular job at a particular company against the rewards of being in that job at that company. We have a minimum level of compensation that we'll accept, and our employers have a minimal level of productivity that they'll accept. Culture, then, can be a cost that turns some people away, or a reward that encourages productivity. Some of us will thrive in the competitive, unrelenting culture of Amazon; some of us dream of the colorful, fun offices of Google. The trick is to recognize an organizational culture when we see it, and decide whether we will thrive or be crushed in that environment. The answer will be different for each of us.

CHAPTER 14

GROUPTHINK AND GROUP FUNCTIONS IN MEDIATED GROUPS

OUTCOMES

- *Knowledge:* Learn the symptoms and outcomes of groupthink and the functions of group communication.
- *Skill:* Recognize the symptoms of groupthink and enact effective virtual team management strategies to promote bonding and productivity.

🗨 INTRODUCTION

Groups are three or more people working together to meet some objective, such as making a decision, solving a problem, or completing a task. Sometimes, great people working together in a group make awful decisions, and sometimes average people working together in groups develop world-changing products. **Groupthink** theory helps us understand how the circumstances of the group affects the communication that occurs, and how communication then affects the quality of outcomes. The **functional approach** suggests that there are things that groups can do that lead to better decisions, and that there is not any one specific procedure that works for all groups. Groups should use the process that works best for them given the individual characteristics of team members. When groups lack a clear process for discussion and decision-making and members feel helpless or stressed due to the circumstances, groupthink may occur, which can lead to bad (and sometimes very dangerous) decisions. Thus, we focus in this chapter on *group processes*, like being open, cohesive, and critical, rather than prescribing a step-by-step *procedure* for effective group interactions.

The good news is that mediated interactions in groups can improve group processes by reducing pressure toward conformity and increasing opinion and information sharing. There are also many emerging technologies that can aid groups in their decisions and tasks. Research suggests that mediated interactions can help groups avoid groupthink and fulfill essential functions, though completely mediated groups may struggle, particularly in the short-term.

MAIN IDEA

Groupthink is what happens in groups that are too cohesive, or too closely bonded, and it leads members to seek agreement rather than engage in critical thinking and open discussion. Janis (1982) defined groupthink as the "deterioration of mental efficiency, reality testing, and moral judgment that results from in-group pressures" (p. 9). Put another way, groups can create pressure to "get along" and this may undermine members' critical thinking. One of the benefits of working in a group *should* be that each member employs his or her unique skills, experience, and knowledge to help a group critically evaluate information and possible solutions. Groupthink undermines this potential. From a **functional perspective**, there are specific things groups can do to reach better decisions, such as understanding the problem or task, developing criteria for solutions, critically analyzing options, and considering the costs and benefits of the outcome.

KEY PREDICTIONS OF GROUPTHINK (JANIS, 1972, 1982)

Janis (1982) argued that "the more amiability…among members of a policy-making in-group, the greater is the danger that independent critical thinking will be replaced by groupthink, which is likely to result in irrational or dehumanizing actions directed against outgroups" (p. 13). When groups are too closely bonded, they fail to critically evaluate the problem and the possible solutions, thus leading them to make bad decisions. But simply being a close-knit group won't necessarily lead to groupthink. In fact, a certain amount of cohesion and bonding is needed for groups to work together. Rather, there are conditions outside the group that can affect group members, and there are specific communication processes that are symptoms of groupthink and lead to defective decision-making.

1. *Conditions of groupthink.* There are specific elements of the group's circumstances that increase the chances of groupthink. For example, group leaders may have an agenda, such that the group lacks **impartial leadership**. Another condition that leads to groupthink is when a group doesn't have clear **processes or norms** for discussion and decision-making, which may stifle people's opportunities to express ideas and opinions. Also, when group members are **homogenous**, or members are all very similar, there may be more social pressure to conform. Cohesive, bonded groups may **insulate** themselves from outside opinions, including expert opinions and important stakeholders.

   Bad group outcomes aren't just the leader's fault. Sometimes there is pressure from the circumstances that leads group members to feel stress. When the group feels a sense of threat that they might lose something like status or power, the **stress** from that feeling can lead to faulty decision-making, particularly when the group has lost hope that a good outcome is possible. The group may not feel like it has a lot of options because of what's going on in the broader context (**lack of feasible options**), and this can make people feel like they have already failed and cannot do anything to fix the problem (**low efficacy**).

Group's Conditions	Consequences

Contextual features:

The group is insulated against outsiders' ideas and perspectives.

The group doesn't have an impartial leader.

The group doesn't have clear processes/ procedures for decision-making.

The group members are too similar (homogeneity).

There is a lot of stress from outside the group, such as threats.

Low morale in the group from failures, a lack of efficacy, or a lack of good options.

Symptoms within the group:
- Overestimation
- Sense of being invulnerable
- Sense of the group as moral/righteous
- Close-mindedness
- Rationalizing decisions
- Stereotyping outsiders
- Pressure toward uniformity
  - Censoring oneself so as to conform
  - The illusion that decisions are unanimous
  - Pressure on people who may disagree to "go along"
  - Mindguards shut down opposition

Flawed **decision-making** processes:
- Failure to explore alternatives
- Failure to understand objectives of the group
- Failure to consider the consequences of decisions
  - Failure to reconsider previously rejected ideas
  - Failure to adequately search for information
  - Failure to objectively analyze information
  - Failure to develop plans for when things go wrong

Group is unlikely to reach a good decision; there's potential for a dangerous decision.

Courtesy of Rebecca Curnalia.

Summary of the groupthink process outlined by Janis (1982, p. 344)

2. *Symptoms of groupthink.* Janis focuses on **concurrence-seeking behaviors**, or the things we say and do as group members that look for agreement and confirmation of the group while silencing opposing viewpoints. Some symptoms of groupthink include the group **overestimating its power**, such as believing that they are **invulnerable** to failure or are inherently **moral** in their decision making. The group may also become **closed-minded**, and fail to think critically about the situation and the pros and cons of the decisions. When this happens, groups focus on rationalizing their decisions rather than critiquing decisions, and they **stereotype outsiders** in unflattering ways to differentiate "us" from "them."

In this environment, people are unlikely to speak up, even when they see the group making a potentially bad decision (**self-censorship**). Because people aren't speaking up to point out flaws in the processes or decisions, there can be an illusion that people are all in agreement (**illusion of unanimity**). Even when group members do speak up and critique a process or idea, other members of the group may shut them down and **pressure them to conform**, or **mindguards** may actively stop relevant but conflicting ideas, perspectives, or information from even getting to the group.

3. *Outcomes of groupthink.* Janis points out that group members conform to and protect the group in this way to protect their own sense of confidence and because of their desire to maintain their social relationships with fellow group members. So, groups caught in groupthink aren't comprised of bad people per se, they just get caught in a flawed process where they do not fully explore the options available to them, they aren't objective, don't take in enough relevant information, don't consider the repercussions of their decisions, and fail to plan for fallout.

Insight into Innovation Example: Are We Groupthinking About Teamwork? Chances are, most of you can think of groups you have been part of that have been less than effective. One interesting idea, discussed in *The New York Times*, is that the current professional focus on teams and collaborative environments is, in and of itself, groupthink (Cain, 2012).

With the shift to new technologies and widely dispersed organizations, teamwork and collaboration have risen in importance because many tasks require skilled professionals working together to complete projects, such as software developers, designers, quality testers, and marketers working to create and promote products. Thus, the trend toward using teams has taken over in American corporations and very few people seem to be questioning whether or not that is improving outcomes and productivity.

Some argue that we have taken it to the point in some workplaces that teamwork is considered the cure-all for many problems, decisions, and tasks, even tasks that could be handled individually. Group work and teams are so ubiquitous that it may be controversial to even question whether forming a team or committee is an appropriate thing to do—this is a perfect condition for groupthink to occur.

Copyright © Monkey Business Images/ Shutterstock.com

In an effort to promote collaboration, some workplaces have moved to open-plan office spaces where there are no walls to divide workspaces. Though the intentions behind creating collaborative spaces are certainly admirable, some research suggests that open-plan offices reduce employees' satisfaction at work and their self-reported performance when their workspace is converted to open-plan (Bergström, Miller, & Horneiji, 2015). Compared to people who work from home, people who work in open spaces have also been found to take up to 70 percent more sick time and report a lot more stress from the environment in which they work (Offices linked to poor health, 2014).

Thinking about this from a groupthink perspective, it makes some sense to move to open-plans: it should reduce insulation and promote input from outsiders. On the other hand, *deciding* how to physically arrange office space should be done thoughtfully based on knowledge of the workers' habits and preferences, their tasks, the environment, and workplace norms. To decide which type of arrangement is good for a particular organization, the decision-making team needs to begin without a forgone decision or personal agenda, look at the alternatives, consider what their objectives are, collect information on their options, carefully weigh the benefits and the drawbacks of their options, and develop a plan if it turns out that their choice doesn't work out.

Chances are, in some workplaces, it is *assumed* at the outset that open space and collaboration are best. Rather than critically thinking about their decision, they may *rationalize* their choice ("everyone else is doing it!"), *stereotype* outsiders ("other approaches are 'old fashioned'; we're a 'modern workplace'"), and *avoid* conflicting information and even their own personal concerns ("would I enjoy and be able to work in this kind of environment?").

Read more about the "Rise of the New Groupthink" here: http://www.nytimes.com/2012/01/15/opinion/sunday/the-rise-of-the-new-groupthink.html?_r=0

OVERCOMING GROUPTHINK: FULFILLING HIROKAWA'S (1985) GROUP FUNCTIONS

Gouran and Hirokawa (1996) suggested the following essential group functions, or tasks, that groups complete to help overcome the constraints of groupthink:

1. Have a clear and accurate understanding of the problem: What do we know and how do we know it?

2. Establish criteria for sufficient solutions: What, exactly, do we need to accomplish? What are the minimum standards for a solution?

3. Explore realistic alternatives. This may include brainstorming for solutions, or collecting alternatives that seem feasible.

4. Examine the alternatives in terms of the criteria by using decision-making and problem-solving processes, such as cost-benefit analyses, that focus on the issue at hand and asking people to play devil's advocate.

5. Choose the solution that best fits the criteria after thoroughly exploring the positives and negatives associated with the alternatives.

"Today's theme is 'Getting Beyond Group Think'."

Copyright © Cartoonresource/Shutterstock.com

Not all groups complete all of these functions in order, and not all of the functions are necessarily equally important in all group processes. Routine tasks, for example, may not require all of these elements. Also, groups do not always have to follow a set procedure to reach a good decision.

Individual differences. Individual differences in traits, such as preference for procedural order may affect whether following a prescribed pattern for group decision-making actually results in better group decisions (Hirokawa, Ice, & Cook, 1988). There are four dimensions or elements of **preference for procedural order** (Putnam, 1979):

High preference for procedural order:	Low preference for procedural order:
• Preference for using plans and patterns to organize a group's activities • Practicing time management • Practicing "predictable procedures" • Preference for keeping group members on-task and reiterating the procedures in group meetings	• Preferring a less orderly process • Not being concerned about time constraints • Being flexible and open to changing agendas in group meetings • Focusing on both tasks that need to be accomplished and the social aspects of the group

Insight into Innovation Example: Build a "Winning Team" Rather Than a "Team of Experts." Team roles theory suggests that putting together effective teams should focus on individuals' characteristics, such as how the members think, behave, and feel when working in a team (Belbin, 1993). Effective teams have members who are of three general types: thinkers, people-oriented members, and producers. The thinkers are creative and analytical, the people-oriented members can bring the group together and secure resources through social connections, and the producers can implement the team's decision. Belbin argues that having people with a balance of these characteristics in a team will help them achieve higher quality outcomes. This video covers Belbin's team roles: https://youtu.be/-efhOLVgEvM.

People are frequently selected for work teams and committees because they hold a certain position in the organization or because they are an expert in an area relevant to the team's task. I'm sure we have all heard the phrase "team of experts" countless times in the news, at work, and at school, and the underlying assumption seems to be that experts working together in a group will lead to the best possible outcomes.

As Janis' groupthink theory points out, a team of experts can sometimes make very bad decisions. It can also lead to more conflict (Belbin, 1993). A person's role in the broader organization and his or her expertise doesn't necessarily lead to him or her fulfilling specific, necessary functions within a group (Senior, 1997). Rather, individual characteristics—having team members who are creative, critical, outgoing, have social capital, and are able to produce real outcomes—may be more important than the titles of the team's members.

Copyright © Ellagrin/Shutterstock.com

Belbin argues that good bosses know how to coordinate people based on their individual characteristics, and can build productive teams to solve complex problems by following four steps:

1. Begin building a team with an expert;

2. "Look for a manager who can relate well" to the expert;

3. Then select team members "so that all the Team Roles, together with any special skills, are well represented" (p. 102) while also

4. Use the fewest number of team members possible to fulfill the roles and accomplish the task, particularly by making use of people who can fulfill multiple roles within the group.

If we think about team roles from a functional perspective, it makes sense that having people with different skills and traits, who are likely to contribute to one or more of Hirokawa's functions, would lead to more successful work teams. Similarly, having team members with different characteristics should also help avoid groupthink, as the group wouldn't be too homogenous and, thus, there would be helpful perspectives on the group's task.

What do you think? Is our frequent reliance on "teams of experts" a good idea? When is it a good idea to use a group versus an individual expert? You can read more about Belbin's team roles at www.belbin.com.

Conflict. Individual differences, such as preference for procedural order and individual team member roles, can lead to conflict in groups. Groups may also experience conflict surrounding the nature of the task at hand or procedures for completing the task at hand, such as who does what and the sharing of resources (Hollingshead et al., 2005). Conflict over routine tasks, or person-centered conflict is not productive. Thus, "in-fighting" and personal attacks among group members can undermine the group's productivity because too much conflict and nonproductive conflict can interfere with the group completing the task, and may signal that the group is not cohesive enough.

Problem-focused conflict, on the other hand, can be productive. *A moderate amount of task and process conflict can be good for a group* because some conflict is a signal that the group is not too cohesive and not feeling pressure to conform (a symptom of groupthink). Conflict is ok as long as it isn't so intense that it undermines motivation and satisfaction within the group. In fact, one of the reasons so many organizations have turned to mediated groups to complete tasks and make decisions is because some research suggests that people will be more willing to openly disagree via mediated channels (Walther, 1996).

Levels of conflict when completing complex or creative tasks:			
Level of task/ procedural conflict	*None*	*Moderate*	*A lot*
May indicate	*Groupthink:* People conforming to avoid disrupting the group	*Critical thinking:* People analyzing the groups task, alternatives, and process	*Dysfunction:* People-centered problems and dissatisfaction
And may lead to	Risky, faulty decisions	Well-reasoned decisions	Imposed, unpopular, or no decisions

METHODS IN GROUPTHINK RESEARCH

Copyright © Zack Frank/ Shutterstock.com

Case studies. Janis' (1972, 1982) original conceptualization of groupthink theory and the related concepts were described using a series of historical "fiascos" where groups of otherwise brilliant and powerful people made very bad decisions. Though the processes he describes are grounded in traditional psychological research, such as experiments and observational studies of group behavior, he uses illustrative cases to demonstrate concepts.

For example, Janis used the Vietnam War as one of several examples of how close-knit presidential cabinets, faced with stressful situations and pessimism about their options, made "colossal misjudgments" and had an underlying assumption that "everything will be alright" (p. 104–105). He made a compelling case that groupthink was at work in President Johnson's administration in particular, such as failing to consider the consequences of decisions, caving in to pressure to use military rather than diplomatic options, and failing to take advantage of opportunities to get out of Vietnam. Thus, Janis concluded that these bad decisions were the result of group cohesiveness, commitment to the group and their previous decisions, pressure to conform, the sense that the group was in complete agreement (unanimity), and failure to think carefully and critically about potential drawbacks or consequences for their decisions.

Given the convincing case that Janis made for groupthink using case studies, it makes sense that subsequent researchers also looked at similar "fiascos" through the lens of groupthink (Esser, 1998). Groupthink has also been used to explore infamous disasters such as Watergate, the spaceship Challenger explosion, and the Iran-Contra affair.

Experiments. Groupthink and the functional perspective make clear predictions about when groups will reach good versus bad decisions, so a significant amount of research has used experiments to test these causal assumptions (see Esser, 1998 for an excellent review of 25 years of groupthink studies). For example, researchers can control the **antecedent conditions** in groupthink theory, such as stress, cohesion, individual member accountability, and leadership style. Then researchers can compare the groups in different conditions to explore how their group processes and group outcomes are different.

In experiments, particularly online experiments where groups interact via text, chat, or IM, researchers can code group members' individual messages for concepts from groupthink and functional theory. For example, we could go over a transcript of a group's interactions and look for group functions and symptoms of groupthink in either an experiment or in a mediated group we're part of:

- Do people disagree with each other? How much?
- Do people bring new information to the group? How much?
- Did people ask for clarification of the problem?
- Do people suggest what an "ideal" solution would look like? How many suggestions were made?
- How many possible solutions did the group consider?
- Did people discuss the pros and cons of the final decision?
- Were there messages that pressured people to conform?
- Were there messages that shut people down when they expressed conflicting ideas?
- Was there really consensus on the decision, or was consensus assumed?

Group outcomes can be difficult to quantify. In experiments, groups are typically given a problem to solve or decision to make and researchers already know the best solution. One such example is the NASA exercise, where group members get a list of items that they must rank in order of importance for their survival during an emergency landing on the moon. The best answers are supplied by NASA. Thus, researchers can control the conditions of the group, monitor interactions for symptoms of groupthink or fulfillment of group functions, then objectively determine which conditions and group processes led to the best and worst decisions.

Insight into Innovation Example: Complete NASA's "Problems in Space" Exercise. You can complete NASA's "Problems in Space" activity here and receive a score based upon NASA's conclusions about what would be most and least useful to people in this situation: http://starchild.gsfc.nasa.gov/docs/StarChild/space_level2/activity/problems_space.html

After completing the activity, consider how your score might have been better working in a group: What skills, knowledge, or resources might group members have had to improve your score? If you were in this situation, do you think you would do better alone or in a group? Why?

In the online environment, experimenting with groups and testing groupthink is getting easier compared to traditional experiments in the lab, but it is still a very difficult undertaking. This is partly because there are many **confounding variables** in groups, or variables that affect how people interact in groups that are difficult to anticipate and may interfere with finding clear, causal relationships between situational variables, processes, and outcomes. For example, some people have anxiety about talking in groups and would be less likely to speak up in group settings regardless of whether they were placed in a highly cohesive group or a less cohesive group. Further complicating things, people's self-perception of their team roles, preference for procedural order, and other individual differences like culture, gender, and personal background can affect how they behave in group settings. In all, figuring out how much of a group's process is affected by stress and constraints in the environment can be a very difficult task. In general, experiments have found support for groupthink's assumptions, and there is also some support for the importance of fulfilling the group's functions in complex problem-solving and decision-making groups.

APPLYING GROUP THEORY IN WEB 2.0: CAPITALIZING ON THE BENEFITS OF CMC IN GROUPS

So, we've learned that groups may be prone to groupthink due to stress from the situation and group member characteristics, and that groupthink leads to ineffective processes within the group and faulty outcomes. We also learned that groups can work toward fulfilling certain functions to improve their processes, and that the composition of groups can be done thoughtfully to improve group processes. Thinking about this in terms of computer-mediated groups, using mediated channels for group projects may help reduce groupthink by reducing peer pressure, but it may make fulfilling essential group functions less efficient.

Benefits of CMC for Group Work. Undeniably, mediated group work is an essential aspect of many employees' lives. As organizations become more geographically dispersed, rely on consultants, and build teams of people from multiple divisions within the organization, employees are often part of multiple groups as part of their daily jobs. Using computer-mediated communication (CMC) to meet, share information, and share ideas and opinions makes group work more manageable for individual members.

Some scholars were optimistic, and expected that CMC would be "liberating," empowering, and an "equalizer" in groups (Spears & Lea, 1994, pp. 429–430). For example, power and status differences can lead to conformity in face-to-face (FTF) teams, but those differences may be less impactful via CMC. Early research suggested that using software to communicate among group members may reduce the silencing of women in work groups when the members can interact at the same time (**synchronous**) and are unidentifiable (**anonymous**) (Herschel, 1994). Also, lower status group members may be more willing to express dissent in anonymous, mediated-group interactions (Walther, 1996).

Anonymity can also liberate people from social constraints; it may make people feel less inhibited, feel less anxious about others' judgments, and less sensitive to self-presentational needs. So when group members are anonymous, they may feel more freedom to express their opinions, which should reduce groupthink (Walther, 1996). For example, Walther observed that anonymous mediated groups may experience greater conflict, "but it is substantive rather than interpersonal conflict, and decision making may be enhanced" (p. 14).

Some research has suggested that "less rich media," or channels that have fewer cues such as chat and IM, can reduce cohesion compared to groups that interact via videoconference or FTF (Hambley, O'Neill, & Kline, 2005). The reduced cohesion may help groups avoid the affiliative constraints that lead to groupthink. On the other hand, having too few cues can also reduce the efficiency of group interactions.

Drawbacks of CMC for Group Work. Of course, in the real world, people often know the people that they work with in a group, even when the group communicates via CMC and is geographically distant. One study that looked at the evidence from 22 studies conducted between 1989 and 1999 found that, when compared to FTF groups, mediated groups who are not anonymous performed *worse* than FTF groups (Baltes, Dickson, Sherman, Bauer, & LaGanke, 2002). The authors attribute this to the possibility that mediated groups may not be fulfilling the group functions outlined in Hirokawa's functional perspective. Anonymity and having unlimited time improved mediated groups' effectiveness. In other words, having more time to work together may help groups fulfill group functions and reach a good decision.

Indeed, time is a very important consideration for mediated groups. CMC can take longer and reduce the overall amount of communication in group interactions which is called a "**floor effect**." People who would communicate a lot via FTF groups may actually contribute *less* via CMC because of the limitations of the channel (i.e., we type fewer words than we would typically speak) (Spears & Lea, 1994). Also, in text-based CMC, there is the potential for confusion as group discussion occurs and so group members are sometimes less satisfied with the process and outcome even when the outcome is ok (Thompson & Coovert, 2003). Thus, purely text-based group interactions are not always ideal because it slows the group down and may reduce some members' contributions. Fortunately, there are many options available that have features to help overcome this, such as video conferencing.

Hybrid Groups: The Best of Both Worlds? One possible solution to the CMC versus FTF paradox is to have hybrid groups, or groups that work both via mediated channels and via FTF. Indeed, teams have many tools available to them to collaborate via CMC, such as e-mail, chat, videoconferencing, and so on. Further, the channels that teams use vary in the extent to which they allow for synchronous communication and the ease of sharing information via the channel (Mesmer-Magnus et al., 2011). For example, websites like GoToMeeting allow you to share your desktop, which is one way to share a lot of information. On the other hand, some group tools, like chats and discussion boards in Blackboard, allow you to share individual files, but it is a more labor-intensive process to share information that way, particularly during a live chat. But, Blackboard keeps a record of interactions, including shared files, that people can refer back to. Given that mediated channels have very different capabilities, it makes sense that using *multiple channels* could improve information sharing, participation, and help people keep track of their group's process and decisions.

In a meta-analysis of 94 studies on virtual teams, Mesmer-Magnus et al. (2011) found that "high virtuality teams," or teams that use more mediated tools to interact, shared more unique information than FTF teams and teams that used fewer CMC tools. Though highly virtual teams' information was more unique, they did tend to be less open about sharing information. Thus, Mesmer-Magnus et al. concluded that "although virtual teams do well with unique information sharing, it is actually open information sharing that is most strongly predictive of their performance. Conversely, although FTF teams are predisposed to openly share information, it is unique information sharing that will promote their performance" (p. 221).

Mesmer-Magnus et al. (2011) suggest that managers consider **hybrid teams** that use both FTF and various mediated tools to maximize team outcomes. They explained that managers should:

- Encourage openness, trust, and ongoing interaction among team members via CMC.
- Provide a variety of tools to teams, such as e-mail, chat, videoconferencing, and areas for sharing content such as databases (I would add cloud storage to this recommendation, such as Google Drive or Dropbox).
- Have teams keep a record of their interactions to refer back to so members can go back to those notes for reference and are also accountable for their contributions.

There are hybrid tools currently available, such as Google, which integrates recorded videoconferencing (Google Hangouts), and document sharing (Google Drive). GoToMeeting also allows people to share their computer screens and video conference; there is also the option to record the meeting to refer back to later. Thus, multimedia tools are emerging that may make hybrid teams a practical solution that alleviates the normative pressure to conform, which is common in FTF meetings, while also helping overcome some of the challenges of CMC in groups. In short, blended groups can use a combination of anonymous, text-based CMC (ideal for brainstorming and critiquing ideas because people are uninhibited), FTF or videoconferencing interactions (to build cohesion), and file sharing software (to share information) to capitalize on the benefits of each channel when completing a group project.

CONCLUSION

In our Web 2.0 world, it is essential to be able to work in mediated groups to produce and market new, innovative products in a rapidly changing environment. Further, organizations are dispersed throughout the world, so the ability to collaborate via mediated channels is that much more imperative to modern professionals. In this chapter, we've covered some pointers we can all use when we are working with a group of people:

- Recognize the contexts that lead to and symptoms of groupthink as they occur.
- To avoid the pitfall of groupthink, focus on fulfilling the essential group functions for the task at hand.
- Pay attention to team composition; understand and capitalize on your own and others' roles within the team.
- Use technologies that enable information sharing, encourage interaction, and to maintain records of interactions.

From a managerial perspective, organizing virtual teams and groups may be time-consuming, but it is a necessary task in our increasingly mediated professional lives and also allows us to capitalize on the benefits of new technologies. Hertel, Geister, and Konradt (2005) recommend the following steps:

1. **Prepare** the team by clarifying their mission, selecting members who will work well together and be able to use the technology, outlining the task (i.e., to generate ideas, make decisions, negotiate solutions, or complete a task), clarifying rewards for quality outcomes, and providing the technology.

2. **Launch** the team with a training workshop, encouraging them to become acquainted with each other and build identification among members, clarifying the goals of the project, and establishing rules for the team process.

3. **Manage team performance** with clear and effective leadership, ongoing monitoring of the team's interactions, responding to the team member's motivations and emotions, providing feedback on the team's process, managing conflicts, and managing knowledge-sharing in the team so that people are openly contributing information.

4. **Develop the team** by assessing their needs and what is missing, providing ongoing training, and assessing the effectiveness of the training.

5. **Disbanding** the team when their work is done, recognizing them for what they have accomplished, and integrating team members back into the organization.

Though group research is particularly difficult to conduct given the task, contextual, individual trait, and channel variables that affect processes and outcomes, groupthink theory offers a solid framework for recognizing and correcting unhealthy group processes. The functional perspective gives us a lens through which we can consider our own and others' contributions to group projects, and pointers on what groups should do to avoid groupthink and reach well-reasoned, informed decisions. Further, CMC is a promising avenue for improving group processes if it is used thoughtfully by managers who compose teams, provide technological resources, and set expectations for the teams. Technology also needs to be used constructively by group members, who should be mindful of how they communicate so that they promote and participate in open discussion, critical thinking, and information sharing and capitalize on the features of CMC channels to help them work through their task.

ASSIGNMENTS

Build a Winning "Comm. Theory" Team

1. Thinking about the syllabus, textbook, and assignments for this class, do you think having a team to work with throughout the semester would help or hinder your progress in the course? Why?

2. Thinking about your classmates, what students would you like to work with on a Comm. Theory team? Which classmates do you think would fulfill the specific roles Belbin suggested? Give their names, the role(s) you'd expect them to fulfill, and your rationale for choosing them for their specific role(s).

3. Explain what you think your role in the Comm. Theory group would be and why you see yourself as fitting that role.

4. Are there features of this class, or this situation, that might increase the likelihood of groupthink if you were assigned to work with this Comm. Theory team for the semester?

5. Lastly, imagine that you were required to work with the Comm. Theory team you just created. What technologies would you use to study together and complete course assignments together? How would the features of the technologies you recommend help your group collaborate throughout the semester?

Teamwork Practice: Choose a New Technology to Use in this Course

Team objective: Discover and recommend a new technology that a) is not currently used in this course and b) would improve students' learning and participation.

Team composition: Work in groups of 3–5

Team interaction: Use mediated channels (i.e., e-mail, online chat, recorded videoconferencing) to explore your options, make a selection, and write a recommendation.

Team submission: As a group, submit a final recommendation to your instructor via e-mail with a) instructions for accessing the technology and b) a brief overview of the technology and c) why your team recommended it. Also submit the recording or transcripts of your interactions to your instructor as an attachment.

Individual Submission: Assess Group Processes and Outcomes:

1. What mediated channel did your group use to communicate? Did the features of this channel improve your group interactions or make them more difficult? How so?

2. What technology did your group recommend? Do you agree that this should be adopted by your instructor? Why or why not?

3. Look over the transcripts or listen to the recording of your group's interactions. What evidence of groupthink did you observe in your group's interactions?

    a. Were there elements of the context or situation that may have led to groupthink?

    b. Did you observe behaviors or messages during group interactions that may be symptoms of groupthink?

    c. Looking at the interactions in your group, do you see flaws in your decision-making process?

    d. What would you do differently as a group member given your observations about the group processes?

4. Referring to specific team members (including yourself), consider who fulfilled which of Belbin's team roles in the group. Use specific examples from the transcripts and recordings to discuss each team member's role.

    a. Who was the "thinker"?

    b. Who was "people-oriented"?

    c. Who was "the producer"?

5. Lastly, referring to the recording of your group's interactions, look for fulfillment of the group functions. Give specific examples/evidence from the recording to support your responses.

    a. Did your group discuss and clarify the problem?

    b. Did your group discuss criteria for recommending a new technology? What were your decision criteria?

    c. Did your group thoroughly explore realistic options to recommend? What options, other than what you recommended, did your group consider?

d. Did your group use criteria to evaluate different new technologies? How did your group choose the technology that you recommended?

e. If your instructor adopted the technology that your group recommended, do you personally think it would help you as a student in this course? Why or why not?

REFERENCES

Seminal Texts:

Janis, I. L. (1974). *Groupthink: Psychological studies of policy decisions and fiascoes.* Boston: Houghton Mifflin.

Hirokawa, R. Y. (1985). Discussion procedures and decision-making performance: A test of a functional perspective. *Human Communication Research, 12,* 203–224.

Academic Articles:

Baltes, B. B., Dickson, M. W., Sherman, M. P., Bauer, C. C., & LaGanke, J. S. (2002). Computer-mediated communication and group decision making: A meta-analysis. *Organizational Behavior and Human Decision Processes, 87,* 156–179.

Belbin, R. M. (1993). *Team roles at work.* Burlington, MA: Elsevier.

Bergström, J., Miller, M., & Horneiji, E. (2015). Work environment perceptions following relocation to open-plan offices: A twelve-month longitudinal study. *Work, 50,* 221–228.

Esser, J. K. (1998). Alive and well after 25 years: A review of groupthink research. *Organizational Behavior and Human Decision Processes, 73,* 116–141.

Gouran, D. S., & Hirokawa, R. Y. (1996). Functional theory and communication in decision-making groups and problem-solving groups. In R. Y. Hirokawa & M. S. Poole (Eds.), *Communication and group decision making* (2nd ed., pp. 55–80). Thousand Oaks, CA: Sage.

Hambley, L. A., O'Neill, T. A., & Kline, T. J. B. (2005). Virtual team leadership: The effects of leadership style and communication medium on team interaction styles and outcomes. *Organizational Behavior and Human Decision Processes, 103,* 1–20.

Herschel, R. T. (1994). The impact of varying gender composition on group brainstorming performance in a GSS environment. *Computers in Human Behavior, 10,* 209–222.

Hertel, G., Geister, S., & Konradt, U. (2005). Managing virtual teams: A review of current empirical research. *Human Resource Management Review, 15,* 69–95.

Hirokawa, R. Y. (1980). A comparative analysis of communication patterns within effective and ineffective decision-making groups. *Communication Monographs, 47*(4), 312–321.

Hirokawa, R. Y., Ice, R., & Cook, J. (1988). Preference for procedural order, discussion structure and group decision performance. *Communication Quarterly, 36*(3), 217–226.

Hollingshead, A. B., Wittenbaum, G. M., Paulus, P. B., Hirokawa, R. Y., Ancona, D. G., Peterson, R. S., Jehn, K. A., & Yoon, K. (2005). A look at groups from the functional perspective. In M. S. Poole & A. B. Hollingshead (Eds.), *Theories of small groups: interdisciplinary perspectives* (pp. 21–62). Thousand Oaks, CA: Sage.

Mesmer-Magnus, J. R., DeChurch, L. A., Jimenez-Rodriguez, M., & Wildman, J. (2011). A meta-analytic investigation of virtuality and information sharing in teams. *Organizational Behavior and Human Decision Processes, 115,* 214–225.

Offices linked to poor health. (2014). *Occupational Health, 66*(6), 5.

Poole, M. S., Seibold, D. R., & McPhee, R. D. (1986). A structural approach to theory-building. In R. Y. Hirokawa & M. S. Poole (Eds.), *Communication and group decision making* (pp. 237–264). Thousand Oaks, CA: Sage.

Putnam, L. L. (1979). Preference for procedural order in task-oriented small groups. *Communication Monographs, 46,* 193–218.

Senior, B. (1997). Team roles and team performance: is there "really" a link? *Journal of Occupational and Organizational Psychology, 70,* 241–258.

Spears, R., & Lea, M. (1994). Panacea or panopticon? The hidden power in computer-mediated communication. *Communication Research, 21,* 427–459.

Thompson, L. F., & Coovert, M. D. (2003). Teamwork online: The effects of computer conferencing on perceived confusion, satisfaction, and postdicussion accuracy. *Group Dynamics: Theory, Research, and Practice, 7,* 135–151.

Walther, J. B. (1996). Computer-mediated communication: Impersonal, interpersonal, and hyperpersonal interaction. *Communication Research, 23,* 3–43.

Examples:

Cain, S. (2012, January 13). The rise of the new groupthink. *The New York Times.* Retrieved from http://www.nytimes.com/2012/01/15/opinion/sunday/the-rise-of-the-new-groupthink.html?_r=0

ORGANIZATIONAL CULTURES

INTRODUCTION

Organizational culture theory takes our understanding of human culture and applies it to organizations. Recall from the chapter on accommodation and politeness that we defined culture as the values shared by a group of people. Organizations also have distinct values, and the cultural approach argues that these values emerge through organizational members' interactions with each other, much like culture emerges through interactions in geographic regions.

If you have held similar jobs at different companies, or have been a student at more than one college, chances are you have observed differences in organizations. As a result, you likely felt differently about those organizations and behaved differently in those organizations. Organizational culture theory gives us a lens through which we can interpret our organizational experiences and understand how we affect and are affected by organizational cultures.

Thus, according to organizational cultures theory, we are not passive victims of an organization's culture; we cocreate culture through our interactions and behaviors. So organizational culture isn't just your company's mission statement or college's strategic plan: it is how every member of the organization behaves and "fits" with the values of the organization.

MAIN IDEA

The cultural approach describes organizations as "tribes" rather than systems (Pacanowsky & O'Donnell-Trujillo, 1983, p. 127). In these tribes, members participate in performances, where they enact their roles during their interactions with coworkers. These interactions, like all human communication, are affected by context, they are episodic, and there is an element of improvisation to most of our interactions. In other words, our interactions at work occur in the broader *context* of our role, power, and the history of the organization. Our interactions are often identifiable *episodes* that have beginnings and endings. And though some rituals are scripted, much of it is *improvisational*, which is to say that we "make it up as we go." There are two levels of meaning to observe in organizational communication as we observe these improvised episodes: a) what is actually done or said and b) the underlying meaning of what is done or said in terms of what it implies about people's perceptions.

KEY CONCEPTS OF ORGANIZATIONAL CULTURES
(PACANOWSKY & O'DONNELL-TRUJILLO, 1983)

1. **Rituals**. Organizational communication involves personal, task, social, and organizational rituals. **Rituals** are repeated patterns for doing things. For example, your professor probably has a specific way he or she starts each class, and this is his or her **personal ritual**. **Task rituals** are how we go about completing our job requirements. For example, my classes follow a relatively typical pattern: I review what we covered in the last class, remind students of upcoming due dates, then delve into the material we are scheduled to cover for that day, then preview what we will cover in the next class and offer one last reminder of upcoming due dates. There are also **social rituals** in many workplaces, such as happy hour get-togethers on Fridays. Lastly, there are **organizational rituals**, such as holiday parties, or annual family picnics.

2. **Passion**. Passion is how we describe organizational activities. **Storytelling** is one way we communicate organizational life. We may tell **personal stories** that make us look good or reiterate our identity within the organization. People tell **collegial stories** about the good and the bad experiences they've had with coworkers, which reveal how the organization "really" is in the eyes of its employees. We also tell corporate stories about how the organization works and indicate how organizational members perceive the organization's structure, processes, and its history.

3. **Sociality**. Organizations also have formal and informal "codes of behavior" for how employees interact (p. 139). For example, there are **courtesies**, or the small favors we do for others or things we say to be courteous, such as always saying "hello" and "goodbye" when we're coming and going from the office. We also exchange **pleasantries**, such as small talk, that can help us get to know our coworkers. **Sociabilities**, such as joking, gossiping, and talking about work can also help coworkers become closer. These pleasantries and sociabilities are also balanced with individuals' **privacies**, or interactions that are private because they are appraisals, confessions, or consolations among coworkers.

4. **Politics**. Coworkers also promote their own self-interests and influence others through politicking. For example, when people command others, take credit for good outcomes, or exercise control over a particular aspect of the organization, they are showing their **personal strength** in the organization. We also seek allies in organizations, such as people who agree with us, offer support, and who pass tests of loyalty. We also **bargain**, or negotiate, in organizations to meet our needs and goals. We have to negotiate when our goals or needs are different from someone else's, and the processes for bargaining are an element of organizational culture.

5. **Enculturation**. Part of "fitting" in an organization is enculturation, or learning about and adapting to an organization's unique culture. We learn our own role within the organization and also learn the organization's processes. Through observing rituals, hearing passions, observing and participating in socialities and politics, we learn what an organization is and what it is not.

METHODS FOR RESEARCHING ORGANIZATIONAL CULTURES

Geertz's (1973) ideas about culture were the foundation of the organizational cultural theory that Pacanowsky and O'Donnell-Trujillo explained. In particular, Geertz wrote that his definition of culture is "semiotic." In other words, "man is an animal suspended in webs of significance he himself has spun" and "I take culture to be those webs, and the analysis of it to be therefore not an experimental science in search of law but an *interpretive* one in search of *meaning*" (p. 5, emphasis added).

Ethnographic studies. Geertz's recommendation that culture be observed and described is an ethnographic approach to research. That is to say, the researcher goes into the organization, observes, talks to people, and tries to see the organization from their perspective. In general, researchers analyze the rituals in the organization, their traditions, the system of formal and informal rewards and punishments, and observe the language that people use in their descriptions and observations about the physical environment in the organization to make inferences about the culture. Thus, cultural research, including research on organizational cultures, uses **thick description** of people's behaviors to interpret the culture as it is created, recreated, and perceived by members of the organization.

Generally, organizational cultures are researched qualitatively. This research involves observing an organization, interviewing employees, and taking detailed notes on observations (Ott, 1989). In terms of what to look for, Ott offers things that we can pay attention to when we are getting a sense of an organization's culture:

1. *Look at the physical space.* Things like buildings, the furnishing and decorations, the arrangement of office space, and logos reflect organizational values.

2. *Listen to the language used by members of the organization.* The myths and stories people tell and retell communicate organizational values. Many stories imply a lesson or a "moral" and give insight into people's perceptions of what is important, valuable, or not acceptable within an organization. Similarly, the unique jargon used by people in an organization can offer insight into what is considered good or bad, right or wrong.

3. *Look for patterns of behavior to infer norms.* Things such as rites, rituals, traditions, and rewards and punishments in the organization tell us what is valued and what is punished.

4. *Infer the values and beliefs of the organization* from all of the collected observations, trying to reflect the organization as it is perceived through the eyes of the members of the organization.

After taking in this rich, detailed information within an organization, researchers infer or interpret the organizational culture, or the organizational values. Organizational culture, therefore, is a web comprised of all of these elements of employees' and managers' communication and behaviors, and people create and recreate this culture through communication about and within the organization.

EXAMPLE OF THEORY IN WEB 2.0: ORGANIZATIONAL CULTURE AT AMAZON

An interesting example of "thick description" of an organization's culture was *The New York Times* report on the corporate atmosphere at Amazon. *The New York Times* report on Amazon's culture included interviews with over 100 people who had worked there. The resulting description of the business practices within Amazon and some employees' descriptions of the work environment makes it clear that Amazon has fostered a unique, "all-in" culture within the organization. Amazon's culture is strikingly different from other West Coast tech companies like Google. In short, the *Time*'s report argued that, "Amazon is where overachievers go to feel bad about themselves" (Kantor & Streitfeld, 2015, para. 55).

Here are some of the examples offered in the *Time*'s article about the organizational culture at Amazon:

Rituals/Rites:

- There are orientations for new hires to Amazon's 14 leadership principles and the expectation is that they will memorize these principles and refer to them often.
- Organizational level review occurs annually. This is when employees are ranked by a group of managers who place employees' names on a chart, then negotiate ranking them from best to worst. Each manager is charged with "defending" his or her most valuable employees with data and facts. Lowest ranking employees are cut. This is called "rank and yank."

Traditions and Rewards/Punishments:

- Conflict and criticism are encouraged to bring about change and innovation.
- Business reviews are data-driven reviews of employees that occur weekly or monthly without forewarning to the employee.

- Data is used to evaluate employees, and each year the bottom tier of employees are fired; employee turnover may be very high.
- Successful employees are given stocks that may be equal to their annual pay.

Verbal Symbols:

- *Narratives* from former employees include:
  - People crying at their desks.
  - Working through holidays like Thanksgiving, through personal vacations and at night.
  - Sabotaging coworkers to try to get their resources.
  - Firing people for, or otherwise discouraging them from, caring for sick family members, taking time off due to their own illnesses, or having children.
- *Language/Jargon* at Amazon:
  - "Purposeful Darwinism" refers to the regular firings among the staff.
  - "Cold pricklies" are the e-mails that Amazon.com sends to customers when their packages don't arrive on time.
  - "I'm Peculiar" is a compliment given to new employees who can recall all 14 Amazon leadership principles.
  - "Customer obsession" is being focused on what will make customers happy.
  - "Vocally self-critical" is being someone who openly criticizes him- or herself.
  - "Ambot" is someone who has internalized the culture and practices at Amazon.
  - "The full paste" is when coworkers' comments and evaluations of an employee are copied and pasted directly into performance reviews.

Physical Symbols:

- The Amazon logo (as seen in the image on the previous page) is a smiling arrow. Perhaps this implies their goal of customer satisfaction.
- There is a new 10-million-square-foot campus in Seattle, which indicates their financial success and growth.
- "Anytime Feedback" is a directory of employees where any employee can offer positive or negative feedback on their peers directly to the management.
- Desks are bare to highlight the importance of a frugal workplace.

Values:

- Brutal honesty and dissent
- Frugality
- A focus on only retaining "star" employees
- Goal of becoming the first trillion-dollar retail corporation
- Making data-driven decisions

As you can see from the example of Amazon based on the *New York Times* report, there is a culture at the company that is evident in their rituals, traditions, verbal symbols, and visual symbols. This "web" of meaning is as much about how the employees behave (i.e., coworkers sabotaging each other; managers participating in the annual "rank and yank") as it is the processes within the company (14 principles they are taught; the anytime feedback system; the annual rank and yank). In fact, in reaction to the *New York Times* article on Amazon, Amazon founder and CEO Jeff Bezos responded that the culture described in the article was not what he had observed and that instances like the ones cited in the story should be reported to human resources (Noguchi, 2015). This may be because the behaviors that create the culture aren't *mandated* per se, so much as they emerged over time through people's perceptions and interactions.

So, who is right about Amazon's culture, the CEO or the former employees cited in the article? Herein lies one of the issues with the cultural approach to organizations: both the CEO and the former employees may be correct in their perceptions. Perceptions of reality, as we discussed earlier in this book, vary from person to person. In particular, narrative accounts of events can be affected by a person's standpoint. Thus, the CEO may not actually see these things happen and thus may perceive the culture as ambitious and innovative. On the other hand, employees who are interacting everyday may be cocreating a culture that is competitive and stressful in response to the policies and organizational principles espoused by that CEO.

Ethnographic research is about seeing things through someone else's eyes, and if we take a step back, we can see the situation at Amazon through the eyes of the CEO and of the employees. The CEO wants to build a massive, competitive company using the best and most productive employees; the employees want to be part of that powerful company and work fiercely to keep their jobs, thus setting an unreasonably high standard for employee performance.

Insight into Innovation Activity: Is Amazon helping or hurting its bottom line? Read *The New York Times'* report on Amazon. Thinking about this from a cost-benefit perspective, how might the norms and values at Amazon ultimately help and hurt the company's bottom line? Do the costs outweigh the benefits for Amazon? Thinking about this from the employees' perspectives, do you think that the costs of working at Amazon outweigh the benefits? Why or why not?

The *New York Times* report is available here: http://www.nytimes.com/2015/08/16/technology/inside-amazon-wrestling-big-ideas-in-a-bruising-workplace.html?_r=0

Survey Studies. Though qualitative studies of organizational cultures are common, organizational culture research in business and organizational psychology also uses survey methods. On the basis of observations of cultures, for example, we can create typologies of organizational cultures, or a list of general types of organizational cultures, such as Cameron and Quinn's four culture types described below. Using the general types of organizational cultures as a guide, we can develop surveys to measure whether people perceive an organization as having the characteristics and values associated with one or more culture types. Indeed, numerous scale measures of culture exist for that purpose (Ashkanasy, Broadfoot, & Falkus, 2000). Developing these measures helps researchers and practitioners assess an organization's culture, and address questions about the outcomes or effects of organizations: Which cultures improve employee satisfaction, commitment, and productivity? What types of people fit best in which types of organizational culture?

APPLIED RESEARCH: ORGANIZATIONAL CULTURE AND ROLES IN A FLEXIBLE WORKPLACE

Not all employees are dissatisfied with Amazon; indeed, many people report that they thrive in this environment. This, of course, raises a lot of questions about organizational culture, particularly how we can choose an organization with a culture that works for us and how we can promote a culture that attracts and retains top talent but also ensures profitability and productivity. Not surprisingly, organizational culture, particularly issues of "fit" in an organizational culture, are related to employees' productivity, dedication, and satisfaction at work. One key distinction between organizational cultures is the extent to which they are flexible versus controlled.

Organization-Level Cultures. Cameron and Quinn (2006) describe four general types of organizational cultures and the values associated with those cultures. Hierarchy and market-focused cultures tend to be more controlling; clan and adhocracy cultures tend to be more flexible and allow workers more discretion in their day-to-day jobs.

- **Controlling cultures**:
  - **Hierarchy cultures** are bureaucracies. They value "rules, specialization, meritocracy, hierarchy, separate ownership, impersonality, and accountability" (p. 37).
  - **Market cultures** are competitive. They value external relationships with customers and clients, and focus primarily on achieving sales, acquiring contracts, and making profits.
- **Flexible cultures**:
  - **Clan cultures** are collaborative. They value team building, communication among members, and facilitating outcomes.
  - **Adhocracy cultures** are creative. They value innovation, change, and adaptability.

Culture and Organizational Outcomes. In the changing technological environment that organizations exist in today, some researchers have suggested that adhocracy cultures may be better suited to adapting to advances in technology (Srinivasan, Lilien, & Rangaswamy, 2002). Adhocracies tend to embrace change and innovations, whereas hierarchies tend to be slow to respond and less agile. Thus, the agility and adaptability of adhocracies is appealing. In terms of the innovation needed to come up with "the next big thing," adhocracies may have the advantage there too. In adhocracies, employees report more participation and being more creative in the workplace (Schepers & ven den Berg, 2007).

A recent meta-analysis looked at the data from 84 studies that had researched Cameron and Quinn's organizational culture types and they found that market cultures seem to outperform both adhocracies and clans in terms of innovative products and profits (Hartnell, Ou, & Kinicki, 2011). On the other hand, employees in adhocracies and, even more so, in clan cultures, were more satisfied in their jobs and were more committed to their employers compared to employees in market cultures.

So, we have research that points to two different conclusions: some research suggests that adhocracies are best for creativity and innovation. Other research suggests that, overall, adhocracies are satisfying to employees, but their outputs are not as high quality and profitable as market cultures. The inconsistency in these findings may come down to cultural "fit", or whether the culture in the organization is one in which the types of people they need are likely to thrive and be productive.

Professional Subcultures. The type of organizational culture that will lead to both organizational outputs and employee outcomes may be a result of the type of industry. For example, Schein (2010) explains that different professional specializations and occupations also have cultures, which can, in turn, affect the organization's culture. Thus, software developers often have a subculture, health-care professionals have a subculture, and even we professors have a subculture related to our respective occupations. These subcultures affect how we fit and interact in the broader organizational culture. As a result, culture in higher education organizations tends to be different from culture in technology companies or in hospitals. Having an overall organizational culture that fits with or accommodates the professional cultures represented in the organization may promote commitment, satisfaction, and productivity.

Individual Differences and Identification. Another important consideration is that there are individual differences in organizational fit, and employees who feel a sense of identification and fit may be more committed and productive. Organizational **identification** is the extent to which we identify with, or see ourselves as "fitting" within the organization (Stinglhamber et al., 2015). Put another way, it is whether the values within the organization's culture fit with our own personal preferences and values.

Organizational identification is also related to our commitment to the organization. Whether or not you would fit best in a more controlled versus more flexible organization depends on your own personal preferences and identity. You may see your profession as defining "who you are" or you may see your profession as "what you do" or as a "means to an end." Also, you may work better in a structured environment with clear objectives, or you may work better when the desired outcomes are unclear. Thus, whether or not a particular organizational culture will "work" for you depends on both culture and traits.

Using a large, international survey of employees at companies, Übius and Alas (2009) found that people from different countries were affected by organizational cultures differently. In other words, each of these organizational cultures can lead to better outcomes for the company and the employees when they *fit the larger national culture.* For example, if we have an individualistic culture and capitalist values, a market culture may be productive for the company and also satisfying for the employees.

Further research applying Cameron and Quinn's culture types found that perceptions of organizational culture "fit" also depends on people's personalities (Gardner et al., 2012). Not surprisingly based on our discussion of personality traits earlier in this book, extraverts fit well in clan cultures, conscientious personalities fit well in hierarchies, people who were low in agreeable personality characteristics fit well in market cultures, and openness was related to fit in adhocracy cultures. This may be why so many organizations use personality tests as part of their hiring processes: certain individual traits may influence whether or not we fit in the existing culture of a company.

Insight into Innovation Activity: What is your "flex style"? Though we may think of flexible employers as the "ideal," not all people like the idea, or practice, of flexible workplaces. *The Washington Post* reported on the link between organizational culture, employee burnout, and work-life fit (Schulte, 2015). The researcher interviewed for the story, Ellen Ernst Kossek, reported a host of emotional and physical consequences for worker burnout. Though teleworking and flextime may be a good option for some people to avoid burnout, the blending of work and home can be stressful for other people.

Consider her recommendations for reflecting on your own flex style, and how that may influence where you would "fit" best as an employee:

1. In terms of your identity, are you more work-life, personal-life, or dual focused?

2. What is your need to control the boundaries between family interrupting your work life and work interrupting your family life?

3. In terms of the role of technology in your life, do you prefer that work and personal communication be separate, or is it ok with you to blur the lines between work and nonwork communication?

On the basis of your responses to these questions, consider whether you are an integrator, volleyer, or separator:

- **Integrators** are more satisfied with combining their work and home lives.

- **Volleyers** prefer to go back and forth while maintaining some boundaries between work and home.

- **Separators** prefer that work and home be completely separate.

Which of these best describes your preferred work-life boundaries?

Would you do well with a more controlling culture or more flexible culture given your preferred boundaries?

What does this tell you about the type of organizational culture that would fit your boundary preferences?

What type of work arrangement do you think would work best for you given your work style: teleworking, a blend of teleworking and working in an office, or working exclusively in an office?

You can read the interview with Professor Kossek here: http://www.washingtonpost.com/news/inspired-life/wp/2015/08/10/the-wrong-boss-can-also-ruin-your-home-life-heres-how-to-make-sure-that-doesnt-happen/

Taken together, the research on the link between organizational cultural values, productivity, and individual differences in occupations, regional culture, employees' personalities, and work styles, suggests that deciding whether or not an organization's culture is "good" versus "bad" or "effective" versus "ineffective" may not be the best approach to applying organizational culture research. Rather, we might be better off considering whether all of these elements "fit" together in a way that is productive for both the company and the employees. Arguably, tech companies likely do need more flexibility, agility, and adaptability, because their goal (technological innovations), occupations (software developers, testers, etc.), the "Silicon Valley" culture, and the types of people they employ (e.g., young, ambitious, STEM grads, etc.), might very well thrive in adhocracy cultures such as Google.

On the other hand, retail companies that focus on selling products, such as Amazon, make sense as market cultures. Their goal is to generate product sales with external consumers. Thus they employ people to create, test, and promote products and services in a highly competitive retail environment, and measure employees' success by that standard.

Insight into Innovation Activity: Google versus Amazon. Check out this CBS video about working at Google: https://youtu.be/_QqT38QRA84 (or, for more in-depth look at Google, watch the National Geographic look at Google https://youtu.be/7vPJT5KZLtM).

Compare CBS' description of life at Google with the *New York Times'* description of life at Amazon:

- How are the descriptions of Google's and Amazon's cultures different in terms of being more controlling versus flexible?

- Is Google more of a hierarchy, market, clan, or adhocracy culture? How about Amazon, which type does it best fit into?

- Now thinking about the flex styles and personality types discussed in this chapter, what type of people would likely fit best at Google? What type of people would likely fit best at Amazon? Why?

LEADERSHIP CHARACTERISTICS AND FLEXIBILITY

If we think critically about organizational culture, it is understandable that the cultures of Google and Amazon are so very different because their leaders are so very different. At Amazon, Bazos wrote and stressed 14 leadership principles (http://www.amazon.jobs/principles). At Google, they have the motto, "don't be evil," and they focused on "culture fit" and personality even in the earliest days of their corporate hiring. As a result of these early differences in the vision of the organizational founders, we see two very different organizational cultures emerge. Employees at Google describe the open and free flow of information within the organization, though they are very guarded about sharing information and details about different projects with people outside the organization. Amazon's culture, on the other hand, is one that promotes competition, and as a result, information and resources are not free and open. The controlled versus flexible cultures that resulted from these leadership styles are fundamentally different.

Schein (1983) argued that the goals, beliefs, and characteristics of corporate founders establishes organizational culture early in a corporation's formation. Later, Schien (2010) linked leadership characteristics to the cultures that emerge. Further, Schein argued that when a culture begins to undermine the effectiveness of the organization in reaching its goals, it is the responsibility of the leadership "to recognize and do something about this situation" (p. 11). So, the last thing we will consider in this chapter is how the characteristics of organizational leaders and managers shape organizational culture and work habits.

X versus Y Theories of Management. One consideration in terms of leadership characteristics is whether the leaders of an organization have more Theory X (people are lazy and are motivated by money) versus Theory Y (people are self-motivated) beliefs. McGregor (1960) argued that managers' beliefs and attitudes toward their subordinates were reflected in their communication and behaviors: Some managers believe that people want to do well, be creative, innovative, and productive (Theory Y), while other managers believe that people are not personally responsible and close supervision is necessary to ensure that people do their jobs (Theory X). Thus, holding these beliefs about employees creates either a supportive climate where people are trusted and empowered (Theory Y) or an untrusting climate where there is an emphasis on supervision and people feel controlled (Theory X).

Theory X	Theory Y
• Managers create productive organizations to meet economic goals using money and materials. • People should be controlled, their behaviors monitored and changed to meet the goals of the organization. • Managers must be proactive because employees are passive, lazy, self-centered, likely to resist changes, unambitious, and not very smart.	• People's motivation and initiative has been dampened by managers' control; people are not inherently lazy and passive. • People are motivated, can be responsible, and can be developed. • Effective managers recognize the potential in their employees and help employees develop their best characteristics to work toward the goals of the organization.

Theory X and Theory Y really boil down to how much trust we have in people to do their jobs. Whether a leader is more X- or Y-oriented affects the amount of independence they allow their subordinates as a result of this trust. If we embrace Theory Y, we give people *autonomy* to control the time and place of their work (Maitland & Thomson, 2011).

Maitland and Thomson argue that meeting the demands of modern work requires adoption of a Theory Y approach to leadership: focusing on what employees produce rather than when and how they produce it and empowering employees to choose the work conditions that best suit their own needs, goals, and work habits. They argue that there are numerous positive outcomes for the company when this approach to work is adopted. People are more productive, responsive to changes in the business environment, and customer service improves. Business costs are also reduced, as there is less employee turnover and absenteeism, and the material costs of running a business (workspace, business supplies, and travel costs) are reduced.

Employees can perceive when their employers have Theory X beliefs about employees, and this can undermine efforts to create a flexible, and thus productive, workplace. When first being introduced as an option, employees report being skeptical of the flexible options offered by their employers because of the culture of the organization itself and their own misgivings (Hylmö, 2006). Thus, by maximizing people's choice to use flexibility options, productivity can be improved by offering flextime and teleworking as an option. When teleworking is a choice and is seen as a flexible, informal arrangement, it leads to employees feeling more of a sense of responsibility (Hall & Atkinson, 2006). In all, we cannot just espouse Theory Y beliefs and offer people flexible schedules and telework options; we must have and enact Theory Y beliefs

Once we've made the leap to a more autonomous work environment where people can choose what works best for them, then we must consider the leadership qualities that will promote ongoing productivity, commitment, and satisfaction. Leader-Member Exchange (LMX) is one approach to leadership that is particularly fitting for a flexible organizational culture and workplace.

Leader-Member Exchange. The leadership of the organization can also set a pace and tone that either encourages or discourages telework productivity and flexibility. For example, **LMX** can affect productivity in both face-to-face and telework arrangements (Golden & Veiga, 2008). High LMX relationships are marked by an open exchange of ideas, knowledge, and resources that promote trust, loyalty, bonding, and productivity between leaders and the people they lead. LMX leaders are particularly effective at promoting commitment, job satisfaction, and improving job performance for people who telework.

It makes sense that high LMX would be related to increased productivity, particularly among teleworkers: allowing teleworking should be empowering to employees.

Also, it seems that full-time teleworking, rather than teleworking as part of one's work life, may be the best option for some people (Golden & Veiga, 2005). But this may only be the case for jobs where teleworking is comfortable given the employee's job requirements. When teleworkers rely on other people to get their jobs done, teleworking is somewhat less satisfying. On the other hand, when employees have a lot of discretion in terms of when and how to do their jobs, more teleworking seems to lead to more satisfaction.

In all, the research suggests that promoting teleworking can be helped by having flexible leaders who empower employees to choose whether or not they prefer to telework and to what extent they should take their jobs online. Thus, a high LMX style, where the leader is familiar with and dedicated to his/her employees, should be responsive to the concerns, work style preferences, and traits of employees, as well as the culture of the organization.

CONCLUSION

In our Web 2.0 world, it is easier than ever to observe organizational cultures, both as they are constructed and how they are perceived. We have new forms of work, and the diversity of organizational cultures reflects the diversity of jobs in the new economy. In the *New York Times* report on Amazon, one person recalled receiving negative feedback from her peers because she wasn't present in the office, even though she had an agreement with her supervisor that she would telework. The *National Geographic* description of Google reported that some people don't show up for work until after 9 and showed employees taking midday breaks to play games, and everyone was ok with that as long as the work gets done. These are clearly two very different companies with two very different cultures resulting from the leadership styles of their founders and the personalities and work styles of the people in the organization.

Organizational culture is a complex web, spun through human interactions in the workplace. What emerges can be a culture that is innovative, agile, and able to change as technologies and consumers' needs change. The culture in an organization affects how people think and feel about their jobs, and ultimately their productivity. What type of organizational culture will work best for each of us depends on myriad things, such as our own values, work styles, personality, culture, and our relationship with our leaders. Good leadership in an organization is responsive to both the culture and goals of the organization and the skills and needs of its employees.

Having a self-aware, responsive approach to leadership and an organizational culture that fits the environment and goals of the organization, as well as the employees, is essential now more than ever. Organizations face an ever-changing environment, and must adapt their approach to organizing and managing human resources to meet those changes, lest they go the way of Blockbuster and Circuit City and find that their business models are obsolete in the Web 2.0 world.

Insight into Innovation Example: Why We Need to Rethink Work. In a *New York Times* article, Schwartz (2015) reports that as much as 90 percent of the American workforce doesn't feel engaged at work. Schwartz, a professor of psychology, argues that many companies still have outdated beliefs about employees, and that the focus on wages is misplaced. He argues that people need to feel empowered, that companies should invest in cultivating employees, and that employees need to feel that the work they do is important. What do you think? Is how much money we make as important as whether we like we what do? Thinking about this from a social exchange perspective, where rewards and costs are unique to each of us, what do *you* expect to get out of your "ideal" job other than a paycheck and benefits package?

Read Schwartz' opinion piece in the *Times* here: http://www.nytimes.com/2015/08/30/opinion/sunday/rethinking-work.html?_r=0

ASSIGNMENTS

1. **Conduct a cultural analysis of your university**. For one day, carefully observe your university: how professors and staff interact with students, how professors talk about the university, and how students talk about the university; research the traditions at your university, and think critically about the physical symbols on your campus.

   a. What are the cultural values of your university? Give examples from each of the following to support your conclusion:

      i. Student's verbal symbols

      ii. Faculty and staff's verbal symbols

      iii. The university's physical symbols

      iv. The university's traditions

      v. The rewards and punishments for students at your university

      vi. The rewards and punishments for faculty and staff at the university

b. Overall, do you think your university is more a hierarchy, market, clan, or adhocracy culture?

   c. What professional subcultures did you observe among the faculty and staff at your university? Support your response with examples.

   d. In terms of students, do faculty seem to have a more Theory X or Theory Y beliefs about students? Support your response with examples.

   e. In terms of faculty, does the university administration seem to have a more Theory X or Theory Y beliefs about faculty? Support your response with examples.

2. **Self-reflection: Would you enjoy being and do well as a DE student?** Some people are good at working from home, and some people fail to thrive in that arrangement. Thinking about your own work/school *flexstyle*, your *interactions* with other students and professors, and your *identification* with your program of study and university, do you think you would do well as a distance learner in online classes? Why or why not?

REFERENCES

Seminal Texts:

Geertz, C. (1973). *The interpretation of cultures: Selected essays.* New York: Basic Books.

Pacanowsky, M. E., & O'Donnell-Trujillo, N. (1983). Organizational communication as cultural performance. *Communication Monographs*, 50, 126–147.

Academic Articles:

Ashkanasy, N. M., Broadfoot, L. E., & Falkus, S. (2000). Questionnaire Measures of organizational culture. In N. Ashkanasy, C. P. M. Wilderom & M. F. Peterson (Eds.), *Handbook of organizational culture and climate* (pp. 131–145). Thousand Oaks, CA: Sage.

Cameron, K. S., & Quinn, R. E. (2006). *Diagnosing and changing organizational culture based on the competing values framework.* San Francisco, CA: John Wiley & Sons.

Gardner, W. L., Reithel, B. J., Cogliser, C. C., Walumbwa, F. O., & Foley, R. T. (2012). Matching personality and organizational culture: Effects of recruitment strategy and the five-factor model on subjective person–organization fit. *Management Communication Quarterly*, 26(4), 585–622.

Golden, T. D., & Veiga, J. F. (2008). The impact of superior–subordinate relationships on the commitment, job satisfaction, and performance of virtual workers. *Leadership Quarterly*, 19(1), 77–88.

Golden, T. D., & Veiga, J. F. (2005). The impact of extent of telecommuting on job satisfaction: Resolving inconsistent findings. *Journal of Management*, 31(2), 301–318.

Hartnell, C. A., Ou, A. Y., & Kinicki, A. (2011). Organizational culture and organizational effectiveness: A meta-analytic investigation of the competing values framework's theoretical suppositions. *Journal of Applied Psychology*, 96(4), 677–694.

McGregor, D. M. (1960). *The human side of enterprise*. New York: McGraw Hill.

Schien, E. H. (1983). The role of the founder in the creation of organizational culture. *Office of Naval Research*. Retrieved from http://oai.dtic.mil/oai/oai?verb=getRecord&metadataPrefix=html&identifier=ADA126356

Schein, E. H. (2010). *Organizational culture and leadership* (4th ed). San Francisco, CA: John Wiley & Sons.

Schepers, P., & Berg, P. T. (2007). Social factors of work-environment creativity. *Journal of Business & Psychology, 21*(3), 407–428.

Srinivasan, R., Lilien, G. L., & Rangaswamy, A. (2002). Technological opportunism and radical technology adoption: An application to e-business. *Journal of Marketing, 66*(3), 47–60.

Stinglhamber, F., Marique, G., Caesens, G., Desmette, D., Hansez, I., Hanin, D., & Bertrand, F. (2015). Employees' organizational identification and affective organizational commitment: An integrative approach. *Plos ONE, 10*(4), 1–23.

Übius, Ü., & Alas, R. (2008). Can organizational culture predict individual and organizational level factors? *EBS Review*, (25), 39–60.

Examples:

Kantor, J., & Streitfeld, D. (2015, August 15). Inside Amazon: Wrestling big ideas in a bruising workplace. *The New York Times*. Retrieved from http://www.nytimes.com/2015/08/16/technology/inside-amazon-wrestling-big-ideas-in-a-bruising-workplace.html?_r=0

Noguchi, Y. (2015, August 17). Amazon CEO Jeff Bezos dismisses claims in *New York Times* article. NPR. Retrieved from http://www.npr.org/2015/08/17/432619125/amazon-ceo-jeff-bezos-dismisses-claims-in-new-york-times-article?utm_medium=RSS&utm_campaign=business

Schulte, B. (2015, August 10). The wrong boss can also ruin your home life. Here's how to prevent it. *The Washington Post*. Retrieved from: http://www.washingtonpost.com/news/inspired-life/wp/2015/08/10/the-wrong-boss-can-also-ruin-your-home-life-heres-how-to-make-sure-that-doesnt-happen/

INFLUENCING PEOPLE ONLINE

In Unit 5 we cover theories of persuasion and social influence. We cover six theoretical approaches to understanding sales, marketing, and social influence via Web 2.0 technologies: The elaboration likelihood model, theory of planned behavior, stages of change, diffusion of innovations, cognitive dissonance, and rhetoric. All of these theories focus on one or more elements of persuasion.

For a great overview of common persuasive tactics, check out this video from *Influence at Work* based on the Robert Cialdini's research: https://www.youtube.com/watch?v=cFdCzN7RYbw

Persuasion is the process of influencing people's attitudes, values, beliefs, and behaviors. It is helpful to think of **attitudes** as existing on spectrum from very favorable to very unfavorable. We have attitudes toward many, many things, including products, people, and behaviors. **Values** are slightly different but are also related to behavior because they tell us what is right and what is wrong. **Beliefs** are what we believe to be true: what is real, factual, and accurate. **Behavior**, which is related to attitudes, values, and beliefs, is what we actually do. Think of it this way: We have attitudes toward specific technology products, such as Apple, Android, and Windows operating systems, that are favorable, ambivalent, or negative. We also have values surrounding technology in terms of how important new technology is and how it should be used. We also have beliefs about how technology has affected people and what will happen if we use one type of technology versus another—such as using Apple products versus Android or Windows. These attitudes, values, and beliefs are related to our purchasing behaviors when we shop for technology, and are therefore common targets of persuasive campaigns to influence those behaviors.

Clearly, persuasion is not an easy task and the relationship among these variables is still unclear. The nature of the relationship among attitudes, values, beliefs, and behavior has been debated for half a century: Do attitudes determine behavior? Or do our behaviors drive our attitudes? Are attitudes shaped by values and beliefs or personal experience? Where do attitudes come from; are they emotional or cognitive? Each of these theories answers these questions somewhat differently. The elaboration likelihood model and theory of planned behavior focus more on the cognitive basis of attitudes, and suggest that attitudes determine behavior. On the other hand, cognitive dissonance theory suggests that our behavior can drive our attitudes. Rhetoric focuses less on the cognitive and more on the social and emotional tactics used to influence others.

227

As you read through these chapters, notice how similar these theories are and also the unique insight that each of these theories offers in terms of changing, shaping, and reinforcing people's attitudes, values, beliefs, and behaviors. These theories teach us about internal motivation and peer pressure, our sense of our own skills and resources, and the cognitive and emotional processes that affect our attitudes and behaviors. Though no one theory can definitively explain how to change people's behaviors, looking at these theories together gives us a toolbox we can use so that we choose the best possible tactics given our persuasive goals, the situation, and the people we are trying to influence. These theories also help us understand persuasive attempts that we see in our everyday lives, identify the tactics being used, and evaluate their effectiveness.

As a whole, theories of persuasion and social influence teach us that we are both cognitively and emotionally driven. New communication media has the unique ability to blend together informative and emotional content to influence us and, as a result, shape our society. Marketers have new ways to appeal to us, friends have new ways to influence us, and we have new sources of social influence that didn't exist 20 years ago.

CHAPTER 16

THE ELABORATION LIKELIHOOD MODEL

OUTCOMES

- *Knowledge:* Learn about the types of motivation and ability that increase or decrease how closely people think about content.

- *Skill:* Apply knowledge of your audience's motivation and ability to develop multimedia, use cues within websites, and use website layout to promote ease of use.

INTRODUCTION

This chapter covers Petty and Cacioppo's (1986) Elaboration Likelihood Model (ELM). The ELM explains how people's thoughts while they are watching or reading a message determines the extent and direction of attitude change. Sometimes very subtle changes in a message—whether it is a news story, blog post, or advertisement—can change how people think about, or cognitively elaborate on, and respond to a message. This is particularly important for online marketing, advertising, and sales. We begin by going over some of the basic tenets of the ELM, then apply concepts from the model to explore why Electronic Word of Mouth (eWOM) is so important for online sales, and then go on to discuss elements we can incorporate into websites that accommodate Internet users' motivation and ability, or lack thereof.

The ELM offers many insights relevant to new media:

- *The ELM identifies message features that increase **motivation** to think critically, such as involvement (Johnson & Eagly, 1989).*

- *The ELM identifies content in all communication formats, particularly new media, that affects **ability** to critically think, such as the presence of distracting content (Newhagen & Reeves, 1992) and the fact that we can read or watch online content at our own pace, when we are the least distracted (Booth-Butterfield & Gutowski, 1993).*

- *The ELM identifies message elements that can serve as **central and peripheral cues**, such as source credibility, citing sources, and message length and quality. Incorporating different message elements into posts, websites, ads, and online product descriptions can improve attitudes toward a product or idea.*

Therefore, the ELM has been applied to help practitioners understand word-of-mouth campaigns and online advertising, and to explain how people may be influenced online in relation to consumer products, health, current events, and politics. This is not to say that the ELM is without criticism: It has been criticized for being *unfalsifiable* (Stiff, 1994). As you will see in the discussion of the ELM below, this theory explains that any one type of message content can serve different functions for different people. Therefore, no matter what the outcome of a message, the ELM can be used to explain the outcome.

OVERVIEW OF THE ELM

KEY PREDICTIONS OF THE ELM (PETTY & CACIOPPO, 1986)

1. **Motivation and ability are both internal and external.** Motivation includes **involvement** in the message. **Involvement** is feeling like the topic is important in terms of people's impression of you, resonating with your values, or the outcomes being important (see Johnson & Eagly, 1989). **Need for cognition** is also an internal source of motivation, and it is a trait related to enjoying critical thinking. Lastly, external motivation includes things like social **expectations** to be informed and make a good decision. Ability includes whether you easily understand the topic and **language** used, have prior **experience** and background **knowledge**, and have enough **time** to think about the message.

   Think about it this way: how much careful thought you give to a post that shows up in your social media feed probably depends on whether it is something you care about (involvement), whether you enjoy scrutinizing those things (need for cognition), whether you think you'll need to know about it later (expectations), whether it's something that you undersand and have experience with, and whether you have time to actually read it and think about it. If you aren't internally or externally motivated to think about it, you'll probably scroll past it without giving it much thought.

2. **Motivation and ability determine elaboration on cues in a message. Cues** are elements in the message that may be persuasive, including the source, content of the message, images, even use of color. Cues that are perceived as positive lead to attitude change that is positive.

When a person is motivated and able, they will process cues centrally. **Central processing** involves more elaboration, or active thinking related to the content of the message. It involves scrutinizing the arguments and message cues and comparing and contrasting message content with what you already know, such as whether the sources cited are high quality, whether the argument is balanced, whether the source has the credentials to speak on the topic, and so on.

When a person is either unmotivated or unable, they will rely on peripheral cues. **Peripheral processing** is easy, less effortful thinking that involves using simple cues in the message to make a decision, like relying on source credibility, source attractiveness, the mere presence of cited sources, and mere message length, to make a decision.

Thinking again about posts in our social network feeds, there are many cues that can affect our attitudes whether we are thinking carefully about what we are seeing or not. An attractive, seemingly knowledgable spokesperson's picture next to a sponsored post may reflect well on the product being advertised. Similarly, the use of a simple, visually compelling infographic that communicates information using bright images and simple language can be persuasive to both active central processors and passive peripheral processors.

Types of cues used in persuasive messages that affect motivation, ability, and serve as persuasive cues	
	Message Elements
Message Source Cues	Credibility and Expertise: Is this person knowledgeable?
	Attractiveness: Is this person socially or physically attractive?
	Likeability: Is this person friendly?
	Similarity: Is this person like me?
Message Content Cues	Message Length: Do they give a lot of details?
	Cited Sources: Do they cite evidence to support conclusions?
	Argument Quality: Do they present strong arguments?
	Relevance to Audience: Is this topic relevant to me?
	Repetition: Am I familiar with the message content?
	Sidedness: Do they present both sides of the issue?
	Message Order: What is presented first and last?
Modality: Implications for Motivation and Ability	Print: Can I read it at my own pace?
	Video: Can I watch it over and over again? Is it interesting or distracting?
	Audio: Can I listen closely to it? Is it interesting?
	Hyperlinks: Do they link to other, relevant information?
	Images: Do the images reinforce the argument or distract?

3. **Elaboration determines attitude change.** The **valence** (positivity or negativity of one's thoughts) determines the direction of attitude change. When elaboration, whether it is peripheral or central, is favorable, then positive attitude change occurs. So more positive thoughts lead to more positive attitudes. When elaboration is unfavorable, then negative attitude change occurs. So, if I evaluate the source of a post as lacking expertise because they do not have credentials, I am having a negatively valenced thought. On the other hand, if I like a post because the person seems to know what he or she is talking about, I am having a positively valenced thought.

The extent of **content-relevant elaboration** determines the extent of attitude change. Peripheral attitude change tends to be short term and less predictive of behavior. Central attitude change tends to be longer term and more predictive of behavior.

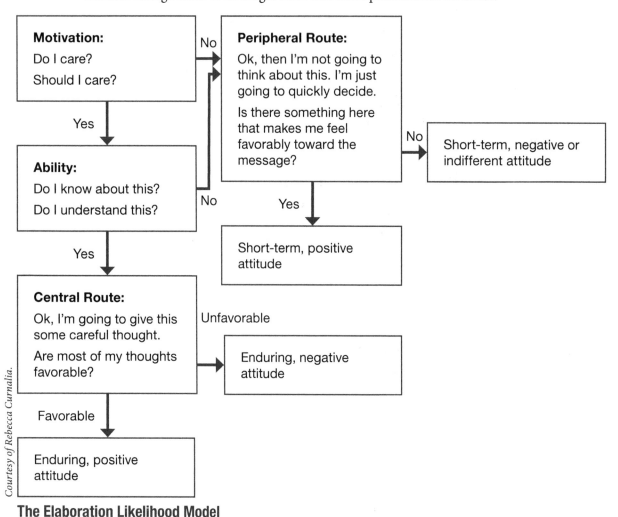

Courtesy of Rebecca Curnalia.

The Elaboration Likelihood Model

EXAMPLE OF THE ELM IN WEB 2.0

Say, for example, I want to buy a pair of shoes online. Imagine all of the things I *could* consider when shopping for shoes: the brand name, style, where they were made, materials they are made from, other people's reviews of the brand and the specific shoe, price, outfits the shoe would match, potential durability, features related to comfort, and so on. If I read through the product description and online reviews, then considered the price and reviews of that shoe versus similar products, I would be centrally processing to form an opinion and make a decision.

But we cannot do this for most decisions, particularly most consumer decisions. We simply don't have the time to labor over small purchases (low ability) and typically these purchases aren't that important to us (low motivation). So, the extent to which I centrally process this information while shopping depends on how important the decision is to me and whether I know enough to thoughtfully weigh my options.

Now consider how online retailers like Amazon.com present products to help us make decisions peripherally. We are shown the "regular retail" price and the reduced online price. Price is a peripheral cue that we use to determine the value of the product, quality of the brand, and so on. We also see the number of "stars" the product has received. More stars means more people liked it, a peripheral cue we can use to judge popularity, value, and quality. If there are limited quantities, Amazon tells us how many are left in stock and to "Order soon!" This increases pressure to make a fast decision while also reiterating that it is a popular, in-demand product. So, Amazon uses a variety of peripheral cues that I can quickly, easily use to determine whether a shoe—or any other product—is a decent product and a good price.

Insight into Innovation Activity: Look up a product you're interested in buying on Amazon. Look at the item description, pictures, and other elements (cues) on the product's page. What potential peripheral cues do you see that would make your purchasing decision easy? How might you design an experiment to see which peripheral cues on the page are most and least effective?

METHODS IN ELM RESEARCH

Experiments. Researchers will create several versions of a message. In the experimental messages, they will typically vary one element of a message such as citing versus not citing sources, using simple versus complex language, or incorporating simple cues (see the "Types of Cues" table) to affect people's motivation and ability to think about the content. They will measure elaboration using a **thought listing task** where people list everything they were thinking about, measure motivation on scale items, and measure attitudes on scale items. Sometimes, after a few days have passed, they will measure attitudes again to see if the attitude change lasted. Researchers can also use online survey software, like SurveyMonkey or Qualtrics, where people read one of several experimental versions of an advertisement, website, or news article, then answer open questions and survey items about the topic of the message.

Surveys. Survey studies of elaboration are increasingly popular in media research. These surveys include scale items. For example, Perse (1990) developed a scale measure of elaboration that is used in media research to measure elaboration on informational media content like the news. The scale includes a) thinking about what the content means to myself and my family; b) thinking about how the content relates to other things I know; c) thinking about what the content means to other people; and d) thinking about the content over and over again. In survey studies, people will be asked about the amount of exposure to a message or type of media content, how much they elaborated on the content, and about media effects (like attitudes, perceptions, etc.) that may be affected by media messages.

ELM methods provide helpful insight for marketing, advertising, and web design professionals. We can use background surveys to assess people's motivations and abilities to process content related to the products or ideas we're trying to promote. We can then use this information to plan our campaign. We can also use the experimental methodology to test our message before mass dissemination to see whether it elicits predominantly positive or negative thoughts in our target audience and make adjustments based on what we observe in their responses. Lastly, we can look at user statistics on our websites to see whether or not people are taking time with our content, such as how long people stay on a website, whether they click on hyperlinks, and so on. These user statistics can give us insight into whether or not people seem to be engaged in our online material.

ONLINE MARKETING AND PURCHASING: THE AGE OF eWOM

The ELM is a useful framework for understanding the implications of the many cues in online marketing and sales. In the first quarter of 2013, e-commerce sales represented over 6 percent of all consumer purchases, or around $58 billion (U.S. Census Bureau, 2013). So, it is no wonder that retailers are trying to figure out how to tap the e-commerce market, and are exploring new ways to reach this growing group of consumers. One relatively new method of marketing products is **eWOM**, or electronic word of mouth (Park & Kim, 2008). eWOM includes customer reviews, like the star and comments sections on Amazon.com, "liking" and rating products and services on Facebook, and even product reviews and endorsements by bloggers.

eWOM is a persuasive cue. eWOM can be both a peripheral cue about the quality of the product by simply looking at the number of positive versus negative reviews to make a judgment. It can also provide central cues, as comments can provide specific information about the features of a product. So, online reviews serve two functions: to **recommend** and to **inform** (Park & Kim, 2008). The *number* of reviews serve as a cue about whether or not others recommend a product. The *types* of reviews and the informational content they contain serve an informer role. Just like the ELM predicts, different types of content in eWOM serve different functions for people, depending on their motivation and ability to make an informed purchasing decision.

Ability and use of eWOM to make purchasing decisions. When people are **experts** about the product (high ability), they tend to prefer reviews that discuss the attributes of the product (Park & Kim, 2008). On the other hand, when people are **novices** (low ability), they prefer reviews that focus on the benefits of the product. Having reviews that fit the level of prospective customers' expertise increased their purchase intentions.

Novice customers who lack expertise in the product are more likely to want to purchase a product as the number of reviews increases (Park & Kim, 2008). Therefore, for people who are low in ability, having *more* online reviews that focus on the *benefits* of the product increases the likelihood that they will purchase that product. That being said, even people with low expertise consider whether online reviews seem credible or not by looking at whether the review was entirely one-sided or includes the pros and cons of the product (Chueng, Sia, & Kuan, 2012). In order for eWOM campaigns to increase purchasing intentions, they must focus on both the *quality* of the reviews and the *quantity* of reviews (Park, Lee, & Han, 2007).

So, it is clear what an online promoter should do: generate online reviews for their products to increase purchases. To generate reviews, promoters may purchase reviews or supply reviewers with the product to encourage reviews.

As one example of how this works, Todd Rutherford created a business, gettingbookreviews.com, where authors could pay to have their books reviewed. People could order anywhere from 1 to 20 reviews of their books. At its height, his website earned $28,000 a month and he had several people reviewing for him. The *New York Times* noted, "reviews by ordinary people have become an essential mechanism for selling almost anything online…In many situations, these reviews are supplanting the marketing department, the press agent, advertisements…" (Streitfeld, 2012, para. 8).

Professional reviews of products, including books, can meet the demands of both central and peripheral processors. They may contain information to satisfy people who are both motivated and able to carefully consider their purchases. They also increase the number of reviews for the product, which serves as a peripheral cue for people who are lower in motivation or ability.

Though "purchasing reviews" is ethically questionable at best, many major brands and retailers have engaged in this practice for years. Consider the number of offers—such as coupons for free food or free samples—you can only receive if you "like" a certain product on Facebook. In essence, you are serving as a favorable online review for that product and you are being "paid" to do it in the form of a coupon. Moreover, you are serving as a peripheral cue for your Facebook friends, as product advertisements in their Facebook feeds tell them that you "liked" a particular product or company. Also, increasing the number of "likes" a page has on Facebook is a persuasive cue, as it is an indication of the popularity and possibly the quality of the product being promoted.

Beyond Facebook "likes" and Amazon.com reviews, there are entire websites devoted to online reviews: Yelp, TripAdvisor, Angie's List, eOpinion, and Google Reviews, to name just a few. Even retailers like Target are allowing product reviews on their websites because these reviews can improve sales. These reviews are an important source of information for motivated and able shoppers and an important peripheral cue for less motivated and able shoppers.

Insight into Innovation Example: Listen to NPR's Planet Money report about Amazon's Vine program, where super reviewers are given free products to review: *Top Reviewers on Amazon Get Tons of Free Stuff*. Consider the implications of thorough, detailed, responsive reviews for appealing to both experts and novices. Is this a good sales strategy? Is it an ethical sales strategy? Why or why not?

MOTIVATION, ABILITY, AND INTERNET BROWSING

Beyond explaining how the number and types of online reviews may affect online shoppers, the ELM is also useful to help us understand the best ways to present information online to accommodate less motivated and able web surfers and more active information seekers. Website content has been diversified significantly, and this can appeal to users at varying levels of motivation and ability.

Websites contain a combination of text, images, videos, and hyperlinks. Therefore, there are **modalities**, or means of communication, available online that can affect processing. It is also important to consider how reading online, even when print is the primary communication mode on a website, is fundamentally different compared to reading traditional print content or even watching TV or listening to the radio. There are numerous distractions online, people are prone to multitasking, and these situational differences *decrease* ability to process content, particularly when users are not motivated to focus. This has many implications for how best to structure website content.

Insight into Innovation Activity: Compare White House Webpages. Which of the two White House websites would appeal to someone with low motivation and ability (peripheral processors)? Which would appeal to someone with high motivation and ability (central processors)? Is there one version that is more likely to appeal to both central and peripheral processors? Why?

Check out the first White House website, launched by the Clinton Administration in 1994, and compare it to the White House website from Obama's Administration in 2014:

Clinton White House website from: http://clinton1.nara.gov

Obama White House Website from: http://www.whitehouse.gov on March 10, 2016

You can see more "early" websites here: http://www.pewinternet.org/2014/03/11/world-wide-web-timeline/

Online, we have all the time we need: Modality and processing. Print modalities allow people the time they need to carefully think about and elaborate on message content. When people read print content, they are most influenced by the quality of the arguments that they are reading (Booth-Butterfield & Gutowski, 1993). Audio and particularly video modalities introduce peripheral cues, like source attractiveness, that users can use to reach conclusions more easily. Audio and video may also contain distractions that diminish people's ability to pay attention. On the other hand, audio and video may be more appealing to low-motivation/low-ability web users. The key to developing effective websites is incorporating modalities that appeal to people who are both high and low in motivation and ability (Braverman, 2008). Thus, a combination of text, visually rich content, and multimedia content is ideal.

Multitasking, distraction, and online skimming and scanning. We call it "browsing" the internet for a reason. People tend to scroll through, skim, and graze online content rather than sitting and carefully focusing their attention. We have an immense amount of content available to us, leading to **information overload**. We also have a lot of things that can distract us on the website itself, in our other browser windows, and in our external environments.

Distracting content reduces the ability to centrally process. Not surprisingly, in the age of smartphones, tablets, and streaming TV, we are doing a lot of things at once and we are very distracted. This **multitasking** has implications for how closely people are going to watch, read, or listen to an online message. When people multitask, they comprehend less of the message and are less scrutinous of the message when it is a **secondary** activity (Jeong & Hwang, 2012). So, for example, if watching TV is your **primary** activity, or what you are most focused on while reading this book, then reading is your secondary activity, which you are less focused on. Skimming content as a secondary activity decreases active processing, so you are less likely to counterargue and also less likely to comprehend and retain what you are reading—so turn the TV and phone off and close your other browser windows if you're going to be tested over this material later!

Further complicating the situation online, and reducing active processing as well, people are more prone to **scan, skim, and be selective** about what they click on when consuming content online versus content in traditional print modalities (Eveland & Dunwoody, 2002). So, even though research suggests that there is a lot of potential for increasing active processing online versus traditional print, the *way people use websites* undermines this potential. Thus, we see the rise of simple infographics, memes, "click-bait" headlines, and so on, as a way to capture people's attention even momentarily in the hopes of promoting a product or campaign.

🗨 HOW TO ADJUST YOUR ONLINE MESSAGE: MESSAGE CUES, MULTIMEDIA, AND LAYOUT

Promoters should keep their target audience and their product/idea in mind when designing persuasive messages: Who is my audience, how much do they know, and how much do they care about what I'm trying to market? Consumers vary widely in both internal and external motivation and ability, and not all decisions warrant close, careful scrutiny. Adjust your message accordingly.

That being said, there are some cues we can incorporate in online campaigns that will appeal to both central and peripheral processors. In short, website content should be informational, entertaining, and easy to navigate (Kang & Kim, 2006).

Informational message cues. Incorporating simple but effective cues throughout a website can improve people's perceptions of the products or ideas that the website promotes. For example, merely including a **seal** on a website from a recognizable and trusted organization, such as the Better Business Bureau, can increase people's purchase intentions (Hu, Lin, & Zhang, 2003). Similarly, incorporating **credible news stories** can also increase the effectiveness of online marketing efforts (Micu & Iryna, 2014). Thinking about these simple message cues in terms of the ELM, seals of approval and credible news coverage can serve as peripheral cues for less involved or less able web browsers and can serve as central cues (argument and evidence) for central processors.

Having certain written elements within the website can also signal trustworthiness. Explaining **warranties** for products, details about the **quality** of customer service and products, and assurances that the site is **secure** also increase users' satisfaction with and subsequent trust of the website (San Martín, Camarero, & San José, 2011).

Clearly, the **images** incorporated throughout any message can also affect elaboration. Having appropriate, emotionally involving, and relevant pictures can increase the persuasiveness of messages (Miniard, Bhatla, Lord, Dickson, & Unnava, 1991). Images that stir people's emotions appeal to low-involvement users, and images that provide visual evidence in support of the product or idea appeal to high-involvement users.

Engaging interactivity and multimedia content. Having interactive and multimedia elements throughout a website can also enhance persuasion by accommodating people with varying levels of motivation and ability. The ability to interact, such as providing a chat between a customer service representative and consumer or allowing consumers to post content, can improve people's perceptions of the quality of the website and the brand being marketed (Ko, Cho, & Roberts, 2013). People who are experienced web users prefer interactive website features when they are highly involved. People who are not particularly involved (peripheral processors) also like interactive features because the "bells and whistles" of the website itself can serve as a persuasive cue (Liu & Shrum, 2009, p. 65).

Easily navigated layout and design. There are many options when designing a website, from the use of columns, integration of hyperlinks, and options for navigation ranging from "forward" and "back" buttons, to detailed tabs along the top or side of the page. When thinking about a website and its features, and why we stay on a site or navigate away from it, the website's "flow" is very important. Flow involves giving users a sense of control, maintaining their attention, sparking their curiosity, and providing interesting content (van Noort, Voorveld, & can Reijmersdal, 2012). There are four features of website flow:

1. perceiving control over the interaction,
2. the extent to which one's attention is focused on the interaction,
3. the curiosity aroused by the interaction, and
4. the extent to which the user experiences the interaction as intrinsically interesting (p. 224).

Website "flow" is a way of increasing user involvement. As the ELM predicts, improving the flow of website content and interactivity increase product-relevant thoughts. This increased elaboration may lead to improved attitudes toward the product being sold and increase purchase intentions.

Insight into Innovation Activity: Write a Website Critique. Choose a website and apply concepts from the ELM to critique how well the content and layout accommodate central and peripheral processors. What type of textual, visual, and multimedia content are used to engage both motivated and able, and unmotivated and unable, users? Does the layout and navigation tools offer "deep" information and also enable surfing? Is the website interactive? Does it have a sense of "flow"?

CONCLUSION

In this chapter, we've reviewed three primary assumptions of the ELM: Motivation and ability are both internal (traits and relevance) and external (from the message and peers); motivation and ability determine cognitive elaboration (central versus peripheral processing); and elaboration determines the effects of a message (positive, negative, or no attitude change). We've covered a couple of applications of the ELM to understand how people use customer reviews and websites, and pointed out some ways that we can use our knowledge of motivation, ability, and cognitive processing to create online content.

If you think about it, the applications of the ELM to new technologies are seemingly endless. It has implications for how we should put together our LinkedIn profiles when looking for a job, build our Pinterest boards, put together our online dating profiles, and even for what we post on Facebook and Twitter if we want to reach the broadest audience:

- Incorporate both informational and simple, visual cues so that our message accommodates both experts and novices, the highly involved and passive users.
- Have both quality content and a sufficient quantity of content.
- Make people feel a sense of involvement.
- Make content accessible to as many people as possible using layout, images, and multimedia.

ACTIVITIES AND ASSIGNMENTS

1. **Website critique.** Write a one-page critique of a commercial website using the ELM-based suggestions for website development. In the review, discuss a) the use of modalities, b) presence of peripheral/simple cues, c) layout and formatting to make the website easy to skim. Based on your analysis, critique how well the content of the website accommodates a) expert versus novice users and b) involved versus passive users.

2. **Write a product review.** Write a product review for something you have recently purchased. The review should include both informational content and critique the quality/benefits of the product. Label the parts of the critique designed to persuade motivated/able users (central processors) and unmotivated/unable users (peripheral processors).

REFERENCES

Seminal Text:

Petty, R. E., & Cacioppo, J. T. (1986a). *Communication and persuasion: Central and peripheral routes to attitude change.* New York: Springer-Verlag.

Academic Articles:

Booth-Butterfield, S., & Gutowski, C. (1993). Message modality and source credibility can interact to affect argument processing. *Communication Quarterly, 41,* 77–89.

Braverman, J. (2008). Testimonials versus information persuasive messages: The moderating effect of delivery mode and personal involvement. *Communication Research, 35*, 666–694.

Cheung, C. M.-Y., Sia, C.-L., & Kuan, K. K. Y. (2012). Is this review believable? A study of factors affecting the credibility of online consumer review from an ELM perspective. *Journal of the Association for Information Systems, 13*, 618–635.

Eveland, W. P., Jr., & Dunwoody, S. (2002). An investigation of elaboration and selective scanning as mediators of learning from web versus print. *Journal of Broadcasting & Electronic Media, 46*, 34–53.

Hu, X., Lin, Z., & Zhang, H. (2003). Trust promoting seals in electronic markets: An exploratory study of their effectiveness for online sales promotion. *Journal of Promotion Management, 9*, 163–179.

Jeong, S.-H., & Hwang, Y. (2012). Does multitasking increase or decrease persuasion? Effects of multitasking on comprehension and counterarguing. *Journal of Communication, 62*, 571–587.

Johnson, B., & Eagly, A. H. (1989). Effects of involvement on persuasion: A meta-analysis. *Psychological Bulletin, 106*, 290–314.

Kang, Y. S., & Kim, Y. S. (2006). Do visitors' interest level and perceived quantity of web page content matter in shaping the attitude toward a website? *Decision Support Systems, 42*, 1187–1202.

Ko, H., Cho, C.-H., & Roberts, M. S. (2013). Internet uses and gratifications: A structural equation model of interactive advertising. *Journal of Advertising, 34*, 57–70.

Liu, Y., & Shrum, L. J. (2009). A dual-process model of interactivity effects. *Journal of Advertising, 38*, 53–68.

Micu, A. C., & Iryna, P. (2014). Integrating advertising and news about the brand in the online environment: Are all products the same? *Journal of Marketing Communications, 20*, 158–175.

Miniard, P. W., Bhatla, S., Lord, K. R., Dickson, P. R., & Unnava, H. R. (1991). Picture-based persuasion processes and the moderating roles of involvement. *Journal of Consumer Research, 18*, 92–107.

Newhagen, J. E., & Reeves, B. (1992). The evening's bad news: Effects of compelling negative television news images on memory. *Journal of Communication, 42*, 25–41.

Park, D.-H., Lee, J., & Han, I. (2007). The effect of online consumer reviews on consumer purchasing intention: The moderating role of involvement. *International Journal of Electronic Commerce, 11*, 125–148.

Park, D.-H., & Kim, S. (2008). The effects of consumer knowledge on message processing of electronic word-of-mouth via online consumer reviews. *Electronic Commerce Research and Applications, 7*, 399–410.

Perse, E. M. (1990). Audience selectivity and involvement in the newer media environment. *Communication Research, 17,* 675–697.

Petty, R. E., & Cacioppo, J. T. (1986b). The elaboration likelihood model of persuasion. *Advances in Experimental Psychology, 19,* 123–205.

San Martín, S., Camarero, C., & San José, R. (2011). Does involvement matter in online satisfaction and trust? *Psychology & Marketing, 28,* 145–167.

Stiff, J. B. (1994). *Persuasive communication.* New York: Guilford Press.

Van Noort, G., Voorveld, H. A. M., & van Reijmersdl, E. A. (2012). Interactivity in brand websites: Cognitive, affective, and behavioral responses explained by consumers' online flow experience. *Journal of Interactive Marketing, 26,* 223–234.

Examples:

Chow, L. (2013, October 29). Top Reviewers on Amazon get tons of free stuff. *Planet Money.* Retrieved from http://www.npr.org/blogs/money/2013/10/29/241372607/top-reviewers-on-amazon-get-tons-of-free-stuff

Streitfeld, D. (2012, August 25). The best book reviews money can buy. *New York Times.* Retrieved from http://www.nytimes.com/2012/08/26/business/book-reviewers-for-hire-meet-a-demand-for-online-raves.html?pagewanted=all&_r=0

U.S. Census Bureau. (2013, May 15). Quarterly retail e-commerce sales: 1st quarter 2013. Retrieved from www.census.gov/retail/mrts/www/data/pdf/ec_current.pdf

Further Reading Online:

Petty, R. E., & Cacioppo, J. T. (1996). *Attitudes and persuasion: Classic and contemporary approaches.* Boulder, CO: Westview Press.

CHAPTER 17

COGNITIVE DISSONANCE THEORY

OUTCOMES

- *Knowledge:* Learn about dissonance and how and why people avoid it.
- *Skill:* Apply dissonance to understand online campaigns.

INTRODUCTION

Leon Festinger (1957) developed cognitive dissonance theory to explain why, when we know what we should do, we don't always do it, and why we sometimes do things that we know we shouldn't do. Typical examples include smoking when we know it is unhealthy, eating foods we know are fattening, and generally doing things we know to be unhealthy, immoral, illegal, or unwise. In the Web 2.0 environment, we are uniquely able to avoid dissonant information and seek out confirming information to make ourselves feel better about our behaviors and to reinforce our existing opinions and justify our behaviors.

Cognitive dissonance theory focuses on two key concepts: **dissonance**, which is being inconsistent, and **consonance**, which is being consistent (Festinger, 1957). The theory emphasizes dissonance and consonance in **cognition**, which Festinger defined as "any knowledge, opinion, or belief about the environment, about oneself, or about one's behavior" (p. 3). *We prefer consonance, and cognitive dissonance that comes from inconsistent thoughts, opinions, or behaviors motivates us to change to restore consonance.*

Dissonance in thoughts, attitudes, beliefs, or behaviors motivates people to change because dissonance is uncomfortable for us (Festinger, 1957). Dissonance can occur for several reasons:

1. When we get new information that challenges what we already know or believe.
2. When we make decisions that force us to choose between alternatives.

There are also ways to reduce dissonance when it does occur:

1. We can change our behavior to make it consistent with our new knowledge, beliefs, and opinions.
2. We can change how we think about the topic to rationalize the inconsistency.

There are numerous ways that dissonance theory applies to our Web 2.0 lives, particularly when you consider user control over exposure to content, the ability to seek out confirming information, and the potential for selectivity online. When we make up our minds to do something, or have already done something that could cause dissonance, we can go online for information and opinions that support our choice, thereby reducing dissonance. Further, once we have made up our minds about something, we can actively avoid information that challenges our decision, thereby avoiding dissonance. We have more control over what we see, read, and hear, and more access to diverse opinions and insights than ever before in history. This has profound implications for our experience of dissonance and how we maintain consonance individually, and also important effects on attempts to persuade people who are Web 2.0 users.

OVERVIEW OF COGNITIVE DISSONANCE

MAIN IDEA

There are two basic assumptions underlying dissonance theory (Festinger, 1957): First, when people experience dissonance they are motivated to reduce it. Second, people will avoid situations or information that will cause them to feel dissonance. This assumes that people are aware of the dissonance, and that is not always the case. This is also a causal argument—that dissonance *causes* changes in thoughts or behaviors—and these types of hypotheses can be very difficult to prove.

 You can preview Festinger's seminal text, A Theory of Cognitive Dissonance, here: http://books.google.com/books?id=voeQ-8CASacC&printsec=frontcover&source=gbs_ViewAPI#v=onepage&q&f=false

KEY ASSUMPTIONS (FESTINGER, 1957)

1. **Making decisions can increase dissonance.** When we make a decision, whether we are buying something, voting, choosing relationships, or making life choices, we are often faced with equally positive options, such choosing among Apple, Android, or Windows smartphones. When we make our final decision, such as choosing an Android over other options, we are rejecting two other good options. This can create dissonance, particularly if we see that most of our friends chose a different type of phone, or if the phone we chose ultimately doesn't do what we wanted or needed it to do. The magnitude, or extent of dissonance, depends on three things:

   - the *importance* of the decision increases the potential for dissonance;

- the *attractiveness* of the alternatives not chosen increases the potential for dissonance;
- the *cognitive overlap*, or how similar we think the options are, decreases dissonance.

So, when we make a decision about something like buying a smartphone, we are more susceptible to feeling dissonance when we feel the decision was really important, the other options were also attractive, and the options were different. If we do end up experiencing dissonance right after a decision, we could try to reverse our decision, but chances are we'll try to change our thoughts about the phone we chose and the phones we didn't choose. One way to do this is through increasing cognitive overlap, or focusing on how the options were similar, or we can tell ourselves that the decision wasn't that important after all. These are methods of mentally *justifying* the decision to ourselves so that we can reduce or avoid dissonance.

Insight into Innovation Example: Check out this song about how we justify our inconsistencies: https://www.youtube.com/watch?v=bp39qSdyTc4

2. **Forced compliance isn't persuasive** because it serves as an external justification. When we discuss "**forced compliance**" we mean that a person was either coerced through the threat of punishment, or bribed through the offer of rewards, to do something. When people are coerced or threatened to do or say something against their own beliefs, attitudes, or typical behaviors, it does not lead to dissonance and change (Festinger, 1957). The same is true when we offer big incentives to get people to comply. The more incentive we offer, the less attitude change we see. This is because people do not have to change their attitudes to reduce dissonance when there is some external justification for why they did what they did. We refer to this as the *ratio of consonant to dissonant elements*. When we threaten or offer a huge incentive, we are giving others consonant elements that will help them justify their behavior.

For example, when a cell phone company offers us a really great incentive to purchase one of their plans—such as free phones or huge rebates—we may not feel dissonance about the decision even if we end up not liking the phone or plan because we can justify our decision: We were essentially paid to select the phone and plan we chose, so it isn't our fault. Similarly, if we were forced to have a particular phone, because the person paying for it limited our options or we were bound by an existing contract, we would not experience dissonance after getting the phone because we could blame those external causes. The key to offering incentives is to offer just enough to get people to comply, but not so much that the incentive becomes the primary, or most important reason people make the purchase.

Insight into Innovation Example: See a video overview of Festinger and Carlsmith's (1959) study here: https://www.youtube.com/watch?v=korGK0yGIDo

3. **Feeling dissonance and a desire for consonance can motivate information seeking perception, and recall.** When we have to take action on something important to us, we will often seek out information to inform our decision, which is called **information seeking**

(Festinger, 1957). If we don't have much of an opinion or existing knowledge about the decision we face, we will generally be **nonselective**, or be open to information from diverse perspectives. Having purchased something, like a cell phone and a data plan, one of three things could happen:

- If I don't experience dissonance from my decision, I don't have to seek information to reduce dissonance or avoid information that may challenge my decision. So, I will still be open to new information.
- If I feel a little dissonance as a result of my decision, I may try to find information that further *supports* my decision so that I feel more consonance, and I may avoid information that would increase dissonance. This is **selective exposure**.
- If I feel a lot of dissonance as a result of my decision, I may actually seek out information that *increases* my dissonance to the point that I change my behavior, such as purchasing another product to replace the one I was disappointed in.

So, once we have made up our minds about something or made a decision, we will generally try to avoid dissonant information, particularly if the decision is *important* to us and we have *invested* a lot of resources. But we cannot always control the information we're exposed to. Particularly online, we sometimes read something with an interesting teaser only to be exposed to a message we might have otherwise avoided, and so we may end up being exposed to dissonant information anyway. We may not pay as much attention to the dissonant content we are exposed to. This is selective attention. There are also ways that we adjust our thinking to reduce dissonance without having to change our opinions. We can **selectively perceive** information and **selectively recall** the information. First, we may reinterpret the message by thinking of ways that it doesn't apply to us or isn't relevant. Second, we could choose to reject the message by saying that it is inaccurate or incomplete. Third, we could simply ignore the dissonant information, or choose not to remember it at all.

4. **Social networks can create dissonance or help relieve dissonance.** Our social networks are also a source of information and can create dissonance or help relieve it much like other sources (Festinger, 1957). Festinger was, of course, referring to social networks of connected people such as groups of friends, coworkers, and family members. Our social groups can help us relieve dissonance by offering support for our opinions. The more people we know who agree with us, the less dissonance we are likely to feel even when confronted with information that runs counter to our beliefs. On the other hand, when someone in our social network disagrees with us, and particularly when they are important, attractive, and their opinion is very different from our own, there is potential for dissonance. To reduce dissonance from within a social network, we can change our own opinion, look for points of agreement, or start to socially distance ourselves from the person or people who disagree.

Consider, for example the options of "unfriending," "unfollowing," or demoting social connections to "acquaintance" status on Facebook. If I have a very strong opinion and someone in my social network has a very strong opposing opinion that he/she regularly posts about, this could cause dissonance. So, I could engage him or her, and see if I could change his or her mind or maybe my opinion could be changed. I could "unfollow" him or her, which is one way to selectively avoid his or her opinions. To completely distance myself, I could "unfriend" him or her, reasoning that we are just too different to be friends or were never really friends in the first place. In keeping with dissonance theory, I can continue to like, comment on, and strengthen my social ties with my Facebook friends that share my beliefs.

EXAMPLE OF DISSONANCE IN WEB 2.0: DO VACCINES CAUSE AUTISM?

Web 2.0 technology and the ability to control exposure to information and curate our social networks to maximize social support for our opinions has wide-reaching implications for trying to change people's minds about a range of issues from products, to politics and healthy lifestyles. As an example of this process at work, and the very unfortunate repercussions of selective information seeking, interpretation, and recall, let's look at people's ongoing skepticism about vaccines.

The Centers for Disease Control and Prevention (CDC), World Health Organization (WHO), American Association of Pediatrics (AAP), and many other health organizations clearly and strongly endorse vaccinations. For example, the AAP (2014) states "Immunization prevents about 2.5 million deaths a year globally and continues to be one of the most successful and cost-effective life-saving public health interventions of the past century" (para. 1). This chart from the CDC demonstrates the effectiveness of the measles vaccine for example:

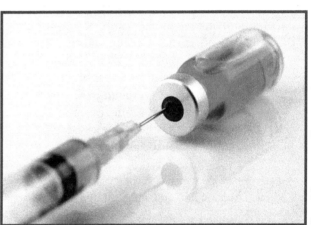

Copyright © jangl4/Shutterstock.com

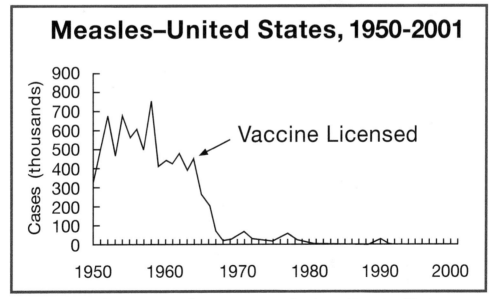

Source: National Notifiable Disease Surveillance System, CDC. Epidemiology and Prevention of Vaccine-Preventable Diseases, 13th Edition, Centers for Disease Control and Prevention, 2015, p. 214.

Given the clear and consistent link between vaccines and the elimination of disease and the very low incidence of reactions to vaccines, why do some people still choose not to vaccinate their children? In 1998, a small study published by Dr. Andrew Wakefield suggested that vaccines were linked to autism. Not long after, celebrities and parent groups in America started promoting the belief that vaccines caused autism. Vaccine rates started to drop, and outbreaks of illnesses such as measles started occurring again.

By 2014, numerous studies found no link between vaccines and autism. Wakefield's study had been retracted and he had been stripped of his medical license when evidence emerged that his data was falsified and that he was paid to conduct his study. Unfortunately, the damage had already been done because people had already made the decision not to vaccinate their children, formed beliefs about the link between vaccines and autism, and held strong opinions about the procedures for formulating, testing, and funding vaccines.

For an interesting review of the Wakefield case, read this CNN article: http://edition.cnn.com/2011/HEALTH/01/05/autism.vaccines/

Cognitive dissonance theory teaches us that once a person has made a decision that is important to him or her, such as choosing not to vaccinate his or her children, he or she will seek out information to confirm that decision and cognitively distort information that challenges his or her conviction in the decision. Also, there is some social support online for this decision, as we see Facebook groups, websites, and personal blogs that continue to report on the alleged link between autism and vaccines, question the ingredients in vaccines, and challenge medical recommendations and research findings that refute the decision not to vaccinate. Even in the face of seemingly irrefutable evidence, people's beliefs can persist and these beliefs are supported by selectively chosen information and a sense of social support.

Insight into Innovation Activity:

Watch this CNN video, "Childhood Vaccines are Safe. Seriously," at http://www.cnn.com/2014/07/01/health/vaccines-for-kids-safe/. Then consider some of the readers' comments, such as:

- Vaccines "contain mercury and other chemicals/toxins! Why has Autism risen in the last 20 years?"

- "Kids have more allergies/illness than ever before due to vaccinations!"

- "Millions have died from cancer caused by those polio vaccines…"

- "The chances of someone having a life threatening reaction to the TDaP vaccine is 5%. The risk of a severe life threatening complication due to the Smallpox vaccine is 17–20%…"

- "Formaldehyde is another ingredient in vaccinations. And other also include aborted baby brains stem cells, cow blood and pig blood to culture the virus they are slamming into your kids…"

- "What role does profitability play into when a vaccine is pulled…therein lies the undeniable, unholy alliance between big pharm, academia and the CDC. Meanwhile, autism rages on, thousands of children appear injured after vaccines."

How does cognitive dissonance theory help us understand people's negative responses to a news story advocating vaccines?

Experiments. Cognitive dissonance theory is typically tested using experiments because the assumptions of the theory are causal. Dissonance theory assumes that dissonance is an uncomfortable state and it motivates people to change. But, this assumption has been debated for nearly 50 years (e.g., Bem, 1967), in part because experimental studies like the one by Festinger and Carlsmith (1959) cannot definitively prove that they created dissonance in the experimental manipulation.

In one of the early studies of this effect, Festinger and Carlsmith (1959) had participants in an experiment perform a boring task, then dismissed them (control condition), or gave them either $20 (high incentive) or $1 (low incentive) to tell other students that the task was interesting. People in the control condition rated the task as boring, reported that they didn't learn much from it, and that they would not like to participate in a similar study. The results were similar for people who were paid $20 to tell others that the study was interesting; they also reported not liking the study. But the people who were *only paid $1* reported finding the study more interesting, important, and they were more likely to want to participate in similar experiments. Why would a small incentive increase attitude change? Because, in the absence of some external justification, people would have to change the way they think about the experiment to achieve consonance. People who were paid $20 (almost $170 in today's money) could justify the inconsistent behavior to themselves without having to change their attitudes toward the experiment. When there wasn't enough external justification, people had to change their attitudes to achieve consonance.

Recent research on selective exposure and selective attention has used Web 2.0 technologies to explore selective exposure and selective attention online (e.g., Garrett & Stroud, 2014, Graf & Aday, 2008; Knobloch-Westerwick & Meng, 2009). Researchers can create "fake" websites to see what types of information people will access online. In these types of studies, they have people answer a series of questions about their existing attitudes, then participants go to the "fake" website that lists both pro- and counter-attitudinal stories. Researchers can record which stories people select and how long they spend reading or watching those stories, then determine whether people select information that supports or challenges their existing opinions and how long people spend on stories that confirm or challenge their opinions. Much of this research has confirmed selective exposure and selective attention online.

Surveys. Some concepts like selective exposure can be explored in surveys. In media research, it is common to have people self-report their attitudes, opinions, and beliefs as well as their use of different media sources (Knobloch-Westerwick, 2015). These types of studies can reveal how people's existing opinions are related to selecting and consuming content, particularly in online contexts.

Survey methods cannot support or refute the argument that dissonance or the desire to avoid dissonance is *causing* selectivity, but they can be a useful tool for helping us understand who is likely to follow which sources. Using this descriptive information, we can design messages to accommodate the types of people likely to use a given source, try to attract people who disagree, and also anticipate responses to our messages. This is particularly useful information in the Web 2.0 information environment, where audiences are self-selected.

WEB 2.0: INCREASING POLARIZATION AND AMBIVALENCE?

There are two ways that the introduction of Web 2.0 technologies could go (Donsbach & Mothes, 2012): The optimistic view is that it could increase people's engagement and access to information. In the pessimistic view, it could increase social fragmentation by allowing people to avoid those things they don't want to face, ignore information contrary to what they already believe, and increase the polarization of people's opinions.

Research findings have been somewhat mixed between the positive and the negative predictions. On the positive side, new media can increase engagement. On the other hand, we do see an increase in selective exposure online, but not necessarily selective *avoidance* (Donsbach & Mothes, 2012). Think of it this way: we have more control over what news stories and advice we read and watch online, so we can be selective about the types of content we see and show bias toward selecting content that supports our attitudes, beliefs, and behaviors. On the other hand, it is very difficult to actively avoid opposing viewpoints online, as our Facebook friends, commenters on online message boards, and so on can post whatever they think or feel. We may or may not agree with it but we're exposed to it anyway.

So, in terms of dissonance, Donsbach and Mothes (2012) suggest that online communication has the potential to polarize people who tend to be very selective. **Polarization** is when our attitudes become much more extreme. On the other hand, people who are exposed to opinions that contradict what they believe may actually be immobilized because they may become unsure or **ambivalent**. Thinking about this in terms of political attitudes in America, we see more polarization in political attitudes and, at the same time, more people withdrawing from politics altogether.

You can read Donsbach's and Mothes' review of how dissonance theory applies to political communication via new media here:

http://books.google.com/books?hl=en&lr=&id=K_ZY37UXwSoC&oi=fnd&pg=PR1&dq=%22th e+dissonant+self%22+Communication+Yearbook&ots=B4GLsl7I4y&sig=bPV_8jKJusT8RLijNg V_j_PkHh8#v=onepage&q=%22the%20dissonant%20self%22%20&f=false

USER CONTROL MEANS MORE SELECTIVITY ONLINE

Much has been written about partisanship in American politics, and we often point our finger at the news media and blame them for polarized coverage. As we will discuss in the unit on Mass Media (Unit 6), the media affect what people think are the important issues in politics and how people think about political issues. But the news media cannot control who uses their content and how people use their content, particularly online. There is an increased potential for selective exposure online, so in terms of informing and persuading people about important issues, including politics and health, the continued shift toward the use of online information can make it much more challenging to reach people.

There are two dimensions to selective exposure: *actively seeking* information that confirms our opinions, and *actively avoiding* information that could challenge our opinions (Garret & Stroud, 2014). The internet makes actively seeking confirming information easier, but Web 2.0 technologies, such as social networks, makes avoidance more difficult in some ways. We compensate for this by being selective about the amount of attention we pay to dissonant messages posted online.

Insight into Innovation Example: Why does selective exposure matter? When we go directly to a particular information source, we tend to spend more time and look more in-depth at that source (Mitchell, Jurkowitz, & Olmstead, 2014). So, if we are selectively choosing news, and we are choosing outlets that support our existing knowledge, opinions, and behavior, that has important implications for what we know. Check out Pew Research's report on *Pathways to Digital News*: http://www.journalism.org/2014/03/13/social-search-direct/

Selective Exposure to Politics. There is solid evidence that we tend to gravitate toward online sources that we expect will confirm our existing political opinions. Studies that involved tracking people's information seeking online confirm that people tend to seek content that agrees with their opinions (Jang, 2014). The user control that we have online has allowed even more selective exposure. Looking at election coverage, people who have a clear political affiliation have steadily increased their reliance on news sources that support their existing opinions (Smith, 2011).

Online news with a political point of view

% of online political users who typically get online campaign news from sites that...

	2004	2006	2008	2010
Share my point of view	26%	28%	33%	34%
Don't have a point of view	32	34	25	30
Differ from my point of view	21	20	21	21
Don't know / Refuse	21	18	21	15

Source: The Pew Research Center's Internet & American Life Project, November 3-24, 2010 Post-Election Tracking Survey. N=2,257 national adults ages 18 and older, including 755 cell phone interviews; n=1,167 based on online political users.

"The Internet and Campaign 2010," Pew Research Center, Washington, DC (March, 2011) http://www.pewinternet.org/2011/03/17/the-internet-and-campaign-2010/.

When people are selective about their consumption of political information and use mostly partisan sources, they tend to know less about the range of social issues and focus instead on a few key political issues (Chan & Lee, 2014).

Selective Attention to Politics. Even online, people cannot completely control what information they are exposed to, but they can still limit how much attention they pay to information that challenges their existing attitudes. When people are multitasking online, they are less selective and less likely to avoid information from dissonant sources (Jang, 2014). It is also difficult to truly avoid dissonant political information online, particularly on social networks, because a growing number of people are sharing and posting about politics via social networks (Smith, 2014).

People do tend to group together via networks like Twitter with like-minded individuals and their ties tend to be stronger with people who share their political viewpoints (Himelboim, Smith, & Shneiderman, 2013). But, **social endorsements**, or the number of people who recommend a news story, can diminish the selectivity effects caused by partisanship (Messing & Westwood, 2012). Even when we have very clear and strong opinions on a topic, if a lot of other people have shared, liked, or recommended an online story, we are more likely to click on that story and read it even if that story is from a source that we may not agree with. This is why we see so much "click bait" online, or story headlines that make vague or shocking statements to get us to click on a link and read more. Also, people are attracted to stories that are listed prominently and include multimedia elements, so these features of political news can diminish the effects of selective exposure (Iyengar, Hahn, Krosnick, & Walker, 2008).

But even when we are lured into reading or watching a story due to click bait tactics, flashy media elements, or social pressure, we aren't necessarily persuaded by the content. When we are exposed to attitude-inconsistent information, we tend to spend less time reading it. Graf and Aday (2008) found that people spent 13 percent to 25 percent less time on articles that were inconsistent with their attitudes. Knobloch-Westerwick and Meng (2009) found that people spent 36 percent less time on articles that were inconsistent with their attitudes. Thus, even when people are exposed to content that challenges their existing beliefs, they appear to pay less attention to that information.

Insight into Innovation Activity: Look through the PPT from Pew Research on *Politics and Advocacy in the Social Media Era* (Smith, 2014). What are the implications for the diversity of opinions and information people are exposed to? How do you think their findings are related to the selective exposure and selective avoidance tenants of dissonance theory?

Access the PowerPoint here: http://www.pewinternet.org/2014/07/29/politics-and-advocacy-in-the-social-media-era/

Unfortunately, exposure to dissonant information as a result of online news use does not seem to have the positive effects we would hope for. Instead, following online news sometimes decreases selective exposure *and* decreases political participation (Knobloch-Westerwick & Johnson, 2014). Experimental research suggests that exposure to diverse political opinions makes us less certain of our political self-concepts compared to exposure to attitude-consistent information (Knobloch-Westerwick & Meng, 2011).

Selective Interpretation of Political Information. Further complicating things, even when we get people to click on a link to information that is counter to their opinions and we reduce selective attention by getting them to stay and consume information, recent research suggests that exposure to counter opinions actually *increases* political polarization (Arceneaux, Johnson, & Cryderman, 2013). That is, when someone who is politically partisan is exposed to information from the opposition, they become even more entrenched in their political ideology. So, though we often complain about partisan divides in the media, the fact that we have so many options available and can selectively "tune out," avoid, or be inattentive to partisan information may actually be a good thing.

Clearly, there are consequences for online selectivity in terms of political attitudes and having an informed electorate. As Donsbach and Mothes (2012) argued, there are good things and bad things resulting from this trend. On the positive side, we have the potential for exposure, if not attention, to diverse opinions and sources of information. On the negative side, exposure to diverse content appears to immobilize some people and exposure to dissonant information can have a "boomerang" effect and actually increase polarization for some people.

In terms of applying what we know to design a campaign, the evidence seems to support the common political tactic of targeting independent or undecided voters. In an environment where people can be selective in terms of exposure and attention, and where exposing people to opposing viewpoints seems to solidify their opinions even more, the best option for changing people's minds is to target those who are ambivalent or undecided. This is generally a small portion of the electorate: in September 2012, two months before the presidential election, only about 22 percent of registered voters were "swing voters" (Pew, 2012). At this point in the campaign, we see people who typically vote along party lines solidify their support for the candidate by becoming strong supporters of their party's candidate.

Health Topic Avoidance. The same issues with selectivity that increase both political polarization and immobilize voters are also a roadblock when we try to persuade people to adopt healthy behaviors. Online, it is even easier to avoid topics that may make us feel dissonance about our lifestyle choices. In 2013, over one-third of Americans went online for health information (Fox & Duggan, 2013). According to WebMD (2014), in 2013 their website attracted around 156 million visits per month. But in our selective, information- and opinion-saturated environment, just because we get people to go to a health website doesn't mean that they will click on, pay attention to, or agree with and ultimately adopt the health advice offered there. Further, the information available online can support any number of different beliefs. Take dieting for example: There's the Atkin's diet, Mediterranean diet, the whole foods diet, wheat busters diet, low fat diet, Weight Watchers, and countless others. So if I like carbs, I can find information that tells me carbs are okay as long as my diet is low fat. If I like fatty proteins, I can find a diet online that tells me saturated fats are okay as long as I avoid carbs. And if I think dieting is a waste of time, I can skip information on healthy eating altogether.

On the positive side, online health information may be useful for bolstering people's positive health behaviors (Knobloch-Westerwick, Johnson, & Westerwick, 2013). For example, people who eat a lot of vegetables select and pay attention to online content that advocates eating fruits and vegetables. But, in keeping with selective avoidance, when people are strongly dissatisfied with their health they do not select health topics as often (Knobloch-Westerwick, Hastall, & Rossman, 2009). Similarly, in emotional health contexts, when people are dissatisfied in their romantic lives, they tend to avoid reading about romance. So, as with strong political opinions, strong opinions about health guide our selection of and attention to physical and mental health information online.

CONCLUSION

Cognitive dissonance theory is a robust theory that helps us understand people's reactions to information and explains how our preference for consistency motivates us to think and act in sometimes biased and seemingly irrational ways. It contributes to our understanding of Web 2.0 users in particular, and applies broadly to curation of our social networks, the types of information we seek out or avoid, how closely we pay attention, and even how we think about the information we receive. Concepts from the theory, particularly selective exposure, have received increased attention from scholars and practitioners as the number of information sources and channels has increased over the past 20 years.

The research applying dissonance theory to online users paints a very complex picture: there are people who seek information to bolster their behavioral choices, people who will avoid types of information as a result of their personal or emotional state, and some evidence that getting people to pay attention to diverse information may actually reduce engagement rather than promote informed decisions and open dialogue. That being said, understanding the range of responses people may have to our social media posts, blog posts, and even the campaigns we design, are a great starting point for reaching audiences.

There is also very useful advice in the literature to help us reach out to people, such as using social networks and social endorsements to promote accurate, useful information and incorporating multimedia to increase exposure. We can also work on gradual social change. If we target people with moderate opinions—those who are ambivalent or undecided—we can promote change through social networks that way. Hopefully, research that explores selective exposure will eventually catch up to our more socially connected lives and clarify how we can use online social groups to promote positive, healthy, and prosocial beliefs gradually in a social network without activating dysfunctional cognitive reactions in strong opinion holders, like selective attention, perception, and recall.

ACTIVITIES AND ASSIGNMENTS

1. **Keep an online diary.** Instructions: For one day, write down every news article/video, blog post, or website link that you click on from social media. Note whether you read/watched just the introduction, skimmed/kind of listened to the entire thing, or paid very close attention to the entire piece. After the one day diary is complete, reflect on your attention to informational content:

   - Did you take in a lot of new information? What new information were you exposed to?
   - Was most of the information consistent with what you already believe/do?
   - What, if any information did you hear or listen to that was dissonant with what you believe/do?
   - What does your diary tell you about how much new information you take in and what information you avoid?

2. Read the Brookings "Primaries Project" report (http://www.brookings.edu/blogs/fixgov/posts/2014/09/30-primaries-project-understanding-party-factions) and use concepts from cognitive dissonance theory to explain why people say they "vote 'for the person, not the party'" but then consistently vote along party lines.

REFERENCES

Seminal Text:

Festinger, L. (1957). *A theory of cognitive dissonance*. Stanford, CA: Stanford University Press.

Academic Articles:

Arceneaux, K., Johnson, M., & Cryderman, J. (2013). Communication, persuasion, and the conditioning value of selective exposure: Like minds may unite and divide but they mostly tune out. *Political Communication*, *30*, 213–231.

Bem, D. J. (1967). Self-perception: An alternative interpretation of cognitive dissonance phenomena. *Psychological Review*, *74*, 183–200.

Chan, M., & Lee, F. L. F. (2014). Selective exposure and agenda setting: Exploring the impact of partisan media exposure on agenda diversity and political participation. *Asian Journal of Communication*, *24*, 301–314.

Donsbach, W., & Mothes, C. (2012). The dissonant self: Contributions from dissonance theory to a new agenda for studying political communication. *Communication Yearbook*, *36*, 3–44.

Festinger, L., & Carlsmith, J. M. (1959). Cognitive consequences of forced compliance. *Journal of Abnormal and Social Psychology*, *58*, 203–210.

Fox, S., & Duggan, M. (2013, January 15). Health online 2013. *Pew Research Internet Project*. Retrieved from http://www.pewinternet.org/2013/01/15/health-online-2013/

Garrett. R. K., & Stroud, N. J. (2014). Partisan paths to exposure diversity: Differences in pro- and counterattitudinal news consumption. *Journal of Communication*, *64*, 680–701.

Graf, J., & Aday, S. (2008). Selective attention to online political information. *Journal of Broadcasting & Electronic Media*, *52*, 86–100.

Himelboim, I., Smith, M., & Shneiderman, B. (2013). Tweeting apart: Applying network analysis to detect selective exposure clusters in Twitter. *Communication Methods and Measures*, *7*, 195–223.

Iyengar, S., Hahn, K. S., Krosnick, J. A., & Walker, J. (2008). Selective exposure to campaign communication: The role of anticipated agreement and issue public membership. *The Journal of Politics*, *70*, 186–200.

Jang, S. M. (2014). Challenges to selective exposure: Selective seeking and avoidance in a multitasking media environment. *Mass Communication & Society*, *17*, 665–688.

Knobloch-Westerwick, S., Hastall, M. R., & Rossman, M. (2009). Coping or escaping? Effects of life dissatisfaction on selective exposure. *Communication Research, 36*, 207–228.

Knobloch-Westerwick, S., & Johnson, B. K. (2014). Selective exposure for better or worse: Its mediating role for conlines news' impact on political participation. *Journal of Computer-Mediated Communication, 19*, 184–196.

Knobloch-Westerwick, S., Johnson, B. K., & Westerwick, A. (2013). To your health: Self-regulation of health behavior through selective exposure to online health messages. *Journal of Communication, 63*, 807–829.

Knobloch-Westerwick, S., & Meng, J. (2009). Looking the other way: Selective exposure and attitude-consistent and counterattitudinal political information. *Communication Research, 36*, 426–448.

Knobloch-Westerwick, S., & Meng, J. (2011). Reinforcement of the political self through selective exposure to political messages. *Journal of Communication, 61*, 349–368.

Messing, S., & Westwood, S. J. (2012). Selective exposure in the age of social media: Endorsements trump partisan source affiliation when selecting news online. *Communication Research*, 1–23.

Pew Research. (2012, September 19). Democrats narrow engagement gap: Obama ahead with stronger support, better image and lead on most issues. *The Pew Research Center for the People & the Press*. Retrieved online from http://www.people-press.org/files/legacy-pdf/09-19-12%20Political%20release.pdf

Smith, A. (2014). Politics and advocacy in the social media era. Pew Research Center: Internet Science, & Tech. Retrieved from http://www.pewinternet.org/2014/07/29/politics-and-advocacy-in-the-social-media-era/

Examples:

American Academy of Pediatrics. (2015). Immunizations. Retrieved from https://www.aap.org/en-us/advocacy-and-policy/aap-health-initiatives/immunization/Pages/About.aspx

Smith, A. (2011, March 17). The Internet and political news sources. *Pew Research Internet Project*. Retrieved from http://www.pewinternet.org/2011/03/17/the-internet-and-political-news-sources/

Mitchell, A., Jurkowitz, M., & Olmstead, K. (2014, March 13). Social, search and direct: Pathways to digital news. *Pew Research Journalism Project*. Retrieved from http://www.journalism.org/2014/03/13/social-search-direct/

WebMD. (2014, February 10). WebMD announces preliminary fourth quarter and full year 2013 results. Retrieved from http://investor.shareholder.com/wbmd/releasedetail.cfm?ReleaseID=824582&CompanyID=WBMD

Further Reading Online:

Festinger, L. (1957). *A theory of cognitive dissonance.* Stanford, CA: Stanford University Press. Limited preview via Google Books: http://books.google.com/books?id=voeQ-8CAS acC&printsec=frontcover&source=gbs_ViewAPI#v=onepage&q&f=false

Knobloch-Westerwick, S. (2015). *Choice and preference in media use: Advances in selective exposure theory and research.* New York: Taylor & Francis. Limited preview via Google Books: http://books.google.com/books?id=2RwWBAAAQBAJ&pg=PA407&lpg=PA407& dq=Coping+or+Escaping?Effects+of+Life+Dissatisfactionon+Selective+Exposure&source =bl&ots=RVN9L1SPuo&sig=QGf6XjAqXJnXunxfYiXAXY0zi88&hl=en&sa=X&ei=VJM-VKinCJWwyASk6YLICQ&ved=0CCwQ6AEwAw#v=onepage&q=new%20media%20 contexts&f=false

THE THEORY OF PLANNED BEHAVIOR

💬 INTRODUCTION

This chapter covers Fishbein and Ajzen's (1975) research on the expectancy value approach to human behavior. It began with the theory of reasoned action, and today it is known as the theory of planned behavior (TPB). The TPB is used to predict people's *planned* behavior based on expected outcomes and evaluations of outcomes, social norms, and perceived ability to control or perform the behavior. Like the elaboration likelihood model, the TPB looks at motivation (norms) and ability (perceived behavioral control). The TPB, however, focuses specifically on behavioral plans and also includes people's existing attitudes in the model (beliefs and evaluations of beliefs). A lot of our daily behavior is impulsive and spontaneous, and theories like the TPB don't predict those behaviors very well. On the other hand, our major purchases, life choices, and decisions—such as adopting new technologies, making health-related decisions, and voting—can be predicted using the TPB.

The TPB offers many useful insights for changing people's behavior and applies in many ways to new communication media. There are three key ideas that the TPB contributes to understanding people's behaviors (Ajzen, 1985):

- *The TPB explains that we consider the **outcomes of behavior** and **evaluate those outcomes**.* Outcomes and evaluations determine attitudes toward the behavior. For example, if we're considering whether or not to adopt technology, we think about what the outcomes will be and whether or not those outcomes will be good. If our attitude is positive due to the anticipated positive outcomes, we are more likely to adopt new technologies.

- *The TPB explains that some human behavior is driven by norms, or **social pressure and the expectations** of our peers.* If new media has highlighted anything for us, it is normative pressure: pressure to purchase and use new technologies; pressure from observing others via social networking sites; and normative lessons taught through blogs, Internet memes, and viral videos and posts. We get normative information from all of these sources, and that pressure can motivate us to adopt new technologies.
- *The TPB explains that we must feel a sense of efficacy and control, or feel like we are **able to do something**.* Each new technological development requires us to learn new things. Whether it is shopping online, joining a new social network, or adopting a new operating system, our sense that we can and will be able to use it determines whether or not we try.

Clearly, the TPB is useful for understanding why some people use certain technologies while other people do not. It also points out specific things we can target if we want to persuade people to do something or to stop doing something by explaining the relationship between beliefs and attitudes, norms, efficacy, and behavior.

💬 OVERVIEW OF THE THEORY OF PLANNED BEHAVIOR (TPB)

MAIN IDEA

The TPB is a quantitative equation used to predict people's behavioral intentions. It is helpful to think of the TPB as asking three general types of questions to help predict people's behaviors: Should I? Could I? Would I?

- *Should I do this, based on what I expect to happen and what others expect of me?* People's **attitudes** are a combination of **beliefs** about the outcomes of performing the behavior and the **evaluation** of those outcomes as positive or negative. The TPB also includes **subjective norms**, which are a combination of **normative pressure** to perform or not perform a behavior and **motivation to comply** with those norms.

- *Could I do this, based on the skills and resources required?* The TPB includes **perceived behavioral control**, or the perception that we are able to perform the behavior.

- *Would I do this, based on my attitude, norms, and sense of control?* As a summative model, the TPB suggests that attitudes, norms, and behavioral control work together to predict intentions.

Should I?	Should I?	Could I?	Would I?
Attitudes: Consider the outcomes. What will happen? Are the outcomes good?	**Norms:** Consider what others would want you to do. Do others want you to do it? Do you want to do what they want you to do?	**Control:** Consider whether or not you believe you can do it. Do you have the knowledge / skills? Do you have the resources?	**Intention:** Planning to (or not to) perform the behavior.

Courtesy of Rebecca Curnalia.

Considerations that influence our intention to do something

You can read Fishbein and Ajzen's seminal text, which is the foundation for the TPB, here: http://people.umass.edu/aizen/f&a1975.html

KEY CONCEPTS IN THE THEORY OF PLANNED BEHAVIOR

1. **Beliefs are the building blocks of attitudes and they predict behavior.** According to the TPB, the key concept that we have to understand in order to explain attitudes and predict behavior is people's **beliefs**. If people don't believe that they should or could do something, they will not. Fishbein and Ajzen (1975) argued that attitudes are learned evaluations of something or someone. They reasoned that *attitudes are affective because they reflect people's feelings. A belief is information that we have stored in memory that "links an object to some attribute"* (p. 12). In other words, beliefs are cognitive information (though not objectively true) about the **attributes**, or characteristics, of something.

   The associations between the object and the attribute can range from strong to weak. Also, the attributes themselves can be evaluated on a range of positive to negative. In the TPB view, *attitudes stem from beliefs and evaluations of beliefs.*

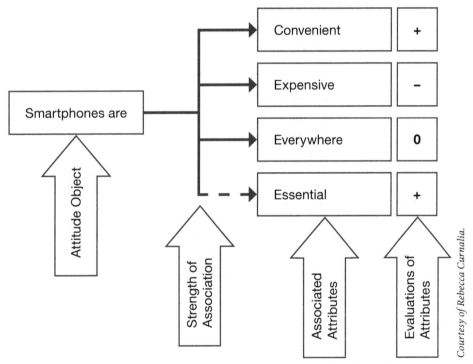

Courtesy of Rebecca Curnalia.

Example of an attitude object (smartphones), associated attributes (they are convenient, expensive, everywhere, and essential), belief strength (solid line for strong beliefs and broken line for weak beliefs), and evaluation of attributes (0 for neutral, + for positive, and – for negative). Judging by what you see here, what is the person's attitude toward smartphones likely to be? Would this hypothetical person intend to buy a smartphone? Why or why not?

2. **There are different types of beliefs.** Fishbein and Ajzen argued that attitudes are based on beliefs and that there are different *types of beliefs* that affect behavior: beliefs about outcomes and beliefs about norms. Ajzen (1985) later added beliefs about behavioral control. So, people have an internal list of beliefs about the attributes of things, *these associations can be strong or weak, positive or negative, and they fall into three categories*: beliefs about outcomes, norms, and control.

   Looking at the figure above, there are beliefs about outcomes (smartphones are "convenient"), about norms (smartphones are "everywhere"), and about behavioral control (smartphones are "expensive"). All of these beliefs work together to predict adoption of smartphone technology.

   There are numerous specific, measurable variables that fit in each category of beliefs in the TPB. For example, subjective norms can be either injunctive or descriptive (Rimal & Real, 2003). **Injunctive norms** are those things that are perceived as acceptable or unacceptable in a social group. **Descriptive norms** are inferred from observing others' behaviors. Continuing with the example of adopting smartphones, injunctive norms would be when friends and family tell us we should have a smartphone. Descriptive norms are when we see many people around us using their smartphones, and we infer social pressure. Not everyone gives in to all social pressure, though. Norms are moderated by **motivation to comply**, or our desire to conform to others' expectations.

   There are also specific variables that comprise perceived behavioral control. Think of perceived behavioral control as the perception that there are "barriers" that might stop you from doing something (Ajzen, 1985). Those barriers may be **internal** (i.e., lacking the skills or ability) or **external** (someone or something standing in the way). It is a person's sense of **efficacy**, or ability, to perform a behavior. So, in terms of buying and using a smartphone, we may feel we lack the skills to use that technology (internal) or we may not think there will be a signal where we live (external). Thus, our sense of efficacy would be low.

3. **Behavioral intention is a belief that predicts behavior.** The final key concept to understand from Fishbein and Ajzen's (1975) early work is **intention**. They argued that our *intentions to do something are a type of belief that should predict behavior*. Intentions are predicted by attitudes, norms, and control beliefs.

   So, taken together, the TPB argues that attitudes (beliefs about outcomes and evaluations of those outcomes), norms (beliefs about what others want us to do and motivation to comply with others' expectations), and control (beliefs about whether we can do/not do the behavior) predict our intention to do the behavior. Lastly, our intention to do the behavior (our *plan*) then predicts our actual behavior.

EXAMPLE OF TPB CONCEPTS AND WEB 2.0 TECHNOLOGY

The TPB is often used to explain health-related behaviors. Researchers, government agencies, and nonprofits have used the TPB to explore people's existing beliefs about the outcomes, norms, and behavioral control people perceive regarding things like following a healthy diet, exercising, quitting smoking, and using condoms. Thinking about this from a Web 2.0 perspective, the TPB gives us a lot of insight into how to reach people with healthy, prosocial messages via new media and also pointers for the types of messages that will be most effective in promoting positive behaviors.

Concept	Definition	Variables
Attitudes	*Beliefs* about what will happen and *evaluation* of those outcomes.	Beliefs Evaluation of beliefs
Norms	*Beliefs* about other people's expectations for our behavior and whether we want to conform.	Injunctive norms Descriptive norms Motivation to comply
Perceived Behavioral Control	*Belief* in our ability to do the behavior.	Internal control: Efficacy and Skills External control: Resources
Behavioral Intention	What we plan to do.	Intention to perform the behavior

Consider, for example, the 2014 ALS "Ice Bucket Challenge." According to the ALS Association, which is devoted to supporting research in amyotrophic lateral sclerosis (ALS), the Ice Bucket Challenge raised nearly $90 million in one month from previous donors and from 1.9 million new donors.

When considering this and other successful viral campaigns, the TPB helps explain why this was successful. It also provides an example that we can learn from to design similarly successful campaigns.

First, it made use of social norms. The challenge spread by people nominating each other via social media to either dump a bucket of ice water over their heads or to skip the ice bucket and donate $100 to ALS research. When people completed the challenge, they posted pictures or videos of themselves dumping a bucket of ice water on themselves and then they nominated friends to do the same. This campaign clearly benefited from direct appeals to both injunctive norms (seeing other people getting "likes" on social media for their posts and expecting there to be social consequences for not participating) and descriptive norms (social media feeds filled with videos of friends dumping water on themselves and #IceBucketChallenge hashtags).

Copyright © wanphen chawarung/Shutterstock.com

Second, it was something people could easily do. Since people who accepted the challenge were only asked to donate a small sum of money compared to refusing the challenge and donating $100, it was something that people likely felt a sense of efficacy about completing. Most people on social media have access to a camera, bucket of water, and $10 to donate. So, the "challenge" was something people *could* complete.

Third, the outcomes that people may have associated with completing the challenge were most likely overwhelmingly positive: personal validation and visibility in the form of "likes" from social media followers, supporting an admirable cause, raising awareness about a devastating terminal disease, showing support for people who have ALS, and many other personal and social benefits. Though all of these outcomes may not have been realized, the TPB teaches us that it is the perception that these positive things may happen that motivates us to act.

In terms of long-term belief change, viral campaigns like the ALS Ice Bucket Challenge may benefit other charities as well. These types of social media events may make people feel more efficacious about contributing to charity and participating in money-raising efforts for charity. Though the ALS Ice Bucket Challenge had its critics, such as *Chicago Tribune*'s Will Oremus (2014), it was clearly an effective viral campaign, even though it wasn't a formal campaign initiated by the ALS Association.

TPB research has clarified that past behavior is a very good predictor of future behavior in general, and in terms of charitable giving specifically (e.g., Knowles, Hyde, & White, 2012). In addition to typical TPB variables, such as behavioral control and attitudes toward the behavior, having given money to a charity in the past year was also a predictor of intention to donate money again to a charity for others in need of assistance. So, in terms of the Ice Bucket Challenge, viral charity campaigns such as these have the potential for influencing future behaviors in addition to the short-term benefit to the specific charity whose campaign became a short-term Internet sensation.

METHODS OF RESEARCH IN THE TPB

Though the TPB can clearly be used to explain people's behaviors after-the-fact, it is most useful at the beginning of a persuasive campaign to assess what the target audience already believes, their evaluations of those beliefs, and to guide how we create a message that addresses or capitalizes on people's existing belief structures.

TPB research is typically done using quantitative surveys. These studies are either **confirmatory**, a direct test of the predictions of the TPB, or **exploratory**, exploring the beliefs people have about a behavior.

Confirmatory surveys are used to examine a specific behavior, determine whether or not the TPB predicts that behavior well, and discover which type of beliefs outlined in the TPB best predict the behavior. Then, using that information, researchers know which beliefs to focus on if they want to change or reinforce the behavior. For example, some behaviors are affected more by social norms, but other behaviors are predicted more by a person's sense of efficacy.

Exploratory surveys, on the other hand, are used to discover people's beliefs about a behavior. Exploratory TPB surveys are useful to both researchers and practitioners who want to more fully understand what beliefs people already have about a behavior. Data from these types of studies give us insight into the beliefs people have that we may not have been aware of and also give us information about the accuracy of people's beliefs, the strength of their beliefs, and whether outcome, normative, or control beliefs are influencing people's behaviors.

Dr. Ajzen has put together a brief document to help you design a TPB questionnaire. You can download the pdf here: http://people.umass.edu/aizen/pdf/tpb.measurement.pdf.

Insight into Innovation Activity: Use Dr. Ajzen's guide to put together a brief TPB survey related to something you care about and would want people to do (or not do). Define the target behavior, consider what beliefs would be related to the outcomes, norms, and people's sense of control over the behavior, and create two survey items for each type of belief.

There is some concern among researchers that TPB studies are largely correlational. In other words, survey studies show that TPB variables are related to each other but do not explain what *causes* changes in beliefs and behaviors (e.g., Sniehotta, Presseau, & Araújo-Soares, 2014). This is due, in part, to the reliance on survey methods to determine how well variables from the TPB predict intention and behavior. There have been some experimental tests of the TPB to see whether or not changing outcome, normative, and control beliefs can change intentions and behavior, but these experiments have been somewhat less successful in terms of supporting the utility of the TPB. In other words, the assumptions of the TPB seem to hold up better in survey studies compared to experimental studies of behavior.

That being said, meta-analyses of the TPB, or research studies that look at the findings of a large sample of related studies, support the TPB and point to some issues with measures used in TPB studies (Armitage & Conner, 2001). For example, the measure used in survey studies to assess norms is not particularly strong. But, overall, meta-analyses confirm that the TPB is a good predictor of behaviors including exercise (Hagger, Chatzisarantis, & Biddle, 2002) and smoking (Topa & Moriano, 2010), and if we are able to change people's intentions, we can influence their behaviors (Webb & Sheeran, 2006).

APPLYING THE TPB TO UNDERSTAND ADOPTION OF TECHNOLOGY

Experimental research that applies the TPB has found specific strategies that are effective at changing people's behavior (Webb & Sheeran, 2006):

1. Offering incentives and social support for the behavior;
2. Giving people information, a behavioral model, instructions, targets to reach, and skills training to perform the behavior;
3. Having people plan and practice behavior;
4. Extended monitoring of the behavior.

Thinking about these strategies from the perspective of new technology, the TPB offers us some insight into how to get people to adopt and use new technologies.

So, as previously mentioned, the TPB is often used to research the beliefs behind people's health-related behaviors, but it also applies to media use and people's adoption of new technologies. In fact, new theories, such as the **technology acceptance model** (Davis, 1989), were built upon the TPB to predict adoption of new technologies using concepts such as attitudes toward the uses of the new technology and beliefs about the usefulness of the new technology (Yousafzai, Foxall, & Pallister, 2010). The technology acceptance model focuses on three concepts: ease of use, perceived usefulness, and intention to use the new technology. Subjective norms were not included in the initial technology acceptance model, in part because, at the time, norms were not likely to predict the types of technology that were in use. Of course, with the advent of Web 2.0 technology such as social networks, online gaming, and the like, norms are important for the adoption of specific *types* of technology.

There is a growing body of applied research that uses the TPB to understand the beliefs about outcomes, norms, and behavioral control that determine the use of specific types of technology. The TPB has been used to explore using technology in the classroom, participating in online learning, using online shopping and banking, and participating in online social media. In keeping with the traditional application of the TPB to promote healthy behaviors, it has also been applied to develop and target online health campaigns.

ONLINE LEARNING

Teachers' attitudes toward delivering lessons online is predicted by their attitudes toward online instruction in terms of their perception of it affecting the quality of teaching, helping students' achievement in courses, and maintaining students' attention (Lee, Cerreto, & Lee, 2010). To a lesser extent, normative pressure from students, administrators, and parents, and control beliefs about having the time, skills, and needed resources, were related to intention to provide computer-mediated lectures. The findings are similar for the adoption of Web 2.0 technologies to enhance instruction: attitudes about usefulness and compatibility with instruction determine intention to use the technology (Hayes Capo & Orellana, 2012).

Though behavioral control wasn't as important in determining teacher use of technology to deliver lectures, research has suggested that behavioral control *is* the most important determinant of whether students will use mobile technology for college classes (Cheon, Lee, Crooks, & Song, 2012). For students, the perceived ease of using the technology, perceived usefulness of the technology (Cheon, Crooks, Chen, & Song, 2011), and students' sense of efficacy (Shih, 2008) determine using technology to complete college courses.

You may wonder why the beliefs that determine teachers' behaviors and the beliefs that determine students' behaviors are different. Recall at the beginning of this chapter that beliefs vary in their perceived relevance, valence, and strength. That is, we make associations about the attributes of the behavior, evaluate whether the attributes are positive or negative and which associations are the most true. For teachers, certain attributes related to the outcomes are clearly most important when considering alternative methods of instruction, particularly whether or not it will help their students. For students, on the other hand, the most relevant beliefs are control-related: whether they are able to actually take a class that way.

ONLINE COMMERCE

Much like students and teachers have different types of beliefs guiding their adoption of online and mobile learning, as consumers we also have different beliefs that guide our adoption of online commerce, such as online shopping and banking. Chances are that you know people who use mobile technology to shop, do their banking, and pay their bills. You probably also know people who are skeptical of the security of online commerce. Because of these very different beliefs, people's intentions and subsequent behaviors are very different.

In terms of shopping online, people must feel a sense of personal efficacy and feel that they can trust in the security of the technology before they shop online (George, 2004). Trust is also essential to predicting online banking (Yousafzai, Foxall, & Pallister, 2010). The ease of using a website to purchase items (ease of navigation and speed) and having the time, money, and skills to use the technology increase intentions to shop online (Pavlou & Fygenson, 2006). Further, to encourage continued online shopping behaviors over time, people's positive beliefs should be confirmed so that they feel satisfied with their experience using the technology and the service provided (Hsu, Yen, Chiu, Chang, 2006). Norms are not important determinants of online shopping behaviors, which makes sense because online shopping is a private activity. Private activities are not subject to public scrutiny so they are typically not affected by norms.

ADOPTION OF NEW TECHNOLOGY

Unlike taking classes online or shopping online, adopting new technologies—particularly posting videos online and joining social networks—are very public activities. Therefore, they are influenced by normative beliefs. For example, having the sense that one's peers upload videos online increases intentions to upload videos (Park, Lee, & Jung, 2010). Also, both attitudes and subjective norms predict intentions to use social networking sites, and norms are the strongest predictor of intention (Pelling & White, 2009). Both injunctive and descriptive norms are related to social network use when looking at participation in *specific* online behaviors, such as following sports on social media (Wang, 2013).

In all, private online behaviors, such as taking classes, shopping, and banking, are driven more by outcomes and efficacy. On the other hand, public online behaviors, like creating user generated content and participating in social networks, are driven more by norms. This has important implications for marketing online services and websites, because people's behaviors are going to be motivated by different beliefs depending on the nature of the product or service being marketed.

PROMOTING HEALTHY BEHAVIORS

Technology provides us with new ways to increase people's sense of efficacy, share information that may change beliefs, and ultimately change people's behaviors. Consider, for example, websites like Pinterest (www.pinterest.com). On Pinterest, people "pin" projects and design ideas to different boards. Users can share their pins with others and see other people's pinned projects and boards. Many pins link directly to recipes, step-by-step instructions, blog posts, or articles. Websites like Pinterest can make people feel a sense of efficacy about doing different types of projects and activities, including cooking healthy meals. It can also increase a sense of normative pressure, as people follow each other on Pinterest, repin each others' pins, and see their friends' pins.

When you think about it, there are millions of behaviors that we could promote or try to change using new technologies like Pinterest, YouTube, Twitter, Buzzfeed, Tumblr, Reddit, and Facebook. Because Web 2.0 messages can be disseminated quickly and easily, we can use them to share information to change beliefs, provide instructions in diverse media formats to improve efficacy, and even increase normative pressure toward healthy behaviors as people's friends post and pin healthy advice.

Even the US government has started using social media to promote healthy lifestyles. For example, the Centers for Disease Control used Facebook, Twitter, e-mail, and YouTube to reach people with information about the symptoms, treatment, and ways to prevent the spread of H1N1, then used new media to disseminate information about the vaccine in 2009 (Walton, Seitz, & Ragsdale, 2012). The United States Department of Agriculture's "Choose My Plate" campaign includes a website with healthy-eating cookbooks, a YouTube channel, Facebook page, and Twitter account. There are three-minute workouts depicted in images on BuzzFeed and posted on YouTube that you can pin, tweet, and share via Facebook. The most difficult part is cutting through the online clutter to reach the people who truly need the information to promote positive beliefs and healthy lifestyle changes.

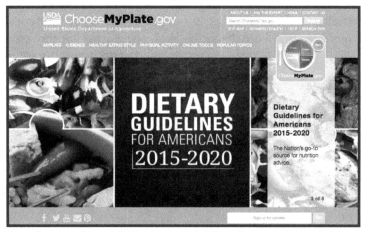

Source for screen shot and MyPlate image: United States Department of Agriculture. (2016). Resources for nutrition and health. Retrieved from www.choosemyplate.gov.

The USDA's choosemyplate.gov website

Insight into Innovation Activity: Check out the USDA's choosemyplate.gov website. Thinking about this website, is the way this is presented likely to help people live healthier lifestyles in terms of addressing people's beliefs about outcomes, norms, and behavioral control? Why or why not? What could they do to improve their message and promote more healthy behaviors?

CONCLUSION

The possibilities for changing people's behaviors are seemingly endless and stretch well beyond health contexts. The TPB has a long history of application to health-related behaviors and has been extended to predict adoptions and uses of new communication technologies as well. Though some have argued that the TPB should be "retired" (e.g., Sniehotta, Presseau, & Araújo-Soares, 2014), the continued relevance of the TPB and many extensions and adaptations, such as the technology acceptance model, suggests that it is still a fruitful and applicable theory to guide our understanding of human behavior, particularly the adoption of new technologies. That is not to say that the TPB is perfect. There are still some measurement and methodological issues in terms of the research being produced. But, it is a helpful starting point for considering how we can promote positive and prosocial behaviors, and when we consider how we might market products.

The important contribution of the TPB for us as Web 2.0 communicators is the focus on our own and others' beliefs. The TPB offers a typology of beliefs about outcomes, norms, and efficacy that is a useful lens for us to apply when we want to change people's behaviors. Whether we are trying to promote a healthy lifestyle change, convince people to support a politician or cause, or promote a particlar product or technology, it is useful to think about our message in terms of our audience's beliefs: What outcomes do they expect and do they think the outcomes will be favorable? What would others want them to do? Do they have the time, skills, and resources to do this? Based on our audience's beliefs, we can build a message strategy that focuses on forming or supporting beliefs to promote the behavior change we are seeking: focus on positive outcomes, develop a sense of normative support for the behavior, and promote the belief that they can do what we are asking them to do.

ACTIVITIES AND ASSIGNMENTS

1. **Learning about others' beliefs.** Choose a prosocial behavior to promote (recycling, reducing your carbon footprint, volunteering, donating to charity, etc.). Ask a couple of classmates about their beliefs about the outcomes, evaluations of those outcomes, their beliefs about what others do and what others would want them to do, and their beliefs about their own ability to do it. Write a brief report on your findings: What beliefs about outcomes, norms, and behavioral control did you find that surprised you? What beliefs do you think you would need to target to promote the behavior among your peers in the class?

2. **TPB case study.** Write a brief case study of a recent marketing campaign for a new tech product (such as a new phone, tablet, software, or app.). Explain which beliefs from the TPB would be most relevant to the product (e.g., outcomes, norms, and/or control). Evaluate how well the campaign addressed those beliefs.

REFERENCES

Seminal Texts:

TPB

Ajzen, I. (1985). From intentions to actions: A theory of planned behavior. In J. Kuhl & J. Beckman (Eds.), *Action-control: From cognition to behavior* (pp. 11–39). Heidelberg, Germany: Springer.

Expectancy value approach

Fishbein, M., & Ajzen, I. (1975). *Belief, attitude, intention, and behavior: An introduction to theory and research*. Reading, MA: Addison-Wesley. Retrieved from http://people.umass. edu/aizen/f&a1975.html.

Academic Research:

Armitage, C. J., & Conner, M. (2001). Efficacy of the theory of planned behaviour: A meta-analytic review. *British Journal of Social Psychology*, *40*, 471–499.

Capo, B., & Orellana, A. (2011). Web 2.0 technologies for classroom instruction: High school teachers' perceptions and adoption factors. *Quarterly Review of Distance Education*, *12*(4), 235–253.

Cheon, J., Crooks, S. M., Chen, X., & Song, J. (2011). *An investigation of mobile learning readiness and design considerations for higher education*. Paper presented at The Annual Convention of the Association for Educational Communications and Technology in Jacksonville, FL. Retrieved online: http://files.eric.ed.gov/fulltext/ED528860.pdf#page=54

Cheon, J., Crooks, S. M., Chen, X., & Song, J. (2012). An investigation of mobile learning readiness in higher education based on the theory of planned behavior. *Computers & Education*, *59*(3), 1054–1064.

George, J. F. (2004). The theory of planned behavior and Internet purchasing. *Internet Research*, *14*, 198–212.

Hagger, M. S., Chatzisarantis, N. L. D., & Biddle, S. J. H. (2002). A meta-analytic review of the theories of reasoned action and planned behavior in physical activity: Predictive validity and the contribution of additional variables. *Exercise Psychology*, *24*, 3–32.

Hsu, M.-H., Yen, C.-H., Chiu, C.-M., & Chang, C.-M. (2006). A longitudinal investigation of continued online shopping behavior: An extension of the theory of planned behavior. *International Journal of Human-Computer Studies*, *64*, 889–904.

Knowles, S. R., Hyde, M. K., & White, K. M. (2012). Predictors of young people's charitable intentions to donate money: An extended theory of planned behavior perspective. *Journal of Applied Social Psychology*, *42*, 2096–2110.

Lee, J., Cerreto, F. A., & Lee, J. (2010). Theory of planned behavior and teachers' decisions regarding use of educational technology. *Educational Technology & Society*, *13*, 152–164.

Park, N., Lee, K. M., & Jung, Y., (2010). *Determinants of uploading user-generated video content on the Internet: Toward an integrated model."* Paper presented at the annual meeting of the International Communication Association, Suntec Singapore International Convention & Exhibition Centre, Suntec City, Singapore.

Pavlou, P. A., & Fygenson, M. (2006). Understanding and predicting electronic commerce adoption: An extension of the theory of planned behavior. *Management Information Systems Quarterly, 30,* 115–143.

Pelling, E. L., & White, K. M. (2009). The theory of planned behavior applied to young people's use of social networking sites. *Cyberpsychology & Behavior, 12,* 755–759.

Rimal, R. N., & Real, K. (2006). Understanding the influence of perceived norms on behaviors. *Communication Theory, 13,* 184–203.

Shih, H. (2008). Using a cognition-motivation-control view to assess the adoption intention for Web-based learning. *Computers & Education, 50*(1), 327–337.

Sniehotta, F. F., Presseau, J., & Araújo-Soares, V. (2014). Time to retire the theory of planned behavior. *Health Psychology Review, 8,* 1–7.

Topa, G., & Moriano, J. A. (2010). Theory of planned behavior and smoking: Meta-analysis and SEM model. *Substance Abuse and Rehabilitation, 1,* 23–33.

Walton, L. R., Seitz, H. H., & Ragsdale, K. (2012). Strategic use of YouTube during a national public health crisis: The CDC's response to the 2009 H1N1 flu epidemic. *Case Studies in Strategic Communication, 1,* article 3. Retrieved from http://cssc.uscannenberg.org/v1/v1art3

Webb, T. L., & Sheeran, P. (2006). Does changing behavioral intentions engender behavior change? A meta-analysis of the experimental evidence. *Psychological Bulletin, 132,* 249–268.

Yousafzai, H. Y., Foxall, G. R., & Pallister, J. G. (2010). Explaining Internet banking behavior: Theory of reasoned action, theory of planned behavior, or technology acceptance model? *Journal of Applied Social Psychology, 40,* 1172–1202.

Examples:

The ALS Association. (2014, August 26). *ALS Association is grateful for outpouring of support.* Retrieved online http://www.alsa.org/news/media/press-releases/ice-bucket-challenge-082614.html

Codecademy. (2014). *Learn to code interactively for free.* Retrieved from www.codecademy.com.

Oremus, W. (2014). Say "No!" to the ice bucket challenge. *Chicago Tribune.* Retrieved from http://www.chicagotribune.com/news/opinion/commentary/ct-oped-icebucket-0819-20140819-story.html.

Pinterest. (nd). Retrieved from www.pinterest.com.

Wang, X. (2013). Applying the integrative model of behavioral prediction and attitude functions in the context of social media use while viewing mediated sports. *Computers in Human Behavior, 29*(4), 1538–1545.

United States Department of Agriculture. (2014). *Resources for nutrition and health.* Retrieved from www.choosemyplate.gov.

Further Reading Online:

Attia, A. M., Aziz, N., & Friedman, B. A. (2012). Impact of social networks on behavioral change: A conceptual framework. *World Review of Business Research, 2*, 91–108. Retrieved from http://www.wrbrpapers.com/static/documents/March/2012/7.%20Nergis.pdf

Davis, F. (1989). Perceived usefulness, perceived ease of use, and user acceptance of information technology. *MIS Quarterly, 13*, 319–340. Retrieved from http://iris.nyit.edu/~kkhoo/Spring2008/Topics/TAM/PercieveUsefulness_MIS.pdf

CHAPTER 19

DIFFUSION OF INNOVATIONS

OUTCOMES

- *Knowledge:* Learn how new technological advances are spread via social networks.
- *Skill:* Identify e-Influentials to promote new products and technologies.

💬 INTRODUCTION

In the previous chapter, we discussed the theory of planned behavior, which links beliefs about outcomes, norms, and behavioral control to behavioral intention. In this chapter, we look more closely at the social process of changing behavior, particularly adopting new technology. **Diffusion theory** explains that we learn about the features of technology from the media and our adoption of technology is affected by our peer groups. **Multistep flow** theory, also called two-step flow, helps to inform our current understanding of diffusion by highlighting the importance of interactions in social groups in the process of disseminating information. Though diffusion of innovations and two step flow were developed over a half century ago, the processes they outline for informing and persuading people about technology are very informative in terms of understanding the adoption of today's new communication technologies.

Rogers ([1995](#)) explains diffusion as "the process by which an *innovation* is communicated through certain *channels* over *time* among members of a *social system*" (p. 5, emphasis added).

- *Characteristics of the innovation determine adoption.* When we consider whether or not to adopt a new technology, we consider how new it is, the attributes of the technology, and what outcomes we expect from adopting the new technology.

- *We are influenced via many communication channels.* Rogers (1995) argues that "diffusion is a very social process" (p. 18). Chances are, friends or family in your social network have influenced your adoption of technology in the past. You may find out about new technology from ads, blogs, social media, and interpersonal discussions.

- *Diffusion takes time.* We don't always adopt new technology as soon as it is released, and the process of disseminating information through media and social networks can take time. Some people are early adopters, but most people need more time before adopting.
- *Our social system affects diffusion.* The process of diffusing information and influence through a social network is affected by the size and structure of the system. The social system may be any group of individuals, collection of interrelated groups, or even an entire region or society targeted by the new technology. These systems have a set structure that determines the flow of information and direction of influence about adopting new technologies.

Given diffusion theory's clear explanation of people's appraisal of new innovations and of the larger social process that drives adoption, this theory is widely applied to adoption of new communication technologies.

You can see Everett Roger's speech about diffusion theory, given at the University of Illinois at Urbana-Champaign, here: https://www.youtube.com/watch?v=j1uc7yZH6eU

Watch a brief review of diffusion theory here: https://www.youtube.com/watch?v=VtTSoMfzvi8

 # OVERVIEW OF THE DIFFUSION OF INNOVATIONS

MAIN IDEA

Diffusion is a multidirectional, sometimes slow process by which new ideas, behaviors, and technologies are adopted or rejected by a social group (Rogers, 1995). Adoption occurs over time in an "S-shaped" curve, and is a result of individual differences, opinion leadership in the social network, and normative pressure. Characteristics of the innovation itself and of individuals affect the rate of adoption.

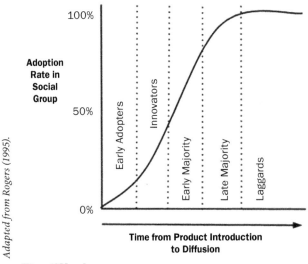

The diffusion process

KEY CONCEPTS IN DIFFUSION THEORY

In 1962, Everett Rogers published *Diffusion of Innovations*, one of the most cited books in the social sciences, that explained the diffusion process. He outlined the stages that people go through when considering adopting an innovation, the types of adopters, and the role of opinion leaders in influencing people the social group.

1. **There are stages to the innovation decision process**. Rogers (1995) argued that there are specific stages of the "innovation decision process" that groups and individuals go through when introduced to a new technological innovation: Knowledge, persuasion, decision, implementation, and confirmation. These stages are motivated by **uncertainty** and **dissonance**. We feel uncertain about new technologies when they are first introduced: How does it work? Is it useful to me? We also want our behaviors to be consistent with our values and existing attitudes to avoid feeling dissonance.

   - *Knowledge of characteristics of the innovation*: We learn about the innovation and how it works. This process is affected by our socioeconomic status, interactions with other people, other sources of information, and our personality.

   - *Persuasion regarding characteristics of the innovation*: We develop an attitude toward the innovation by seeking information about the advantages/disadvantages from peers. This is when we consider the characteristics, or attributes, of the innovation such as

     - *advantages* over other options and the link between the innovation and social status;

     - *compatibility* with our existing values, beliefs, ideas, and needs;

     - *complexity* or ease of use;

     - *triability*, or having the opportunity to experiment with the technology;

     - *observability*, or visibility, of the innovation.

   - *Decision to adopt or reject*: We make a choice about using the technology or not using it. Sometimes we will "try it out" or observe others to make our decision.

   - *Implementation of adoption*: We begin to use the technology and integrate it into our lives. As we become comfortable with the innovation, we may even reinvent it, or use it for our own novel purposes.

   - *Confirmation of decision*: We look for confirmation of our decision and possibly change our minds based on feedback and our experience with the technology.

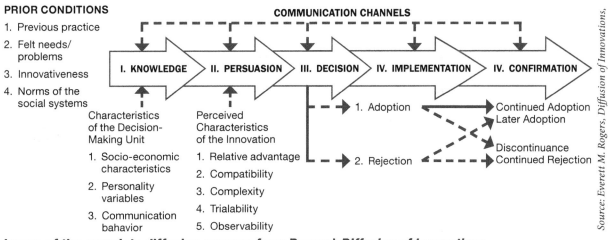

Source: Everett M. Rogers, Diffusion of Innovations, 5th Edition. Free Press: 2003, p. 170.

Image of the complete diffusion process from Rogers' *Diffusion of Innovations*, Chapter 5; copyright The New Press.

2. **There are clear types of adopters**. Each person will go through the decision process outlined above in his or her own time and at his/her own pace. This leads to individual differences in adoption; some people tend to be very early adopters and some people tend to be very late adopters. Most of us fall somewhere in the middle as mass adopters.

Where we fall on the range of adopters depends on our **innovativeness**, or how early we adopt technology compared to others in our social systems (Rogers, 1995). The ability and desire to adopt new technology early is linked to age, education, social status, social mobility, and social group. Younger, more educated, and wealthier people adopt innovations earlier. Keeping in mind these individual differences, Rogers developed five categories of adopters:

- *Innovators* are "venturesome," or enjoy trying out new things. They are comfortable with uncertainty and have the resources to be innovative.

- *Early adopters* are "respectable," integrated members of their social systems, and serve as opinion leaders for other people in their social groups who are going through the decision process.

- *Early majority* adopters are "deliberate;" they serve as a link between the opinion leaders and the majority, but need more time to carefully consider an innovation compared to innovators and early adopters.

- *Late majority* adopters are more "skeptical" and typically adopt due to peer pressure in their social group.

- *Laggards* are "traditional" because they are suspicious of new innovations and they also have the fewest resources, making them the last people to adopt a technology.

Insight into Innovation Example: It may be difficult to believe, but 20 percent of Americans—about 60 million people—do not use the Internet (Dewey, 2013). In keeping with the predictions of diffusion theory, nonusers tend to be older, have a lower income, and live in rural areas. Read more about the Internet divide here: http://www.washingtonpost.com/blogs/the-switch/wp/2013/08/19/the-60-million-americans-who-dont-use-the-internet-in-six-charts/

3. **Opinion leaders are key to the multistep flow of information. Opinion leaders** are central to beginning the diffusion process in a social group as they set the stage for later adopters (Rogers, 1995). The key to successfully launching new technology is to identify opinion leaders, who then serve as a model for other people in their social networks. *Opinion leaders are informal leaders in a social group who are in a position to influence others' opinions and behaviors.*

Rogers (1995) reasoned that opinion leaders were essential to the diffusion process in part because of the two-step flow process discovered by Lazarsfeld, Berelson, and Gaudet (1944) decades earlier. Two-step flow suggests that the media provides *information* to opinion leaders and opinion leaders who, in turn, *influence* people in their social networks. The premise of two-step flow is not a complete picture of the flow of information because people get information from both the mass media and peers in the knowledge and persuasion stages. We now understand that there is multistep flow, and people get information from many sources. Even so, opinion leadership is an important takeaway from Lazarsfeld's research.

How and whether information and influence flows from opinion leaders depends on the social network (Rogers, 1995). **Homophilous** social networks, where all members are very similar, tend not to have clear opinion leaders and, therefore, innovations tend to be difficult to diffuse in those types of systems. **Heterophilous** social groups, where members vary in attitudes, beliefs, and status, tend to have opinion leaders who are higher status that aid in the diffusion of an innovation throughout the group. Opinion leaders tend to be distinct, or different from, other members of their social groups: They follow the media more closely, socialize more, are higher in socioeconomic status, and are more innovative.

EXAMPLE OF DIFFUSION IN WEB 2.0: ADOPTION OF SOCIAL MEDIA

Consider, as an example of diffusion theory, the adoption of social media. In 2005, only about 8 percent of adults who had the Internet were using social media (Duggan & Smith, 2013). These innovators were the first users and began the diffusion process. Between mid-2006 and mid-2012, adoption went from 15 percent to 70 percent, so this is when the majority adopted the technology, likely as a result of peer influence. Now, the number of social media users is tapering off with around 73 percent of all Internet users in the United States using social media.

Looking at the early adopters, we see that people aged 18 to 29 years were the most rapid first adopters, followed by people aged 30 to 49 years. It wasn't until 2009—3 years later—that we saw a marked increase in social media use by people aged 50 and over. So, young people tended to be early adopters, whereas older people tended to be late majority and laggard adopters. Also, notice that reaching the point of mass adoption took 4 years, and generally followed the "S-shaped" pattern that diffusion theory suggests.

Lastly, notice that there have been peaks for adoption and dips. Even after we adopt an innovation, such as joining a social network, we may decide we do not like the experience or may receive feedback that challenges our decision, and we may discontinue our use of the innovation.

Insight into Innovation Activity: When did you join a social network? Are you an early, mass, or laggard adopter? Who influenced your decision to join or not join a social network? How many of your friends have "quit Facebook"? Have you considered it? Why?

METHODS FOR DIFFUSION RESEARCH

Tracking trends in adoption and using surveys can confirm the "S-shaped" curve proposed by diffusion theory and confirm the categories of adopters defined in the theory. For example, the Pew Internet & American Life Project does an exceptional job of using random samples and brief surveys to track adoption trends over time. In the chart below, we see the "S-shaped" adoption curve for social networking from Pew's ongoing research.

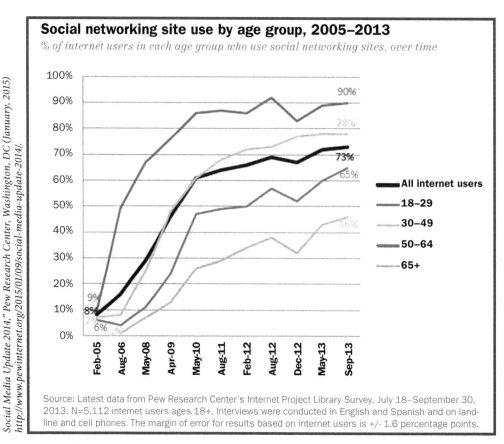

Social networking site use by age group, 2005–2013

% of internet users in each age group who use social networking sites, over time

Social Media Update 2014," Pew Research Center, Washington, DC (January, 2015) http://www.pewinternet.org/2015/01/09/social-media-update-2014/.

Legend:
- All internet users
- 18–29
- 30–49
- 50–64
- 65+

Source: Latest data from Pew Research Center's Internet Project Library Survey, July 18–September 30, 2013. N=5,112 internet users ages 18+. Interviews were conducted in English and Spanish and on landline and cell phones. The margin of error for results based on internet users is +/- 1.6 percentage points.

Image from Pew Research Internet Project (2013)

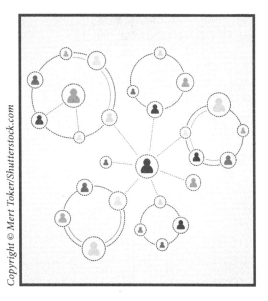

In terms of looking closely at the diffusion process within a social group, **network analysis** is a common method used to map the social structure of a group (Rogers, 1995). It looks at the **proximity** of connections in a social group (close or distant) and **individuals' social networks** (interlocking versus radial). When conducting a network analysis, we look at the communication proximity of members, or how much their interpersonal connections overlap. Chances are, with your significant other and long-term friends, you have many shared connections on social networks like Facebook. They are "close" in social proximity. You may also have friends that have few or no shared connections with you, which would be a "distant" social proximity. We also have **interlocking personal networks**, or people that we interact with on a regular basis, and **radial social networks**, or those people that we know but do not interact with frequently.

Having a lot of weak ties aids the diffusion process. So, when your friends—or you—have hundreds or thousands of Facebook friends and Twitter followers, there is a large, radial, distant social network. People in those positions tend to hear about innovations first, get a lot of insight into innovations from their social networks, and are able to disseminate information and opinions to a lot of people, thereby influencing a wide social network. This aids the diffusion process.

But just having a lot of friends and followers in a social network does not necessarily mean that a person is an opinion leader. To be an opinion leader, other people in the social network must be influenced by the information and opinions being shared. There are several ways to identify the opinion leaders in a social group:

- **Sociometric**. This method involves simply asking people in a social group to name the people they would ask for advice about a particular innovation. The names that are provided most frequently by social group members are the opinion leaders in that group.
- **Key informants**. This method involves asking people who are knowledgeable about their social group to identify the opinion leaders.
- **Self-designation**. We can also ask people if they are the opinion leaders in their social groups using survey items or interview questions about whether others rely on them for information and insight.
- **Observation**. This is most time-intensive, and involves observing a social group and discovering which members of the group are most sought out for information and advice.

IDENTIFYING E-INFLUENTIALS: THE MODERN OPINION LEADERS

Modern opinion leaders have gone online to spread information and opinions. Given the wide reach of online opinion leaders, they are a common target for industry professionals who want to promote new products.

Change Agents are people employed by an organization or group to promote the diffusion of an innovative product or idea (Rogers, 1995). These are formal roles within an organization, and change agents promote their organization's innovations by interacting and building relationships with clients, being empathetic and responsive to their needs, providing information and, later, supporting clients who adopt their products. Change agents tend to be in direct contact with innovators and early adopters within their clients' social groups to help promote their products. So, the methods outlined above for researching the social networks of clients and identifying influential opinion leaders is an important starting point for the roll out of new technology.

In our Web 2.0 environment, one of the challenges faced by change agents is identifying the innovators and potential early adopters who can serve as online opinion leaders and develop a client base for new products. Many people have 1,000 or more friends and followers via social media, and many bloggers have posts that go viral. This does not necessarily mean that those popular people on social networks and popular bloggers are opinion leaders, and people who are opinion leaders in one area are not necessarily opinion leaders in other areas. But, online opinion leaders are more likely to be open to and try out new products (Kwak, Fox, & Zinkman, 2002). So once they are identified, they may prove to be very willing consumers and promoters.

The challenge for change agents is separating popularity from opinion leadership and identifying the people who are opinion leaders for the product being rolled out. Online opinion leaders who influence others' technology adoption are **e-influentials**.

BLOGGERS

Blogs, also called web logs, are user generated content that include thoughts, feelings, opinions, insights, and information. Bloggers tend to write blogs because they *want* to be influential, and people read their blogs to be entertained, pass time, and seek information (Segev, Villar, & Fiske, 2012). Bloggers and their followers constitute a social group, because the need for belonging is a key motivation behind both blogging and following. Therefore, bloggers with large followings can be a great resource for public relations and marketing professions if they are able to identify the bloggers who meet the needs of their followers. But, not all bloggers are good, and so not all bloggers are influencers.

When we are considering who the opinion leaders are in a network, we look at **network centrality**, or how socially connected people are (Dubois & Gaffney, 2014). This can be determined by looking at the number of followers and the importance of a person within a social network. We know from the definition of opinion leadership that just having a lot of social connections is not sufficient to be an opinion leader; opinion leaders *influence* others. Interestingly, centrality in a social network may not be the most important deciding factor of whether one is an opinion leader. Credibility/expertise, trust, and interaction with people in the social network are essential for bloggers to influence their readers.

Influential blogs tend to be well written, focused, have a large following, integrate technology such as microblogging on Twitter, and are generally trusted by their readers (Uzunoğlu & Kip, 2014). Li and Du (2011) recommend the BARR approach—looking at blogs, authors, readers, and relationships—to identify e-influentials.

1. Look at the content of the **b**log to see if a review of your product would fit.
2. Examine the **a**uthor's expertise regarding the product being marketed, based on number of views and followers.
3. Consider the **r**eaders of the blog, particularly whether they reblog content or post responses.
4. Explore the strength of the blogger's **r**elationship with their readers by finding out how often they interact.

MICROBLOGGERS

One way to engage with and strengthen relationships among followers is through microblogging. **Microblogging** is blogging brief snippets and links via Twitter in 140 characters or less. Much like analyzing the opinion leadership of traditional blogs, influential microbloggers are socially connected and involved (Xu , Sang, Blasiola, & Park, 2014). On Twitter, people follow certain accounts and are also followed by other users. More connected Twitter microbloggers have many followers and also influence the flow of information. Microblogging influencers also tend to be involved in the topic they are tweeting about, including having "interest, enthusiasm,

Copyright © GAnnette Shaff/Shutterstock.com

excitement, and personal relevancy" regarding the product (p. 1282). Twitter opinion leaders tend to be motivated to express their opinions, seek information, mobilize others, and are effective in increasing their followers' involvement (Park, 2013).

Once influential blogs are identified, marketers can send bloggers samples of their products, build and maintain relationships with the bloggers, and assess the sales outcomes from those relationships (Uzunoğlu & Kip, 2014). In addition to their motivation to be leaders in their social networks, online opinion leaders are also motivated by extrinsic rewards, such as monetary incentives and product samples (Shi & Wojnicki, 2014). So, to get e-influentials to promote a product, it may be most effective to offer them some financial or material incentive. Interestingly, research has suggested that online opinion leaders are particularly susceptible to being influenced (Lee, Cotte, & Noseworthy, 2010). People who are central to their social networks—who have the most connections to others—want to maintain their leadership position in the social network and, therefore, are more susceptible to influence.

Insight into Innovation Example: Read the *Forbes* article about Shi and Wojnicki's (2014) study of monetary incentives and online opinion leaders here: http://www.forbes.com/sites/avaseave/2014/03/26/opinion-leaders-much-more-willing-to-be-paid-for-social-network-referrals/

 **CONCLUSION**

The spread of Web 2.0 technology has both changed the flow of information in society and also breathed new life into "old" communication theories, such as diffusion theory and two-step flow. Opinion leadership in particular is important to understand, as these everyday, influential people now have a wider reach than ever before via blogs, microblogging, and social networks. They have the potential to promote new technologies and products (Uzunoğlu & Kip, 2014), and also to influence people's political knowledge and opinions (Campus, 2012). The diffusion process is still typically slow, as evidenced by the adoption of social networking technologies. Diffusion theory helps us understand the characteristics of the people who are likely to adopt early, en masse, and late in the process.

Diffusion theory reinforces the importance of social networks in our decisions to adopt new technologies and ideas. Whether we are trying to get people to purchase a new product, promote a lifestyle change, or influence political opinions, knowing the opinion leader in the target population is essential to our efforts. Diffusion research gives us a lot of insight into who online opinion leaders are and also how to identify them by looking at the size of their following, the quality of the content they produce, and also the strength of their ties within their networks.

Another interesting takeaway from recent diffusion research is how we, ourselves, can be effective bloggers by identifying those topics that we have expertise in, building a following, generating high quality content, and engaging our followers in ongoing interactions. There is clearly social capital that can be gained by becoming an opinion leader in a specific area, and there are also financial rewards. But the research also tells us that this is not going to be an easy task: we need to have resources, knowledge, expertise, a wide social network, and dedicate ourselves to ongoing relationship building to become an online opinion leader. All of this takes effort and time.

ACTIVITIES AND ASSIGNMENTS

1. **Map your social network**. Create a map of your social network at school.
   a. List everyone you know in your major or program..
   b. Circle the people you interact with frequently.
   c. Draw lines between people in your social network who know each other.
   d. Which of the people you know are the closest in social proximity to you?
   e. Is your social network more interlocking or radial?
   f. Who is the person with the most interconnections in your social group? Are they an opinion leader in your program? Why or why not?

2. **Determine the opinion leadership potential of a blogger**. Use the BARR approach to assess a blog. Choose a blog to review.
   a. Look at the content of the blog to see what products seem most appropriate given the topic of the blog.
   b. Examine the author's expertise regarding the products being discussed.

282   **Insight into Innovation**

c. Consider the **r**eaders of the blog, particularly whether they reblog content or post responses.

d. Explore the strength of the blogger's **r**elationship with their readers by finding out how often they interact.

e. Write an overall assessment of whether the blog is likely to be a source of opinion leadership, the types of products they may be good at marketing, and how influential you think could be given the strength and number of connections they have made.

REFERENCES

Seminal Text:

Rogers, E. M. (1995). *Diffusion of innovations* (4th ed). New York: The Free Press.

Lazarsfeld, P., Berelson, B., & Gaudet, H. (1944). *The people's choice: How the voter makes up his mind in presidential elections*. New York: Columbia Press.

Academic Articles:

Campus, D. (2012). Political discussion, opinion leadership and trust. *European Journal of Communication, 27*, 46–55.

Dubois, E., & Gaffney, D. (2014). The multiple facets of influence: Identifying political influentials and opinion leaders on Twitter. *The American Behavioral Scientist, 58*, 1260–1277.

Flynn, L. R., Goldsmith, R. E., & Eastman, J. K. (1996). Opinion leaders and opinion seekers: Two new measurement scales. *Journal of the Academy of Marketing Science, 24*, 137–147.

Kwak, H., Fox, R. J., & Zinkhan, G. M. (2002). What products can be promoted and sold via the internet? *Journal of Advertising Research, 42*, 23–38.

Lee, S. H., Cotte, J., & Noseworthy, T. J. (2010). The role of network centrality in the flow of consumer influence. *Journal of Consumer Psychology, 20*, 66–77.

Li, F., & Du, T. C. (2011). Who is talking? An ontology-based opinion leader identification framework for word-of-mouth marketing in online social blogs. *Decision Support Systems, 51*, 190–197.

Park, C. S. (2013). Does Twitter motivate involvement in politics? Tweeting, opinion leadership, and political engagement. *Computers in Human Behavior, 29*, 1641–1648.

Segev, S., Villar, M. E., & Fiske, R. M. (2012). Understanding opinion leadership and motivations to blog: Implications for public relations practice. *Public Relations Journal, 6*. Retrieved from http://www.prsa.org/intelligence/prjournal/documents/2012segev.pdf

Shi, M., & Wojnicki, A. C. (2014). Money talks…to online opinion leaders: What motivates opinion leaders to make online referrals? *Journal of Advertising Research, 54*, 81–91.

Uzunoğlu, E., & Kip, S. M. (2014). Brand communication through digital influencers: Leveraging blogger engagement. *International Journal of Information Management, 34*, 592–602.

Xu, W. W., Sang, Y., Blasiola, S., & Park, H. W. (2014). Predicting opinion leaders in Twitter activism networks: The case of the Wisconsin recall election. *American Behavioral Scientist*, 58, 1278–1293.

Examples:

Dewey, C. (2013, August 19). The 60 million Americans who don't use the Internet, in six charts. *The Washington Post*. Retrieved from http://www.washingtonpost.com/blogs/the-switch/wp/2013/08/19/the-60-million-americans-who-dont-use-the-internet-in-six-charts/

Duggan, M., & Smith, A. (2013, December 30). Social Media Update 2013. *Pew Research Center*. Retrieved from http://www.pewinternet.org/2013/12/30/social-media-update-2013/.

Seave, A. (2014, March 26). Opinion leaders: Much more willing to be paid for social-network referrals. *Forbes*. Retrieved from http://www.forbes.com/sites/avaseave/2014/03/26/opinion-leaders-much-more-willing-to-be-paid-for-social-network-referrals/

Further Reading Online:

Rogers, E. M. (1995). *Diffusion of innovations* (4th ed). New York: The Free Press. Retrieved from http://books.google.com/books?id=v1ii4QsB7jIC&dq=diffusion+of+innovations+eve+rogers&source=gbs_navlinks_s

RHETORICAL THEORY

🗨 INTRODUCTION

As we discussed in the first chapters in this text, communication studies has its roots in the study of rhetorical theory. So far in this unit, we have looked at theories from psychology, such as the elaboration likelihood model, cognitive dissonance theory, and the theory of planned behavior, as well as diffusion of innovations from sociology. We will end the unit by looking at theories from the rhetorical tradition, and explore how specific rhetorical tactics identified by classical rhetorical theorists such as Aristotle, and modern rhetorical theorists such as Burke and Fisher, contribute to our understanding of influencing people via Web 2.0 technologies.

Rhetorical theory is not one unified theory of rhetoric; it is *a body of research that discovers, describes, and critiques rhetorical tactics and effects.* In this chapter, we review some of the most influential rhetorical tactics that scholars have identified and used to understand human communication. Rhetorical theory focuses on (Kuypers & King, 2009):

- How people use symbols;
- People's goals, or motivations, in terms of the audience and the context;
- Evaluating the effects and effectiveness of messages given the audience and context.

The study of rhetoric is helpful to us as we interact with people via Web 2.0 technologies. Rhetoric provides us with a toolbox of persuasive tactics that we can use to influence others, and that we can recognize when they are used to influence us. Studying rhetorical tactics should make us more competent Web 2.0 communicators and more aware, critical consumers of Web 2.0 content by challenging us to think about the person who created the message, their motivations and biased view of reality, and how their messages shape our social reality.

MAIN IDEA OF RHETORICAL THEORY

There are many options available to people when they try to persuade others, and the choices that people make when persuading—the words they use, the images they create, even the production of the message—reveal their motivations and their views of reality. These rhetorical choices also have the potential to change or to reinforce how we see the world and our social structure by selectively including or excluding people or issues and framing people or issues in a particular way.

KEY RHETORICAL CONCEPTS

Types of Proof: Ethos, Pathos, and Logos (Aristotle). Aristotle sought to identify the rhetorical tactics used in Ancient Greece, and explained that there are three types of proof used to persuade: ethos, pathos, and logos. **Ethos** is when communicators establish their goodwill toward others, their own competence, and expertise as a type of proof. **Logos** is an appeal to logic, and includes building valid arguments to prove a point. Some proofs require a syllogism with a major premise (main idea) and minor premise (supporting points) that lead to a clear conclusion. Lastly, **pathos** appeals to people's emotions, such as hope, fear, pride, and so on.

Many people post political and social opinions and memes via social networks like Facebook. If you have, chances are it was something related to your background (ethos). On social media, you can find your niche, or your own area of ethos, and invest time and energy in building an audience of followers. The opinions you post may focus on the evidence that supports your opinion (logos), such as linking to statistics or reliable sources that support your opinion. Posts may also express the emotions behind your opinion (pathos), such as linking to emotional blog posts or sharing memes with images that inspire emotions.

Narrative (Fisher, 1987). We also use **narratives** to influence others through accounts of what could happen, is happening, or has happened. Narratives are also a type of proof. Fisher argued that we use narratives to make sense of our world. When we tell a narrative, whether it is a story to our kids or a blog post online, there is a plot with characters and a setting. **Plots** are the sequence of events that unfold and **characters** are the people involved. This all takes place in a **setting**, or a particular context or situation. When we tell a story, causes and effects are implied in the plot: we are explaining what caused something to happen. Similarly, how we frame the characters and describe their roles in the plot, as well as the characteristics of the characters, reflect how we see the people involved. So, narratives are a reflection of the communicator's view of reality. But we don't believe every story we hear; we consider whether the story holds up when compared to other stories (**coherence**) and whether it seems realistic based on our experience (**fidelity**). Many blog posts and opinion articles that go viral are narratives that depict situations and people in particular ways. These can be influential because it gives us personal stories that we can relate to, and it shapes our understanding of ourselves and others.

As an example of how narratives can reflect our social reality, and how receptive we are to narratives, consider a couple of false stories that have gone viral, only to find out later that they were untrue (e.g., Weigel, 2013). There was the story of Elan, traveling on Thanksgiving in 2013, who allegedly taunted and shamed a woman on his flight who was being huffy and rude. Elan posted, play by play, a mean-spirited exchange between himself and a woman in seat 7a on his flight. Then there was the waitress who posted a picture of a receipt that was allegedly left by a family that didn't leave a tip because they "don't agree" with her "gay lifestyle." Like the "live tweeted" feud between Elan and the woman in seat 7a, the story about the waitress was also false. How did these stories go viral? Shouldn't they have failed the tests of coherence and fidelity? Maybe not. Both of these examples fit with things that really happen: People do get irrationally angry when traveling by plane and there have been numerous news stories about passengers getting into fights with each other on crowded flights. Servers have been stiffed by people for many callous reasons, and we know that ongoing discrimination against people who are in same-sex relationships still exists within the United States. So, when considering the fidelity and coherence of the characters, setting, and plot, it is not surprising that people believed these narratives.

Identification (Burke, 1969). Part of the effectiveness of social media celebrities and bloggers is our ability to **identify** with them, or see them as being similar to ourselves. Burke referred to this as **consubstantiation**, or when the substance of someone overlaps significantly with the substance of someone else. When the opposite is true, and two people are described as being very different, then **division** occurs. Division is when we point out how someone is fundamentally different from, or distinct from, someone else. Think of it this way, if you wanted to endorse a political candidate on social media, you could stress how that candidate's goals, values, and background are similar to your own and your followers'. This would create consubstantiation. On the other hand, you could stress how the opposition is "out of touch" with people like you and your social circle to create division.

Metaphors. We can link things together through **metaphors**, or by comparing two things, to reach a conclusion or frame a person or event. Metaphors influence how we see the world and what we do (Lakoff & Johnson, 1980). When we call student debt a "bubble," for example, that metaphor has implications for how we view student debt: It is fragile; it could burst. Through this process of identifying one thing with another, we are framing it, or promoting a particular view of the situation. It can also affect our behavior; maybe we'll be more hesitant to take out loans for school, or choose a school where we will go into less debt. Metaphors are useful, because they can clarify an abstract idea, but they can also be misleading because they are not always accurate comparisons. So, the bubble metaphor used to describe the debt crises is helpful, because it demonstrates how the situation is volatile, but it is also potentially misleading because it isn't as fragile as a bubble per se.

Insight into Innovation Activity: Metaphors for student debt. Check out this video where Mark Cuban discussed student loans as a "bubble" and what's likely to happen: http://www.inc.com/mark-cuban/video-student-loans-bubble.html

Is "bubble" a good metaphor for student debt? Why or why not? How would the meaning be different if he had used another metaphor—such as a "time bomb waiting to go off"? What other metaphors can you think of?

Guilt and Redemption (Burke, 1969). Much like identification can influence how we think and feel about people and issues, negative feelings we have about our own circumstances can motivate us as well. Burke referred to this as the process of creating **guilt**, or discomfort, shame, or embarrassment, from things not being what they should be. Part of persuading people often includes convincing them that there is a problem; this is focusing on the **negative**, or what is wrong. Burke argued that when we want to purge our guilt and be redeemed, we can engage in **mortification**, or blame ourselves. Or we can **scapegoat**, which is blaming someone or something else.

So, thinking about student debt again, is the situation truly dire? If so, this should create a sense of guilt. Who, then, is to blame for this situation: is it students who are not being responsible when taking out loans (mortification) or is it predatory lending or higher education institutions taking advantage of students (scapegoat)? If we look at the blogosphere, opinions abound: it is students for wasting time and money on 5- and 6-year degrees; it is higher education for increasing tuition and fees; it is the availability of loan money and predatory schools. Whom bloggers point the finger at depends on who the blogger is: we in higher education tend to point at state funding, the federal government points at wasteful spending in higher education, and students point to tuition, books, and fees. The sources we listen to can define for us whether or not there is something wrong in our social order and tell us whether we are to blame and need to change (mortification) or whether it is someone else's fault and we need to change them (scapegoating).

Ideology. Many narratives, attempts at identification, metaphors, and uses of guilt in our social and political discourse reflect ideology. **Ideology** is a key concept for both rhetorical scholars and critical researchers, because it is the idea that our common view of reality—our values, beliefs, and perceptions of how things are—is communicated through discourse. Discourse is our public communication. We have a unique sense of who we are, but we also have a collective sense of who we are as a society in terms of what is good, right, and just. We learn this, in part, through discourse (Barker, 2008). Like Burke and Fisher argued, discourse shapes our view of reality. Ideological analysis focuses our attention on the ways that communication creates and reinforces social structures through specific rhetorical choices.

At the heart of critical ideological approaches is the idea of power and **hegemony**, or one group of people influencing the ideology of other people. This important idea is borrowed from **Marxism**, which focuses on the social control that powerful people and institutions have because they reinforce social order and culture by dominating discourse (Foss, 2004). For example, our consumer culture in the United States is part of our ideology because we want the best, newest, biggest, and fastest of everything. Arguably, these values are the result of corporations, who want us to buy their products, influencing our ideology through advertisements, political messages, mass media messages, and even affecting the flow of information online.

Ideology is not just economic; it is also social. Our views of others are shaped through public discourse, including our perceptions of social classes, gender, and race. Foss (2004) pointed out that ideology is a useful lens for analyzing messages because it makes "visible the dominant ideology or ideologies…and [gives] voice to those whose interests are not represented" (p. 243). Public discourse is a combination of our political messages, news coverage, blog posts, viral memes, advertisements, and entertainment media. We frame class, gender, and race in particular ways in our public discourse, and create a common ideology that affects our perceptions of these groups.

For example, **classism**, or judging people based on social class, is evident in media depictions, viral memes, and political discussion about "welfare queens." Inherent in these messages is dislike of, and belittling, people who are poor. It reinforces the middle class as the ideal standard. Also inherent in the label "welfare queen" is **sexism**, or stereotyping of people based on gender, because the label communicates that it is manipulative *women* who are taking advantage of the system. Lastly, use of "welfare queen" also perpetuates **racism**, which includes stereotyping people based on race, as the label is disproportionately applied to people who are African American. Our views of social class such as idealizing the middle class, our perceptions of gender norms and roles, and our perceptions of other races are shaped continually through our public discourse, which critical scholars argue is controlled by a powerful few people in society. Thinking about the hegemonic power behind the label "welfare queen," who do you think is punished, and who do you think benefits from, the use of this label?

Snap logo from: http://www.fns.usda.gov/sites/default/files/SNAP_Basics_LogoGuidelines.pdf

EXAMPLE OF THEORY IN WEB 2.0

As an example of how one person's rhetoric can at once appeal to our common ideology and challenge it, take Peter Thiel's "20 Under 20" program. Thiel was a cofounder of Paypal who subsequently invested in Facebook and is now a billionaire. He holds degrees from Stanford University, and was initially a lawyer before going into tech fields. In 2012, he created a "20 Under 20 Fellowship" where he competitively selected 20 students to drop out of college and paid them $100,000 each to pursue an innovative project (CBS News, 2012). In an interview, Thiel argued that "we have a bubble in education" that was similar to the housing bubble that burst and sank the U.S. economy (para. 3). He argued that some colleges are like "subprime mortgage lenders" and that students are "conned" into going to college but end up "worse off" because of student debt (para. 5). In his argument for skipping college and going straight into the workforce, he pointed to prominent billionaires like Bill Gates from Microsoft, Mark Zuckerberg of Facebook, and the late Steve Jobs from Apple, who never finished college.

If you take a look at the interview with Thiel, you'll see many of the rhetorical tactics we've covered in this chapter at work. He uses *narrative*, in terms of his own success and the success of people who didn't finish college, as proof that entrepreneurship pays greater dividends than education. He also uses the "bubble" and "subprime mortgage" *metaphors* to demonstrate how student debt is not sustainable. He avoids *division* with his audience by playing down his own Ivy League education and argues that his education at Stanford was different and other schools would have led him astray. Though what he is advocating in the interview runs contrary to common beliefs in America about higher education being a valuable investment, he also appeals to ingrained American values by focusing on entrepreneurship and innovation as the pathways to success.

Lastly, in terms of power and *hegemony*, take a step back and ask yourself why anyone cares what Peter Thiel thinks about higher education. Why does he get interviews on *60 Minutes*? One answer is his wealth. Wealth and business success build *ethos*, particularly given America's values. So he didn't necessarily directly pay for air time, but investing $2 million in start-up funds for young entrepreneurs and being a successful billionaire allows his opinion to be heard. Thiel is part of an elite, powerful handful of people who can get interviews as a platform for telling others what we should or should not value, believe, and do. Also, in terms of gender, race, and class, what does Thiel have in common with the people he cites as evidence of his argument against higher education, such as Bill Gates, Mark Zuckerberg, and Steve Jobs? They are all wealthy men. It would be difficult to generalize their experiences to all people, particularly people living in poverty, people of other races, and women. In fact, African Americans, Latinos, and women are grossly underrepresented in STEM fields, such as technology and computer science (Landivar, 2013).

Image from http://www.census.gov/prod/2013pubs/acs-24.pdf

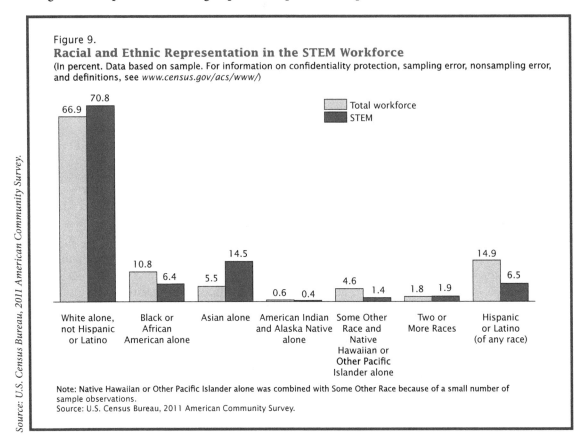

Figure 9.
Racial and Ethnic Representation in the STEM Workforce
(In percent. Data based on sample. For information on confidentiality protection, sampling error, nonsampling error, and definitions, see *www.census.gov/acs/www/*)

Note: Native Hawaiian or Other Pacific Islander alone was combined with Some Other Race because of a small number of sample observations.
Source: U.S. Census Bureau, 2011 American Community Survey.

Source: U.S. Census Bureau, 2011 American Community Survey.

 METHODS FOR APPLYING RHETORICAL THEORY

Rhetorical analysis involves choosing a method, either by choosing a lens or using open analysis; considering the context of the communication; and evaluating the choices that were made, the effects, and the effectiveness of those choices (Kuypers & King, 2009). We will look at each step in some detail.

Being a Rhetorical Critic: Question Choices and Effects. Here's a great video that discusses rhetorical analysis as considering two things when you see or hear a message: choices and effects. http://youtu.be/9sOLqAdqkV0

1. **Choosing a Method: Lenses vs. Close Analysis.** Rhetorical tactics are typically used as **lenses** through which rhetorical analysts view messages. We can choose any set of tactics we think might be at work in a message, then *look for those tactics in the verbal, visual, and production elements of the message.* The tactics we choose to look for are the lens through which we see the message. Or, as I did above with the Thiel interview, we can look closely at a message and see which rhetorical tactics are at work in a message, which is **close analysis**.

One directed method for close analysis is **dramatism** (Burke, 1945). We can explore identification, guilt, and redemption in discourse using Burke's **pentad**, which is also called dramatism. The pentad looks at five elements in discourse: The act, scene, agent, agency, and purpose. The **act** includes the events that are described, which occur within a **scene** that includes the circumstances. The people that are described are the **agents**, who have **agency**, which are the things that they do and say, and **purpose**, or motivations that led to behave the way they did. Looking at how the communicator describes these things gives us insight into their worldview, and also insight into how people's views of reality may be affected by rhetorical choices.

Consider Mark Cuban's explanation of the student debt situation: http://www.inc.com/mark-cuban/video-student-loans-bubble.html. He explained that the federal government kept giving low interest loans to a lot of people during the Great Recession, and a lot of colleges and universities raised tuition because of the amount of money available, and students took out a lot of loans. In this example, we have *agents* (the government, universities, and students) who have *agency* (to give money, to spend money, and to borrow money, respectively), and distinct *purposes* (to fund students, to make money, and to get an education). This *act* of ballooning student debt is occurring in a larger economic *scene* (a down economy with high un- and underemployment). This explanation of the student debt crisis creates *guilt*, because something is wrong; it uses *division* to make the interests of the government, universities, and students seem at odds; and universities are the *scapegoats*. The persuasive tactics of identification and guilt are revealed by applying the Pentad to the explanation. When we look closely at the division, guilt, and scapegoating, it is clear who is to blame. Now, think for a minute about *who else* could be to blame. What does applying the pentad tell us about Mark Cuban's view of reality given his description of the agents, their agency, and purpose?

Mark Cuban

2. **Context.** The process of rhetorical analysis, whether it is systematic and objectively guided by a lens or more critical in its approach, begins with an analysis of context. The context is the communication situation: the social and historical context, audience, and the genre of the message. The social and historical context helps us interpret the choices that were made in terms of the symbols used, because we know from semiotics that signs and symbols evolve. Signs and symbols also have different meanings for different people, so we consider who the intended audience for the message was so that we can better critique the effectiveness of symbol choices.

   Genre is the category, or type, of communication it is: persuasive, informative, and celebratory speeches, for example. Aristotle introduced genres for public speeches, including **deliberative** rhetoric that argues over what we should or should not do, **judicial** rhetoric about past events to establish blame, and **epideictic** rhetoric where we focus on celebration or values. There are now established genres for speeches, commercials, television, and movies. The genre of the message affects the rhetorical choices of the communicator, which is why it is such an important part of the context.

Insight into Innovation Activity: Go through your Facebook news feed. What genres emerge in the posts you see there? How are the genres different and similar? How does the genre affect people's rhetorical choices?

3. **Analysis and Evaluation.** The final step in rhetorical analysis is analyzing the communication using the lens and chosen method, and evaluating the effects and effectiveness of the message. Here is where our understanding of communicators' motives, the context, and the social implications of rhetorical choices all come together. As we analyze the message and discover or confirm the rhetorical tactics that were used, we consider whether these tactics were effective or ineffective given the audience, social context, and genre: Were proofs used effectively? Did narratives hold up under scrutiny? Did the communicator use guilt, blame, and redemption effectively? We also consider the view of reality—the ideology—created and reinforced in the communication choices. Was there evidence of classicism, sexism, or racism in the message? What values does the message teach?

Insight into Innovation Activity: Choose one rhetorical tactic, and look for evidence of that tactic in Barack Obama's responses to Reddit users' questions: http://www.reddit.com/comments/z1c9z. What rhetorical tactics did Obama use? Were the tactics effective given the situation, genre, and audience? Why or why not?

APPLIED RESEARCH

Given the diversity of tactics that rhetorical scholars have identified, only a few of which we cover in this chapter, it is not surprising that rhetorical theory can be used to inform our understanding of rhetorical choices and effects in new media. Two fruitful areas of research borne out of rhetorical theory that apply very clearly to our Web 2.0 lives are electronic eloquence and image repair.

ELECTRONIC ELOQUENCE

We see many of these rhetorical tactics at work in our mediated communication. Even as we all have the ability to disseminate our messages to a mass audience via Facebook, Twitter, YouTube, and blogs, these mediated messages all make use of rhetorical tactics such as narrative and identification. **Electronic eloquence** focuses on the interpersonal, informal nature of mediated rhetoric in the electronic age (Jamieson, 1988). Electronic eloquence involves *personifying* issues and ideas, *self-disclosing* to build intimacy, having an informal *conversational style*, *distilling* our ideas and arguments down into sound bites, and *dramatizing* our posts with attention-getting visual images and videos. Electronic eloquence explains how the rhetorical tactics we use via new media to influence are somewhat different - they're more visual, shorter, more interpersonal - but at the same time they are consistent with building identification, using narrative elements to frame people and issues, and using ethos, pathos, and logos in snippets.

Consider, for example, popular memes posted online. Memes use GIFs or images of people, settings, cartoons, or other graphics with some sort of textual element that is supposed to be inspirational, informational, or funny. Inherent in many of these memes are social messages or political opinions, but they are delivered using electronic eloquence. They are eloquent because they make use of dramatizing images, distill an argument down to less than a sentence, and make use of conversational style including sentence fragments and informal language. In other words, memes can appeal to logos, elicit pathos, imply a narrative or metaphor that frames a person or issue, or promote consubstantiation or division. Though memes are often funny, they can also be misleading and inaccurate, and can distract people from real problems, issues, and causes (Choney, 2012). Memes are visual and distilled arguments, thus they may lack coherence, fidelity, or sound evidence.

In terms of practical applications, electronic eloquence challenges us as communicators to consider both the verbal and the visual elements of our Web 2.0 messages. To effectively use Web 2.0 technology, we need to understand graphic art and how to visually represent ourselves and our ideas (Cyphert, 2007) as well as how to distill our messages to fit the character limits of social media and attention spans of online natives. It also challenges us as consumers of Web 2.0 content to consider the viral messages we see, such as memes, to consider how the limitations of electronic eloquence affect the accuracy and usefulness of the content we see.

ONLINE IMAGE REPAIR

Insight into Innovation Example: Dr. Benoit. You can watch Dr. Benoit discuss image repair theory here: http://youtu.be/7GaZAe_3L9Q

Benoit (1995) identified **image repair strategies** that companies and people use when faced with a public crisis: **denial** of the allegation or of accountability, **evasion** of responsibility by blaming the situation, **reducing offensiveness** by making the offense seem less terrible, **corrective action** by explaining how the situation will be fixed, and **mortification** by accepting responsibility. Public crises are instances when celebrities, politicians, or organizations are caught doing something unethical, socially unacceptable, or illegal. These strategies for image repair in the face of a crisis go back to Burke's concepts of guilt and redemption, as those caught in a public scandal can use mortification or denial through scapegoating. Those affected by the crisis may also use identification to reduce offensiveness (e.g., "we've all made mistakes" and "nobody's perfect") and narratives to evade responsibility, reduce offensiveness, and explain corrective actions. And, if we think about it, what these image repair strategies really get at is rebuilding ethos to restore the public's liking and trust.

Via social media, there are many opportunities for celebrities, politicians, and organizations to go directly to their supporters and repair their images when they face a crisis. BP used social media extensively during the crisis in the Gulf of Mexico when one of their rigs spewed oil into the ocean (Muralidharan, Dillistone, & Shin, 2011). Celebrities, like Jon and Kate Gossling, from the now canceled *Jon & Kate Plus Eight* reality show, also used Twitter throughout their very public separation and divorce, and their use of image repair strategies led to Kate being successful at making herself a "victim" in the situation while Jon looked irresponsible and foolish (Moody, 2011).

On the flip side of that, social media is increasingly becoming a source of crises for public figures and companies. People can post videos, images, and reviews on social media and blogs, and these can go viral before the affected company or person even knows there's a problem (Pang, Hassan, & Chong, 2014). There have been numerous instances of bloggers taking major corporations to task for issues such as selling inappropriate or offensive clothing to young girls, customer service disasters, cases of discrimination, and mistreatment of employees. Once these go viral via social media, the mainstream media picks up on the issue and the accused have to engage in image repair.

For example, one angry blogger went after Target for sexualizing young girls by selling shorts with as little as a 1" inseam, forcing Target to apologize and take corrective action by reviewing their clothing line for girls (Fashingbauer Cooper, 2014). Politicians' and celebrities' sexual texts and IMs, gaffes, and inappropriate comments have been posted online, requiring them to engage in image repair with varying degrees of success. For example, Congressman Anthony Weiner's sexting scandals were revealed via social media, and it eventually ended his political career when he repeated the behavior after assuring the public and his wife that he had stopped sexting with other women. Similarly, Mitt Romney's comment to supporters that 47 percent of Americans saw themselves as "victims" who were "entitled" and "paid no income tax" were similarly damaging to his political career when a video of those comments was posted online. Romney tried to minimize the damage by saying that it was an off-the-cuff remark that wasn't well stated (Shear & Barbaro, 2012), but arguably the damage was done. Similarly, celebrities' bad and odd behaviors have been caught on audio or video and gone viral, such as actor Alec Baldwin's angry voicemail left for his daughter in which he insulted her and her mother. In all, social media can be both the cause of, and the channel used to correct, public image crises.

CONCLUSION

Given its flexibility and long history in communication, rhetoric has a lot to offer students and scholars as we grapple with questions about effective communication choices and influencing people online. Rhetoric also has the potential to inform us about strategies and methods for critical thinking as we navigate our information and image-saturated world by asking us to consider the types and merits of the proofs we see, the context, and the limitations of the worldview of message creators. In other words, rhetoric challenges us to think about messages as a series of choices and to consider the effects of those choices, particularly in terms of ideology.

That being said, rhetorical theory has a tradition of being grounded in analysis of historical arti-facts, which has made it slow to address and apply to changes in communication technologies (Lunceford, 2011). Part of this slow application of rhetorical theory to new communication tech-nologies is the outcome of the research and publication process itself, but some of it is also due to the long history of rhetoric as a method for looking back and explaining what happened. As we know from our review of the World Wide Web's history at the beginning of this book, web tech-nology changes quickly and in ways we don't always anticipate, so researchers, including rhetori-cal theorists, must rethink their research paradigms and adjust to the new and diverse ways that people communicate.

ACTIVITIES AND ASSIGNMENTS

1. **Learn the history of the "Welfare Queen."** Read the *Slate* article by Josh Levin about the use of the label "welfare queen": http://www.slate.com/articles/news_and_politics/his-tory/2013/12/linda_taylor_welfare_queen_ronald_reagan_made_her_a_notorious_ameri-can_villain.html. After reading the article about the history of the label, apply narrative coherence and fidelity to critique Levin's narrative about Linda Taylor. How does the use of "welfare queen" in our political and social discourse elicit pathos, identification, and divi-sion; guilt and scapegoating; and reinforce the dominant ideology in America?

2. **Create an Internet meme.** Create a meme to teach one of the rhetorical tactics covered in this chapter.

   - It should include an image or GIF and text that uses humor to demonstrate the concept.

   - You can use a website to create your meme, such as http://memegenerator.net/

   - Share your meme on the *Insight into Innovation* Facebook page: https://www.facebook.com/CommTheoryForSocialMedia.

REFERENCES

Seminal Texts:

Burke, K. (1945). *A grammar of motives.* Berkley, CA: University of California Press.

Burke, K. (1969). *A rhetoric of motives.* Berkley, CA: University of California Press.

Cyphert, D. (2007). Presentation technology in the age of electronic eloquence: From visual aid to visual rhetoric. *Communication Education, 56,* 168–192.

Fisher, W. (1987). *Human communication as narration: Toward a philosophy of reason, value, and action.* Columbia: University of South Carolina Press.

Lakoff, G., & Johnson, M. (1980). *Metaphors we live by.* Chicago: University of Chicago Press.

Academic Publications:

Barker, C. (2008). *Cultural studies* (3rd ed.). Thousand Oaks, CA: Sage.

Benoit, W. (1995). *Accounts, excuses, and apologies: A theory of image restoration strategies.* Albany: State University of New York Press.

Jamieson, K. H. (1988). *Eloquence in an Electronic Age.* New York: Oxfprd University Press.

Kuypers, J. A., & King, A. (2009). What is rhetoric? In J. A. Kuypers (Ed.), *Rhetorical criticism: Perspectives in action* (pp. 1–12). New York: Lexington.

Lunceford, B. (2011). Must we all be rhetorical historians? On relevance and timeliness in rhetorical scholarship. *Journal of Contemporary Rhetoric, 1,* 1–9.

Moody, M. (2011). Jon and Kate Plus 8: A case study of social media and image repair tactics. *Public Relations Review, 37*(4), 405–413.

Muralidharan, S., Dillistone, K., & Shin, J.-H. (2011). The Gulf coast oil spill: Extending the theory of image restoration discourse to the realm of social media and beyond petroleum. *Public Relations Review, 37,* 226–232.

Pang, A., Hassan, N. B. B. A., & Chong, A. C. Y. (2014). Negotiating crisis in the social media environment: Evaluation of crises online, gaining credibility offline. *Corporate Communications: An International Journal, 19,* 96–118.

Examples:

CBS News. (2012, May 21). Dropping out: Is college worth the cost? *60 Minutes.* Retrieved online from http://www.cbsnews.com/news/dropping-out-is-college-worth-the-cost/

Choney, S. (2012, April 21). The ugly dark side of Facebook memes. *Today: Money.* Retrieved from http://www.today.com/money/ugly-dark-side-facebook-memes-727490

Fashingbauer Cooper, G. (2014, October 7). Target responds to mom's complaints about girls' clothing sizing. *Today: Parenting.* Retrieved from http://www.today.com/parents/target-adjust-girls-clothing-sizing-thanks-moms-blog-post-2D80198052

Landivar, C. L. (2013). *Disparities in STEM employment by sex, race, and Hispanic origin.* U. S. Census Bureau. Retrieved from http://www.census.gov/prod/2013pubs/acs-24.pdf

Shear, D. M., and Barbaro, M. (2012, September 17). In video clip, Romney calls 47% " dependent" and feeling entitled. *The Caucus.* Retrieved from http://thecaucus.blogs.nytimes.com/2012/09/17/romney-faults-those-dependent-on-government/?_r=1.

Weigel, D. (2013, December 3). If you want reporters to check stories before they publish, you're a hater. *Slate.* Retrieved from http://www.slate.com/blogs/weigel/2013/12/03/buzzfeed_and_elan_gale_s_internet_hoax_too_good_to_check.html

Further Reading Online:

The Journal of Contemporary Rhetoric is an open, online journal that publishes rhetorical scholarship. You can read their articles here: http://contemporaryrhetoric.com/archive.html

MASS MEDIA

In Unit 6, we will discuss three perspectives on theory and research in mass media: the media environment, media audience, and media effects perspectives. This marks a move away from theories of persuasion, which focus on explaining the tactics used to persuade and people's cognitive, emotional, and behavioral responses. Persuasive messages are formulated with the specific intent to persuade. Mass media messages—such as TV shows, movies, and news—are not always overtly persuading us, though the messages we receive via mass media can affect our perceptions of ourselves, others, society, and politics.

The first view, media ecology, is that media is an environment, new media technologies affect power structures and human relationships, and these changes are not always for the better. Therefore, *media ecology focuses on media channels*. The second view we will discuss, ***uses and gratifications***, *focuses on audiences*. Uses and gratifications research looks at the reasons people choose media, and views audiences as active, selective, and participatory. The third and final view we will discuss is the ***media effects perspective***, *which includes theories about how media messages affect people's thoughts, opinions, feelings, and behaviors*.

In terms of media effects, we will cover theories focused on the cognitive effects of media, such as agenda setting, framing, and priming. These theories teach us that the media can affect how we think about issues and, therefore, influence our political attitudes and behaviors. The media also tells us what is socially acceptable and unacceptable, and the spiral of silence theory and social learning theory explain that the media is a source of information and behavioral lessons that can affect what we do. Lastly, cultivation theory explains that media depictions of other people, regions, races, and social classes can skew our perceptions of reality.

These three perspectives, and the theories and concepts associated with each perspective, help us more fully understand implications, uses, and effects of new media technologies. From the media ecology perspective, we are challenged to consider how media shape our social structure and to question the value and usefulness of advances in technology. Rather than blindly embracing new technology, we should consider the implications of advancements on individuals' power, social capital, and participation in our society. Interestingly, each advancement may actually increase disparities between the wealthy and upwardly mobile and the working classes.

Uses and gratifications challenges us to consider why and how people use technology. Individual differences in situational and personal motivations shape whether and how we use technology, which has implications both for the societal-level implications of new technology and the effects of technology on individuals. Further, understanding media audiences, particularly how and why they use technology, should help us develop mediated messages that meet people's needs and expectations.

Lastly, the media effects perspective challenges us to consider individual-level effects of mediated messages in terms of people's thoughts, attitudes, beliefs, emotions, and behaviors. Media messages, particularly messages that are repeated online, can shape our worldview, our view of ourselves and others, and therefore how we act. Particularly as media becomes more interactive, this has serious implications given the violent, sexual, and stereotyping content we are exposed to via media.

Taken together, these three perspectives should inform our use of media for personal entertainment, how we select media channels and create media messages, and how we interpret the media messages we receive. These perspectives should improve **media literacy**, or our ability to understand and use media technology.

MEDIA ECOLOGY

Media ecology is the study of media as an "environment" (Strate, 2006) and it is often referred to as **medium theory** because it focuses on how changes in the mediums available to us change who we are and our society (e.g., Ellis, 2009). It is sometimes described as a **deterministic** view of technology because it asserts that changes in mediums from oral, to print, to electronic, to mobile media, *determine* how we feel, think, and behave. In this chapter, we will review some of the positives and some of the negatives of Web 2.0 technology, including empowering some people and disadvantaging some people.

Media ecology challenges us to be critical, even skeptical, of the implications of each new technology:

- *Consider the implications of new mediums* rather than just media content. Mediums determine the production features available for creating messages and affect how we experience messages, hence Marshall McLuhan's (1965) infamous phrase "the medium is the message." They also limit access to certain people while increasing access and opportunity for other people.

- *Think of the media as an environment that changes.* Each new technology changes our personal and social environment, and this is not always for the better. Postman (1993) wrote, "new technology does not add or subtract something. It changes everything" (p. 18). Therefore, he argued, it is an "ecological" change when a new technology is introduced. Each change in the environment also means that we, as people existing in that environment, must change as well by learning new skills.

- *Changes in the media environment lead to changes in people's behavior and social structure.* Some people benefit from advances in technology and some people are disadvantaged. McLuhan also argued that media shapes human history and that the advances in media technology lead to shifts in society. Postman (1993) argued that there are clear winners and disadvantaged losers when new technologies are introduced. Indeed, research on who uses Web 2.0 technology and how they use it suggests that even our Web 2.0 society is divided into "haves" and "have nots."

There is evidence that advances in new media technologies do disadvantage some people who may not have access to those technologies, thereby creating a **digital divide**. This divide in access leads to **knowledge gaps**, where some members of society have access to a lot of information and resources and other members of society do not have access. But it isn't all doom and gloom either, as social media advances have aided important social movements.

OVERVIEW OF MEDIA ECOLOGY

MAIN IDEA

Media ecology is as much a **paradigm**, or way of thinking about and theorizing about media, as it is a theory. It challenges us to shift our thinking away from studying genres, specific types of media, and isolated media effects to thinking about the broad implications of mediums themselves: mediums affect who can communicate and how mediated messages are formulated, sent, and received. Therefore, new mediums influence human behavior, social order, power, and public discourse. In the new media environment, older, impoverished, and rural populations may be disadvantaged by the proliferation of new media.

Insight into Innovation Activity: Read more about two of the founders of media ecology: Marshall McLuhan and Neil Postman. Both of them passed away before the proliferation of Web 2.0 technology, and yet some of their ideas are just now being more fully realized:

- Read more about Neil Postman here: http://neilpostman.org

- Read more about Marshall McLuhan here: http://www.marshallmcluhan.com

MCLUHAN'S (1964) KEY CONCEPTS

McLuhan's concepts get at the changes that occur as a result of technological advancements, from the development of language, to print, and then electronically mediated communication. His concepts are ways of thinking about each technological advancement: how it shapes messages, changes us as people, changes our social order, affects how we experience messages, and even reshapes our relationships with one another.

1. *The medium is the message.* That is to say, the introduction of new mediums have more impact on people and society than the mere messages they are used to transmit. So, for example, smartphones themselves have had an impact on each and every one of us who uses them. The effect isn't from any one message that we receive through our smartphones; the effect is from the presence of the smartphone itself.

2. *Media are extensions of people.* McLuhan describes technology as an "extension" of people, like one of our senses. Here, too, the example of smartphones is on point. Our smartphones tend to be with us all the time and everywhere—next to our beds at night, on the

table or desk in front of us, in our pockets, or in our hands. Much like sight, sound, and smell, smartphones are becoming part of how we experience the world. They are extensions of our physical selves.

Copyright © Leremy/Shutterstock.com

3. *Media is an environment that changes: From tribal, to oral, print, and now electronic.* Innis (1951) and McLuhan (1964) contended that there are four **media epochs**, each with its own literacy, social organization, and culture. The tribal era relied on the spoken word; the literate era introduced writing; the print era introduced mass dissemination of printed content; and the electronic era allowed for dissemination of spoken and written words and video. Each of these changes in the media available to people changed how they interacted, who their messages reached, and how people responded. Now, with social media and smartphones, we interact differently, by being able to disseminate our thoughts, feelings, and experiences in the moment with countless people.

4. *There are "hot" and "cool" mediums.* **Hot mediums** extend one human sense in "high definition," and require little participation from the receiver (p. 36). **Cool mediums**, on the other hand, require a lot of participation from users, and receivers have to fill in a lot of information. McLuhan contended that TV was a cool medium compared to movies, for example, because TV required more activity and had less intense sensory information than a movie. So our smartphones may be more cool than our computers. Though they have similar functions, the more stripped-down mobile versions of websites and apps require us to fill in more information compared to the full websites and apps on our computers.

5. *New mediums increase fragmentation.* Mediums eliminate constraints of time and space. Society becomes increasingly decentralized as new mediums are introduced, no longer requiring us to physically be together to accomplish tasks. We are, therefore, more fragmented with the introduction of new technologies.

6. *We are creating a global village.* In keeping with fragmentation, we are no longer part of one physical, geographically situated community; rather, we are part of a global community. The people who follow our Tweets, who are our Facebook friends, and who write the blogs that we follow are our "neighbors" in the global village. So now, we are all linked together as part of a single online community, and we affect and are affected by those links.

Insight into Innovation Activity: McLuhan's Interview on The Today Show (1976). Watch McLuhan's interview with Tom Brokaw where they discuss TV debates: https://www.youtube.com/watch?v=ZF8jej3j5vA. McLuhan doesn't think the format of political debates are suited for the TV medium and that the medium overtook the message. Do you agree? Are political debates not suited to TV? What modern format may be better for debates: Twitter? YouTube? Some other social media?

POSTMAN'S (1993) KEY CONCEPTS FROM TECHNOPOLY

Postman is more openly critical of technological advances than McLuhan, and challenges us to think about the good and the bad that comes with each advancement. His work focuses on values—our cultural values as they are affected by and reflected in each technological advancement. In many ways, the issues that Postman raise are ethical, such as considering whether technology is now more important to us than people. Postman asks us to stop and consider who each advancement helps and who each advancement hurts.

1. *Technocracy.* In the United States, we focus on progress, see technology as a way to achieve freedom, and use technology to do things faster. We are "driven by an impulse to invent" (p. 41), and so we focus on "how to invent things" but not "why we invent things" (p. 42).

2. *Technopoly.* Postman defined technopoly as "the submission of all forms of cultural life to the sovereignty of technique and technology" (p. 52). Put another way, technological advancement is more important than people and has replaced culture.

3. *Knowledge monopoly.* New technologies shift power from one group to another group. Therefore, when a new technology is adopted, there are "winners and losers" (p. 9). Postman uses the example of computers, arguing that people are being tracked and controlled, and that the only people benefiting from their use are large organizations and researchers. Technology also allows for increased information control. Postman argued that computers "have solved very little of importance to most people and have created at least as many problems for them as they may have solved" (p. 161).

 Insight into Innovation Activity: Watch Neil Postman's explanation of *Technopoly*: https://www.youtube.com/watch?v=KbAPtGYiRvg. He discusses how merging the telephone, TV, and computer will enable us to shop, vote, and interact from home so we have technologies that "keep us private." Do you agree that each of these advances is "taking away something"? Are we wrong in our optimism about technology? Why or why not?

🗪RESEARCH METHODS IN MEDIA ECOLOGY

Media ecology is credited with the rise of media criticism as a method of inquiry. **Media criticism** is the careful critique of media. Postman (1986, 1993) and Innis (1951) use historical anecdotes as evidence for their claims about how technological advances affect society. In fact, Postman (1993) was cynical about scientific approaches to understanding human behavior, citing their "common sense" findings, reliance on artificial experimental conditions, and use of arbitrary counting to *appear to be* more like science. He argued that moral evaluations are diminished by **scientism**. Scientism is the faith our society has in statistics and scientific evidence. He contended that there was no way to predict how a new technology would affect society, but we should be *critical* of the personal and social repercussions of new technologies as they are introduced.

McLuhan, on the other hand, seemed to believe that we could critique and anticipate cultural changes resulting from new technologies as they were occurring by applying the **tetrad**. The tetrad is a lens through which we can view a new technology. The tetrad directs us to critically consider how technology *enhances* existing technology; *obsoletes*, or makes earlier technology outdated; *retrieves*, or brings back to life old technologies; and *reverses*, or eventually evolves into something new (McLuhan & Powers, 1992). It challenges us to think about both the good and the bad when considering a new technology (Hanke, 2003).

Insight into Innovation Activity: Applying the Tetrad to Tablets. Take, for example, tablet computers such as the iPad.

Timeline of Tablet Technology (Bort, 2013)

http://www.businessinsider.com/history-of-the-tablet-2013-5#

- 1987: Linus Write-Top tablet that recognized handwriting and included a stylus

- 1989: Gridpad ran MS DOS, and also used a stylus

- 1993: Apple MessagePad still used a stylus, but included some apps

- 1997: PalmPilot was an affordable, touchscreen personal digital assistant (PDA)

- 2000: Microsoft demonstrates a tablet PC prototype

- 2010: iPad introduced by Apple

  - Android tablets introduced

  - Kindle Fire was rolled out for $199, forcing down tablet prices

- 2012: Microsoft Surface Tablet released

When the iPad was introduced in 2010, we already had desktops, smartphones, netbooks, PDAs, tablets, and laptops. What was *enhanced* by the introduction of the iPad? What was made *obsolete*? Are there iPad features that *retrieve* features of "old" technology? What is this likely to *reverse*, or turn into? Use the timeline of tablet technology to consider where the tablet came from and where it may go next. Overall, do you think tablets are good or bad for people and society?

Though the tetrad is a clearly outlined method for critiquing technological advances, we do not see much research generated that applies this method explicitly. That being said, looking to other areas of study, such as research on adoption rates, usage statistics, and other social and societal trends, we see evidence of many of Postman's predictions about technology in society and the concerns that both McLuhan and Postman raised about the effects of technology on our social structure.

💬 SOCIETAL IMPLICATIONS OF NEW TECHNOLOGY: DIVIDES AND GAPS

As with most debates, there is some evidence to support the idea that technological advances are good for society by empowering people. For example, young activists using Twitter are credited with the Arab Spring. Young people in the midst of the movement used social media due to their fear of authority and skepticism of traditional media (Sayed, 2011). So social media platforms can empower people to overcome tremendous political oppression. In Europe and the United States, young people's use of social media for political engagement encourages involvement in politics as well (Holt, Shehata, Strömbäck, & Ljungberg, 2013; Xenos, Vromen, & Loader, 2014). This is particularly valuable because American youth tend to be disengaged when it comes to politics, so using social media may be a way to inform and motivate young voters. Participation in online social and political debates is affected by whether young people feel that they have the background knowledge and social media skills to participate (Warner, McGowen, & Hawthorne, 2012). So, though there is significant promise that social media can get people involved and empower people, not all people are equally empowered.

There are also repercussions of the mass adoption of new technologies that disadvantage and disempower people due in part to the persistent digital divide in America. After the groundbreaking report, "Falling through the net," was released in 1998 outlining the divides in access to technology between the haves and the have nots, communication researchers in the early 2000s began to grapple with digital divides: what they are, how they happen, and the individual and social implications of these divides (Norris, 2001). The primary concern is that divides in access and use lead to gaps in knowledge which have social, professional, and political consequences. There is a clear division between the "haves" and "have nots" that is accentuated and perpetuated by unequal access to and use of digital technologies.

The (many) digital divides in America. **The digital divide** in general refers to the differences in access to new technology among sociodemographic groups. People who are economically disadvantaged, older, handicapped, less educated, and racial minorities tend to have less access to new technology. For example, only 42 percent of people who make $10,000 or less have access to broadband Internet at home, but 90 percent of people making $100,000 or more have access to broadband (Raine, 2013).

Some may point to the rise of mobile technology, such as smartphones, as a way to break down the digital divide and increase access to the Internet among our most economically disadvantaged citizens. There are several issues with this technology as a person's sole access to the Internet (Strover, 2014). The functions we can access and use on our phones are still limited compared to having access to broadband Internet and a PC. Also, data plans are expensive, and often have data caps, that limit the number and types of functions people can use mobile devices to complete. Imagine, for example, trying to fill out a long, online job application or trying to take an online class using only a smartphone.

There are clearly still access divides, but the digital divide is much more nuanced and complicated than early definitions suggested. As mentioned in our discussion of diffusion theory, people who are economically well-off tend to be early adopters of new technology and they are also the opinion leaders that influence other people's adoption. In terms of using new technologies to create Web 2.0 content, research suggests that people lower in socioeconomic status tend to create less content, even when they have access to the needed tools. Thus, the primary divide is a **usage divide**, or a fundamental difference in how people from different socioeconomic backgrounds use Internet technologies. Consider, for example, what a person needs to know to effectively use the internet and how this might affect the usability of the internet, even when people have access:

Medium-related internet skills	
Operational internet skills	*Operating an internet browser:* Opening websites by entering the URL in the browser's location bar; Navigating forward and backward between pages using the browser buttons; Saving files on the hard disk; Opening various common file formats (e.g., PDFs); Bookmarking websites.
	Operating internet-based search engines: Entering keywords in the proper field; Executing the search operation; Opening search results in the search results lists.
	Operating internet-based forms: Using the different types of fields and buttons; Submitting a form.
Formal internet skills	*Navigating on the internet, by:* Using hyperlinks embedded in different formats such as texts, images, or menus.
	Maintaining a sense of location while navigating on the internet, meaning: Not becoming disoriented when navigating within a website; Not becoming disoriented when navigating between websites; Not becoming disoriented when opening and browsing through search results.
Content-related internet skills	
Informational internet skills	*Locating required information by:* Choosing a website or search system to seek information; Defining search options or queries; Selecting information (on websites or in search results); Evaluating information sources.
Strategic internet skills	*Taking advantage of the internet by* Developing an orientation toward a particular goal; Taking the right action to reach this goal; Making the right decision to reach this goal: Gaining the benefits resulting from this goal.

From Van Deursen and Van Dijk (2010) page 896. © Sage

There are numerous divides in our society between socioeconomic groups (Brake, 2014):

- **Motivation divides** are differences in *wanting* to use Web 2.0 technologies, seeing their usefulness and their benefits.
- **Material divides** are differences in *access* to the technologies needed to create Web 2.0 content.
- **Skills divides** include differences in the ability to *perform* activities online, find and interpret *information* online, and make *strategic* decisions about what to create and how to share content online.
- **Usage divides** are differences in how much people use technology and the different ways they use technology.

These divides begin at a young age, as families' socioeconomic situations affect kids' access to technology while they are growing up. One study of elementary schools in Ohio also pointed out that the economic situation of the school districts in the state determined the technological resources teachers had and the use of computers in their classrooms (Wood & Howley, 2012). Divides in childrens' homes and schools may disadvantage people throughout their lives, contributing to an ongoing cycle of poverty. In adulthood, both access and usage divides create issues with social inclusion, social position, citizenship and participation in American politics, and even employability (Tsatsou, 2011).

The persistent knowledge gap. As early as the 1970s, scholars recognized that each new media advancement had the potential to increase, rather than decrease, differences in access to information and knowledge (Tichenor, Donohue, & Olien, 1970). This unequal access to and use of technology serves to widen the **knowledge gap**, which is the difference between being information "rich" and information "poor."

Even in our information-rich society, people do not always use the tools available to them to get useful information. In our chapter on uses and gratifications, we look at differences in how people use media: whether a person's technology use is active versus passive and informational versus entertaining. These differences in use lead to differences in knowledge. Socioeconomic variables like education predict how people use the Internet and, as a result, how much they know (Wei & Hindman, 2011). In areas that have higher entertainment orientations, such as the United States, the content that people seek out online tends to be entertainment focused rather than informational (Segev & Ahituv, 2010). So, though people have access to unimaginable amounts of information and resources to build knowledge, that is not necessarily how they are using these online tools.

Insight into Innovation Example: Income Inequality. The digital divide and resulting knowledge gap are important for many reasons. Consider, for example, the evidence about the personal, social, and political effects of income inequality in the United States. **Income inequality** is the difference between people's earnings. Differences in income impact long-term wealth. At the end of 2014, the median wealth of upper income families was 7 times more than wealth in middle-income families and 70 times more than wealth in low-income families. This inequality in income and wealth may be related to the changes in our media environment and the subsequent knowledge gap. How, for example, would you look for a job if you needed to find one? Chances are, you would go online and search through monster.com, careers.com, or indeed.com. If you wanted to start a business or sell goods that you produced, how would you sell them? Chances are, you would sell items online and promote your business through social media and websites. But for the economically disadvantaged, creating, uploading, and disseminating documents, images, and videos may be difficult or even impossible. Thus, the wealthy have access to resources to build more wealth, while the poorest among us are excluded from those opportunities. This is an issue of access, usage, and skill.

Copyright © Apoint/Shutterstock.com

DIGITAL LITERACY IN MODERN AMERICA

Back in the 1980s, in an interview on PBS, Postman argued that the rise of electronic media was leading to the death of reading and literacy and McLuhan made similar claims in some of his interviews. Both the new digital divides and the persistent knowledge gap in our society support their critique: there is a genuine lack of digital literacy that is holding people back. The National Communication Association Statement on the Digital Divide makes it clear that the divide is less about access to technology and more about use of technology. Put another way, we can have access to the riches of the Internet, but we still may not use it productively. And this division in technology use is an underlying factor in the continuing digital divides and knowledge gap in our society.

To make productive use of the Internet and Web 2.0 technologies, we must have access to technology *and* be literate new media users. **Digital literacy** is the ability to use technology to *find* content, *evaluate* content, *participate* in interactions online, and *create* mediated messages (Sora, 2012). Thus, there are two separate skill sets we need to foster to build equality in our society: **Internet skills** for finding and evaluating information and reducing the knowledge gap; **Web 2.0 skills** to help people participate in online dialogue and create messages to reduce social and political exclusion.

Education is an important determinant of how people use the Internet and, as a result, their knowledge (Wei & Hindman, 2011). Even in countries where there have been clear, government-funded initiatives to improve access to the Internet, people still do not always adopt it and use it well, thus limiting the government's ability to address the usage divide and knowledge gap (Brandtweiner, Donat, & Kerschbaum, 2010). This is because sociodemographic variables, such as education, affect people's attitudes about using technology, which may explain why use is different (Graham, 2009). Education is also related to people's ability to use technology to retrieve needed information (Van Deursen & Van Dijk, 2011). Think of it this way, lacking digital literacy and then trying to use the Internet is like standing in the middle of the world's most robust library and not knowing how to find, let alone open and read, a book.

Internet skills. To make use of information resources online, Van Deursen and Van Dijk (2010) provide a review of skills we can observe in ourselves and others. They argue that there are necessary operational skills and formal skills people need to have in order to use the Internet for informational purposes. **Operational** Internet skills include being able to use an Internet browser to search for needed information. **Formal** Internet skills include navigating the Internet by being able to read websites, follow hyperlinks, and navigate search result lists.

But, just because a person can search the Internet doesn't mean that they will learn more and close the knowledge gap. Literacy also includes higher order critical thinking skills: **informational skills**, such as being able to sift through and evaluate information found online, and **strategic skills**, such as setting and achieving goals when seeking information. The cognitive skills help people avoid being duped by things such as satirical posts, inaccurate memes, or clearly biased content posted by someone with a political or social agenda.

Web 2.0 skills. Beyond being able to access content, Web 2.0 demands that we also be able to create content so that we can participate in online interaction. Using multimodal technologies (e.g., multiple online modes such as video, images, and text) has a snowball effect: The more types of online activity we engage in, the more we try out new things, and the more we continue to add to our repertoire (Wei, 2012). The ability to *create* user generated content—post videos to YouTube, share images via Instagram, create and share blog posts, post thoughts and opinions to Facebook or Yik Yak, and so on—is essential to reducing the social and political divisions between the haves and the have nots (Sora, 2012).

That being said, just being able to create Web 2.0 content is still not enough to be fully digitally literate. Many people know how to use their devices to, for example, take a picture or record a video. On the other hand, they may not have the analytical skills to consider the "social impact, cyber etiquette and ethics" of sharing content (Sora, 2012, p. 5).

Insight into Innovation Activity: Internet and Web 2.0 Skills Self-Check. Put a check mark next to each Web. 2.0 skill you possess (adapted from Lee, Park, & Hwang, 2015). Calculate your skill score: Give yourself 1 point for each checked item. Sum your score for the instrumental, creative, and networking skill sets. Divide the number of points you have for each skill set by the total number of points possible in that set. What do your percentage scores tell you about your Web 2.0 skills? Where are your strengths and weaknesses? How might the weaknesses you see hold you back socially and professionally?

Instrumental skills:

I can

_____ identify text, video, and image files.

_____ upload files online.

_____ store and share content I found online.

_____ store and share MP3s.

_____ change the options on my Internet browser.

_____ find the information I need online.

Instrumental Skill Score: _____ / 6 = _____ percent

Creative skills:

I can

_____ use editing software.

_____ express myself via user-generated content.

_____ make video/audio clips of people from the media.

_____ remix online video and audio content.

_____ use image editing software.

_____ use digital recorders and/or cameras.

_____ use pictures and video clips to express myself.

Creative Skill Score: _____ / 7 = _____ percent

Networking skills:

I can

_____ leave comments on news articles online.

_____ leave comments on bulletin boards online.

_____ share links via social networks.

_____ share videos and photos via social networks.

_____ create and manage blogs.

_____ search through Wikipedia.

_____ contribute to wikis.

_____ create and share content via social networks.

Networking Skill Score: _____ / 8 = _____ percent

# CONCLUSION

Concepts from media ecology explain that the media is an environment in which we all exist, and that changes in the technologies available change our entire environment: how we think, interact, and work. These changes in our environment affect us as people and society as a whole.

In this chapter, we've focused on the societal and social implications of Web 2.0 technologies, focusing in particular on the widening gap between the "haves" and the "have nots." Changes in the media environment have led to certain groups of people being more, rather than less, excluded. This exclusion extends to information, political participation, and even social inclusion. There is no one cause for the persistent divides and knowledge gaps in our society, and merely providing access to underprivileged groups will not, in and of itself, bridge divides and close gaps in our Web 2.0 society. Rather, digital literacy, in terms of fostering the skills needed to participate in this new environment, is essential to reducing the gaps that perpetuate inequality. In keeping with the critical/cultural nature of media ecology, this is as much an area of research as it is a moral and social issue for us to debate and address. What do you think we should do to improve the Web 2.0 environment and close knowledge gaps? What can *you* do to help?

ASSIGNMENTS

1. **Social critique of a new technology.** Trace the history of a new technology (such as Facebook, Twitter, or smartphones). Write a critique of the technology in terms of:

   a. How it has or could become an extension of people

   b. Whether it is a "hot" or "cool" medium

   c. How it has or could contribute to fragmentation

   d. Who is advantaged or disadvantaged by the technology.

2. Go online to find an answer to the question: *What is the current status of income inequality in the United States?* Write a report on your answer, and reflect on how you found that answer:

   a. Summarize the current state of income inequality in the US.

   b. Which browser did you use to find your answer?

   c. Which search engines did you use to find your answer?

   d. What search terms did you use when you searched for the answer?

   e. What limiters within the search engine did you use?

   f. What operators did you use in your search phrase?

   g. How many websites did you look at?

   h. What source(s) did you use to decide on an answer to the question? Give the complete hyperlink.

   i. Why did you choose the source(s) you selected?

   j. Submit a pdf of the source with your report.

REFERENCES

Seminal Texts:

McLuhan, M. (1964). *Understanding media: The extensions of man*. New York: Signet.

Postman, N. (1986). *Amusing ourselves to death: Public discourse in the age of show business*. New York: Penguin Books.

Postman, N. (1993). *Technopoly: The Surrender of culture to technology*. New York: Vintage Books.

Innis, H. (1951). *The bias of communication*. Toronto: University of Toronto Press.

Academic Sources:

Brake, D. R. (2013). Are we all online content creators now? Web 2.0 and digital divides. *Journal of Computer-Mediated Communication, 19*, 591–609.

Brandtweiner, R., Donat, E., & Kerschbaum, J. (2010). How to become a sophisticated user: A two-dimensional approach to e-literacy. *New Media & Society, 12*, 813–833.

Ellis, D. (2009). Medium theory. In S. Littlejohn & K. A. Foss (eds.) *The encyclopedia of communication theory* (pp. 644–648). Thousand Oaks, CA: Sage.

Graham, R. (2009). Group differences in attitudes towards technology among Americans. *New Media & Society, 12*, 985–1003.

Hanke, B. (2003). McLuhan, Virilio and electric speed in the age of digital reproduction. In G. Genosko (Ed.), *Marshall McLuhan: Renaissance for a wired world* (pp. 121). London: Routledge.

Holt, K., Shehata, A., Strömbäck, J., & Ljungberg, E. (2013). Age and the effects of news media attention and social media use on political interest and participation: Do social media function as leveller? *European Journal of Communication, 28*(1), 19–34.

Lee, H., Park, N., & Hwang, Y. (2015). A new dimension of the digital divide: Exploring the relationship between broadband connection, smartphone use and communication competence. *Telematics & Informatics, 32*(1), 45–56.

Mcluhan, M., & Powers, (1992). *The global village: Transformations in world life and media in the 21st century*. New York: Oxford University Press.

National Communication Association. (2013). *The digital divide*. Retrieved from https://www.natcom.org/uploadedFiles/Public_Engagement/Digital%20Divide%20Press%20Kit%20-%20Oct%202014.pdf

Norris, P. (2001). *Digital divide: Civic engagement, information poverty, and the Internet worldwide*. Cambridge, MA: John F. Kennedy School of Government.

Sayed, N. (2011). Toward the Egyptian Revolution: Activists' perceptions of social media for mobilization. *Journal of Arab & Muslim Media Research, 4*(2&3), 273–298.

Segev, E. & Ahituv, N. (2010). Popular searches in Google and Yahoo! A "digital divide" in the information uses? *The Information Society*, *26*(1): 17–37. Available at: http://www.informaworld.com/smpp/content~db=all~content=a918686087

Strate, L. (2006). *Echoes and reflections: On media ecology as a field of study*. Cresskill, NJ: Hampton Press.

Strover, S. (2014). The US digital divide: A call for a new philosophy. *Critical Studies in Media Communication*, *31*, 114–122.

Tichenor, P. J., Donohue, G. A., & Olien, C. N. (1970). Mass media flow and differential growth in knowledge. *Public Opinion Quarterly*, *34*, 159–170.

Tsatsou, P. (2011). Digital divides revisited: What is new about divides and their research? *Media, Culture, & Society*, *33*, 317–331.

Raine, L. (2013, November 5). The state of digital divides. *Pew Research Internet Project*. Retrieved from http://www.pewinternet.org/2013/11/05/the-state-of-digital-divides-video-slides/

van Deursen, A., & van Dijk, J. (2010). Measuring Internet skills. *International Journal of Human–Computer Interaction*, *26*, 891–916.

van Deursen, A., & van Dijk, J. (2011). Internet skills and the digital divide. *New Media & Society*, *13*(6), 893–911.

Warner, B. R., McGowen, S. T., & Hawthorne, J. (2012). Limbaugh's social media nightmare: Facebook and Twitter as spaces for political action. *Journal of Radio & Audio Media*, *19*(2), 257–275.

Wei, L. (2012). Number matters: The multimodality of Internet use as an indicator of the digital inequalities. *Journal of Computer-Mediated Communication*, *17*(3), 303–318.

Wei, L., & Hindman, D. B. (2011). Does the digital divide matter more? Comparing the effects of new media and old media use on the education-based knowledge gap. *Mass Communication & Society*, *14*(2), 216–235.

Wood, L., & Howley, A. (2012). Dividing at an early age: The hidden digital divide in Ohio elementary schools. *Learning, media, and Technology*, *37*, 20–39.

Xenos, M., Vromen, A., & Loader, B. D. (2014). The great equalizer? Patterns of social media use and youth political engagement in three advanced democracies. *Information, Communication & Society*, *17*(2), 151–167.

Examples:

Bort, J. (2013). The history of the tablet, an idea Steve Jobs stole and turned into a game-changer. *Business Insider*. Retrieved from http://www.businessinsider.com/history-of-the-tablet-2013-5#

Further Reading Online:

You can read Chapter 1 of McLuhan's Understanding Media here: http://web.mit.edu/allanmc/www/mcluhan.mediummessage.pdf

You can read more about digital literacy here: http://www.digitalliteracy.gov

Brown, R. H., Barram, D. J., & Irving, L. (1995). *Falling through the net: A survey of the "have nots" in rural and urban America*. Washington, DC: National Telecommunications & Information Administration. Retrieved from http://www.ntia.doc.gov/ntiahome/fallingthru.html

CHAPTER 22

THE USES AND GRATIFICATIONS PERSPECTIVE

OUTCOMES

- *Knowledge:* Learn the relationship between needs, motives, media uses, and effects.
- *Skill:* Recognize and adapt to the diverse needs that motivate use of different technologies.

💬 INTRODUCTION

Much like media ecology from the previous chapter, uses and gratifications (U&G) is a paradigm, or way of thinking about media and media effects, rather than one unified theory. As the name implies, U&G focuses on **uses**, why people use the media they do, and **gratifications**, or what people get out of their media use. U&G has been called the **limited effects perspective** because it argues that media effects are limited by people's unique uses of media (Klapper, 1960). More recently, U&G has been called an **active audience approach** because it focuses on the many different reasons people have for their media use and people's unique media use behaviors. In other words, U&G considers what people use the media for (Katz, Blumler, & Gurevitch, 1974).

So, U&G encompasses three interrelated concepts: the functions the media serve, audiences, and effects:

- *The media serve functions for people.* These functions, or unique media-use motives, stem from individual differences, such as personality and circumstances, which create needs. One key feature of U&G research is discovering and measuring the different types of functions that different media fulfill.
- *Audiences choose media to fulfill their needs.* Therefore, audiences are actively choosing and avoiding media content. We may need to know something, so we choose informational media and pay close attention. Or we may be using media to pass time, which is still a choice that fulfills a need, but we may choose content that we only have a moderate interest in as background noise or to graze.

- *How people use media determines media effects.* If we are simply killing time and glossing over content, we may not retain much of the information that we gloss over but we may experience effects. On the other hand, if we are carefully paying attention to content because we want to learn from it, we may recall more of the content but experience fewer perceptual effects because our use of that content is more active.

U&G has become particularly relevant in the Web 2.0 environment because new media has increased users' control and interactivity during media use (Ruggiero, 2000). We have more options than ever before in terms of choosing media to fulfill our needs by bookmarking, creating playlists and watchlists, pausing, re-watching or reading, binge watching, subscribing to, following, and skimming, skipping or blocking content. Also, new media is more interactive, so we can comment, tweet about, share, and follow links within content. So the idea of a selective, active audience is particularly relevant in our new media environment. On the practical side, it is useful to understand the motivations that lead people to seek out media content since that will help us understand how they are likely to use that content, what we should include when we develop it, and what (if any) the possible effects might be.

💬 OVERVIEW OF USES AND GRATIFICATIONS

MAIN IDEA

The basic, underlying assumption of U&G is that media audiences are motivated by individual and situational needs and select media to fulfill their needs. The needs, or media-use motives we have, determine how we engage and interact with media content, which in turn determines media effects.

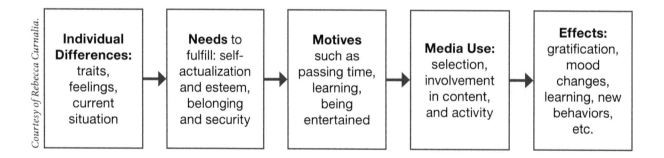

Courtesy of Rebecca Curnalia.

Individual Differences: traits, feelings, current situation → **Needs** to fulfill: self-actualization and esteem, belonging and security → **Motives** such as passing time, learning, being entertained → **Media Use:** selection, involvement in content, and activity → **Effects:** gratification, mood changes, learning, new behaviors, etc.

KEY CONCEPTS IN U&G

1. *Traits, states, and situations create needs, which we sometimes fulfill using media.*
   - We all have **personality traits**, or individual dispositions, such as being outgoing (extrovert), emotionally stable (neuroticism), preference for being planned and orderly (conscientiousness), being interpersonally warm (agreeableness), and enjoying new things (openness). These personality traits may be related to the types of media we enjoy. For example, extroverts may really like social media as a way to build their circles of friends and people who are more open may enjoy diverse types of media.

- We all experience moods, whether we are lonely or excited, and we can use media to enhance or repair our mood. This is **mood management**. For example, you may have an upbeat music playlist or station on Spotify or Pandora that you turn to when you're in a good mood or need to feel better, and you may have a calmer playlist for when you're feeling reflective.

- There are also situations in our lives, such as when we are uncertain, that we may turn to media for information, distraction, or support. For example, when we are sick, our first inclination may be to Google our symptoms to find out what may be wrong. This is also true on the societal level. When there is a disaster or some other news item we are concerned about, this activates **media dependency**, where we must rely on the media for information about what's going on.

2. *There are different needs that lead to media use* (Katz, Gurevitch, & Haas, 1973). People have **cognitive needs** such as wanting information, **affective** needs are emotional such as wanting entertainment, **personal needs** such as wanting credibility and status, **social needs** such as building relationships, and the need to **release tension** such as passing time. These needs lead us to use media in particular ways, such as reading blogs and websites for information and inspiration (cognitive and personal needs) or creating a blog to build our network and pass time (social and release needs).

3. *There are many types of motives; motives are either active or passive* (Rubin, 1984). A lot of U&G research has focused on finding and confirming typologies of motives. A **typology** is a list of types or categories. **Motives** are the different reasons we have for using media. For example, eight motives for media use that are often applied in research are passing time, diversion, learning about oneself, learning about the world, emotional arousal, to relax, for companionship, and out of habit (Greenberg, 1974). Thinking about this early typology, consider your own use of new media, such as social media. Chances are, you sometimes use it when you're bored (pastime), when you feel lonely (companionship), when you need to escape (diversion), to find out what's going on (learning), to be amused (arousal), or even as part of your daily routine (habit). These are all motives for using social media, and some of them are more active (i.e., to learn) while some are more passive (i.e., pastime).

4. *Motives lead to audience selectivity, activity, and orientation* (Rubin, 1993). Generally, media-use motives can be broken down into two categories depending on whether the motives are more active or more passive: intentional and selective **instrumental media use** or habitual and passive **ritualized media use**. Think of this as the difference between looking for information online (instrumental use) versus browsing (ritualized use). There are likely situations and needs that lead you to use the Internet in fundamentally different ways depending on why you chose to open your browser in the first place. If you're in line and want to kill some time, you may graze content more ritualistically. If you are looking for product information so you can make a decision, you may look for and read information more instrumentally. In those two different scenarios, you will have different orientations toward the content that you access.

5. *Orientations can increase or diminish media effects* (Rubin, 1993). When we use media instrumentally, we tend to be more **involved**: we pay closer attention and think more about the content. When we are using it more ritualistically, we are less involved, so we pay less attention and think less about the content. Thinking about this in terms of media effects, when we are instrumentally seeking information we may think more about what we see or read and therefore retain more. On the other hand, when we are ritualistically grazing through Internet content, we may be less likely to remember what we read but be more

affected by it. Why would we *remember less* but be *more affected*? If we're not thinking actively and critically about what we're consuming, we're less likely to reject the content we're consuming, even if it is faulty, unrealistic, biased, or irrelevant.

Insight into Innovation Activity: Personality and Media Use. Take a personality test, then relate the results to the types of media you enjoy using. How do your traits help explain the types of media content to enjoy and use most often?

Take the a quick self-assessment of the Big 5 personality test here: http://drphil.com/shows/bigfivepersonalityquiz

Americans More Attached to Internet, Cellphones

Percent who say ... would be very hard to give up

INTERNET
53% of internet users

CELLPHONE
49% of cellphone owners

48%

44%

43%

TELEVISION
35% of all adults*

38%

LANDLINE TELEPHONE
28% of landline telephone owners

2006   2014

*Only 12% of those ages 18-29 say television would be very hard to give up.

PEW RESEARCH CENTER

Americans increasingly view the internet, cellphones as essential," Pew Research Center, Washington, DC (February, 2014) http://www.pewresearch.org/fact-tank/2014/02/27/americans-increasingly-view-the-internet-cellphones-as-essential/.

EXAMPLE OF THEORY IN WEB 2.0: WHY WE LOVE (AND MAY BE ADDICTED TO) THE INTERNET

When was the last time you weren't able to get online? How did it make you feel? If you were angry, or upset, you may have an addiction. We all have reasons, or motives, for using the Internet that range from wanting a sense of belonging, to getting information, to passing time. Our motives for using the Internet are linked to our personality traits (Amiel & Sargent, 2004). Sometimes our use of media, like the Internet or social media sites, can be so involving that it affects other aspects of our lives, such as our productivity, personal relationships, and even our own sense of well-being. In other words, it may be addictive.

One recent study suggests that personality traits and personal circumstances along with motives for Internet use are related to three aspects of **Internet addiction**: the Internet *intruding* on our activities (losing track of time online, staying online a lot, and it interfering with our other activities); using the Internet to *escape* or as a distraction from reality; and being *attached* to the Internet, including becoming upset if we don't have Internet access (Kim & Haridakis, 2009). Research by Pew (2014) indicates that over half of people who use the Internet regularly say it "would be very hard to give up" using it. This exceeds people's reliance on, or potential "addiction" to, earlier media such as television. What do you think? Are we Internet addicts?

 METHODS IN U&G RESEARCH

Early research on U&G used interviews with people about why they like the media they consumed and how they felt when that media was no longer available (Herzog, 1944; Berlson, 1959). These early approaches to studying U&G were useful for exploring the uses people had for mass media, like radio and newspapers. They also set the stage for the ongoing exploration of people's uses, motivations, and feelings about new and emerging technologies.

Survey methods. U&G research is typically survey research that employs scales. These scales are used to measure people's motives by employing an existing or newly developed motive typology. Researchers also use scale items to measure personality traits, personal circumstances, and media use. This is one of the interesting and unique features of U&G research, but also one of the challenges in terms of building a coherent, testable theory: Because researchers frequently develop their own motives measures, it is hard to reach general conclusions about exactly which motives are related to specific media use. For the research findings from these studies to be practical and useful to media professionals, there would need to be more consistency in approaches so that we could reach clearer conclusions to guide our development of new media messages.

There are several ways to go about developing a typology of media use motives. Some researchers use brainstorming or rely on existing research to create scales for their studies, then use statistics to create a typology of motives by seeing which scale items fit together into clear categories. Early motives typologies were developed using interviews and open questions, by asking people about their feelings and reasons for using media (e.g., Berelson, 1959; Greenberg, 1974). On the basis of interview responses, scale items were developed and statistically analyzed to develop a typology of motives (Rubin, 1981). As an example of the diversity of motive typologies available just for the Internet, check out the table below from Foregger (2008). As you can see, research has explored numerous types of motives for different types of Internet use: general Internet use, consumer sites, and social media such as blogs.

 Insight into Innovation Activity: Questions to Ask Before Designing a Course Website. Imagine you were tasked with making recommendations about how to design and what to include in a new website for your college course. What questions would you ask to discover people's motives for using and orientations during use of course websites? Who would you ask? How might their responses affect the content of your website, such as layout, features, and use of multimedia?

Measuring media use: Surveys, diaries, and tracking software. One issue with reliance on surveys of motives and media use is that people are notoriously bad at self-reporting their media use. Think of it this way, if your professor asked you "how many minutes did you spend using your phone yesterday," chances are your response would not be accurate because we aren't always aware of how often and for how long we check our phones.

Researchers have also used diaries to have people track their media use, which gives a slightly different and possibly more complete picture of how often people are using media and what types of media they use, but even these can be incomplete (Greenberg et al., 2005). Particularly for new communication media, tracking software and website traffic tracking are somewhat better measures of how people are using media. For instance, websites can track whether people are first-time or returning visitors, how people landed on their websites (whether they went there directly

Factors Found in Selected Internet Uses and Gratifications Research				
Authors	**Year**	**Terminology**	**Channel**	**Uses and Gratifications Factors Found**
Eighmey & McCord	1998	Factors	Product website	Entertainment value, personal relevance, information involvement, personal involvement, continuing relationship
Ko, et al.	2005	Motivations	Product website	Information, social interaction, and convenience
Kaye & Johnson	2004	Motives	Bulletin boards, Chat forums, WWW	Political guidance, entertainment/social utility, convenience, information seeking
Parker & Plank	2000	Motivations	General internet	Companionship/social interaction, surveillance/entertainment, and relaxation/escape
Charney & Greenberg	2002	Gratification Factors	General internet	Keep informed, diversion/entertainment, peer identity, good feelings, communication, sights/sounds, career, and coolness
Papacharissi & Rubin	2000	Motives	General internet	Interpersonal utility, pass time, information seeking, convenience, and entertainment
Ferguson & Perse	2000	Motives	General internet	Entertainment, pass time, relaxation/escape, social information, and learning
LaRose & Eastin	2004	Expected Outcomes	General internet	Entertainment, social interaction, information, 'pass time', monetary, status motivations, and habit
Stafford & Stafford	2004	Gratifications	AOL/General internet	Process gratifications, content gratifications, and social gratifications
Leung	2001	Motives	ICQ Chat	Relaxation, entertainment, fashion, and inclusion, affections, sociability, and escape
Recchiuti	2003	Motives	Instant messaging, Chat rooms, Email	Entertainment, information seeking, and interpersonal utility (for chat room, IM, and email)
Li	2005	Motives	Blogs	Self-documentation, improving writing, self-expression, medium appeal, provide information, pass time, and socialization

Source: Sarah K. Foregger, "Uses and Gratifications of Facebook.com" (Unpublished Doctoral Dissertation), 2008.

or arrived there from a search engine, or social media post), and how people navigated their site (whether they clicked on multiple links, how long they stayed, etc.). They can collect some of this data by storing cookies on people's web browsers. There are, of course, accuracy issues with this kind of data too because more than one person may use the same computer, so it is impossible to know that someone is a returning user. It is also not possible to measure motives using tracking software, though we might infer motives from how a person landed on a page. Thus, there is a lot of potential for research on U&G in the new media environment, and new tools are emerging to analyze data to better understand and adapt to new media audiences.

TRAITS, CIRCUMSTANCES, MOTIVES, AND SOCIAL MEDIA USE

People use the Internet and mobile technology for a variety of reasons, and the U&G perspective has provided a framework for understanding how and why people are using Web 2.0 technologies. From an applied standpoint, understanding the people who are using your website or following you on social media should make you more effective at meeting their needs and, hopefully, strengthen your personal or professional connections. In general, people use the Internet for researching information, communicating and socializing with other people, shopping, and surfing (Rodgers & Sheldon, 2002). The motives people have for using the Internet predict the types of content they are likely to click on, so understanding the traits, circumstances, and motives of our web audience should help us develop messages that are more likely to appeal to them.

Apprehension, shyness, and use of new media Some people use mediated channels to avoid the anxiety of face-to-face interactions (Keaton & Kelly, 2008). Other people use mediated channels to help them overcome their shyness (Valkenburg, Schouten, & Peter, 2005). So, as U&G proposes, individual differences in traits and social needs lead to specific uses of new media. People's perceptions of their own communication skills (competence), anxiety when communicating (communication apprehension), reluctance to speak out (reticence), and being introverted are related to the uses and outcomes of using computer-mediated communication channels (Keaton & Kelly, 2008).

Though it seems that certain people are drawn to new media as a way to avoid or help manage their apprehension and overcome their introversion, the jury is still out on whether or not mediated channels actually *help* them (Valkenburg, Schouten, & Peter, 2005). The **rich-get-richer** view is that people who are extraverted actually benefit more from new media compared to introverts because extraverts build even broader social circles via new media, thus making them more "socially rich." The **social compensation explanation**, on the other hand, suggests that people who are introverted may use new media to overcome their communication obstacles.

There is evidence to support both of these explanations. People who are already satisfied in their face-to-face relationships tend to disclose more via social media and in turn are more satisfied with their online social network friendships as well (Pornsakulvanich, Haridakis, & Rubin, 2008). On the other hand, people who are already "rich" on social media like Twitter, for example, tend not to tweet more as their number of followers increases; but people with fewer followers tend to respond by posting more as followers increase (Toubia & Stephan, 2013). This means that people who are already socially "rich" do not seem to be affected by their increases in popularity online. People who are less "rich" seem to benefit from the positive feedback from increased followers though.

Of course we all know that not all feedback we get online is positive. Social media may actually make the isolation that sometimes comes along with being more apprehensive about communicating *worse* rather than better. People who are apprehensive tend to have less active motives for Facebook use, and therefore use the features of Facebook less often than their peers who are more comfortable communicating (Hunt, Atkin, & Krishnan, 2012). Therefore, people who are shy, introvert, or anxious may use social media less often, thus experiencing fewer of the social and self-esteem benefits associated with making online social connections.

Loneliness. The answer for people who feel isolated and lonely may not be to turn to social media sites such as Facebook and Twitter, but rather to seek social support from blogs. Blogs are helpful to people in terms of reducing their feelings of loneliness and offering them a sense of social support (Jung, Vordere, & Song, 2007). Hollenbaugh (2011) found that people in general blog to help others and lonely people tend to blog in an effort to make social connections as well. And there is some evidence that these motives for blogging are gratified. Preliminary research suggests that people who blog feel more social support, social integration, and friendship satisfaction than people who don't blog (Baker & Moore, 2008).

MOTIVES LINKED TO SPECIFIC TYPES OF SOCIAL MEDIA

In the previous section, we discussed how personality traits and circumstances lead us to use social media in particular ways. There are also motives related to each type of social media we currently use.

Online video. **Podcasts**, or downloadable video and audio files, are a popular way to create and save broadcasts. People use podcasts to build a library of titles, to use media when it is convenient for them (time shifting), and also as a source of conversation (McClung & Johnson, 2010). Similar to podcasts, YouTube is a video website where people can create, edit, and share videos. Like podcast users, people use YouTube because it is a convenient way to pass time and get information, and because there is a social element to it as people watch YouTube videos together and

use videos to interact with each other through comments, sharing, and posting videos (Haridakis & Hanson, 2009). The motives we have for using sites such as YouTube also affect how we interact with the content. People who got their news from YouTube tended to be more motivated by interpersonal uses of YouTube, compared to the information motives common among traditional news users (Hanson & Haridakis, 2008).

Twitter. People use Twitter for both information and social reasons. As people build a group of followers and interact with more people on Twitter, their needs for social connection are gratified (Chen, 2011). People tweet for more informational reasons as well, to share and receive feedback on information that others might find useful and to promote their own work and the work of people they know (Holton et al., 2014).

Blogs. Much like users of podcasts and YouTube, bloggers also use blogs because they are convenient, a way to get and share information, personally and socially useful, and to help them express themselves (Kaye, 2005). They are also useful for getting guidance and opinions and serve as an alternative to traditional media (Kaye, 2010). Compared to using traditional sources like the news, people use blogs for more social reasons: to engage in discussions and socialize (Mitchelstein, 2011).

Taken together, research on the use and gratifications of online video, social networks, and blogging suggests that Web 2.0 media is fulfilling informational, diversionary, and social motives for its users.

APPLYING U&G: ADAPTING TO PEOPLE'S SOCIAL MEDIA USE MOTIVES

Understanding motives to design social media messages. We see that U&G research into Web 2.0 technologies such as podcasting, YouTube, Facebook, and Twitter gives us some insight into users of these new media channels. First, an important use of social media is *interpersonal*: making connections with people, interacting, and building a group or community of friends and followers. The uses of social media are also *personal*. Social media is a way to learn about yourself, try out different identities, promote yourself, express yourself, and build social capital. People also reported getting *information* as a motive for using each of the types of social media. There were different types of information that people were looking for—from getting news to finding out information about their friends. Also, across the types of new media, people use it because it is *convenient*. As mobile technologies become more widely used, people are able to control when they watch or read online content, so they can access whatever they want when it is convenient for them.

Insight into Innovation Activity: Why is @TacoBell #winning Twitter? Check out the article on *Huffington Post* about Taco Bell's widely lauded Twitter account. Looking at the tweets in this article, can you use our conclusions from U&G research to explain *why* Taco Bell's tweets are so popular? What motives for social media are they fulfilling? How are they gratifying those motives?

http://www.huffingtonpost.com/2014/02/28/taco-bell-tweets_n_4856259.html

Thinking about this in terms of how we should and should *not* use social media to interact, we see why some people are so very annoying on Facebook. Mashable posted a Top 20 List of annoying posting habits on Facebook that included the humblebrag, vaguebooking, marketing, check-ins, TMI, vanity, rants, urban legends, and redundant links. If we consider these social media complaints from a U&G perspective, it makes sense why we should not do these things. Social media users are looking for a blend of personal, interpersonal, and informational content in a convenient social media feed. If people overpost, have posts that are too long, or otherwise meaningless check-ins, it clutters people's feeds, making them less convenient to browse. If people post too many selfies, too much bragging, or too much marketing material, not only are they cluttering feeds but they are also focusing exclusively on the personal aspects of social media—using it exclusively for self-promotion—and not on building interpersonal connections or providing information. Posting empty statuses, like vaguebooking and humblebragging, are not interesting to people seeking to build interpersonal connections and looking for information about what their friends are up too.

If we know the reasons, or motives, people have for following us via social media, we can get insight into what we should be posting: interesting or important information, disclosures, images, and thoughts that people may find entertaining, useful, or that maintain social connections.

Applying motivations and orientations to choose communication channels. U&G research findings can also help communication professionals and individuals interested in self-branding choose the social media channels that will be most effective for disseminating their messages. People use online video, Twitter, Facebook, and blogs slightly differently. Followers' expectations and preferences for content vary according to their motives for using these different types of social media. As a content creator, your message should be created to gratify the motives and accommodate the uses of your followers via each specific social media channel.

For some social media formats, like blogs, providing information and social support to people is an important motive. Blogs are a great place to go into detail with long posts that provide people information that is presented in an interpersonal, conversational way. On the other hand, the potential for interaction and feedback is better more immediate via Facebook and Twitter. So we can quickly share, retweet, and respond via these channels to build connections and keep pace with constantly updating feeds. It is more difficult to time shift via those social media feeds because the feed changes in real time as people post content and, on Facebook, the feed order is manipulated. So Twitter and Facebook will give you timeliness and immediacy for people who prefer that, but blogs allow for time shifting and detail. U&G challenges us to think about how people are using the technology, which should inform the technology we choose and how we construct messages to meet our own and our followers' needs.

Using U&G surveys to learn about your audience. One of the takeaways from U&G is their research methods, which focus on learning why an audience is there in the first place. U&G offers useful tools for communication professionals, as there are many existing scales and typologies of motives practitioners can use to develop their own audience analysis surveys. Particularly via social media, we can distribute online surveys with open questions (i.e., Ask people "what kind of content do you enjoy seeing me post?") and closed questions (i.e., Ask people, "On a scale of 1 to 10, 1 being not at all and 10 being very much, do you prefer posts that are funny?"). Looking back at Foregger's (2008) table that reviews motives for social media use, professionals could create scale items to explore people's motives for following them and ask whether or not their posts are meeting the needs of the audience. These scales can be relatively short and provide practitioners a wealth of information about their followers' motives and uses.

CONCLUSION

Not surprisingly, as an approach to media that focuses on individual users' motivations, control, and activity, U&G has increased in popularity in the past decade. Even though the theory's assumption that mass media has limited effects remains controversial, the U&G approach has proven to be a fruitful way to explore new media and understand how and why people are using it. These findings provide valuable personal insight into our own uses and the likely implications of our own new media use, and also provide a framework for understanding how best to communicate with people via social media in a way that meets their needs.

Though research on U&G suffers from a lack of consistency, as different researchers develop and apply different motive typologies, it is also useful that there are so many typologies available as it gives us insight into the broad range of reasons people have for using these new technologies. U&G also clarifies that the reasons people use media determine the effects of that media as a result of differences in audience orientations, which can help us choose the channels that are best for us to convey our message.

ASSIGNMENTS

1. Track your Internet use for one day. Write a self-reflection paper and explain how (instrumental or ritualized) and why (cognitive, affective, personal, social, or tension release) you use the Internet throughout the day and whether you are or are not addicted to the Internet.

2. Read the paper *The e-mail is down! Using a 1940s method to research a 21st Century* problem: http://web.missouri.edu/~bentleycl/Research_Papers/Emaildown.htm.
   a. Is this "old" method of discovering motives still useful for researching Web 2.0 technology? Why or why not?
   b. How could we use Berelson's method to study Web 2.0 technology?
   c. Do you think Berelson and the authors of this paper found evidence of media *addiction*? Why or why not?

REFERENCES

Seminal Texts:

Berelson, B. (1959). What "missing the newspaper" means. In W. Schramm (Ed.), *The process and effects of mass communication* (pp. 36–47). Urbana: University of Illinois.

Herzog, H. (1944). Motivations and gratifications of daily serial listeners. In W. Schramm (ed.) *The process and effects of mass communication* (pp. 50–55). Urbana, IL: University of Illinois.

Klapper, J. (1960). *The effects of mass communication*. New York: Free Press.

Academic Articles:

Amiel, T., & Sargent, S. L. (2004). Individual differences in Internet usage motives. *Computers in Human Behavior, 20,* 711–726.

Baker, J. R., & Moore, S. M. (2008). Blogging as a social tool: A psychosocial examination of the effects of blogging. *CyberPsychology & Behavior, 11,* 747–749.

Berelson, B. (1949). What "missing the newspaper" means. In P. F. Lazarsfeld & F. N. Stanton (Eds.), *Communications Research, 1948–1949* (pp. 111–128). New York: Harper & Brothers.

Chen, G. M. (2011). Tweet this: A uses and gratifications perspective on how active Twitter use gratifies a need to connect with others. *Computers in Human Behavior, 27,* 755–762.

Foregger, S. K. (2008). Uses and gratifications of Facebook.com. Unpublished Doctoral Dissertation. Retrieved from http://books.google.com/books/about/Uses_and_Gratifications_of_Facebook_com.html?id=0idbf365YBkC

Greenburg, B. S. (1974). Gratifications of television viewing and their correlates for British children. In J. G. Blumler & E. Katz (Eds.), *The uses of mass communications: Current perspectives on gratifications research* (pp. 71–91). Beverly Hills, CA: Sage.

Greenberg, B. S., Eastin, M. S., Skalski, P., Cooper, L., Levy, M., & Lachlan, K. (2005). Comparing survey and diary measures of Internet and traditional media use. *Communication Reports, 18,* 1–8.

Hanson, G., & Haridakis, P. (2008). YouTube users watching and sharing the news: A uses and gratifications approach. *Journal of Electronic Publishing, 11,* 6.

Haridakis, P., & Hanson, G. (2009). Social interaction and co-viewing with YouTube: Blending mass communication reception and social connection. *Journal of Broadcasting & Electronic Media, 53,* 317–335.

Hollenbaugh, E. E. (2011). Motives for maintaining personal journal blogs. *Cyberpsychology, Behavior, and Social Networking, 14,* 13–20.

Holton, A. E., Kang, B., Coddington, M., & Yaschur, C. (2014). Seeking and sharing: Motivations for linking on Twitter. *Communication Research Reports, 31,* 33–40.

Hunt, D., Atkin, D., & Krishnan, A. (2012). The influence of computer-mediated communication apprehension on motives for Facebook use. *Journal of Broadcasting & Electronic Media, 56,* 187–202.

Jung, Y., Vorderer, P., & Song, H. (2007). *Motivation and Consequences of Blogging in Social Life.* Paper presented at the annual meeting of the International Communication Association, San Francisco, CA.

Katz, E., Gurevitch, M., & Haas, H. (1973). On the use of the mass media for important things. *American Sociological Review, 38,* 164–181.

Kaye, B. L. (2005). It's a blog, blog, blog world: Users and uses of weblogs. *Atlantic Journal of Communication, 13,* 73–95.

Kaye, B. L. (2010). Going to the blogs: Toward the development of a uses and gratifications measurement scale for blogs. *Atlantic Journal of Communication, 18,* 194–210.

Keaton, J. A., & Kelly, L. (2008). "Re: We really need to talk": Affect for communication channels, competence, and fear of negative evaluation. *Communication Quarterly, 56,* 407–426.

Kim, J., & Haridakis, P. (2009). The role of Internet user characteristics and motives in explaining Internet addiction. *Journal of Computer-Mediated Communication, 14,* 988–1015.

McClung, S., & Johnson, K. (2010). Examining the motives of podcast users. *Journal of Radio & Audio Media, 17,* 82–95.

Mitchelstein, E. (2011). Catharsis and community: Divergent motivations for audience participation in online newspapers and blogs. *International Journal of Communication, 5,* 2014–2034.

Pornsakulvanich, V., Haridakis, P. M., & Rubin, A. M. (2008). The influence of dispositions and internet motivation on online communication satisfaction and relationship closeness. *Computers in Human Behavior, 24,* 2292–2310.

Rodgers, S., & Sheldon, K. M. (2002). An improved way to characterize Internet users. *Journal of Advertising Research, 42*(5), 85.

Rubin, A. M. (1981). An examination of television viewing motivations. *Communication Research, 8,* 141–165.

Rubin, A. M. (1984). Ritualized and instrumental television viewing. *Journal of Communication, 34,* 67–77.

Rubin, A. M. (1993). Audience activity and media use. *Communication Monographs, 60,* 98–105.

Ruggiero, T. E. (2000). Uses and gratifications theory in the 21st century. *Mass Communication & Society, 3,* 3–37.

Toubia, O., & Stephen, A. T. (2013). Intrinsic vs. image-related utility in social media: Why do people contribute content to Twitter? *Marketing Science, 32,* 368–392.

Valkenburg, P. M., Schouten, A. P., & Peter, J. (2005). Adolescents' identity experiments on the internet. *New Media & Society, 7,* 383–402.

Examples:

Caumont, A. (2014, February 27). Americans increasingly view the Internet, cellphones as essential. *Pew Research Center Fact Tank*. Retrieved from http://www.pewresearch.org/fact-tank/2014/02/27/americans-increasingly-view-the-internet-cellphones-as-essential/

Further Reading Online:

Buck, S. (2012, August 14). 20 Things your most annoying friends do on Facebook. Retrieved from http://mashable.com/2012/08/14/facebook-annoying/#gallery/20-things-your-most-annoying-friends-do-on-facebook/5269a99812d2cd39fc0002ac

CHAPTER 23

AGENDA SETTING

OUTCOMES

- *Knowledge:* Learn about how the media influences people's opinions and how they think about issues.
- *Skill:* Recognize how social media users reframe issues and start social movements.

🗨 INTRODUCTION

In the previous chapter we looked at uses and gratifications, which is an individual-level explanation of people's uses of media and how uses influence media effects. We move on in this chapter to discuss the first of several theories that suggest that there are *mass* media effects. McCombs and Shaw (1972) developed **agenda setting** theory to explain how news coverage makes some issues seem important by giving those issues a lot of coverage, and how other issues are made to seem unimportant because they are not covered as much or not covered at all. Also, how a story is **framed** by the news media, or the angle used to report a news story, influences how people think about issues as well. So, the news media *tell us what is important* (agenda setting) and give us an angle, or perspective, *that tells us how to think about the story* (framing). From a practitioner's standpoint, understanding how to affect the news media's agenda promote a particular frame are important tools for promoting issues, people, products, and events, and also for crisis management. From a societal standpoint, agenda setting helps us understand how news media can influence society's priorities and our understanding of important issues.

The height of agenda setting's popularity was when there were fewer news outlets covering issues and events. In the age of Web 2.0, traditional news media are losing market share as people increasingly go online for their news. This has important consequences for what issues are on people's agendas and the frames that people are exposed to. Our news sources are increasingly **decentralized**—meaning that our news is coming from many different people and outlets—and are therefore less consistent. That being said, there are still agenda setting and framing effects online, but it can now come directly from politicians, organizations, issue campaigns, and even people we are linked to through social networks such as as bloggers, social media opinion leaders, and traditional news media.

MAIN IDEA

McCombs (2004) explains that the news media influences people's issue agendas by telling them which issues are important (first-level agenda setting). The media also frames issues, people, and events in particular ways, which influences how people think about those things (second-level agenda setting).

KEY ASSUMPTIONS/CONCEPTS (MCCOMBS, 2004)

1. *The prominence given to a news story in mass media influences which issues people think are important.* We all have personal agendas, or issues and events that we think are important. These personal agendas change somewhat over time as a result of the news bringing new issues to our attention. Story **prominence**, or whether it is a lead story or buried later in the news coverage, tells us whether a story is important or not. Also, the **depth** of coverage, or how much time and space a news story receives, determines how important we as news users perceive the story to be. Think about the last time you were on a news website. The stories that were posted at the top of the page, with a big headline, and included images or multimedia were likely the ones that you perceived as most important.

2. *Gatekeepers and other media affect news agendas.* Since the media's agenda is important in terms of setting people's personal agendas, it only makes sense that we need to understand who sets the media's agenda. **Gatekeepers**, such as the editors, decide which stories get covered, their prominence in the news, and even the depth of story coverage (White, 1950). Gatekeepers can choose among many different stories from many different sources: news wire services such as Reuters and the Associated Press, other news outlets, press releases, prominent people like celebrities and politicians, and social media are all sources of news stories. As news organizations look more closely at what's trending on social media to decide whether or not a news story is important, bloggers and microbloggers have managed to influence the news agenda in the Web 2.0 environment. Bloggers sometimes post about people and events, their posts go viral, and news media pick up on trending topics. This is a new type of **intermedia agenda setting**, where both legacy media and new media are influencing other media outlets' agendas.

3. *There are issues that are personally important or relevant to people and are part of their personal issue agendas regardless of news coverage.* Whether or not an issue is relevant to us is **issue salience**. **Obtrusive issues** are things that we have personal experience with and these influence our personal agendas. Just because the news media covers a topic at length,

as they do with celebrity deaths and scandals, does not mean that will become part of our personal issue agenda. If we do not see the issue as salient, or relevant to us, we won't incorporate it into our personal agenda. Similarly, there are some things that happen to us or that we have experience with that are obtrusive, and we don't need the media to tell us that it is an important issue. If you have a lot of student loans, for example, you don't need the news media to tell you that there is a student debt crisis. For me, as a professor, higher education policy and funding are part of my issue agenda regardless of what the media reports because it is both salient (relevant to my daily life) and obtrusive (something I have experience with).

4. *How news stories are framed influences how people think about issues.* Even when an issue is obtrusive the media may influence how we interpret or understand it, particularly early in the discussion of a campaign, event, or policy. There are many different ways of seeing an issue. So, there are many different frames, or angles, that can be used to cover news stories. Frames are typically part of the headline, subheading, images, or first paragraph of a news story. They give a way of interpreting, or thinking about, an issue, event, or person. Research suggests that **conflict frames** that focus on disagreements between people dominate American news (Neuman, Just, & Crigler, 1992). In keeping with the emphasis on conflict in American journalism, it isn't surprising that stories about who stands to win or lose, stories that focus on strategies, and stories that frame politics and issues as games or wars are common in American media. Journalists may frame things in terms of **gains or losses** by focusing on whether something will be a benefit that gives people something, or by focusing on what it will cost people or what people stand to lose. Politics, campaigns, and events can also be framed in terms of **strategies or issues** by focusing on either the intention behind an action or on explaining the issues being addressed. Campaigns and events can even be framed as a sport, war, or **game** by focusing on which side is winning versus losing. In addition to conflict-focused frames, we also see frames that focus on people and moral evaluations. **Human interest frames** focus on the suffering of people involved in an issue. **Morality frames** are also common, and these focus on moral evaluations of issues and events. These frames may also support the **status quo or social change** by either explaining why a social movement, policy, or event is hurting people or society or by emphasizing how a movement or event is bringing about needed social changes.

Insight into Innovation Example: How Media Framed a Proposal for Free Tuition. Consider, for example, funding for higher education. In 2015, President Obama announced via social media a plan to offer 2 years of community college free for people who enter public service. Let's consider some of the early frames used to report on the proposal, keeping in mind that these were the lenses through which people learned about the free tuition plan:

- *Gain frames* focused on the tuition money saved by students, such as the *New York Times* headline, "Obama plan would help many go to community college."

- *Loss frames* focused on the cost to taxpayers, such as *Forbes'* headline "Six reasons why Obama's free community college is a poor investment" and similar headlines estimating the cost to be around $60 billion.

- *Strategy frames* looked at the strategic aspects of "selling" the plan, such as ABC News' headline, "Obama's free community college idea may be hard to sell."

- *Human interest frames* focused on the personal impact of the proposal for students, such as *The Washington Post*'s headline "'I want to go further than my daddy did': What free community college means to kids."

- *Status quo frames* supported keeping things the way they are by arguing that free community college tuition would not fix the problem. For example, one *Forbes* article pointed out that this plan does not address the issues facing students from economically disadvantaged backgrounds: "Three problems with President Obama's 'free' community college pitch."

- *Change frames* focused on the ways that the current tuition-based system is not working, such as *The Guardian* headline, "Free community college isn't a joke for families who spend half their income to send a child."

- *Game frames* discussed the free tuition plan as a game, war, or sporting match between Obama and republicans. *The Chronicle of Higher Education*'s (2015) headline about "The players who influenced Obama's free-college plan" and NBC's headline that "Obama says community college initiative 'a game changer'" both make use of the "game" metaphor in covering the proposal.

Insight into Innovation Activity: Frame the Free Community College Proposal. Read through President Obama's proposal to make community college free for "responsible students" by following the link below. Brainstorm a list of 10 story headlines you would use if reporting or blogging about this proposal. From your list of headlines, choose the one that you like the best, that best fits the topic, and that would get people to click on the story to read more. What type of frame (gain, loss, issue, strategy, status quo, change, or game) is implied in the headline you chose? What do you think the effects of that frame would be on people who read your story? (http://www.whitehouse.gov/blog/2015/01/08/ president-proposes-make-community-college-free-responsible-students-2-years)

5. *Agenda setting and framing effects are* **cognitive processes**; *they affect how people think.* Our understanding of how agenda setting works is based on our understanding of cognitive **priming**. Priming is when an idea, feeling, opinion, or knowledge comes to mind quickly and easily. The more quickly and easily something comes to mind, the more it is primed in our memory. Repeated exposure to a message, such as a news story or a specific frame, increases its priming in our memories. So, if we hear about Obama's plans for free tuition a lot through news, social media, and even conversations with other people, it will be primed in our memory and will come to mind quickly and easily. Similarly, the frames used to discuss the issue can be primed, so that, when we think about the issue, the associated frames come to mind too. So if most news outlets and people frame free tuition in terms of gains for students, when we think about Obama's proposal, gains will also come to mind. If most news outlets frame the tuition plan in terms of the cost to taxpayers, then the costs associated with the plan will come to mind.

6. *Agenda setting and framing affect people's attitudes, knowledge, and behavior.* Priming is important because the issues and frames that are primed determine what knowledge we use to form our attitudes and to make decisions. The theory was originally applied to people's voting decisions: media primed issues and people voted based on the issues and interpretations of issues in memory. In keeping with the free tuition example, when we

think about Obama we may think first about his proposal for free tuition and our attitude toward that, which has been shaped by framing of the issue, and that will affect our opinion of Obama. Of course, agenda setting can explain a variety of behaviors beyond just voting, such as health-related behavior and purchasing decisions. For example, the media can form and prime attitudes about retailers by covering controversies about corporations and framing those issues in particular ways.

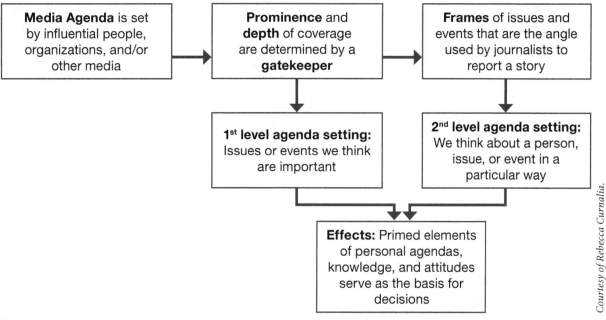

The Agenda-Setting Process

EXAMPLE OF THEORY IN WEB 2.0: BLOGS, SOCIAL MEDIA, AND THE "PINK SLIME" CONTROVERSY

Blogs, such as the *Huffington Post* and *Drudge Report*, and social media such as YouTube, Facebook, and Twitter, are changing the landscape of agenda setting and framing. Take, for example, McDonald's. The media has covered many controversies centering on McDonald's from the foam packaging used in the 1980s, to their employees' wages post Great Recession, to the "pink slime" allegedly used in processing their hamburger. Each of these news stories primes issues related to McDonald's corporate practices, and that coverage can shape our opinions of McDonald's as an organization and our behavior when deciding whether or not to eat there. The pink slime controversy is a case of a celebrity, Chef Jamie Oliver, bringing media attention to an issue with processed foods, popular media picking up on the issue, and

Jamie Oliver

ultimately the news coverage affecting agendas and leading to change in our food industry. Not only was McDonald's affected, but the meat industry as a whole reeled from the coverage of pink slime.

How did this become such a major public relations fiasco? In 2011, on his show *Food Revolution*, Oliver highlighted the use of "lean finely textured beef," which he termed "pink slime," in hamburger. Oliver's goal is starting a "national movement to change the way America eats" (Jamie Oliver Food Revolution, 2014, para. 4), and his criticism of "pink slime" was part of that effort. Industry experts said that a combination of factors helped Oliver's cause and injured the beef industry's ability to manage the public image crisis (Schultz, 2012): the use of the label, "pink slime," was very effective; fast food restaurants like McDonald's and Wendy's quickly responded that they would no longer use the product; "pink slime" news was spread widely via social media; and the beef processors' message that it is "safe" did not successfully counter frames emphasizing that it was "gross." After Oliver's segment on pink slime, popular food safety boggers picked up on the issue, and ABC News ran a series of investigative reports on the issue (Adams, 2014).

Because of the industry's inability to reframe the issue, pink slime was removed from school lunches in the United States, stores including Walmart refused to sell meat containing the product, and several policy changes were debated in Congress (Adams, 2014). So, in this example, we see agenda setting and framing at work. Oliver and social media made pink slime a media agenda item. The news media described the product as "pink slime," a frame that focused more on the texture and appearance of the product than on its safety. This frame shaped people's opinions and feelings about the product, ultimately leading fast food retailers and grocers to stop selling products containing that ingredient. As Adams pointed out, this also led to increases in beef prices, more waste in the beef industry, and lost jobs as meat processors moved away from this method of making ground beef. But these downsides were not a dominant aspect of news coverage—these issues were not part of the dominant frames—so many people may remain unaware of the reasons for using the product and remain focused instead on a yucky-sounding ingredient being removed from their food.

METHODS IN AGENDA SETTING RESEARCH

As the pink slime example demonstrates, agenda-setting processes and framing are different in the user-generated, interactive, social new media environment. So, as news has increasingly moved online, research on agenda setting and framing has incorporated new methods for analyzing news content and effects. The theory was developed at a time that people still read newspapers, and there were only a few sources of broadcast news for people to turn to for information. In today's Web 2.0 environment, there are thousands of sources of news, ranging from websites developed and maintained by legacy news media to user-generated content on sites such as BuzzFeed.

Traditional Method: Content Analysis and Opinion Polls. McCombs and Shaw's (1972) seminal study applied two research methods: interviews and content analysis of news stories. They interviewed people periodically to find out what people felt were the most important issues during the 1968 presidential election. They also conducted a content analysis of broadcast and print news to determine the media's agenda. Using this method, they found a strong correlation between the issues that the news media reported on and what people said were the most important issues. Later research has used similar methods but expanded on their sampling methods by content analyzing news for issue prominence and depth and analyzing large, random samples of voters via opinion polls to determine the relationship between news agendas, the issues people feel are important, and people's voting intentions.

Though studies using Pew and National Election Study data are more generalizable than the targeted method employed in the initial Chapel Hill study, agenda setting's underlying assumptions are causal: changes in the media's agenda and story frames cause changes in people's thinking about issues (Kosicki, 1993). Because the assumptions of the theory are causal, experiments are the best way to test the assumptions about first- and second-level agenda setting.

1980s and 1990s: Experiments. Agenda-setting research in the 1980s and 1990s moved away from relying on opinion polls to applying experimental methods to explore the assumptions about cognitive priming and test the causal assumptions of agenda setting (Iyengar & Kinder, 1987). Iyengar and Kinder conducted 14 experiments where they varied news content and tested for agenda and framing effects. They found that TV news had significant agenda setting effects. Much like research on other theories, field experiments and observational studies have also supported agenda setting's assumptions. For example, researchers have tracked online news coverage and correlated it with the frequency of topics being discussed online via social media and blogs (Roberts, Wanta, & Dzwo, 2002; Heim, 2013).

Web 2.0 Agenda-Setting Research: The Age of Big Data. **Big data** refers to massive datasets that collect information on people's online behaviors. Polls, even national random samples such as Gallup, still rely on self-reports, and experiments are very limited in the amount of insight they provide into the long-term, dynamic agenda-setting process. Big data, such as Google Trends, which tracks searches and news on topics, and tracking social media trends, provide a lot of information about what people are actually searching for and posting about online, referred to as online **buzz**. In terms of agenda setting, online buzz should align with the topics covered in the news media, and big data can be used to test whether or not this assumption holds up, though using online buzz to explore second-level news framing is much more complicated (Neuman, Guggenheim, Jang, & Bae, 2014).

Insight into Innovation Activity: Google Trends. There are useful, practical tools we can use for research online that will give us insight into people's issue agendas. For example, Google Trends can give us a glimpse of news coverage and trending search topics. Take a look at the top "What is" searches conducted via Google in 2014. What do these top searches tell us about the important issues in 2014?

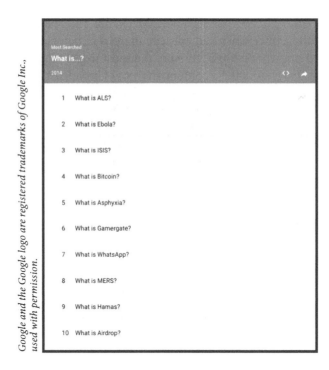

Challenges in the New Media Environment: Sampling and Content Analysis. Content analysis is a common method for analyzing news frames and news frame effects are typically confirmed using experiments (e.g., Iyengar, 1991). Though content studies cannot speak to the effects of frames on people's perceptions, they have been essential to exploring and confirming the different types of frames in news coverage. These content studies may be qualitative or quantitative analyses of the frames used in news stories (Neuman et al., 1992; Gamson, 1989).

One essential aspect of framing research, regardless of whether it is a qualitative exploration seeking to discover the types of frames in news stories or a quantitative study confirming the presence of predefined frames, is sampling news stories. Sampling blogs and news stories is increasingly difficult as search engines, such as Google News, "optimize" search results making the sample nonrandom. On the other hand, databases of news articles and broadcast transcripts, such as Lexis Nexis, have "blind spots" in news coverage (Weaver & Bimber, 2008), which means that there are popular news outlets not included in the databases. Many content analyses will analyze one or two of the most popular news sources to explore the news frames used to cover a specific topic. *The New York Times* and *USA Today* are common targets of analyses because they are regularly in the top 10 newspapers based on circulation (journalism.org, 2014). On the other hand, the top websites for news stories include Yahoo!-ABC and CNN (stateofthemedia.org, 2013), and the frames used by those media are under-researched. So, though experimental research on news frames has demonstrated that framing affects how people think about topics, the new media environment makes it increasingly difficult to identify the news stories people are most likely to have read when researching frames, limiting the generalizability and applicability of the findings from content analytic studies. As we move forward with agenda setting and framing research, looking at indicators such as the number of hits, shares, blog citations, and comments, will become essential to content studies for us to reach generalizable conclusions about the agenda items people are following and the frames that people are exposed to.

AGENDA SETTING AND FRAMING IN THE DIGITAL AGE ARE INTERACTIVE, DYNAMIC PROCESSES

There has been some speculation that agenda setting effects are slowly declining and will ultimately be eliminated in the new media environment. There is evidence that agenda setting effects are reduced in the new media environment because of the diversity of sources available for information online, but that traditional, legacy media still affect the topics that people think are important (Shehata & Strömbäck, 2013). We will discuss important changes brought about by Web 2.0 technology that are reducing, but not eliminating, the agenda-setting effect: People and other news media affect agendas online, but Internet news followers still tend to be more influenced by traditional media. Framing is also different online, as people can avoid frames, impose their own frames on issues, and the news media use different news frames in online news posts.

ONLINE AGENDA SETTING IS A BACK-AND-FORTH BETWEEN NEWS MEDIA AND USERS

News websites like CNN.com or FoxNews.com tend to have agendas that are similar to traditional news outlets, but blog and social media agendas can be very different (Maier, 2010). During the 2008 presidential campaign, for example, social media focused more on social issues like same-sex marriage. Traditional media, on the other hand, focused more on national economic issues and foreign affairs. This finding was replicated in a big data study in 2012, suggesting that the trend in social media toward focusing on social issues is likely to continue (Neuman et al., 2014).

These different agendas may be driven by social media users' preferences. On the social news websites Reddit and Digg, the stories that receive the most votes tend to be emotional, human interest stories and stories about technology, neither of which are national or international issues that are common topics in old media. Older news media tend to focus on conflicts and economics, such as jobs, national security, and the economy (Wasike, 2011). As people's news use continues to shift toward social media and away from traditional media, the implications for people's political and social agendas may prove to be dramatic, particularly if certain types of issues tend to be picked up or ignored by social media users.

The interpersonal, interactive nature of social media is changing the "top down" agenda-setting and framing process. Traditional news agendas drive social media agendas *and* social media drives news agendas (Neuman et al., 2014). Even early on when blogging was emerging as a news trend and citizen bloggers began tackling political issues, it was clear that social media may end up driving legacy media's agendas (Delwiche, 2005). The conversations that people have on social media, such as their Facebook posts, can influence the agendas of news shows (Jacobson, 2013). But, it still appears that traditional, legacy media influence the topics that people discuss on social media such as blogs (Heim, 2013) and they influence each other's agendas (Meraz, 2009). Thus, agenda setting now appears to be a two-way street; it is a dynamic, interactive process.

Though anyone can post "news" online, not all news sources are equally influential when setting people's agendas. People do consider the source of news online, and traditional media have more of an agenda setting effect compared to nontraditional news outlets like blogs (Dillman Carpentier, 2014). That being said, blogs, like the *Huffington Post*, and news aggregators like Yahoo! and Google News are increasingly prominent sources of news for online audiences (stateofthemedia.org, 2013). So, it appears that people may be going to nontraditional news sources, but these sources have less of an agenda setting effect than traditional newspapers and TV news broadcasts.

FRAMING ONLINE FOCUSES ON THE SOCIAL ASPECTS AND USERS CAN REFRAME ISSUES

Framing is also somewhat different online. We discussed cognitive dissonance in the previous unit and explained that people are more selective about news stories online. In particular, the frames used in news stories that are indicated in the headline and the subheads of news articles affect which news stories people choose to read (Zillman, Chen, Knobloch, & Callison, 2004). Even when we are exposed to a news story that we selected, if the issue is important to us personally we are less affected by the frame used in the news story (Lecheler, de Vreese, & Slothuus, 2009). This may explain why news outlets use different frames when posting online. Traditional news outlets tend to use conflict frames, but social media posts from news outlets focus more on human interest and technology frames (Wasike, 2013). Using these more popular online frames may help generate clicks.

We also are not passive consumers of information, and online we can be proactive by countering frames that we disagree with. People can reframe issues as they repost them to Facebook and Twitter, introducing a new, more interpersonal level of influence to the agenda-setting and framing process (Schweisberger, Billinson, & Chock, 2014). When you share a news story via Facebook or Twitter, chances are you editorialize it a bit or choose a quote from the article to highlight. This is an example of you framing issues for your followers. Political bloggers do this often, particularly conservative bloggers. They reject the dominant frames used by traditional news media and instead offer their own interpretations of issues and events (Meraz, 2011).

Similarly, the comments people make on online news stories can serve as a frame that influences how we interpret the content of the article. Both the frames in news stories and the comments people make on the stories affect readers' attitudes (Borah, 2014). Frames and comments also affect people's perceptions of the news content itself, with less civil comments sometimes improving people's perceptions of the news stories (Borah, 2013).

So, much like issue importance, issue interpretation effects are limited online compared to the media environment of the 1960s when agenda-setting theory was developed. We see weakening of traditional media's ability to set people's agendas and establish the dominant frames that guide how people think about news topics. We also see increased potential for individuals to influence the media's and other Internet users' agendas and interpretations through posting via social networks, blogging, and even commenting on news stories.

USING AGENDA SETTING AND FRAMING RESEARCH TO DESIGN SOCIAL MOVEMENTS

Agenda setting and framing are staples of public relations practice, but clearly they are changing in the new media environment. In the Web 2.0 environment, people are empowered to share their own frames and become agenda setters via websites and social media, and activist groups and organizations may be able to bypass the media and take their issues and frames directly to people via social media (Zoch, Collins, Fussell Sisco, & Supa, 2008). This is an important new development because historically social activists have had difficulty getting news media attention, and the frames used to cover protests tend to support the status quo and make activists look like deviants. Evidence for the usefulness of social media to get attention for a cause is offered in the research on recent social movements, such as Occupy Wall Street.

Read more about the history of the Occupy Wall Street movement in this *Vanity Fair* article from 2012: http://www.vanityfair.com/politics/2012/02/occupy-wall-street-201202

There were several ways that Occupy organizers used social media such as Twitter (Penney & Dadas, 2014): for **e-mobilization** to organize their protests; **citizen journalism**, where participants reported on protests in progress; **circulating information** by sharing links and retweeting; **editorializing** by expressing their own opinions; **deliberation** and debate about the issues at the heart of the movement; **strengthening ties** among like-minded people who were also involved in the movement; and employing political **e-tactics**, such as lobbying politicians and creating online petitions to support the cause. Even Occupy's use of YouTube was unique, as protesters used their phones to capture and post video of the protests and uploaded and shared news and entertainment videos related to their cause (Thorson et al., 2013).

The Occupy Movement did well using diverse online tools. Initially, traditional news media were dismissive of the Occupy Movement (DeLuca, Lawson, & Sun, 2012). Within weeks of the initial protests in New York, the news agenda shifted to focus on the very issues that the protestors were bringing to the forefront: income inequality and the stalled U.S. economy. Moreover, Occupy created significant online buzz with its early protests and social media strategies.

Take, for example, this Google Trend analysis of buzz about the Occupy movement and income inequality:

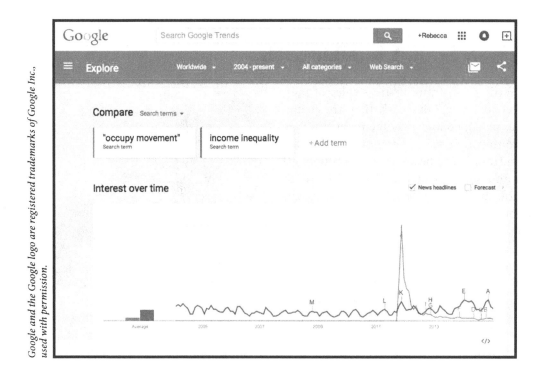

Notice the subtle increase in buzz that occurred at the start of the movement and the heightened buzz about income inequality that persisted into 2015. Thus, Occupy was able to influence both the traditional news media's agenda and the social media agenda.

Though they did well influencing the media's and public's agenda, Occupy did not do well reigning in the frames used to cover their protests. Traditional media framed Occupy as frivolous and disorganized, and right-leaning blogs framed them as social deviants. But, they were able to communicate directly to a wide audience, and their framing of the issue as one of "equality" was effective throughout their new media messages.

There are several takeaways from the Occupy Movement that we can consider as potential participants, practitioners, or even observers of activism. First, there are many *tools* at our disposal to generate buzz around an issue, and using diverse tools together (online petitions, hashtags, social media, websites, and video sharing) can help generate buzz. Second, the *clarity* of the activist cause is important. Even in the absence of central leadership, as was the case with Occupy, having a clear and succinct message (e.g., "We are the 99 percent" as a motto or "equality" as a buzzword) across channels is important. Being "on message" is essential to generating the numbers needed to influence the media's agenda and also supports the frames that the movement wants to promote. That being said, the third insight from the Occupy movement is the importance of *participation*. One person or one small group working alone, even with a sound social media strategy and message, cannot create Internet buzz that will get the attention of traditional news media and the general public. The key features of social media center on participation: users can create media, share it, and comment on it. Occupy got people to participate, this generated buzz, and the buzz got the attention of traditional news media and put their issues on the public's agenda.

CONCLUSION

For years, agenda setting and framing generated hundreds of research articles, most of which pointed to the effects that the news media have on the issues that people think are important and how people think about those issues (McCombs & Shaw, 1993). More recently, research that looked at social media and blog trends suggests that the media's ability to set agendas and frame issues still exists, but is slowly eroding as people take up opinion leadership roles via social media. Gradually, through blogs, comments, and social networks, people are also affecting the media's agenda, leading to a much more complex, dynamic process. This is both a unique challenge and an opportunity for marketers, social activists, and campaigners. Participative social media allows us to take our message—the issues we care about and want to promote—directly to people and, through building an online base of active supporters, we can influence the media's agenda and promote the issue frames that help our cause.

ASSIGNMENTS

1. Work in a group to develop the front page of this week's campus newspaper. After having time for discussion, provide a list of the top three stories on campus, a headline and a lead paragraph for each story, and indicate which of the three stories will be featured above the fold with an image. Present your group's plan to the class. Then reflect on how each group's agendas and frames were different:

   - How are the other group's agenda items different from your own group's agenda items? What are the implications of these differences for student readers?

   - How are the news items framed in other groups' plans? What are the implications of the frames they chose in terms of affecting student readers?

   - Did the other groups list stories your group did not consider? Do you think the stories they listed are more or less newsworthy than the stories your group listed? Why or why not?

2. Look up a recent news topic using Google Trends (www.google.com/trends). Check what correlates with searches for that news topic in Google Correlate (www.google.com/trends/correlate). What do the search trends tell us about the importance of the topic? What do the correlations with the trending topic tell us about what people are thinking about in relation to the topic?

REFERENCES

Seminal Texts:

Gamson, W. A. (1989). News as framing. *American Behavioral Scientist, 33*, 157–161.

McCombs, M., & Shaw, D. (1972). The agenda setting function of mass media. *Public Opinion Quarterly, 36*, 176–187.

White, D. M. (1950). The "gate keeper": A case study in the selection of news. *Journalism Quarterly, 27*, 383–390.

Academic Sources:

Borah, P. (2013) Interactions of news frames and incivility in the political blogosphere: Examining perceptual outcomes, *Political Communication*, *30*, 456–473. http://dx.doi.org/10.1080/10584609.2012.737426

Borah, P. (2014). Does it matter where you read the news story? Interaction of incivility and news frames in the political blogosphere. *Communication Research*, *41*(6), 809–827.

DeLuca, K., Lawson, S., & Sun, Y. (2012). Occupy Wall Street on the public screens of social media: The many framings of the birth of a protest movement. *Communication, Culture & Critique*, *5*(4), 483–509.

Delwiche, A. (2005). Agenda–setting, opinion leadership, and the world of Web logs. *First Monday*, 7.

Dillman Carpentier, F. R. (2014). Agenda setting and priming effects based on information presentation: Revisiting accessibility as a mechanism explaining agenda setting and priming. *Mass Communication & Society*, *17*(4), 531–552.

Heim, K. (2013). Framing the 2008 Iowa democratic caucuses political blogs and sedon-level intermedia agenda setting. *Journalism & Mass Communication Quarterly*, *90*, 500–519.

Iyengar, S., & Kinder, D. R. (1987). *News that matters: Television and American opinion.* Chicago: University of Chicago Press.

Iyengar, S. (1991). *Is anyone responsible? How the television news frames political issues.* Chicago: University of Chicago Press.

Jacobson, S. (2013). Does audience Participation on Facebook influence the news agenda? A case study of *The Rachel Maddow Show*. *Journal of Broadcasting & Electronic Media*, *57*(3), 338–355.

Journalism.org. (2014). Newspapers: Circulation at the top 5 U.S. newspapers reporting Monday-Friday averages (2012–2013). *Pew Research Journalism Project*. Retrieved from http://www.journalism.org/media-indicators/average-circulation-at-the-top-5-u-s-newspapers-reporting-monday-friday-averages/

Kosicki, G. M. (1993), Problems and opportunities in agenda-setting research. *Journal of Communication*, *43*, 100–127.

Lecheler, S., de Vreese, C., & Slothuus, R. (2009). Issue importance as a moderator of framing effects. *Communication Research*, *36*(3), 400–425.

Maier, S. (2010). All the news fit to post? Comparing news content on the web to newspapers, television, and radio. *Journalism & Mass Communication Quarterly*, *87*(3/4), 548–562.

McCombs, M. (2004). *Setting the agenda: The mass media and public opinion.* Cambridge, UK: Polity Press.

McCombs, M. E., & Shaw, D. L. (1993). The evolution of agenda-setting research: Twenty-five years in the marketplace of ideas. *Journal of Communication*, *43*, 58–67.

Meraz, S. (2009). Is there an elite hold? Traditional media to social media agenda setting influence in blog networks. *Journal of Computer-Mediated Communication, 14*, 682–707.

Meraz, S. (2011). The fight for "how to think": Traditional media, social networks, and issue interpretation. *Journalism, 12*(1), 107–127.

Neuman, W. R., Just, M. R., Crigler, A. N. (1992). *Common knowledge: News and the construction of political meaning.* Chicago: Chicago University Press.

Neuman, W. R., Guggenheim, L., Jang, S. O., & Bae, S. Y. (2014). The dynamics of public attention: Agenda-setting theory meets big data. *Journal of Communication, 64*, 193–214.

Penney, J., & Dadas, C. (2014). (Re)Tweeting in the service of protest: Digital composition and circulation in the Occupy Wall Street movement. *New Media & Society, 16*(1), 74–90.

Robert, M., Wanta, W., & Dzwo, T.-H. (2002). Agenda setting and issue salience online. *Communication Research, 29*, 452–465.

Schweisberger, V., Billinson, J., & Chock, T. M. (2014). Facebook, the Third-Person Effect, and the Differential Impact Hypothesis. *Journal of Computer-Mediated Communication, 19*(3), 403–413.

Shehata, A., & Strömbäck, J. (2013). Not (Yet) a New Era of Minimal Effects: A Study of Agenda Setting at the Aggregate and Individual Levels. *International Journal of Press/Politics, 18*(2), 234–255.

Stateofthemedia.org. (2013). The state of the news media 2013: An annual report on American journalism. *Pew Research Center's Project for Excellence in Journalism.* Retrieved from http://www.stateofthemedia.org/2013/digital-as-mobile-grows-rapidly-the-pressures-on-news-intensify/digital-by-the-numbers/

Thorson, K., Driscoll, K., Ekdale, B., Edgerly, S., Thompson, L. G., Schrock, A., Swartz, L., Vraga, E. K., & Wells, C. (2013). YouTube, Twitter, and the Occupy Movement. *Information, Communication & Society, 16*(3), 421–451.

Wasike, B. S. (2011). Framing social news sites: An analysis of the top stories on Reddit and Digg. *Southwest Mass Communication Journal, 27*, 57–67.

Wasike, B. S. (2013). Framing the news is 140 characters: how social media editors frame the news and interact with audiences via Twitter. *Global Media Journal, 6*, 5–23.

Weaver, D. A., & Bimber, B. (2008). Finding news stories: A comparison of searches using LexisNexis and Google News. *Journalism & Mass Communication Quarterly, 85*(3), 515–530.

Zillmann, D., Lei, C., Knobloch, S., & Callison, C. (2004). Effects of lead framing on selective exposure to Internet news reports. *Communication Research, 31*(1), 58–81.

Zoch, L. M., Collins, E. L., Sisco, H., & Supa, D. H. (2008). Empowering the activist: Using framing devices on activist organizations' web sites. *Public Relations Review, 34*(4), 351–358.

Examples:

Adams, R. J. (2014). Consumer deception of unwarranted product disparagement? The case of lean, finely textured beef. *Business and Society Review, 119*, 221–246.

Schultz, E. J. (2012). Beef industry bruised by "pink slime" battle. *Advertising Age, 83*(14), 2–20.

Further Reading Online:

Agenda Setting and Framing Example with Kathleen Hall Jamieson: http://youtu.be/Gp5hEWsJxQA

CHAPTER 24

CULTURAL STUDIES AND CULTIVATION

OUTCOMES

- *Knowledge:* Learn how media depictions affect people's perceptions and ideologies.
- *Skill:* Recognize the mean world effect in mediated messages and how people commodify themselves via social media.

Cultivation theory explains that mediated messages affect our perception of reality because media is the dominant storyteller in our culture (Gerbner, 1998). These stories, or narratives, teach us what people are like and how things are and so we learn from them in much the same way people used to learn culture and norms from the stories told by their parents and grandparents. Similarly, cultural studies explains that mediated messages affect our culture, and add that a small group of powerful media owners control the mediated messages we consume.

Both of these areas of study are focused on **media depictions**, or how the media represents reality in inaccurate, skewed, and self-serving ways. Those misrepresentations have implications for how we perceive reality. In particular, we look at representations of social class, gender, race, sexual orientation, and culture to consider how lessons about consumerism, violence and crime, and other people may lead us to a skewed perception of reality.

Even as we move toward an age of user-generated content, we still live in an environment where relatively few companies control and censor the media content we consume. Whether it is through challenges to net neutrality that affect user experience on websites, algorithms that determine the posts we see on social networking websites, or software that detects and restricts certain types of user-generated content, corporations still control a lot of what we see, hear, and read online and this has implications for our perceptions of reality.

MAIN IDEA

According to cultural studies, major media companies control the media messages that we consume, and therefore the media messages that are shaping our culture are also a form of social control. Cultivation theory explains that inaccurate media depictions cultivate, or develop in people, inaccurate views of the real world because mass media narratives depict a skewed and inaccurate view of reality.

KEY CONCEPTS FROM CULTURAL STUDIES

Many of the concepts from cultural studies come from **Marxism**. The primary concern of this area of study is that there are ongoing class divisions that benefit and serve the interests of rich, powerful, and socially connected people, and exploit and oppress the poor and working class.

- **Media ownership** is about who owns the media and the profit goals of media companies. In traditional media, very few media companies control the majority of the media we consume via TV, movies, newspapers, magazines, and even in books. Thus, relatively few people have a significant amount of power in our culture.

- **Hegemony** is when one social group controls another social group. This is not necessarily done through physical force or direct orders, but can be done subtly by controlling the messages that shape a person's ideology, general complacency and willingness to accept those messages.

- **Ideology** is a system of beliefs and norms that constitute a culture. Getting back to media ownership, if relatively few companies control most of the media messages we consume, and media messages affect our ideology, then those media companies are a hegemonic power in our society that shape our culture *and we let them do it.*

- **Political economy** is one's power in society. Cultural studies theorists argue that the rich maintain their political economy by maintaining their control over the major sources of socialization in society. This, in effect, silences and suppresses the poor and working class, ensuring that they remain poor and working class.

Insight into Innovation Activity: What Data Might Google Have on You? Google owns Gmail, Google search, YouTube, Google+, Google Maps, Google Chrome, and much more. For a list of some of Google's products as of 2014, check out this list: http://www.minterest.org/google-products-services-you-probably-dont-know/. How many Google products do you use? Thinking about how you use these products, what might Google know about you? How might this affect the content they recommend to you when you're searching the Internet or YouTube? How does this affect your access to entertainment and information online?

KEY ASSUMPTIONS OF CULTIVATION THEORY (GERBNER & GROSS, 1976)

Insight into Innovation Activity: Watch George Gerbner summarize cultivation theory.

1. Media as a storyteller with the goal of selling products: http://youtu.be/ylhqasb1chl

2. Violent media content: http://youtu.be/2PHxTr-59hE

3. Desensitization to violence: http://youtu.be/msfu8YCCc8Q

Cultivation theory builds on cultural studies by outlining specific media effects. Like cultural studies, cultivation theory explains that media ownership determines the depictions we see in media content, that media depictions are skewed and inaccurate, and cultivation theory adds that there are specific, testable media effects.

- *The mass media is a dominant story teller in society.* The stories, or narratives that we see in movies and on TV serve as a source of socialization.

- *The media depicts a skewed image of the world and people then perceive the world in keeping with those skewed depictions.* Early cultivation research focused on violence. A systematic study of TV content demonstrated that the media depicted a world that was more violent and people were less trustworthy than in reality (Gerbner & Gross, 1976). Thus, heavy media consumers, or people who consumed the most content, develop a sense that the world is a scary place and they tend to overestimate the likelihood that they would be a victim of a violent crime. This is called the **mean world syndrome**.

- *The media blurs, blends, and bends to create a mainstreamed view of reality* (Gerbner, 1987). It *blurs* the differences between distinct political ideologies; *blends* together social and racial groups into one homogenous mainstream; and *bends* media messages to promote their corporate goals. This leads to **mainstreaming effects**, or one dominant, homogenous, middle-of-the-road view of reality that is not entirely accurate. This includes reinforcing stereotypes of social groups and diminishing differences in perceptions and values commonly associated with different regions, political ideologies, and social groups (see Morgan, Shanahan, & Signorielli, 2009 for a review). Put another way, mainstreaming reduces individual differences in perceptions and worldviews that we would typically expect.

- *There are circumstances that may enhance cultivation, such as **resonance**, or having personal experiences similar to those depicted in the media.* So, people who live in a high crime region may experience more of a mean world effect because crimes depicted in media would resonate with their experiences (Gerbner et al., 1980; Shrum & Bischak, 2001).

- *The cultivation effect may be the result of cognitive processes, whereby seeing vivid depictions in the media makes examples more accessible in memory* (Shrum, 1995, 1996). This is the process of priming that we discussed in the chapter on agenda setting. Having media examples primed repeatedly—both real examples from the news and examples from entertainment media—may make them seem more prevalent when people are making judgments.

EXAMPLE OF THEORY IN WEB 2.0: THE HISTORY OF YOUTUBE

In 2015, YouTube celebrated its 10th anniversary. Here are Pew's five facts about YouTube from that anniversary (Anderson, 2015):

- One-third of adults who use the Internet have posted a video online

- Animals, pets, and everyday people are popular in online video

- YouTube is second only to Facebook in the number of users

- Young people, African Americans, and Hispanics use YouTube the most

- People are getting more and more of their news from YouTube

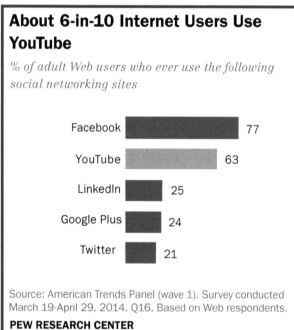

About 6-in-10 Internet Users Use YouTube

% of adult Web users who ever use the following social networking sites

Facebook	77
YouTube	63
LinkedIn	25
Google Plus	24
Twitter	21

Source: American Trends Panel (wave 1). Survey conducted March 19-April 29, 2014. Q16. Based on Web respondents.

PEW RESEARCH CENTER

"5 facts about online video, for YouTube's 10th birthday," Pew Research Center, Washington, DC (February, 2015) http://www.pewresearch. org/fact-tank/2015/02/12/5-facts-about-online-video-for-youtubes-10th-birthday/.

These findings from Pew suggest that YouTube may break down some of the mainstreaming content and effects that cultivation researchers have warned about. Arguably, the ability to post user generated videos should give voice to traditionally underrepresented groups.

Morgan et al. (2009) argued that "even when new digital delivery systems threaten dominant interests, they are quickly swallowed up within existing institutional structure" (p. 44). They used YouTube as an example of this process. The once free online video sharing website was "absorbed by dominant players," specifically Google, and YouTube is "already being exploited" to benefit advertisers (p. 44). They go on to argue that the proliferation of video via the Internet, video on demand, and digital video recordings (DVRs) may intensify cultivation. Morgan et al. expect that there will be "deeper penetration and integration of the dominant patterns of images and messages" that has been repeatedly found in cultivation research (p. 46). This is due, in part, to the continued concentration of media ownership, including concentration of website ownership. Thus, in the on-demand, user-generated, Web 2.0 world, we may experience *more* rather than less of a mean world and mainstreaming effect.

Beyond cultivation, Google's purchase of YouTube and integration of all of Google's services into one user account also raised concerns. Owning so many services and collecting user data from across their products, Google can collect data on billions of people that can be used for tracking and

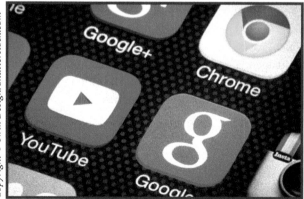

marketing. This is a major concern in the United States, as we confront issues such as surveillance, data use, and data security. Both the U.S. government and major corporations can use big data, such as the information collected about web use across Google products, to track individuals or to target groups of people. Major Internet companies like Google can sell our data, use it for their own marketing purposes, and are charged with maintaining the security of our data. From a cultural studies perspective, this is a particularly troublesome opportunity for social control by increasing Google's social and economic power through control over information and media content.

METHODS: INSTITUTIONAL, MESSAGE, AND CULTIVATION ANALYSIS

Cultural studies is a type of **media criticism** that involves critiquing the ownership, production features, and social consequences of media messages. Cultural approaches critique the ideology created and reinforced in media content, how message content and control affect people's political economy, and how these messages relate to corporate ownership and power. Critical cultural studies is one approach to the institutional analysis that cultivation theory includes.

The **Cultural Indicators Project**, which is an ongoing study of cultivation, involves three elements: looking at the corporate profits that drive specific types of content, looking at media messages to see how reality is depicted, and survey studies of the perceptions that media messages cultivate in media users (Gerbner et al., 2002).

- **Institutional analysis** looks at the ways that media ownership and profit motives affect the media messages we see.
- **Message analysis** is the careful content analysis of media messages to look at trends in media depictions of people and events.
- **Cultivation analysis** looks at how the trends in media messages affect people's perceptions.

In a summary of findings from the Cultural Indicators Project, Gerber concluded:

- Concentrated media ownership decreases the diversity of programming and media depictions.
- Women, the elderly, African Americans, Latinos, people who are physically disabled, and the poor are underrepresented on TV.
- Villains are disproportionately male, poor, young, and Latino or foreign born.
- Being a victim of violence is overrepresented, particularly among main characters.
- Violence is prevalent even in kids' cartoons, and old women, mentally ill characters, and Hispanic characters are often the perpetrators of violence.
- Heavy TV viewers overestimate the likelihood of being a victim of violent crime, are more afraid to walk around alone at night, are more apprehensive, and tend to take more protective actions like buying guns.

So, for example, cultivation studies that look at violence often apply the **violence index** to analyze media content. The violence index looks at the number of programs in a sample that contain violence, the average number of violent behaviors across programs, the average number of violent behaviors per hour, the number of violent perpetrators versus victims, and the percentage of characters killed (Signorielli & Gerbner, 1995). After applying the violence index to a sample of media content, a survey is distributed to determine if is there is a cultivation effect among media users that reflects the trends found in content. So, in a violence study, researchers would ask people to estimate the likelihood that they would be the victim of a violent crime. Results have indicated that people who watch more media, particularly violent media, overestimate the likelihood that they will be a victim of crime. From an institutional standpoint, even though there may be some negative effects on viewers, crime is still a popular element of media messages because it attracts audiences and increases profits.

Insight into Innovation Activity: Check out this list of cultivation research published between 1969 and 2013. Cultivation has been a particularly *heuristic* theory, generating hundreds of studies: http://people. umass.edu/mmorgan/CulturalIndicatorsBibliography.pdf

After looking through publications, what do you think is missing? Is most of the research in cultivation keeping pace with the changes in the media content we consume now? Is it outdated? What areas of study should cultivation researchers expand to include?

Typically, cultivation is assessed quantitatively. Studies that report the results of message and cultivation analysis, when examined as a body of evidence, reveal a small cultivation effect (Morgan & Shanahan, 1997). Experiments, such as Shrum's research program that tests specific media content, have shown relatively consistent cultivation effects as well. The relatively small effect sizes led researchers to argue that cultivation research may benefit from adopting more critical approaches, such as the critical cultural studies approach, and focusing more attention on "political, economic, and legal" issues as part of institutional analysis (p. 42).

There is also the potential for cultivation, particularly the cultural indicators approach, to lose relevance as people turn away from TV to user-generated and on-demand content. At the same time, cultural studies may increase in relevance as power dynamics shift in the new media environment. Cultivation studies of binge watching, viral video, and popular streaming content could sustain the research program, though these individual-level differences in media use may prove to diminish the generalized mainstreaming effect that cultivation predicts.

CULTIVATION AND THE MEAN, SCARY (ONLINE) WORLD

Online news and violent urban legends. Early cultivation research suggested that following a lot of news, particularly local news, can cultivate perceptions of a mean world (e.g., O'Keefe & Reid-Nash, 1987). This is due to the "if it bleeds, it leads" practice in journalism. Crime is easy to cover and frightening content is entertaining to audiences (Altheide, 2000). Thus, rare or isolated crimes are covered extensively in the news, leading to people cultivating exaggerated estimates of the likelihood of being a victim of a crime. Take, for example, Casey Anthony, who was accused of murdering her daughter. In addition to overwhelming media coverage, social media was also abuzz with opinions, content sharing, and details of the trial. These messages may all work together to cultivate the perception that these types of crimes are prevalent given the amount of coverage they receive.

Altheide (2000) argued that coverage of crime has led us to be a more fearful society, even when we find out that the stories are inaccurate or entirely false. There are, of course, negative social consequences of living in fear: people become easier to control and manipulate and become more aggressive. But fear is also profitable for companies because people are drawn to it, are more controllable due to feeling it, and will purchase goods and services to reestablish their sense of security. From the cultural studies view, this increases corporate power in our lives.

It isn't hard to think of examples of viral stories and even urban legends spread through social media and e-mail that cultivate fear of crime. Particular types of real news stories go viral online, such as missing children, animal abuse, and, particularly in 2015, mass shootings and police brutality. Many urban legends have been revived and recirculated via the Internet as well. There are tools like FactCheck websites and Snopes dedicated to correcting misinformation spread online, but it is difficult to combat the misinformation. The combination of violent, viral news stories and urban legends warning about predators can create an online message environment that further promotes perceptions of a mean and scary world.

Insight into Innovation Example: Craigslist and Fear of Online Predators. Check out Snopes' debunked crime stories that have been spread via e-mail and social media: http://snopes.com/crime/crime.asp. Many of these crime stories come in the form of a warning, encouraging people to protect themselves and their children from dangerous predators. These messages are part of a larger *message system* we consume both online and in traditional media, from news coverage of brutal murders, serial killers, and terrorism to entertaining crime dramas and action movies. The entire message system bombards us with messages about a violent and scary world. The Internet is one more vehicle for delivering this frightening content.

Take, for example, stories of "Craigslist killers." There are more than a dozen Snopes entries about Craigslist that investigate viral online posts. A quick Google News search reveals over 33,000 news stories about Craigslist murders. Together, online urban legends and news stories may cultivate a perception that Craigslist is unsafe. There have been around 60 murders linked to Craigslist since 2009 (Law Street, 2014). This sounds like a lot, but let's think about the numbers. As of 2015, Craigslist is the 12th most visited website in America (Alexa, 2015). Now let's look at some of Craigslist's own 2015 stats (Craigslist, 2015):

- There are 60 million people using Craigslist every month.

- There are more than 80 million ads posted to Craigslist every month.

- There are over 700 local Craigslist sites.

Not to be dismissive of the loss of life, or the thousands of other crimes and scams perpetrated using Craigslist, but 60 or so murders out of *billions* of postings over the course of 6 years is a very, very small incidence. Still, in a small, nonrandom study by Gliph in 2012, very few people who used Craigslist strongly agreed that they could trust others who use the site, and users didn't want people on Craigslist to have their phone numbers, e-mail addresses, or to know their full names. Looking at the stats on Craigslist, are people's concerns about the website's safety justified? Why or why not?

WE ARE ALL COMMODITIES BEING BOUGHT AND SOLD

In addition to violent content and the mean world effect, mainstreamed capitalist values are also prevalent online. One glimmer of hope in social media is everyday people participating in journalism, also called **citizen journalism**. Citizen journalism, such as CNN's iReports, or people live tweeting events as they unfold, should increase people's political economy. Balancing out that potential, however, is the profit motive behind citizen journalism: it is free reporting in the service of major media corporations, and it serves to boost news organizations by generating clicks and web traffic (Vujnovic et al., 2014). There also isn't much evidence that online news is overwhelmingly different than traditional news outlets in terms of the stories they cover or giving more or less voice to "average citizens" (Curran et al., 2013).

Audience and Prosumer as a Commodity. Interestingly, in the user-generated environment, the people who create videos and posts may be seen as a corporate commodity (Fuchs, 2012). They are both creating the content that generates traffic and they are part of the traffic that generates revenue for companies. Arguably, this is exploitation of everyday people because people are giving a commodity (their time and the content they created) to media companies, who then profit from that content (Fisher, 2012). The concept of "prosumer commodity" drives this area of research and critique in cultural studies (Fuchs, 2009). **Prosumers** are people who both create and consume content; they play both producer and consumer roles. **Commodities** are those things that can be marketed and/or sold to make a profit.

Though there are noncommodified places to share content, such as nonprofits like Wikipedia, much of the Internet is commodified, or owned by a major media company like Google, Yahoo, or Facebook for the purpose of generating corporate profits. Fuchs (2009) puts it this way:

> The users who "Google" data, upload or watch videos on YouTube, upload or browse personal images on Flickr, or accumulate friends with whom they exchange content or communicate online on social networking platforms like MySpace or Facebook, constitute an audience commodity that is sold to advertisers. (p. 81)

We also are essentially selling our personal information to websites: they give us free access, and we let them have our personal information, such as our location, age, occupation, education, marital status, and so much more (Campbell, 2011). Our Facebook, Twitter, and YouTube account information provides marketable user data in terms of how we use those media, allows us to create content to draw in new users to be marketed to, and provides companies with our personal information, which they can use to sell targeted advertising. Thinking of it this way, all of those "free" accounts we have are worth an awful lot of money.

Cultivation of Consumer and Material Perceptions. So, audiences are a commodity that major media companies, including Internet companies, can buy and sell for advertising purposes. It is common knowledge that media companies create TV content to attract viewers and sell advertising space. But beyond the advertisements, the content on TV and in movies can be "sold" in the form of product placement. **Product placement** is when companies pay to have their products featured in media content: everything from the brands of food that TV and movie characters eat, the beverages they drink, the branded clothes they wear, to the cars they drive, can be placed there by companies as a form of advertisement. From a cultivation theory perspective, seeing characters and situations that resonate with audiences may make product placement that much more effective (Russell, 1998). From a cultivation standpoint, product placement can make consumption of specific brands seem really common. Coca Cola, Ford, and Apple are some of the most commonly placed brands.

There is similar potential for product placement via social networks. The brands and products we "like" on Facebook, for example, can be used to promote that product to our friends. Celebrities with large social media followings are also used as paid product promoters, and they post product endorsements or images of themselves using products. These social media posts also further cultivate consumer culture.

Both cultivation research and cultural studies point to the cultivation of consumer goals and values through media content. More subtle than product placement, media *depictions of lifestyles* reflect material wealth and consumption (O'Guinn & Shrum, 1997). People who watch media content that depicts affluent lifestyles tend to cultivate exaggerated perceptions of others' consumption of luxury goods. Similarly, social media like Pinterest may cultivate inaccurate perceptions of others' lives, as the ideas, projects, and products that people pin can create a perception of other people's lifestyles.

Insight into Innovation Activity: Consumer TV. Take a moment to reflect on how you think other people live. How big and well-designed are their homes? How new is their furniture and decor? Do most people have granite countertops, organized first-floor laundry rooms, and tiled master bathrooms with Jacuzzi tubs? How much does it cost them to have those things?

Chances are, your expectations are linked to your TV use as well as other things, like what you've seen of others' homes on Facebook, Pinterest, and in blogs. Shows like HGTV's remodeling shows make these luxuries seem common and attainable, even though they are very expensive upgrades to have in your own home and often financially impossible to have for lower and middle income homeowners.

Copyright © Dziekan/Retna Ltd./Corbis

HGTV *Design Stars*

🗨 CONCLUSION

As we will discuss in the next chapter on behavioral theories of media effects, perceptual theories of media effects could also generalize to our Web 2.0 lives, though research has yet to catch up with technological changes. Consider, for example, the decades of cultivation research that point to the skewing effects of inaccurate media depictions about class, race, gender, sexuality, and wealth. How might depictions that we see through social media, like personal blogs and Facebook posts, and user-generated content like YouTube videos, cultivate inaccurate perceptions of our society and of other people? How might our regular diet of frightening news and warnings about online predators make us more fearful of others?

Beyond just the behaviors and lifestyles depicted in media content, cultivation and cultural studies also challenge us to think about media ownership and profits. When we were a captive TV audience, we were packaged and sold to advertisers. The same is true online, only now we are both creating the content that attracts the audience (for free!) and we are also the consumer audience being advertised to.

The challenge to be a media literate, informed, and aware consumer is that much more necessary online. Cultivation theory and cultural studies challenge us to consider the corporate ownership of the online content we consume, particularly the things we don't see like cookies used to track our online behavior and algorithms based on our past website use and demographics, as we support corporate profits through generating clicks and ad revenue. Also, we may still culivate skewed perceptions from online media content, and indeed our cultivation of skewed perceptions may be more pronounced as we are able to binge on certain types of content and see the same content repeatedly shared via social networks. So, even though TV may be slowly falling by the wayside, cultivation may be equally, or even more, pronounced in our Web 2.0 lives.

ASSIGNMENTS

1. **Write a cultivation critique.** Find a viral YouTube video with 100 million or more views. Write a cultivation critique of the video:
   a. Does it promote mean world syndrome through showing verbal or physical violence?
   b. Does it depict or promote mainstreamed and / or typical American values?
   c. Does it depict stereotypes of racial or socioeconomic groups?
   d. Who created the video? Did they have a profit motive? How might this have affected the content of the video?

2. **Self-reflection: Self as a Commodity.** Reflect on the ways that you are a commodity to the websites you are registered with: What information have you provided that these websites can sell to third parties? Have you played the role of prosumer on websites? Have you helped attract a larger audience for websites?

REFERENCES

Seminal Texts:

Gerbner, G. (1987). Television's populist brew: The three B's. *Etc., 44*, 2–7.

Gerbner, G., & Gross, L. (1976). Living with television: The violence profile. *Journal of Communication, 26*, 172–199.

Academic Articles:

Altheide, D. L. (2010). Mass media, crime, and the discourses of fear. *Hedgehog Review, 5*, 9–25.

Anderson, M. (2015). 5 facts about online video, for YouTube's 10th birthday. *Pew Research Center Fact Tank*. Retrieved from http://www.pewresearch.org/fact-tank/2015/02/12/5-facts-about-online-video-for-youtubes-10th-birthday/

Campbell, J. E. (2011). It takes an iVillage: Gender, labor, and community in the age of television-Internet convergence. *International Journal of Communication, 5*, 492–510.

Curran, J., Coen, S., Aalberg, T., Hayashi, K., Jones, P. K., Splendore, S., Papthanassopoulos, S., Rowe, D., & Tiffen, R. (2013). Internet revolution revisited: a comparative study of online news. *Media, Culture & Society, 35*(7), 880–897.

Fisher, E. (2012). How less alienation creates more exploitation? Audience labour on social network sites. *TripleC: Cognition, Communication, Co-Operation, 10*(2), 171–183.

Fuchs, C. (2009). Information and communication technologies and society: A contribution to the critique of the political economy of the Internet. *European Journal of Communication*, *24*(1), 69–87.

Fuchs, C. (2012). Google capitalism. *TripleC: Cognition, Communication, Co-Operation*, *10*(1), 42–48.

Gerbner, G. (1998). Cultivation analysis: An overview. *Mass Communication & Society*, *1*, 175–194.

Gerbner, G., Gross, L., Morgan, M., & Signorielli, N. (1980). The "mainstreaming" of America: Violence profile no. 11. *Journal of Communication*, *30*, 10–29.

Gerbner, G., Gross, L., Morgan, M., Signorielli, N., & Shanahan, J. (2002). Growing up with television: Cultivation processes. In J. Bryant & D. Zillman (Eds.), *Media effects: Advances in theory and research* (2nd ed.). Mahwah, NJ: Lawrence Erlbaum.

Signorielli, N, & Gerbner, G. (1995). Violence on television: The cultural indicators project. *Journal of Broadcasting & Electronic Media*, *39*, 278–283.

Morgan, M., Shanahan, J., & Signorielli, N. (2009). Growing up with television: Cultivation processes. In J. Bryant & M. B. Oliver (Eds.), *Media effects: Advances in theory and research* (pp. 34–49). New York: Routledge.

Morgan, M., & Shanahan, J. (1997). Two decades of cultivation research: An appraisal and meta-analysis. In B. R. Burleson (Ed.), *Communication Yearbook*, *20* (pp. 1–45). New York: Routledge.

O'Guinn, T. C., & Shrum, L. J. (1997). The role of television in the construction of consumer reality. *Journal of Consumer Research*, *23*(4), 278–294.

O'Keefe, G. J., & Reid-Nash, K. (1987). Crime news and real-world blues: The effects of the media on social reality. *Communication Research: An International Quarterly*, *14*, 147–163.

Russell, C. A. (1998). Toward a framework of product placement: Theoretical propositions. *Advances in Consumer Research*, *25*, 357–362.

Shrum, L. J. (1995). Assessing the social influence of television: A social cognition perspective on cultivation effects. *Communication Research*, *22*, 402–429.

Shrum, L. J. (1996). Psychological processes underlying cultivation effects: Further tests of construct accessibility. *Human Communication Research*, *22*, 482–509.

Shrum, L. J. (2007). The implication of survey method for measuring cultivation effects. *Human Communication Research*, *33*, 64–80.

Shrum, L. J., & Darmanin Bischak, V. (2001). Mainstreaming, resonance, and impersonal impact: Testing moderators of the cultivation effect for estimates of crime risk. *Human Communication Research*, *27*, 187–215.

Vujnovic, M., Singer, J. B., Paulussen, S., Heinonen, A., Reich, Z., Quandt, T., & Domingo, D. (2010). Exploring the political-economic factors of participatory journalism. *Journalism Practice*, 4(3), 285–296.

Examples:

Alexa. (2015). *Craigslist.org*. Retrieved from http://www.alexa.com/siteinfo/craigslist.org

Craigslist. (2015). *FactSheet*. Retrieved from http://www.craigslist.org/about/factsheet

Gliph. (2012). *Craigslist survey results: Users want privacy, anonymity*. Retrieved from https://blog.gli.ph/2012/08/03/craigslist-privacy-and-anonymity-survey-results/

Law Street. (2014). *Killers of Craigslist*. Retrieved from http://lawstreetmedia.com/killers-craigslist/

CHAPTER 25

BEHAVIORAL MEDIA EFFECTS: SOCIAL LEARNING AND SPIRALS OF SILENCE

In this chapter, we look at theories related to the behavioral effects of mediated content: how we learn what we should and should not do by observing other people both in "real life" and via mediated channels. **Social cognitive theory** (SCT; also called social learning theory) explains that we may **model** the behaviors of others; we see another person do something and we may learn a new behavior. **Spiral of silence** theory explains that we may also infer what not to say or post by observing others and making inferences about their opinions. These theories give insight into the features of mediated messages that may lead to behavioral effects. We do not simply replicate every behavior we see on Facebook, TV, or in YouTube videos. Rather, as people who make judgments and inferences, we are susceptible to behavioral influence in *some* situations.

According to SCT, there are five factors that affect whether we model the behaviors we observe (Bandura, 2001):

1. *Memory* of the behavior,
2. *Forethought* about the consequences and outcomes of the behavior,
3. *Identification* with the person or character who depicted the behavior,
4. Our moral *self-regulation and reflection* on whether or not the behavior is justified, and
5. Our sense of *self-efficacy* in terms of actually doing the behavior.

Much like the elaboration likelihood model and theory of planned behavior in Unit 5, SCT explains that people are information processors: we interpret, evaluate, and decide. We do not blindly follow the lead of others.

We may also infer what we should or should not do, such as whether or not we should express an opinion on a controversial issue, by observing others via social media and traditional media.

Spiral of silence explains that there are particular conditions that affect whether or not some people express their opinions:

- When we feel that we have a **minority opinion**, or that most people disagree with us, we are less likely to speak out. This happens because many of us have a **fear of isolation**, or a fear of being a social outcast as a result of expressing an unpopular opinion.
- We determine whether our opinion is in the minority by looking at the opinions that others express, and get a **quasi-statistical** sense of approximately how popular or unpopular our opinion is.

Though not much research exists that applies SCT to Web 2.0 technologies, we can all probably think of examples of how people's behaviors can be affected by the types of content users post—from informational life hacks, to Pinterest project boards, to online instructional videos from Yumly and Food Network, to the behaviors we see our friends posting on Facebook—we have many new sources of behavioral information via Web 2.0. The spiral of silence, on the other hand, has been the subject of renewed interest as a result of Web 2.0, as researchers explore whether we are more empowered to express controversial opinions online compared to face-to-face.

As a word of caution as we proceed through this chapter: We often think of ourselves as immune to the effects of media and think of others as being greatly affected by that same content. This is called the **third-person effect** (Davison, 1983). But, as we will discuss in this chapter, there are sometimes subtle ways that others' behaviors—either fictional depictions in entertainment media or real-life friends and family members—may influence our own behavior.

 QUICK OVERVIEW OF OF SOCIAL LEARNING AND SPIRAL OF SILENCE

MAIN IDEA

SCT and Spiral of Silence both explain that we look to other people for information about what we ourselves should or should not do. This is a shift from **behaviorism**, or the idea that experiencing rewards and punishments taught people what they should and should not do. In other words, SCT explains **modeling** is one way we learn behavior: we observe and learn from what other people do. Spiral of silence explains that we're socially pressured to conform out of fear of becoming a social outcast.

SCT KEY ASSUMPTIONS (BANDURA, 2001)

The assumptions of SCT have been developed over nearly 50 years of research, beginning in the 1960s. Originally, SCT was used to explain the circumstances under which children learn and model violent behaviors that they see other people engage in, particularly people on TV and in movies. But, as we discussed in the units on the development of self online and in our interpersonal relationships in Web 2.0 environments, we also have many people who may serve as models of good and bad behavior for us via social media. These processes and effects generalize to adults as well. So, to demonstrate how this fits with Web 2.0 technologies, I'll use the example of recipes posted on Facebook—because who doesn't have a friend or family member instagramming their homemade dinners or sharing recipes via social media?

1. *People must remember a behavior that they have observed in order to later model that behavior.* So, if I want to cook a healthy recipe I see a friend share on Facebook, I have to remember it when the time comes for me to grocery shop and make dinner. There are Web 2.0 tools, such as Pinterest and online recipe boxes on AllRecipes, to help me with this. Or people often share these types of things on their own Facebook timelines so that they can refer back to them later.

2. *People have forethought about the consequences and outcomes of the behavior before performing it.* So, I'm not going to cook every recipe that every friend posts via Facebook or that my friends pin on Pinterest. Rather, I'm going to think about whether it is something I will like, something my family will eat, how much it will cost to buy the ingredients, and things like that.

3. *Identification with the person or character who depicted the behavior increases the likelihood of modeling.* When we feel that the people posting content or the characters enacting behaviors are similar to us and likable, we are more likely to model their behavior. So, if one of the people I follow on Pinterest pins a recipe they made and enjoyed, and they are someone I like and think of as having similar tastes to my own, I am more likely to model their behavior.

4. We do not model all behaviors we see, even behaviors from our close friends and family. *We also go through a process of self-regulation and reflection on whether or not the behavior is justified and fits with our values when we are deciding whether or not to do something.* So, if I eat healthy, whole foods, and someone I follow on Pinterest posts a recipe for an unhealthy-looking dessert, my self-regulation and reflection may stop me from making that dessert myself.

5. *Even if it is something we feel is a good idea, promoted by someone that we like, that fits our values and morals, we still have to feel like we can do the behavior in order to model it.* This is our sense of **self-efficacy** in terms of actually doing the behavior. So, thinking one more time of the recipe example, if my friends post a recipe that I would like and fits my typical diet, but seems really complex and involves foreign-sounding ingredients or unfamiliar cooking techniques, I probably would not feel efficacious enough to actually attempt it myself.

Insight into Innovation Activity: What Would You Cook? Check out Ree Drummond's blog, *The Pioneer Woman Cooks* (http://thepioneerwoman.com/cooking/). Looking at her most recent recipe, would you make this? Why or why not? Discuss your decision to model or not model her behavior by referring to a) your thoughts about the consequences and outcomes, b) your identification, or lack thereof, with Ree Drummond, c) your self-regulation, and d) your sense of efficacy.

Modeling can be applied to seemingly insignificant behaviors (such as cooking a recipe) and to important social behaviors (such as how we treat other people). Spiral of silence focuses on issues and behaviors that are *morally and socially important*. Spiral of silence also stresses the importance of what others think of us as an important deciding factor in how we behave. So, according to spiral of silence, there are four factors that work together to silence minority opinion holders on important, moral issues: threat of isolation from society, our fear of that isolation, gauging public opinion to avoid isolation, and adjusting our behavior to avoid being isolated.

1. There is an ongoing **threat** within society that if we do not conform to the majority opinion, we will be socially isolated. A threat is when we stand to lose something, and things like social capital, power, and peer relationships are an asset to us that can be lost. Many, but not all of us, are afraid to take stances on issues that may cause us to lose these important connections.

2. Thus, many of us have a **fear of isolation**; this is essentially a fear of being kicked out of our group. Consider, for example, posting a controversial opinion on Facebook. To a certain extent, since we are socially rewarded for having a large circle of friends, aren't we also potentially facing more backlash if we post something controversial?

"Grab the suitcases, dear, there's been a shift in public opinion!"

3. We gauge the popularity of our opinion using a **quasi-statistical sense** and determine if our opinion is in the minority or in the majority. This sense is our perception of public opinion, and it is not necessarily accurate. One source of our perception of opinion is the mass media, another is our reference group. Before speaking out, we may also consider what public opinion will be like in the future. Our perception of public opinion on important, moral issues determines whether we express our opinions on those issues or if we keep our opinion to ourselves. If we sense that we have a minority opinion, and we do not expect that to change, we will be **silenced** by social pressure. In other words, we will not post our opinion. However, research has clarified that some people—particularly younger, more affluent men—tend to speak out regardless of the opinion climate depicted in the media and perceived within their social group. There are also cultural differences in willingness to speak out (Scheufele, 2008). Thus, due to these individual differences, the silencing effect is relatively small (Glynn, Hayes, & Shanahan, 1997).

Example of Theory in Web 2.0: The Spiral of Silence Goes Viral. Initially, we were optimistic about the rise of social media as an opportunity for people to overcome social barriers and express their opinions online. Research conducted by Pew, however, suggests that the spiral of silence is alive and well online (Hampton, Rainie, Lu, Dwter, Shin, & Purcell, 2014):

http://www.pewinternet.org/2014/08/26/social-media-and-the-spiral-of-silence/

Copyright © Rena Schild/Shutterstock.com

Pew researched people's opinions and posting behavior about whistleblower Edward Snowden, who leaked NSA documents online that revealed an ongoing domestic spying program. Pew found that social media may actually increase, rather than decrease, silencing when people sense that they hold a minority opinion. Some key findings included:

- People were more likely to post their opinions when they felt that others agreed with them; they were unwilling to speak out when they sensed that most people disagreed with them.

- People who frequently used social media were less willing to share their opinions face-to-face.

- People who felt informed on the issue, had strong opinions on the issue, and were very interested in the topic were more likely to share their opinions.

These findings suggest that the spiral of silence may actually be *more* pronounced via social media. Why do you think we may be more silenced online? Is there more pressure toward conformity and cohesion via social media? Perhaps the threat of isolation is more present and immediate online than it is in our face-to-face interactions, as people can unfriend or unfollow us?

METHODS IN SCT AND SPIRAL RESEARCH

The "bobo doll" experiments. Initially, SCT was the outcome of a series of experiments conducted by Bandura (Bandura, Ross, & Ross, 1963a, and b). In these experiments, children were shown films or real-life models who were a) violent toward a Bobo doll, b) nonviolent, or c) shown no model at all. In some experiments, the modeled violence was rewarded with treats or punished with a scolding. In the experiments, after exposure, the children were put in a playroom with toys

and given the opportunity to play. Among the toys was an inflatable Bobo doll. They found that the children who saw violent behaviors showed more aggression and imitated the violent behaviors more than children in the other conditions. Rewarded behaviors were more likely to be imitated. Lastly, seeing violence in real life and being exposed to it via film *both* resulted in increased aggression and imitation. These were groundbreaking findings at the time, and raised serious concerns about the behaviors depicted on TV and in movies and the effects that these behaviors might have on children.

Of course, there are some very reasonable criticisms of this method. First, showing someone punching a Bobo doll and then giving kids a Bobo doll to test for modeling effects was not realistic. It did not necessarily reflect the victims of violence typically seen in media content; Bobo dolls are made to be hit, punched, and kicked; and modeling effects were observed immediately after viewing rather than after a period of time. Subsequent research, of course, improved on this method by testing the effects of real, rather than experimentally made-up, TV content. A substantial body of correlational evidence has accumulated through the use of survey studies.

Correlational survey studies. Both SCT and spiral of silence have been the subject of survey studies. Though SCT was initially developed and tested using experimental evidence, surveys that assess people's media consumption have provided evidence that media characters can serve as real-life models for people's behaviors. Spiral of silence, on the other hand, has traditionally been assessed using survey methods. Noelle-Neumann's (1974) initial research into spiral of silence was what we now refer to as the "**train test**." In this survey method, people are asked about their willingness to discuss their opinion on a controversial issue with a stranger on a train. For example, the

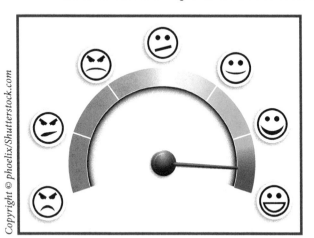

researcher may ask mothers who agree with spanking whether or not they would speak to a mother on a train who disagreed with spanking and vice versa.

Though other measures have been developed, one issue with many survey measures is that they use hypothetical situations to gauge whether or not a person is willing to express his or her opinion (Scheufele, 2008). Subsequent research has been plagued by issues with survey design and measures, often employing very different scale measures of concepts from spiral of silence to test the theory, which may explain the weak overall findings (Scheufele & Moy, 2000).

Insight into Innovation Activity: Assess your Fear of Isolation (Hayes, Matthes, & Eveland, 2011, p. 444).

Answer the following on a scale of 1 (strongly disagree) to 5 (strongly agree):

- Thinking about not being invited to gatherings hosted by people I know is scary to me.

- Being "excluded by the people I know" is "one of the worst things that could happen to me."

- "It would bother me if no one wanted to be around me."

- "I dislike feeling left out of social gatherings."

- It is "important to me to fit into the group I am with."

Sum and average your score. On a scale of 1 (very low) to 5 (very high), what is your fear of isolation? Do you think that may affect your willingness to speak out on controversial issues in face-to-face settings and online?

APPLYING BEHAVIORAL EFFECTS THEORY TO MEDIA

Behavioral effects theories and their associated methods have been applied to many, many media effects. Typically, these theories are applied to traditional media, such as TV, movies, and video games. Arguably, each of these effects may also relate to the videos we see online and the pictures people post online, though more research needs to be done to clarify these possible effects of user-generated content. Our friends and the people we follow on social media could be a profound source of information about attractiveness, violent versus prosocial behaviors, health behaviors and public opinion, and therefore, also have important effects on our behavior.

Angelina Jolie

Copyright © Jaguar PS/Shutterstock.com

Body image studies have looked at how very attractive, thin models on TV and in magazines may lead to unhealthy perceptions of attractiveness. When fashion magazines, movies, and TV shows feature women who are unhealthily thin, women may feel that extreme thinness is ideal and adopt disordered eating habits to try to achieve that thin ideal. Take, for example, Angelina Jolie. In 2012, Twitter lit up during the Academy Awards over Angelina Jolie's weight. When celebrities appear to be unhealthily thin, we have to be concerned about whether or not their extreme thinness serves as an unhealthy model for women and young girls who then may adopt disordered eating to achieve that "ideal."

Another negative effect of the behaviors modeled in traditional media is evidenced in violence and aggression studies. These studies look at modeling **violent** behaviors (physically injuring or killing people) and **aggressive** behaviors (being threatening) that are depicted in TV shows, movies, and video games to determine the extent to which people learn these types of behaviors. For

example, there has been a lot of conjecture and some research about whether or not violent video games, particularly first person shooter games, may serve as a kind of "behavioral training" for would-be murderers and mass shooters. It is difficult to make any generalizable claims about the direct modeling of violent behaviors in video games, but there is evidence that playing these types of games increases aggressive behaviors in *some* people (Anderson, 2003).

Health behavior studies have looked at modeling positive health behaviors, such as healthy eating, exercising, safe sex, and preventative care, in entertainment media. Take, for example, the recent revamping of Cookie Monster's character on *Sesame Street* and his new stance that "a cookie is a sometime food." He raps with Wyclef Jean that "me one healthy dude 'cause me eat healthy food" (see the video here: http://youtu.be/pEvhJKwxsZk). These types of messages are meant to model good behaviors for children.

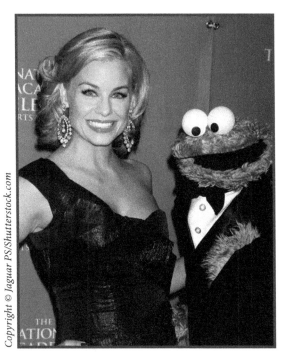

**Jessica Collins and
Cookie Monster**

Similar health messages are in adult media as well, with shows such as *Biggest Loser* that promote identification with people who are exercising and dieting to lose weight and increases viewers' senses of efficacy (Tian & Yoo, 2015). These shows show people enacting the behaviors associated with losing weight, such as restricted diets and regular, strenuous exercize. The people who lose the most weight are praised and rewarded throughout the show, thus reinforcing the social desirability of achieving and maintaining a healthy weight.

Silencing studies have looked at how and when people speak out or are silenced. Spiral of silence has been used to explain people's willingness to speak out on many controversial issues, such as same-sex marriage, abortion, and parenting techniques.

Clearly, both SCT and spiral of silence have been researched and applied extensively in traditional media studies. Key concepts from both SCT and spiral of silence have also been applied to understanding people's use of new technologies and how the messages we receive via new media technologies affect our real-life behaviors. These theories help us understand new media in two ways: first, they explain social conditions that determine new media use. Second, they explain the behavioral implications of the messages we receive via new media.

APPLYING BEHAVIORAL THEORIES TO NEW MEDIA: LEARNING ABOUT AND FROM NEW MEDIA

Internet efficacy from modeling. One important area of research that applies SCT to new communication technologies focuses on **Internet efficacy**: or how we develop people's sense that they can effectively use new technologies. SCT explains that people observe models, and one of the judgments we make before engaging in a modeled behavior is determining our efficacy. We develop a sense of efficacy from both real and mediated models and the modeled behaviors affect both our real-life and mediated behaviors.

Having a sense of self-efficacy and the expected outcomes of use are important determinants of whether or not people use new technologies like the Internet (LaRose & Eastin, 2004). When children are young, parents serve as models of Internet behaviors, which can affect kids' use of different Internet technologies (Vaala & Bleakly, 2015). Much like early research that applied SCT had confirmed, we may also be learning about how to use social media by modeling the behavior of our favorite TV stars as well (Stefanone, Lackaff, & Rosen, 2010). Reality TV viewing is related to having a larger social network that includes more people that have not been met face-to-face and sharing photos via that network. Thus, both real-life models like parents and mediated models in TV shows are demonstrating for people what Internet behaviors they should engage in and how they should behave online.

In adulthood, we still turn to others and model their Internet behaviors in professional and social contexts. In professional contexts, having models whose examples we can follow increases our sense of efficacy when working in virtual teams, and that sense of efficacy leads people to be more dedicated, confident, satisfied, and perform better in online teams (Staples & Webster, 2007). We refer to this as the "**best practices**" approach, or the idea that we share our best practices with others who have similar jobs to perform, and they can learn by modeling our behavior.

Using technologies like Wikis in education contexts are also affected by self-efficacy (Liu, 2010). **Wikis**, such as Wikipedia, are websites where users can post and edit content. Course wikis are useful in education settings as a way for instructors and students to share knowledge and resources about class topics. But, as with any online tool, wikis are only effective for education and participation insofar as people feel a sense of efficacy about using them and, as a result, participate in online knowledge sharing.

Copyright © Evan Lorne/Shutterstock.com

As we introduce new technologies to get people involved in creating and sharing knowledge and opinions online, developing their sense of efficacy will be essential. We discussed this in terms of increasing digital literacy earlier in this unit. Social cognitive theory explains that modeling those online behaviors for people who feel less of a sense of efficacy and sharing best practices among peers are helpful ways to improve efficacy and promote engagement.

Opportunities for entertainment education to promote positive behaviors. Scholars and government agencies have been looking at ways to use new technologies to teach people prosocial and healthy behaviors and to reduce antisocial and unhealthy behaviors. One way to promote positive behaviors using concepts from SCT is through entertainment education. **Entertainment education** is when media developers intentionally incorporate information and modeling of healthy or prosocial behaviors in entertaining media (Moyer-Gusé, 2014). Initially, entertainment education focused on incorporating information about personal health and wellness in sitcoms, soap operas, and other entertaining TV content. These approaches to teaching people positive behaviors are thought to work because entertaining content increases involvement by embedding the target behaviors in a narrative and because people tend to like, identify with, and sometimes see themselves as similar to the characters that they enjoy watching on TV.

More modern approaches are exploring how we can incorporate important health messages in entertaining new media content. For example, role-playing computer games have been designed to help teach people about their ideal weight, how to select foods based on their weight goals, and about the amount of exercise they need to burn calories (Peng, 2009). By embedding information in a fun, interactive game and having people build self-efficacy through role play and observe the results in their avatars, people who participated in the game learned more, felt more self-efficacy, perceived that there were more benefits, and had greater intentions to eat healthy compared to a control group that did not play the game.

Though research has not kept pace with technology, the findings on entertainment education programs suggests that the use of the Internet may be a unique opportunity to teach positive, prosocial, healthy behaviors. Entertainment is a common motive for using the Internet. For example, YouTube, BuzzFeed, and other multimedia online platforms could be pivotal in teaching adults and children new behavior.

Exemplars and modeling social media behaviors. For online magazines and articles to promote positive behaviors such as weight loss, research suggests that specific **exemplars** are useful for promoting self-efficacy (Sarge & Knoblich-Westerwick, 2013). Exemplars are real-life examples that we can look to as models for behavior. People may be more likely to model the behavior in a magazine article about one person who lost 100 pounds than they are to follow the advice of an article that reports the results on a study of 50 people who lost an average of 100 lbs. Having one clear exemplar—one specific person to model—appears to be more effective. In virtual environments, people also model healthy behaviors like exercising when exposed to a visual depiction of themselves shown losing weight and exercising (Fox & Bailenson, 2009). In these types of activities, people's virtual selves serve as an exemplar of healthy habits that they can, in their real lives, imitate to achieve weight loss and other health goals.

Similar to modeling individuals we see depicted in online media like magazines, blogs, and games, we also model the social behaviors we see other people demonstrate online via mediated channels like discussion boards. Seeing positive posting behaviors to model increases our willingness to take part in those discussions (Han & Brazeal, 2015). Interestingly, this very modeling of other people's posting behaviors may serve to exacerbate the silencing effect of social media observed in the Pew (2014) study discussed above. More specifically, if we see that few people are posting their opinions on a controversial issue, that the opinions being posted are different from our own, or we see people being trolled or harassed for posting controversial opinions, we may learn that we should not post our opinions through observing others. In essence, we learn what other people post, the consequences or outcomes associated with those posts, how our opinion would be received by others if we posted it, and decide whether or not it would be a good idea for us to post similar content.

Opinion expression online. Survey research has suggested that in general people were more willing to express their opinions via computer-mediated communication (CMC) compared to face-to-face settings, though willingness to express opinions was affected by the perception that future public opinion would be more supportive (Ho & McLeod, 2008). Later research has clarified that there can be a silencing effect online based on what others post. For example, Yun and Park (2011) conducted an online experiment where they compared people's willingness to post their opinions in a comment section when the existing comments either agreed or disagreed with the participants' opinions. People were more likely to post their opinions when existing comments expressed support for their opinions, even when they were posting anonymously. Thus, there is evidence that we glean information about opinion climate online and that it can affect whether or not we express our opinions.

Online posting of opinions is also affected by our perceptions of the context and our individual traits. Culture affects people's willingness to speak out (Matthes et al., 2012), with people from some cultures being more or less likely to speak out online. In the first study looking at the spiral of silence on social media, Gearhart and Zhang (2014) found that one's self-censorship, perception of the national opinion climate, and one's willingness to speak out were related to expressing opinions via social media. Thus, online, there are both internal factors and external factors that affect whether or not we express our opinions. Some people censor themselves more than others, while other people are very outspoken about their opinions regardless of the climate of opinion. These individual differences affect our online posting behavior, our face-to-face behavior, and whether or not we adjust to different contexts in terms of speaking versus withholding our opinions.

CONCLUSION

Both SCT and spiral of silence offer insight into how other people serve as models of behavior and the implicit social pressure to conform. Research that applies these theories to Web 2.0 technology is just now emerging, and there are many issues that researchers have yet to address.

For example, researchers have not closely examined **binge watching**, or watching long marathons of TV shows or movies, though binge watching through Netflix, Amazon, and Hulu clearly has implications for theories such as SCT. In addition to the potential for pronounced modeling effects resulting from immersed viewing of TV shows, there is also the potential for people in our social networks to serve as behavioral models for us.

Particularly since SCT points out that identification with behavioral models and efficacy are important determinants of modeling, the real-life behaviors modeled in our friends' social media posts may prove to have a significant effect for better or for worse, both in affecting our own social media use and our offline behavior. In terms of body image, consider our current obsession with **selfies**, or pictures that we take of ourselves with our mobile devices and post to social media. Our Facebook friends and people we follow on Instagram who post beautiful selfies, or post pictures of themselves working out, may serve as models of attractiveness for us.

Research on spiral of silence has suggested that we may be more silenced online, but it does not explain why this is happening and has not offered insight into how we might overcome social media silencing. Even so, examples of prosocial online campaigns that seek to empower people and reverse the spiral of silence are emerging as are examples of the types of issues we post about and avoid via social media. Research may reveal that the "feel good" content we like and retweet, the need to be popular on social media, and the fact that we are identifiable and our posts are semipermanent and only semiprivate, may actually accentuate rather than help attenuate the spiral of silence. After all, none of us wants to be that one friend who always goes on Facebook rants.

Thus, behavioral theories have a lot of insight to offer us in terms of understanding the implications of Web 2.0 technologies. Exploring these theories in the context of new media will require important changes in methodology, possibly moving away from lab experiments and in person interviews to more observational studies of people's posting behaviors and effects of others' posts.

ASSIGNMENTS

1. **Online Social Learning.** Look up how-to instructions online to learn a new skill such as a blog post outlining a DIY project or a brief video recipe. Evaluate the likelihood that you will actually do the new behavior using the criteria outlined in social cognitive theory: creating a sense of *efficacy*, the *vividness* of the instructions, *identification* with the creators of the content, and whether the *outcome* was worth the investment of time and resources.

2. **Choose a controversial issue to research.** Find an online news article on the topic, then read the comments section. Write a brief essay summarizing the opinion climate, projecting what the opinion climate will be in the future, and who is likely to be silenced given the current and future opinion climate expressed in the comments.

REFERENCES

Seminal Texts:

Bandura, A., Ross, D., & Ross, S. A. (1963a). Imitation of film-mediated aggressive models. *Journal of Abnormal and Social Psychology*, 66, 3–11.

Bandura, A., Ross, D., & Ross, S. A. (1963b). Vicarious reinforcement and imitative learning. *Journal of Abnormal and Social Psychology*, 67, 601–607.

Noelle-Neumann, E. (1974). The spiral of silence: A theory of public opinion. *Journal of Communication*, 24(2), 43-51.

Academic Sources:

Bandura, A. (1978). Social learning theory of aggression. *Journal of Communication*, 28(3), 12–29.

Bandura, A. (1986). *Social foundations of thought and action: A social cognitive theory.* Upper Saddle River, NJ: Prentice-Hall.

Bandura, A. (2001). Social cognitive theory of mass communication. *Media Psychology, 3,* 265–299.

Davison, W. P. (1983). The third-person effect in communication. *Public Opinion Quarterly, 47,* 1–15.

Fox, J., & Bailenson, J. M. (2009). Virtual self-modeling: The effects of vicarious reinforcement and identification on exercise behaviors. *Media Psychology, 12,* 1–25.

Gearhart, S., & Zhang, W. (2014). Gay bullying and online opinion expression: Testing spiral of silence in the social media environment. *Social Science Computer Review, 32,* 18–36.

Glynn, C. J., Hayes, A. F., & Shanahan, J. (1997). Perceived support for one's opinion and willingness to speak out: A meta-analysis of survey studies on the "spiral of silence." *Public Opinion Quarterly, 61,* 452–463.

Hampton, K., Rainie, L., Lu, W., Dwyer, M., Shin, I., & Purcell, K. (2014). Social media and the "spiral of silence." *Pew Research Center.* Retrieved from http://www.pewinternet.org/files/2014/08/PI_Social-networks-and-debate_082614.pdf

Han, S.-H., & Brazeal, L. M. (2015). Playing nice: Modeling civility in online political discussions. *Communication Research Reports, 32,* 20–28.

Hayes, A. F., Matthes, J., & Eveland, W. P., Jr. (2011). Stimulating the quasi-statistical organ: Fear of isolation motivates the quest for knowledge of the opinion climate. *Communication Research, 40,* 439–462.

Ho, S. S., & McLeod, D. M. (2008). Social-psychological influences on opinion expression in face-to-face and computer-mediated communication. *Communication Research, 35*(2), 190–207.

LaRose, R., & Eastin, M. S. (2004). A social cognitive theory of Internet uses and gratifications: Toward a new model of media attendance. *Journal of Broadcasting & Electronic Media, 48*(3), 358–377.

Liu, X. (2010). Empirical testing of a theoretical extension of the technology acceptance model: An exploratory study of educational wikis. *Communication Education, 59,* 52–69.

Matthes, J., Hayes, A. F., Rojas, H., Shen, F., Min, S., & Dylko, I. B. (2012). Exemplifying a dispositional approach to cross-cultural spiral of silence research: Fear of social isolation and the inclination to self-censor. *International Journal of Public Opinion Research, 24*(3), 287–305.

Moyer-Gusé, E. (2008). Toward a theory of entertainment persuasion: Explaining the persuasive effects of entertainment-education messages. *Communication Theory, 18,* 407–425.

Noelle-Neumann, E. (1993). *The spiral of silence: Public opinion—our social skin* (2nd ed.). Chicago, IL: University of Chicago Press.

Peng, W. (2009). Design and evaluation of a computer game to promote a healthy diet for young adults. *Health Communication, 24,* 115–127.

Sarge, M. E., & Knobloch-Westerwick, S. (2013). Impacts of efficacy and exemplification in an online message about weight loss on weight management self-efficacy, satisfaction, and personal importance. *Journal of Health Communication, 18,* 827–844.

Scheufele, D. A. (2008). Spiral of silence theory. In W. Donsbach & M. W. Traugott (Eds.), *The Sage handbook of public opinion research* (pp. 175–184). Long Grove, CA: Sage.

Scheufele, D. A., & Moy, P. (2000). Twenty-five years of the spiral of silence: A conceptual review and empirical outlook. *International Journal of Public Opinion Research, 12,* 2–28.

Staples, D. S., & Webster, J. (2007). Exploring traditional and virtual team members' "best practices": A social cognitive theory perspective. *Small Group Research, 38*(1), 60–97.

Stefanone, M. A., Lackaff, D., & Rosen, D. (2010). The relationship between traditional mass media and "social media": Reality television as a model for social network site behavior. *Journal of Broadcasting & Electronic Media, 54,* 508–525.

Tian, Y., & Yoo, J. H. (2015). Connecting with the Biggest Loser: An extended model of parasocial interaction and identification in health-related reality TV shows. *Health Communication, 30,* 1–7.

Vaala, S. E., & Bleakly, A. (2015). Monitoring, mediating, and modeling: Parental influence on adolescent computer and Internet use in the United States. *Journal of Children and Media, 9,* 40–57.

Yun, G. W., & Park, S.-Y. (2011). Selective posting: Willingness to post a message online. *Journal of Computer-Mediated Communication, 16,* 201–277.

Examples:

Further Reading Online:

Anderson, C. A. (2003). Violent video games: Myths, facts, and unanswered questions. *American Psychological Association Science Briefs.* Retrieved from http://www.apa.org/science/about/psa/2003/10/anderson.aspx

Hampton, K., Rainie, L., Lu, W., Dwyer, M., Shin, I., & Purcell, K. (2014). Social media and the "spiral of silence." *Pew Research Center.* Retrieved from http://www.pewinternet.org/files/2014/08/PI_Social-networks-and-debate_082614.pdf

CONCLUSION: DIFFERENCES, DIVIDES, AND PARADOXES

OUTCOMES

- *Knowledge:* Explore the intersections among theories and how they work together to help us understand mediated communication.

- *Skill:* Apply theories as lenses for understanding new and emerging technologies.

We have covered theories, concepts, and research methods to explore the impact of Web 2.0 technology on the self, social and professional relationships, and society. Looking broadly across theories and research into Web 2.0 technologies, there are some general themes and specific lessons to take away:

1. *Individual differences* in values, motivation, and circumstances affect how we communicate and respond.
2. We are all caught in *paradoxes of competing needs and goals*, some of our own making, some as a result of society, and still others as result of technology.
3. Being *mindful* of ourselves and others can help us navigate complex, changing contexts and interactions.
4. *Efficacy* is the essential component of human behavior.
5. *Technology can both help and hinder* our understanding of each other and our personal, social, professional, and societal engagement.

Thinking about these five takeaways, theory should help us use the technologies available to us now as we strive to be mindful, critical, responsive communicators. Understanding these theories and the lessons they teach us about effective and ineffective communication should also prepare us for whatever technologies are on the horizon.

TAKEAWAY 1: INDIVIDUAL DIFFERENCES

Individual differences motivate our communication behavior and our *cognitive* and *affective* (emotional) responses to other people's messages. Individual differences in personality, gender, culture, emotions, motivations, standpoint, life circumstances and psychological states, attitudes, beliefs, knowledge, and demographics affect how we interact and respond.

Symbolic interactionism and Goffman's concept of self-presentation teach us that meanings exist within people, and are the result of who we are, our experiences, and our culture. How people talk to and about us shapes our perception of ourselves—the roles we play and the meaning of those roles—which affect how we feel about ourselves, think about ourselves, and thus how we behave. Importantly, how we talk to and about others is similarly impactful on them and their perceptions of themselves.

Culture (politeness theory) and gender (genderlect styles) influence both our values and our communication styles, thus these both affect how we create and how we respond to messages. Culture, gender, and context are also a lens through which we view other people, and this can shape our expectations in an interaction (expectancy violations theory). Further, our status within society shapes what we know and what we do (opinion leadership).

Even knowing that people are unique, our drives for certainty (uncertainty reduction theory) and to "explain" other people's behavior (attribution theory) sometimes make us less able to truly know other people. And so we have our own expectations for interactions (expectancy violations theory), and we often react negatively when our expectations are violated.

> Try to understand people as unique, complex individuals during interactions. Rather than relying on one obvious characteristic such as a person's race, gender, social class, or even a single personality trait, try to consider them as complex and unique individuals.

TAKEAWAY 2: NEEDS

Needs are an essential aspect of human motivation (social exchange theory, uses and gratifications theory). Indeed, many of the theories covered in this text have spoken to some kind of human need:

- Our need to understand (attribution theory),
- Our need to manage others' perceptions of us (presentation of self),
- Our need to be liked and respected (politeness theory),
- Our need to be validated by people similar to us (attraction theory),
- Our need to feel certain and secure (uncertainty reduction),
- Our need for equitable and rewarding relationships (social exchange theory),
- Our need to get along with others (groupthink),
- Our need for consistency (cognitive dissonance theory),

- Our need to do what peers expect us to do (theory of planned behavior),
- Our need to fix what's wrong (Burke's guilt),
- Our needs for entertainment and information (uses and gratifications theory), and
- Our need to fit in (spiral of silence theory).

We are all caught in **paradoxes** based on these needs, and we use communication to manage and navigate competing needs within ourselves and between ourselves and others. Inconsistency makes us uncomfortable (dissonance theory), but still we change over time in response to the changing contexts and relationships (relationship dialectics). We may sometimes need to reduce uncertainty (uncertainty reduction theory) and want closeness (social penetration theory), but at the same time we need spontaneity and privacy.

Some of these paradoxes are due to social norms, such as gender double-binds between the demands of the situation and the demands of gender norms (genderlect styles and muted group theory), or the tension between managing our own and others' face needs (face negotiation theory). Some of these paradoxes are an outcome of our desire to do what's right but to also do what's best for ourselves.

Our individual differences are related to our needs in an interaction, and needs often conflict internally (when we have two competing needs) and externally (when our needs are different from others' needs or different from what the situation calls for). These needs can change over time, and can affect internal, social, and professional relationships. Be aware that your own needs may be in conflict, there may be conflict between your own and others' needs, and others may have internally conflicting needs as well.

TAKEAWAY 3: MINDFULNESS

Mindfulness of ourselves, others, and context is essential to communication competence, but we live much of our lives mindlessly due to a lack of *motivation* and, in some cases, *ability*. Being present and attentive in the moment is essential to recognizing and adapting to individual differences and people's needs. Mindful living can help us navigate the paradoxes we face, recognize the paradoxes that others face, and be more responsive to individual differences. Mindfulness also helps us exist in the moment, which should make us sensitive to group and organizational contexts (organizational cultures), recognize dysfunctional group processes as they occur (groupthink), and help us integrate into or accommodate cultures.

Many theories covered in this text relate directly to mindful communication, or being aware of and attentive to one's own and others' thoughts and feelings:

- They challenge us to practice perspective-taking and see the contextual restraints that others experience (attribution theory);
- They challenge our critical thinking, asking us to consider the "simple decision rules" we use to make decisions, and reflect on how closely we think about messages (elaboration likelihood model);
- They explain that our perceptions are incomplete (attribution theory) and often formed based upon faulty information (cultivation theory);

- They explain that human behavior is complex, influenced by norms, attitudes, and efficacy, which can be very different from one person to the next (theory of planned behavior and social cognitive theory);
- They challenge us to reframe issues (mindfulness) and to consider how others frame issues (framing theory);
- They challenge us to consider the obstacles that others face (muted group theory) and how our communication environment can make those obstacles that much more insurmountable (media ecology).

All of these theories, in one way or another, speak to our general ability or inability and our motivation or lack of motivation to be aware in the moment of the people, context, and messages we are taking in. These theories give us ways to consider our own thought processes and the thought processes of others, and challenge us to think of the many things that influence how people communicate, think, feel, and respond.

Being mindful in our interactions can help us be more sensitive to individual differences and unique needs by increasing awareness of how we are thinking and feeling and how others are thinking and feeling. Mindfulness promotes active, thoughtful listening and responding and also helps us be more critical consumers of content, as we consider the complex reasons behind what we are seeing.

TAKEAWAY 4: EFFICACY

Efficacy is essential to human action and clarifies both motivation and ability. Efficacy is the belief that we can do something (social learning theory) and hinges on our evaluation of whether we can and will achieve the outcomes we seek and the strength of our beliefs (theory of planned behavior).

Efficacy is a combination of our thoughts (what we believe) and our feelings (whether something is good or bad). Whether it is trying a new dating app, voting, quitting a bad habit, or adopting a new healthy habit, the first step is believing that we *can* do it and that the outcomes will be positive. In this text, we have covered concepts such as communication competence, active listening, and digital literacies in an effort to build your sense of efficacy as a communicator in a Web 2.0 world. The more you practice these theory-based skills and try new things, the more efficacy you should feel as you navigate our complex new media environment.

At the start of this text, I described theories as lenses through which we can consider new technologies. Indeed, throughout this book, I've tried to emphasize what theories tell us about the uses, usefulness, and effects of technology. In some chapters, we discussed specific "how-tos," in other chapters we used theory as a lens to understand mediated communication processes or recent events that affect our daily lives. Hopefully, after reviewing these theories and applications, you have developed a sense of efficacy in terms of your own communication, your use of communication scholarship to inform your interactions and media use, and your use of new technologies.

> Build your own sense of efficacy by trying new technologies, new communication styles, and seeking out new experiences. Use the theories in this book as a starting point for understanding how you have formed and project your sense of self, to improve yourself, to build your personal and professional relationships, and to use and respond to mass media.

TAKEAWAY 5: TECHNOLOGY CAN HELP AND HINDER

Lastly, **technology** can help us navigate paradoxes, learn about people who are different from ourselves (cultivation theory), learn about important events (agenda setting), fulfill myriad needs (uses and gratifications theory), help us build relationships (hyperpersonal communication), and build our sense of efficacy (social learning theory) when used mindfully. On the other hand, technology can also create paradoxes and exacerbate silencing (spiral of silence theory) and accentuate or drown out differences as we avoid dissonant content (cognitive dissonance theory).

Technology is possibly the greatest paradox we face in terms of our sense of self, our personal and professional relationships, and in our society.

- It can help us manage our presentation of the self, but breaks down barriers between the public and the private self.
- It helps us build and maintain relationships, but can distract us from our relationships.
- It helps us balance work and home, but increases the potential for intrusion of work into our home lives and home lives into our work.
- It gives us more control over how and when to interact, but controls much of our daily lives as we are constantly connected.
- It is a channel where diverse voices can be heard, but it is also used to shame, harass, and drown out dissent.
- It is a source of infinite information and entertainment, but it blurs the lines between fact and opinion.
- It is everywhere, but still some people are excluded.

Part of being a mindful technology consumer and user is remembering that all of those individual and contextual aspects that affect and constrain our own behavior are also affecting and constraining the behavior of the people consuming and creating mediated messages (media ecology). It is easy to forget the people on the other side of the screen—the developers and other users—because they are out of sight. This challenges us to consider the people behind the online content we use, their goals, and the repercussions of their and our own mediated messages. We must also consider who is excluded—the goals, needs, individual traits, and standpoints that are not represented—and how that affects each of us and our society.

Technology is not just a tool; it is a human creation that reflects cultural values, norms, corporate interests, and the standpoints of its creators and users. Each technological change is framed as progress, but there are also consequences for those advancements in terms of who has access, who can and will participate in new modes of interaction, who benefits, and thus who is left out and left behind in our social, professional, and public lives.

Insight into Innovation Activity: Communication Theory Ted-style Talk. Think about one key takeaway from the theories you've learned this semester. What did you learn from this course that is an "idea worth spreading" such as those in the Ted Talks throughout this book? Create a 5-minute Ted-style talk summarizing that takeaway, explain the evidence for that takeaway, and be sure to focus on the practical importance of that takeaway for our Web 2.0 lives. Upload your Ted-style talk to You-Tube, and share it on our textbook Facebook page: facebook.com/communicationtheoryforsocialmedia

CLOSING THOUGHTS: NOW YOU HAVE THE START OF A THEORY TOOL BOX

In the introduction to this text, I talked about theories as lenses that teach concepts and help us communicate more effectively in our everyday lives. Though I applied these theories to specific technologies and recent events in each chapter, communication theories and methods provide lenses for understanding human communication and relationships in many ways, even as the modes and channels of communication change.

It is difficult to imagine what's on the horizon, as we explore wearable technologies and the potential for an Internet of things. For example, the Internet of things is when our machines and devices can communicate with each other, rather than just the current Internet of people where humans are interacting with each other. So, our kitchen cabinets could communicate with the systems at a retailer and order some supply we ran out of, which could then be automatically ordered, the cost debited from our bank account, and the product delivered to our doorstep without us having to communicate anything.

Consider if the Internet of things materializes: How might communication theory apply to our devices and appliances talking to each other?

Forbes made nine predictions about the Internet of things (Press, 2015):

1. The Internet of things will reshape the global economy.
2. There will be around 30 billion devices linked to the Internet of things by 2020.
3. The majority of the Internet of things will be largely used in enterprises rather than by consumers.
4. North America is the focal point of the Internet of things, and will continue to be.

5. Telecommunications, banks, and utility companies will be the leaders in the Internet of things.
6. Corporate adoption of the Internet of things is taking off across the globe.
7. The Internet of things lowers labor costs and improves customer service.
8. The primary issue with the Internet of things will be security.
9. Microsoft is the leader in the Internet of things market.

Thinking about the theories we've covered this semester, and the takeaways from the theories discussed above, the Internet of things has the potential to improve our lives in terms of offering predictability (I will always know there's milk in the fridge!) and control (we can control devices more easily, reducing accidents, service interruptions, and supply shortages). It will also give us an unimaginable amount of data on people's lives. On the other hand, it is also an intrusion into our privacy, makes our information less secure, and may further disconnect us from each other. Thus, though it may fulfill individual and corporate needs, it is nonetheless another potential paradox that we should approach mindfully as consumers. Indeed, it may make our lives easier in some ways, but only for those people who can afford it and feel efficacy in regard to adopting it. So even as we move to machine-to-machine communication, our theories help us think critically about the individual, relational, and societal implications of that technology.

Thus, if we think about theory and methods in applied, critical ways, we can use it to understand and navigate our changing computer-mediated environment. We can consider the implications of whatever technology is next in terms of our sense of self and our relationships with others, and in terms of mass, societal-level effects.

REFERENCES

Press, G. (2015, July 30). 9 new predictions and market assessments for the Internet of things (IoT). Retrieved from http://www.forbes.com/sites/gilpress/2015/07/30/9-new-predictions-and-market-assessments-for-the-internet-of-things-iot/

GLOSSARY

Ability is whether or not we feel that we are able to think critically about the message

Accommodation is when we adjust our messages to match others' communication styles

Active audience approach focuses on explaining the many different reasons people have for selecting media

Active information seeking strategies are when we talk to others about a person so that we can learn about him or her

Active listening involves trying to understand what the other person is saying, implying, and feeling

Adhocracy cultures are creative

Affect exchange is when we disclose our personal feelings, beliefs, and attitudes

Affective needs are emotional, such as wanting entertainment

Affinity is our liking of a channel

Agenda setting is used to explain how news coverage makes issues important to us

Aggressive behaviors include being threatening

Alternation is prioritizing one need over the other

Ambivalent attitudes are attitudes that are mixed, or not clearly favorable or unfavourable

Anonymous messages are when the communicator is not identifiable

Antecedent conditions are conditions that affect outcomes and can be manipulated in experimental research

Anthropological research looks at communication and rituals within cultural groups

Applied research is guided by theory-based research questions that ask about how specific concepts and assumptions from a theory apply to or explain a specific situation or event

Artifacts are any kind of communication record

Asynchronicity is when CMC allows for delays in responses

Attitudes are people's evaluations or feelings toward something

Attitudes are people's evaluations or feelings, and they range from extremely favorable to extremely unfavorable

Attributes are the characteristics of something

Attributions are our explanations of our own and other people's behavior

Axiomatic theories have very clear and specific axioms, or assumptions

Backstage is some place separate from the work-related performance

Balance is compromising

Bald messages communicate what we want or need directly

Bargain means to negotiate

Behavior control is when you change your behavior, which motivates a change in your partner's behavior

Behavior management is when we control our nonverbal behaviors so that the other person won't recognize that we're being deceptive

(Behavioral) Intentions are what people plan to do; their beliefs about what they will do

Behaviorism is the idea that receiving rewards and punishments taught people what they should and should not do

Beliefs are the information people possess about the attributes of something

Best practices approaches are the idea that we share our best practices with others who have similar jobs to perform, and they can learn by modeling our behavior

Big data refers to massive datasets that collect information on people's online behaviors

"Big 5 Personality Types" are broad trait categories, including extraversion, agreeableness, conscientiousness, neuroticism, and openness

Biological sex is how we are born

Blogs user generated content that include thoughts, feelings, opinions, insights, and information

Body image studies have looked at how very attractive, thin models on TV may lead to unhealthy perceptions of attractiveness

Buzz is what people are talking about and posting online

Canons of rhetoric include invention, arrangement, style, memory, and delivery of public speaking

Case studies are illustrative examples of the processes described in a theory

Causal claims are when theorists argue that one thing *causes* another

Central processing involves more elaboration, or active thinking related to the content of the message

Change agents are people employed by an organization or group to promote the diffusion of an innovative product or idea

Changing contexts is intentionally changing things up

Channel is the means of communication, including face-to-face and our many mediated delivery options

Characters are the people involved in the plot of a narrative

Chronemics is how we use time to communicate

Citizen journalism is everyday people participating in journalism

Clan cultures are collaborative

Classical period includes Ancient Rome and Greece when work began on classifying types of rhetoric and rhetorical tactics

Classism is unfairly judging people based on social class

Close analysis is when rhetorical analysts look closely at a message and see which rhetorical tactics are at work in a message

Close textual analysis is the careful analysis of artifacts to look for evidence of specific rhetorical tactics or to discover new rhetorical tactics

Closed-mindedness in groups is when they fail to think critically and weigh the pros and cons of decisions

Code switching is moving between communication styles

Coding is identifying the trends and themes in field notes, transcripts, or other recorded forms of communication

Cognition is our thoughts, knowledge, opinions, and beliefs

Cognitive complexity is the quality and quantity of constructs we have for people

Cognitive elaboration is how carefully we think about a message

Cognitive load is how much we can think about at any one time

Cognitive needs are wanting information

Cognitive processes are how people think

Coherence is when we consider whether the story holds up when compared to other stories

Collectivist cultural values include building, maintaining, and protecting relationships

Collegial stories are about the good and the bad experiences they've had with coworkers

Commodities are those things that can be marketed and/or sold to make a profit

Communication competence is the ability to "communicate more skillfully"

Communication education communication in the classroom

Communication style includes how long we speak, our rate of speech, use of pauses, use of voice, how long we take to respond, disclosure of personal details, use of jokes, gestures, facial expressions, and our posture

Comparison level is a person's minimum threshold for rewards

Comparison level of alternatives is when people compare relationships to other potential relationships

Concealment is intentionally hiding information

Concepts are abstract ideas that we want to explore in research, such as specific feelings, states of being, attitudes, behaviors, or message strategies

Conceptualization is the process of carefully defining our concepts

Concurrence-seeking behaviors are the things we say and do as group members that look for agreement

Confirmation bias is the potential that, by seeking to confirm what we already believe to be true, we may look for evidence to support that notion and overlook what's really going on

Confirmatory research seeks to confirm the assumptions of a theory and is typically guided by hypotheses that are based on existing theory

Confirmatory surveys test the model

Consonance is being consistent in thoughts, attitudes, and behaviors

Constructivism looks at the complexity of people's understanding of others

Constructs are the unique descriptions we have of people

Consubstantiation is when the substance of someone overlaps significantly with the substance of someone else

Contempt is when we express disdain for the other person

Content analysis is the systematic, objective analysis of communication messages

Context is the situation in which communication occurs

Contradictions are oppositional demands, or opposing wants and needs

Convenience samples are samples of data that we have easy access to

Convergence is when we seek to match others' communication styles

Conversational style includes being animated, relaxed, and attentive during interactions

Cool mediums require a lot of participation from users and receivers have to fill in a lot of information

Costs are the drawbacks, sacrifices, and investments required for a relationship

Costs in a relationship are anything that eliminates benefits or costs us resources

Courtesies are the small favors we do for others or things we say to be courteous

Critical methods look closely at the use of symbols in discourse, are critical of how symbols are related to power structures in society, used to influence, and used to maintain or challenge social order

Critical perspective focuses on how communication reinforces existing power structures and leaves some groups powerless

Criticisms are personal attacks on our partner

Cues are elements in the message that may be persuasive

Cultivation analysis looks at how the trends in media messages affect people's perceptions

Culture is shared values

Culture refers to values shared by a group of people

Cyberbullying is the repeated use of aggressive tactics online to hurt someone whom is seen as having less power

Cybernetics perspective focuses instead on people as rational information processors

Data is anything that can be analyzed to make inferences and reach conclusions

Decentralized news comes from many different people and outlets

Decoding is processing, or thinking about and interpreting, a received message

Defensive messages are when we complain and blame the other person

Deliberative rhetoric argues over what we should or should not do

Denial is denying that there is tension

Depenetration occurs when we move backward in the relationship stages, or when we terminate a relationship

Depth of news coverage is how much time and space a news story receives

Descriptive norms are our observations of what other people do

Deterministic views of technology assert that changes in mediums *determine* how we think and behave

Dialectics are needs expressed in interpersonal communication within a relationship

Diffusion a multidirectional, sometimes slow process by which new ideas, behaviors, and technologies are adopted or rejected by a social group

Diffusion theory we learn about the features of technology from the media and our adoption of technology is affected by our peer groups

Digital divide refers to the differences in access to new technology among demographic groups

Disclosure breadth refers to the number of topics we cover in our disclosures

Disclosure depth refers to how personal, or intimate, the details are that we self-disclose

Discourse and conversation analysis are methods that focus on the topics discussed and omitted; who gets to speak and who doesn't; who dominates the conversation; and the tone, connotations, and implications of the language used in discourse

Discourse is any type of human communication

Disorientation is when we become overwhelmed, and may include leaving the relationship

Dissonance a key motivational variable in diffusion theory that explains that we want to be consistent in terms of our values, attitudes, and behaviors

Dissonance is caused by inconsistency in thoughts, attitudes, and behaviors

Divergence is when we accentuate differences between our own and others' communication styles

Division is when we point out how someone is fundamentally distinct from someone else

Dominant groups hold power and control discourse in society

Double-binds are a lose-lose situation

Dramatism builds on the idea of narrative by explaining that critics should explore the elements of stories that are emphasized and downplayed

Dramaturgical perspective is that we consider how we want to be perceived by others and we perform based on that

e-Influentials are online opinion leaders who influence others' technology adoption

E-mail functions are reasons for emailing, include completing a task, building a relationship, giving excuses, participating, and/or to make a favorable impression

Early adopters are the second group of people who adopt new technologies and are often opinion leaders

Early majority are the third group of adopters who follow the lead of early adopters

Egocentrism is our focus on ourselves when communicating

Elaboration is having thoughts related to the content of the message

Electronic media content study of media content on TV, online, etc.

Electronic propinquity theory proposes that mediated channels can create a sense of closeness between people

Elocutionists studied oral and nonverbal delivery and public speaking in the 1800s

Encoding is creating a message and formulating responses to messages

Enculturation is learning about and adapting to an organization's unique culture

Enlightenment happened in the 1600s; influential philosophers explored the extent to which people are rational, how we maintain order in society, and highlighted the issues of social justice

Entertainment education is when media developers intentionally incorporate information and modeling of healthy or prosocial behaviors in entertaining media

Enthymemes are premises that we all agree on

Entry phase is when we tend to be more guarded and controlled by social conventions

Epideictic rhetoric where we focus on celebration or values

Equity is when our inputs and outcomes are roughly equal to that of our partner's

Equity theory asserts that we perceive that there is inequity in a relationship and seek to fix it

Equivocation is being intentionally unclear

Ethnographic research is when the researcher observes, talks to people, and tries to see the organization from their perspective

Ethnographies are when researchers go in to a group, organization, or setting, observe people in that natural environment, and take extensive field notes

Ethos is the speaker's authority on the subject

Ethos is when communicators establish their goodwill toward others, their own competence and expertise as a type of proof

eWOM is electronic word of mouth

Exemplars are real-life examples that we can look to as models for behavior

Exemplification is an impression management strategy whereby people exceed expectations to be seen as a hard worker

Exit phase is when we indicate to each other whether or not we would like to meet again

Expectations to be informed and make a good decision are an external form of motivation

Experiments create an artificial situation or message, have people participate, then carefully observe or collect self-reported responses

Exploratory research is research that seeks to answer a question that has never been asked before

Exploratory stage is when we slowly disclose more personal information about ourselves

Exploratory surveys explore concepts and variables outlined in the theory

External attributions explain people's behavior as a result of outside causes such as the situation or context

Eye gaze is maintaining eye contact

Fabrication is directly providing false information

Face refers to our self-image needs

Face threats are when we communicate a message that could injure either positive or negative face

Facework is balancing our own face needs with the face needs of others

Facial expressions is the use of the face to communicate, such as smiling or frowning

Facilitation occurs when one relationship partner helps the other reap some kind of reward

Fate control is when you change your behavior in a relationship to affect someone else's outcomes

Fear of isolation is fear of being a social outcast as a result of expressing an unpopular opinion

Fidelity is whether a narrative seems realistic based on our experience

Fields of study in communication focus on different contexts

Focus groups involve the researcher asking open questions of a group of people

Forced compliance is when a person was either coerced, through the threat of punishment, or bribed, through the offer of rewards, to do something

Four horsemen of the apocalypse are negative ways of communicating in a relationship that predict termination

Frame is the angle used to report a news story

Front is the image of self we want to project

Functional approach explains that media serves specific functions for society

Functional approach suggests that there are things that groups can do that lead to better decisions

Gatekeepers such as the editors, decide which stories get covered

Gender is a social construct

Generalizability is how well findings generalize to everyone or everything in the population

Generalized others are our community and social groups

Genre is the category, or type, of communication

Gratifications are what people get out of their media use

Group communication interactions and processes in groups

Groups are three or more people working together to meet some objective

Groupthink explains how groups' circumstances and members' communication affect the quality of outcomes

Guilt is discomfort, shame, or embarrassment, from things not being what they should be

Health behavior studies have looked at modeling positive health behaviors in popular media

Health communication health campaigns; communication between health professionals and patients; health information

Hegemony is one group of people influencing the ideology of other people

Hegemony is when one social group controls another social group

Heterophilous social groups are when members vary in attitudes, beliefs, and status

Hierarchy cultures are bureaucracies

High LMX relationships are marked by an open exchange of ideas, knowledge, and resources

Homogenous groups are when members are all very similar

Homophilous social networks are when all members are very similar

Hot mediums extend one human sense in "high definition," and requires little participation from the receiver

Hybrid groups use both face-to-face and mediated communication

Hyperpersonal communication is more disclosure earlier in CMC relationships that leads to an increased sense of closeness

Hypothesis is a declarative statement about how two or more variables are expected to be related to each other

Identification is when we see something as being similar to something else

Ideology is people's beliefs, values, and perceptions

Illusion of unanimity occurs because people fail to disagree, and it is assumed that they are all in agreement

Immediacy are communication behaviors that bring us psychologically closer to someone

Implicit personality theories are our own ideas about how traits cluster together

Impression management is selective self-presentation

Impression management is what we include in a deceptive message to protect our own face

Increasing discrimination is creating new categories to see people and things in more complex ways

Individualistic cultural values include autonomy, independence, and personal success

Information management is when we knowingly manipulate the information we give others

Information seeking is looking for information about something to make a decision

Ingratiation is an impression management strategy of using flattery and favors

Injunctive norms are what is acceptable or unacceptable in a social group

Innovativeness how early people adopt technology compared to others in their social system

Innovators are the earliest adopters of new technology and enjoy trying out new things

Institutional analysis looks at the ways that media ownership and profit motives affect the media messages

Instrumental media use is active and selective

Instrumentality principle asserts that we are attracted to people who help us fulfill our needs and achieve our goals

Insulate is when groups protect themselves from outside opinions

Integration involves meeting both partners' needs without having to compromise

Integrators are more satisfied with combining their work and home lives

Interactive information seeking strategies are when we converse with the person so as to learn about them

Interdependence we can stand between people and the rewards they seek (*interference*), or we can help them achieve those rewards (*facilitation*)

Interdependent needs are when our understanding of one type of need depends on our understanding of an oppositional need

Interference includes habits, behaviors, and tendencies in the other person that lead to us not getting the response or outcome we want

Interlocking personal networks are people that we interact with on a regular basis

Intermedia agenda setting is when media are influencing each other's agendas

Internal attributions explain people's behavior as a result of their internal traits and characteristics

International/intercultural communication communication between cultures

Internet addiction includes Internet intrusion, escape, and attachment

Internet efficacy is people's sense that they can effectively use new technologies

Interpersonal communication communication between two people

Interpersonal deception theory explains the behaviors that people engage in when they are deceiving others

Interpretive research involves being immersed in data collection through direct observation, conducting interviews, focus groups, or analyzing transcripts or recordings to describe communication as it occurs from the perspective of the people involved

Interviews are interpersonal sessions where the researcher asks a person open questions

Intimidation is an impression management strategy accentuating one's ability to punish or have power over others

Introspective is thinking about who we are and how we feel

Involved in media content means we pay closer attention and think more about the content

Involvement is feeling like the topic is important in terms of people's impression of you, your values, or the outcomes being important

Invulnerability in a group is the belief that the group cannot or will not fail

Issue salience is whether or not an issue is relevant to us

Judicial rhetoric is about past events to establish blame

Justification is the ability to rationalize attitudes, thoughts, and behaviors that are inconsistent

Key informants a method that involves asking people who are knowledgeable about their social group to identify the opinion leaders

Knowledge gap is the difference between being information "rich" and information "poor"

Lack of feasible options is when a group does not have a lot of options because of what's going on in the broader context

Lack of impartial leadership is when group leaders may have an agenda

Lack of processes or norms is lacking structure for discussion and decision making

Laggards are the last people to adopt a technology

Late majority are the fourth wave of adopters that typically adopt due to social pressure

Latitude of acceptance is all of the points of agreement between someone who is trying to persuade and their target

Legal communication communication in legal settings

Lenses are when rhetorical analysts choose tactics to look for in messages

Likert items are survey items on a scale of "strongly agree" to "strongly disagree"

Limited effects perspective is the idea that mass persuasion, propaganda, and mass media effects were relatively limited

Limited effects perspectives argue that media effects are limited by people's unique uses of media

Linguistics is a research method that looks closely at people's language

Linguistics is the close, qualitative study of the messages people use in real-life situations

Logos are appeals to logic, and include building valid arguments to prove a point

Logos are logical appeals

Longitudinal studies are conducted over time to see how things change

Looking-glass self is considering how other people perceive us

Low efficacy is when people feel like they have already failed and cannot do anything to fix the problem

Mainstreaming effects are when one dominant, homogeneous, middle-of-the-road view of reality results from media use

Make-work is when we are at work and we try to *look* busy

Market cultures are competitive

Marxism focuses on the social control that powerful people and institutions exert

Marxism is idea that there are ongoing class divisions that benefit some and exploit others

Mass communication effects individual and social effects of media

Matching hypothesis is that people select partners that are similar to themselves in terms of social and physical attractiveness

Material divides are differences in access to the technologies needed to create Web 2.0 content

Mean is the average

Mean world syndrome is when people who consume the most content, developed a sense that the world is a scary place

Media criticism involves critiquing the ownership, production, and social consequences of media messages

Media criticism is the careful critique of media

Media dependency occurs when we must rely on the media for information

Media depictions are how the media represents reality

Media ecology is the study of media as an "environment"

Media ownership is about who owns the media and the profit goals of media companies

Medium theory is another name for media ecology, because it focuses on how changes in the communication mediums available to us change who we are and our society

Message analysis is the careful content analysis of media messages

Message production involves producing verbal and nonverbal messages that accomplish goals given the person and the situation

Message reception is listening to and processing other people's messages

Messages are what is actually said or done

Metamessages are the underlying relational meaning of what is said or done

Metaphors compare two things to reach a conclusion or frame a person or event

Methodological thinking is thinking of things critically, from different perspectives, and objectively

Microblogging is blogging brief snippets and links via Twitter in 140 characters or less

Mindfulness is choosing to be more aware and thoughtful

Mindguards actively stop relevant but conflicting ideas, perspectives, or information from even getting to the group

Mindlessness leads to behaving automatically rather than thoughtfully

Minority opinion is the opinion on an issue that most people disagree with

Modalities are different means of communication, such as video, text

Modeling behaviors is when we see another person do something and we may learn a new, good or bad, behavior

Mood management is when we use media to enhance or repair our mood

Mortification is blaming ourselves for what is wrong

Motivation divides are differences in wanting to use Web 2.0 technologies; seeing their usefulness and benefit

Motivation is feeling compelled to actively pay attention to and think about the message content

Motivation to comply is our desire to conform to normative influence

Motives are the different reasons we have for using media

Multicommunicating is having interactions via multiple channels at one time

Multidimensional concepts are when there are several different aspects to a concept

Multitasking is when we are doing two or more things at once

Muted groups are defined by and excluded from public discourse

Muting is excluding diverse voices from our public discourse

Narcissism includes believing that one's self is more valuable or important than others and lacking empathy

Narrative analysis asks us to consider discourse as narration, or an *intentionally constructed telling of how things are, were, or should be*

Narratives are used to influence others through accounts of what could happen, is happening, or has happened

Need for cognition is an internal source of motivation, and it is being someone who enjoys critical thinking

Negative face is our need for freedom, choice, and autonomy

Negative is what is wrong

Negative politeness is what we include in messages to protect other people's negative face

Negatively valenced violations signal disconfirmation such as disapproval, dislike, and disinterest

Negotiation/conflict management managing and resolving conflicts

Netiquette is online etiquette

Network analysis is a common method used to map the social structure of a group

Network centrality is how socially connected people are

Noise includes internal and external things that may interfere with the transaction

Nonselective exposure is openness to information from diverse perspectives

Nonverbal behaviors include use of space, eye contact, movement, use of touch, gestures, facial expressions, posture, and body movement

Nonverbal leakage are unintended nonverbal signals

Normative distance is the socially acceptable distance between two people assignments

Norms are stable "rules about behavior"

Objective researchers are detached observers who look to reach generalizable, factual conclusions about the types, processes, and effects of communication

Observational method observing a social group and discovering which members are most sought out for information and advice

Observational studies are studies where we observe people's behavior in a particular situation

Obtrusive issues are issues that we have personal experience with

Off-record messages communicate what we want or need indirectly

Openness is being willing to hear and consider new information

Operationalizing a concept is when decide how to measure it

Opinion leaders are informal leaders in a social group who are in a position to influence others' opinion and behaviors

Organizational communication communication in formal organizations

Organizational identification is the extent to which we identify with, or see ourselves as "fitting" with the organization

Orientation stage is when we begin by disclosing peripheral or basic details about ourselves

Outcome orientations are when we approach a person or situation focused on the outcomes we want

Outliers are individual instances that are far above or far below the norm

Over-accommodation is when we accommodate based upon perceived limitations or stereotypes

Overbenefitted partners get more out of the relationship than their partner

Overestimating group's power is when we think a group has more power than it really does

Paradigm is a way of thinking about and theorizing about something

Paradoxical means two things in direct opposition to each other

Particular others are specific people who are important to us

"Passing stranger" phenomenon suggests that people will disclose more to people they are unlikely to ever see again

Passion is how we describe organizational activities

Passive information seeking strategies include observing how a person interacts with others to learn about him or her

Pathos are appeals to people's emotions

Pathos are emotional appeals

Perceived behavioral control is the belief that we can, or are able to, do something

Perceived outcome value is the perception of the rewards we could get from a prospective relationship

Perception is a process of observing and inferring

Peripheral processing is easy, less effortful thinking that involves using simple cues in the message to make a decision

Personal needs are wanting things for ourselves, such as credibility and status

Personal phase is when we exchange our feelings and attitudes more spontaneously

Personal space is our "preferred distance from others"

Personal stories make us look good or reiterate our identity within the organizational

Personal strength is when employees command others, take credit for good outcomes, or exercise control

Personality traits are individual dispositions

Perspective taking is thinking of things from multiple perspectives

Perspective-taking is our ability to create person-centered messages and to understand others' perceptions by considering their unique perspectives

Phenomenological perspective on communication stresses the subjective nature of communication

Physical attraction includes seeing someone as sexy, good looking, handsome and/or pretty

Physical proximity is how close a person is to you

Pleasantries, such as small talk, can help us get to know our coworkers

Plots are the sequence of events that unfold

Podcasts are downloadable video and audio files

Polarization is when our attitudes become much more extreme

Political communication communication in political systems and political processes

Political economy is one's power in society

Politics are how coworkers promote their own self-interests and influence others

Polysemy is when something has multiple possible meanings

Positive face is our need for others to like and respect us

Positive politeness protects the positive face of others

Positively valenced violations are nonverbal messages that signal confirmation, liking, and interest

Posture is how we position our bodies

Power is our ability to influence people in the relationship

Praxis is the idea that we affect and are affected by changes in our relationships

Preference for procedural order is an individual preference for planning, order, and procedures in groups

Priming is when an idea, feeling, opinion, or knowledge comes to mind quickly and easily

Privacies are interactions that are private because they are appraisals, confessions, or consolations

Process orientation is when we think about how and why things happen

Product placement is when companies pay to have their products featured in media content

Professional subcultures occur when professional specializations and occupations also have cultures

Prominence of news stories includes whether it is a lead story or buried later in coverage

Propinquity is closeness, or similarity

Prosumers are people who both create and consume content; they play both producer and consumer roles

Proximity of connections in a social group (close or distant) is one aspect of network analysis

Public address study of major public speeches

Public relations communication between organizations and their audiences

Punishing people communicate negatively valenced messages and tend to be people that we hold in lower regard

Purposive sample is a sample that is put together for a reason

Pygmalion effect is a self-fulfilling prophecy in which people live up or down to others' expectations of them

Qualitative research can include objective, theory-directed coding of content or open, interpretive approaches to discovering trends and themes

Quantification is the process of assigning numerical values to statistically analyze data

Quasi-statistical is our sense of approximately how popular or unpopular our opinion is

Racism is stereotypes based on race

Radial social networks are those people that we know but do not interact with frequently

Random sampling is a large-scale study where all members of the population have an equal chance of being included

Rapport styles focus on personal connection

Reaffirmation is accepting the tension

Recalibration is when we reframe the tension to change how we think about it

Reciprocation is when we mimic people's verbal and nonverbal cues when we are uncertain

Reframing is considering something in a new way

Regions are the actual, physical space where we perform

Relationship assessment scale is a measure of relationship satisfaction

Relationship development is a dynamic, interactive process of achieving closeness between two people

Relationship dialects focuses on the *conflicting needs* we have in relationship

Relationship maintenance includes things that we do in a relationship to keep relationships at the desired level of intimacy

Release tension needs including wanting to passing time

Reliability is whether or not we get the exact same results over and over again using the same measure

Report styles focus on tasks and relaying information

Research questions are open questions that guide a study

Resonance is having personal experiences similar to those depicted in the media

Return on investment when we invest in something we expect sufficient returns

Rewarding people offer more positively valenced interactions overall and are held in higher regard

Rewards are our benefits from a relationship in terms of need fulfillment

Rewards are those benefits, or needs that are fulfilled, in a relationship

Rhetoric analysis of communication artifacts

Rhetorical criticism tradition is rooted in literary criticism and historical methods

Rhetorical perspective is that communication is an art form that can be critiqued and classified to explore the best ways to persuade people

Rich-get-richer view is that people who are extraverted actually benefit more from new media

Ritualized media use is habitual and passive

Rituals are repeated patterns for doing things

Roles in a relationship are what we are expected to do

Sampling is deciding what and how much data researchers need to look at to reach a conclusion

Scapegoating is blaming someone or something else for what is wrong

Scientism is a term used by Postman (1993) to describe how and why our society puts so much value in statistics and scientific evidence

Segmentation is focusing on a dialectic in one context, but not another

Selective exposure is when we seek out confirming information and avoid disconfirming information

Selective perception is misunderstanding the message or rejecting the message because it doesn't conform to one's existing opinions

Selective recall is choosing to forget or misremember dissonant information

Self includes a person's norms, gender, culture, and traits

Self is who you see yourself as being

Self-censorship is when people are unlikely to speak up, even when they see the group making a potentially bad decision

Self-designation asking people if they are the opinion leaders in their social groups

Self-disclosure is when we tell other people personal information about ourselves

Self-esteem means feeling comfortable with who you are

Self-promotion is an impression management strategy of highlighting one's accomplishments

Selfies are pictures that we take of ourselves with our mobile devices and post to social media

Semiotic perspective focuses on how people use and interpret symbols to convey meaning

Semiotics is the study of the signs and symbols we use to communicate and their associated meanings

Semiotics symbols and signs used to communicate

Separators prefer that work and home be completely separate

Setting is a particular context or situation where a narrative is set

Sexism is stereotyping of people based on gender

Sexting is when people send sexually explicit photos and messages to other people via text messaging

Similarity is a general sense of being like someone

Skills divides include differences in the ability to *perform* activities online, find and interpret *information* online, and making *strategic* decisions about what to create and whom to target

Sociabilities such as joking, gossiping, and talking about work help coworkers become closer

Social and professional relationships includes people's interpersonal, group, and organizational connections

Social attraction includes being someone that people would like to talk to, socialize with, and is fun or pleasant to be around

Social capital is the number and strength of a person's social connections within a community

Social compensation explanation suggests that people who are introverted may use new media to overcome their communication obstacles

Social needs are wanting to have and build relationships

Social penetration theory asserts that relationships become closer and more personal through gradually increasing self-disclosure

Social perception is accurately perceiving the other person and the situation

Social science tradition methods are rooted in sociology and psychology

Sociality is the organization's formal and informal "codes of behavior"

Society includes mass persuasion and mass media

Sociocultural perspective focuses on how communication creates and recreates social order

Sociometric method asking people in a social group to name the people they would ask for advice about a particular innovation

Sociopsychological perspective focuses on discovering clear cause-effect relationships

Speech verbal and nonverbal speech making

Spirals occur when we manage contradictory needs, which brings up new contradictions

Stable exchange is when we disclose intimate details about ourselves that are central to our sense of self

Standpoints are the positions we occupy in society and that affect what we know

Stereotypes are established social expectations

Stereotyping outsiders is when groups discuss outsiders in unflattering ways to differentiate "us" from "them"

Stonewalling is avoiding or withdrawing from interactions

Storytelling is one way we communicate organizational life

Stress in groups happens when there is pressure from the circumstances

(Subjective) Norms are beliefs about other people's expectations for our own behavior

Supplication is an impression management strategy to receive sympathy by highlighting struggles

Surveys are carefully designed questionnaires that ask open and/or closed questions related to the variables being studied

Symbolic interactionism is the idea that the meanings that we have for people and things determine our behavior and are the outcome of interactions

Synchronous is communication that occurs at the same time

Tactile communication is the use of touch to communicate

Task attraction includes whether or not people will help us get what we want, such as being reliable, dependable, and someone we'd be able to work with

Task rituals are how we go about completing our job requirements

Taxonomy is a system for classifying

Technology acceptance model uses beliefs about ease of use and usefulness of new technologies to predict adoption intentions

Tension occurs when relationship partners continually try to balance contradictory needs

Tetrad is a lens through which we can view a new technology

Theory is *a lens for understanding some aspect or type of communication*

Theory X assumes people are lazy and are motivated by money

Theory Y assumes people are self-motivated

Thick description of people's behaviors to interpret the culture as it is created, recreated, and perceived is used in the ethnographic approach

Third-person effect is when think of ourselves as immune to the effects of media and think of others as being greatly affected

Threat threshold is our own unique threshold for what makes us feel uncomfortable

Totality is looking at a relationship as a whole

Train test is a survey method where people are asked about their willingness to discuss their opinion on a controversial issue with a stranger on a train

Transactional means that communication occurs among people

Truth bias is our general expectations that people are honest

Two-step/multistep flow opinion leaders get information from the media and share it with their followers in a social group

Typology is a list of types or categories

Uncertainty a key motivational variable in diffusion theory that explains that we are unsure about new technologies when they are first introduced

Uncertainty reduction theory explains that we feel a lot of uncertainty early in relationships, and so we communicate to try to reduce our feelings of uncertainty

Underbenefitted partners receive less out of the relationship than their partner

Usage divide is the difference in how people from different socioeconomic backgrounds

Uses are why people use the media they do, and are also referred to as motivations or motives

Valence is the positivity or negativity of one's thoughts

Validity is about being accurate; whether a study is actually analyzing what they need to analyze to find out about the variables being studied

Variables can be anything that varies or changes from person to person or situation to situation

Verbal aggression is when people intentionally attack another's face

Violence index is used by cultivation researchers to content analyze media messages

Violent behaviors include physically injuring or killing people

Visual communication communication through visual artifacts

Volleyers prefer to go back-and-forth while maintaining some boundaries between work and home

Warranting information is information that we find online that is not generated by the person we are trying to find out about

Wikis such as Wikipedia, are websites where users can post and edit content

Yale program was a series of experiments to develop models and theories of persuasive messages and media effects

INDEX

397

P

paradoxes, 375
parental leave policies, *174*
participative social media, 341
particular others, 41
passing stranger, 158
passing time, 317
passion, organizational cultures, 212
pathos, 13, 286
Paypal, 289
people's behaviors, 213
perceive, selective, 246
perceived behavioral control, *263*
perceived outcome value, 140
perceptions, 39–40
    posting content and accuracy, *63*
    of reality, 216
peripheral processing, 231
personality, 54–57
    traits, 60, 61, 316
personal needs, 317
personal phase, 150
personal rituals, 212
personal stories, 212
personal strength, 213
person-centered accommodation, 89
perspective taking, 57, 75, 76
persuasion, 227
Pew Research Internet Project, *278*
Pew's five facts about YouTube, 348
phenomenological approaches, 7, *8*
Photoshop, 49
physical attraction, 138, *139*
physical proximity, 141
physical symbol, Amazon, 215
"pink slime" controversy, 333
Pinterest, *20*
planned behavior, 375, 376
Plato, 13
pleasantries, 212
plots, 286
podcasts, 322
polarization, 250
    and ambivalence, 250
"polite" message structures, 85
politeness theory, *90*, 90–92, 93, 374
political communication, 5
political economy, 346
political polarization, 252

politics, organizational cultures, 213
polysemy, 65
positive face, 91
positive interaction, 121
positive politeness, *90*, 92, 98
positivity, *186*
Postman's concepts from technopoly, 302
posture, 122
power, 182
    posture, 122
Power of Mindful Learning, The (Book), 77–78
PowerPoint slides, 73
praxis, 168
predictors of attraction, 140–141
preference for procedural order, 199
prepare, team, 206
presentation, 42
primary activity, 237
priming, 332
privacies, 212
procedural order, *200*
processes, 196
process orientation, 76
product placement, 353
professional networks, 1
professional reviews of products, 235
professional subcultures, 218
prominence, 330, *333*
propinquity, 140
prosumers, 352
proximity of connections, 278
public
    address, 5, 6
    commitments, 48
    crisis, 293
    relations, 5, *6*
Public Speaking Review, The, 14
purpose, 291
"Purposeful Darwinism," 215
purposive sample, 25
Pygmalion effect, 41, 43, 47

Q

quality of customer service, 238
quantification, 33
Quarterly Journal of Public Speaking, The, 14
quasi-statistical sense, 360, 362
Quintilian, 13

R

racism, 289
radial social networks, 278–279
random sampling, 25
"rank and yank" (Amazon), 214
rapport, 103
reaffirmation, 170
recalibration, 170
recall, 246
Reddit, *20*
reducing offensiveness, 293
reframing, 76
region, 44
region-specific behavior, 44
"regular retail" price, 233
relationship(s)
    assessment scale, 185
    under-benefitted, 182–183
    building, 1
    development, 149
    maintenance, 186–187, *186*
    over-benefitted, 182
relationship dialectics theory, 167–169
    defined, 167
    managing, 169–170
    research, 170–171
    work–life balance, 171–175
release tension, 317
reliability, 24, 25
report style, 103
research questions, 26
research studies
    communication studies, 28
    new theories, generation, 26
    testing and applying theories, 27
resonance, 347
return on investment, 180
rewards, 153, 180, 181, *181*
rhetorical criticism tradition, 16
rhetorical theory, 285–289
    applied research, 292
    electronic eloquence, 293
    methods, 290–292
    online image repair, 293–294
    in Web 2.0, 289–290
rhetoric analysis, 5, *6, 7, 8*, 290
ritualized media use, 317
rituals/rites
    Amazon, 214
    organizational cultures, 212
Rogers' diffusion of innovations, *275*

role categories questionnaire (RCQ), 58
roles, 182
romance scams, 160
Rousseau, 14

S

Sacco, Justine, 44–45
sampling, 25
Sandberg, Sheryl, *108*
Sapir-Worf Hypothesis, 3
scan, 237
scapegoat, 288
scene, 291
scientific (empirical) approach, 23
scientism, 302
seal on website, 237
secondary activity, 237
second-level agenda setting, *333*
secure sites, 238
segmentation, 170
selective attention to politics, 251
selective avoidance, 250
selective interpretation of political information,
   252–253
selectively perceive, 246
selectively recall, 246
self, 2, 42
    concept, 39
    inappropriate social media posts, 44–48
    self-presentation, 43–44
    symbolic interactionism, 41–42
self-censorship, 198
self-designation, *279*
self-disclosure, *151*, 151–152. *See also* online,
   self-disclosure/privacy paradox
self-efficacy, 359, 361, 368
self-esteem, 39, 61
self-focus, 85
selfie-obsessed social media culture, 49
self-perception, 204
self-presentation, 43–44, 64, 374
    online, 48–49
    posting pics, 48–49
    social media profiles, 48–49
self-promotion, 46, *46*, 324
self-regulation and reflection, 359
self-reporting, 319
self reports, 123
semiotics, 5, *6, 7, 8*, 29
separators, *219*
SET. *See* social exchange theory (SET)